FOUCAULT AND LATIN AMERICA

Foucault

AND LATIN AMERICA

Appropriations and Deployments

of Discoursive Analysis

Edited by **BENIGNO TRIGO**

Routledge • *New York* • *London*

Angel Rama, "The Ordered City," originally appeared in *The Lettered City*, ed. and trans. John Charles Chasteen, copyright 1996, Duke University Press, pp. 1–15, and is reprinted here with permission. All rights reserved. Román de la Campa, "The Lettered City: Power and Writing in Latin America," originally appeared in *Latin Americanism* (University of Minnesota Press, 1999), pp. 121–147, and is reprinted here with permission. Roberto González Echevarría, "A Clearing in the Jungle: From Santa Mónica to Macondo," originally appeared in *Myth and Archive: A Theory of Latin American Narrative*, copyright 1998, Duke University Press, pp. 1–42, and is reprinted here with permission. All rights reserved. Doris Sommer, "Love and Country: An Allegorical Speculation," originally appeared in *Foundational Fictions: The National Romances of Latin America* (Berkeley: University of California Press, 1993), copyright © 1993, The Regents of the University of California, pp. 1–29, and is reprinted here with permission. Sylvia Molloy, "The Theatrics of Reading: Body and Book in Victoria Ocampo," originally appeared in *At Face Value: Autobiographical Writing in Spanish America* (Cambridge and New York: Cambridge University Press, 1991), pp. 55–75, and is reprinted here with permission.

Published in 2002 by
Routledge
29 West 35th Street
New York, NY 10001

Published in Great Britain by
Routledge
11 New Fetter Lane
London EC4P 4EE

Copyright © 2002 by Routledge
Routledge is an imprint of the Taylor and Francis Group.

Printed in the United States of America on acid-free paper.

Library of Congress Cataloging-in-Publication Data
Foucault and Latin America : appropriations and deployments of discursive analysis / edited by Benigno Trigo.
     p.cm.
Includes bibliographical references and index.
ISBN 0-415-92828-1 (alk. paper)—ISBN 0-415-92829-X (pbk. : alk. paper)
1. Spanish American prose literature—20th century—History and criticism. 2. Latin America—Civilization. 3. Foucault, Michael. 4. Discourse analysis. I. Trigo, Benigno.
PQ7082.P76 F68 2001
860.9'98'0904—dc21   00-046451

Contents

PART 3 SUBJECTIVITY

PART 4 SEXUALITY

Acknowledgments

This volume grew out of a series of panels on the subject of Foucault and Latin America presented at several professional conferences, including Modern Language Association and Latin American Studies Association. My gratitude goes to the students and colleagues whose enthusiastic response and participation confirmed our belief in the timeliness of our venture. My thanks also go to United University Professions of New York for its financial support in procuring the permissions to reprint some of the essays in the volume. I owe many thanks to Román de la Campa for his encouragement throughout the process of assembling this collection and for his insightful feedback. I am also indebted to the tireless work of Sobeira La Torre and Elena Machado who helped to assemble the bibliography and produced the index to the book. Thank you also to Gayatri Patnaik for her unwavering belief in the project and for her wise recommendations. My gratitude also goes to the production staff at Routledge for working so hard to assure that the volume's content and appearance are as close as possible to perfection. My loving gratitude to Kelly for making it all possible.

Introduction

BENIGNO TRIGO

*S*ince the mid-eighties, Michel Foucault's work has informed much of the critical thought about Latin America's cultural, literary, historical, and political events. Influential works written in the United States such as *La ciudad letrada* (1984) by Angel Rama, *Myth and Archive* (1990) by Roberto González Echevarría, *Foundational Fictions* (1991) by Doris Sommer, and *At Face Value* (1991) by Sylvia Molloy draw from Foucault's *The Order of Things* (1966), *The Archaeology of Knowledge* (1969), *Discipline and Punish* (1975), *The History of Sexuality* (1976), and *Technologies of the Self* (1988) to develop concepts like the consciousness of an intellectual elite (or *letrados*), the archive novel, the foundational fiction, and self-writing, all of which are now the common currency of critical analysis in and about Latin America. Thus it is not surprising that a new generation of critics in universities in the United States continues this trend and turns to Foucault in an effort to develop its own insights into Latin American culture, politics, history, and literature.

However, as the division of this volume into Discourse, Government, Subjectivity, and Sexuality suggests, the trend to appropriate Foucauldian topics, strategies, and modes of analysis has been selective rather than wholesale. Indeed, as is made clear in the essays by Elzbieta Sklodowska, Doris Sommer, Román de la Campa, and Kelly Oliver, the impulse toward a selective appropriation of Foucault's work turns into a critical appropriation in some cases.

What explains this selective and sometimes critical appropriation of Michel Foucault's work, and why has Michel Foucault been so popular among these writers? One may begin to answer these two questions by engaging *Latin Americanism*, a recent and fascinating book by Román de la Campa (one of whose chapters is included in this volume). In that book, de la Campa maps "a transnational discursive community" which he calls "Latin Americanism."[1] It is a powerful and indeed convincing mapping of the last thirty years of critical production about Latin America written both from within and from outside that geographical space. In that book, de la Campa identifies two key moments or states of this discursive community. He refers to the first as an "epistemic negation" and to the second as an "episthetic." These two moments or states roughly correspond to a general moment in the history of literary studies: the appearance of "modes of deconstruction of [structuralist] constructs, some strictly from the singularity of key or canonical texts, others with a more extensive model of how textuality and dispersal challenge history as well as literary studies" (128). In other words, the negative epistemic and the episthetic moment are simultaneous but different events that correspond to the deconstructive challenge to structuralism, or to what is otherwise known as poststructuralism. According to de la Campa, the difference between these two modes of the same deconstructive moment is crucial. The negative epistemic tries to engage the "life-world" by calling into question its own linguistic and rhetorical modes of operation and by problematizing its object of analysis. The episthetic only "mimics" the first, but in fact remains content with its unexamined method and object of analysis. Indeed, it even goes so far as to "celebrate" what, for de la Campa, amounts to an aesthetic reduction of the material and spiritual needs of that life-world (19). In short, for de la Campa these two states or moments of Latin Americanism correspond to its postcolonial and to its postmodern respective directions after the poststructuralist turn.

In his book, de la Campa further argues that while the postmodern episthetic has been the dominant moment in Latin Americanism, it is also in a state of exhaustion. He suggests that the way out of the postmodern dead end is not so much fully to embrace the new rhetoric of globalization and its push for cultural studies, but to revisit the postcolonial moment or state and draw useful lessons from it. For de la Campa, one of the last works by the critic Angel Rama (*La ciudad letrada*) contains the useful lessons taught by the negative epistemic within the postcolonial moment of Latin Americanism. Significantly, de la Campa traces Rama's negative epistemic back to Michel Foucault's "discursive epistemology." In turn, Foucault develops this epistemology (according to de la Campa) during his "archaeological moment."

> One ventures to say that *The Lettered City* is a true essay—in the double sense of providing a test as well as a rehearsal—of many theoretical aspects that have fueled debates in the years since it was published, many of which are central to Foucault's own work. It is now well understood that *The History of Sexuality,* or *Technologies of the Self,* for example, constitute profound revisions of the discursive epistemology that was central to *The Order of Things* or *The Archaeology of Knowledge* (125).

Thus, parallel to his description of the poststructuralist turn in Latin Americanism, de la Campa describes Foucault's work as a divided corpus. While the Foucault of *The Order of Things* and *The Archaeology of Knowledge* is akin to the postcolonial direction of Latin Americanism, the Foucault of *The History of Sexuality* on *Technologies of the Self* is akin to the postmodern moment. Following the first Foucault, Rama focuses on discourse in such a way as to suggest simultaneously discourse's potential for empowerment and its constitution of the prison house (124). "This focus" (continues de la Campa) "includes a way of theorizing the arbitrariness of the sign, the so-called abyss between language and world, never quite accepting [it] unconditionally, nor failing to see it as an opportunity to continue to theorize colonialism, imperialism, and agency" (128). By contrast, the second Foucault emphasizes what de la Campa calls "the micropolitics of subjection" (116). Rather than permitting the theorization of colonialism, imperialism, and agency, this Foucault instead leads to a version of the West as self-contained, which de la Campa thinks Gayatri Chakravorty Spivak is right to criticize in her essay "Can the Subaltern Speak."

Despite de la Campa's elegant and sincere attempt to inhabit the middle ground of what he describes as "Latin American entanglements," this description of Foucault's divided corpus clearly falls on the side of the theorization of agency available only through the first Foucault; which emphasis essentially divides Foucault's work into an empowering side, leading to action, and the other side, leading to the cul-de-sac of celebratory aestheticism and self-perpetuating literariness. Thus de la Campa confronts us with two Foucaults rather than one aporetic Foucault: the Foucault of deeds and the Foucault of words, the Foucault of postcolonialism and the Foucault of postmodernism. To be fair, such a characterization runs against the grain of de la Campa's stated purpose, who does not want to turn literary deconstruction (and postmodernity) into a bête noire (viii). And yet one cannot help but conclude that there is in *Latin Americanism* a strong preference to turn away from that direction and embrace instead the postcolonial challenge, which is "defining a struggle against an imperial tradition that encumbers the critic's own contradictory attempts to simultaneously invest and resist it, to 'leave the wound open,' as Spivak is wont to say" (19).

Following de la Campa's logic, one can attempt an initial stab at the two questions asked at the beginning of this essay. Indeed, both Foucault's popularity and his critical appropriation by Latin Americanism could be explained by the very same fact. Foucault's divided corpus, the wounded but active body of his "archaeological moment," and the self-absorbed aestheticism of his later work would explain his attraction to followers of both currents of poststructuralism. By the same token, Foucault's divided work would also explain the criticism that sometimes accompanies the appropriation of his work. And yet, as is made evident in this volume and as de la Campa himself suggests, Foucault has not been appropriated in so straightforward a manner. Moreover, as will be suggested in this introduction (and as I argue in my contribution to this volume), to divide the work of Foucault into such clearly distinct parts is to miss the all-important interconnection between opposites such as word and deed, language and matter, resistance and discipline that is Foucault's definition of discourse.

Roberto González Echevarría's appropriation of Foucault is a case in point. The first chapter of his book *Myth and Archive* (included in this essay) uses the Foucault of the "archaeological moment" despite the fact that, according to de la Campa, González Echevarría's works are on the postmodern side of the poststructuralist divide. De la Campa explains this odd alliance as a corrective attempt to incorporate Foucauldian categories into methods of deconstructionist close readings that have otherwise failed (131). This explanation, however, presupposes the unlikely admission, or at least the suspicion, by González Echevarría that his method has failed, when perhaps one should first consider revising the binary model that makes a failure of deconstruction and a success of "discursive epistemology." Conversely, in a chapter of her book *At Face Value* (also included in this volume), Sylvia Molloy uses the later Foucault of *Technologies of the Self*. But according to de la Campa, Molloy (together with other women writers and critics) occupies a crucially destabilizing terrain for both moments of Latin Americanism; an effect that doesn't quite match Molloy's reliance on the later "postmodern" Foucault. De la Campa significantly describes this terrain as "the blindspot shared by transculturation and postmodern Latin Americanism" (27). But the slippage between Molloy's destabilization of postmodern Latin Americanism and her reliance on Foucault's essay on self-writing "L'ecriture de soi," also excerpted in Foucault's *Ethics*) suggests that perhaps the blind spot identified by de la Campa is bigger than he imagines it to be.

Román de la Campa brilliantly suggests that there is a third space that points to an overlooked but valuable critical terrain that cannot be reduced to either postcolonialism or postmodernism. But this third space also includes a terrain that lies outside the agonistic model that informs aspects of de la Campa's engagement with Foucault's corpus in particular and Latin Americanism in general. Moreover, the search for this third space can be found not only in the work of de la Campa but also in the work of the other contributors to this volume and, more to the point, in the work of Michel Foucault. His notion of "discourse" goes a long way in the direction of that third space, which I have argued elsewhere puts into question the very difference between matter and metaphor, fact and fiction, truth and error (*Subjects of Crisis* 4). Indeed discourse is a material operation at odds with its materiality and a figurative representation uncomfortable and even dismissive of its own figures. Discourse aims to be seen without being material. It wants to represent or signify without figures and without the mediation of signs. Discourse is not a matter of fact, but it aspires to be known and to be seen as a matter of fact. Most importantly, it is discourse's ambivalence or refusal to place subjects in symmetrical or dialectical relations of power and recognition that explains its attraction and the otherwise paradoxical appropriations of Foucault by critics such as González Echevarría and Sylvia Molloy.[2] Indeed, it is the common search for the uncertain ground of discourse and the vicissitudes of that search that explain the attraction of Foucault's theory and his critical appropriation by the critics included in this volume.

De la Campa's *Latin Americanism* is a representative example of the relentless search for the space of discourse in this strong sense. But a close look at the two principles driving his genealogy of Latin Americanism also reveals the vicissitudes often encountered in the hopeful search for that liminal space. On the one hand, de la Campa's primary distinction between a postcolonial and a postmodern direction after the poststructuralist turn (or between a negative epistemic and an episthetic moment) is based on the existence of what he refers to as the "life-world." On the other hand, de la Campa's choice to turn away from the postmodern direction and its episthetic moment and to invoke the state of the negative epistemic is predicated on the need to remain engaged with the "material and spiritual needs" of that life-world. Paradoxically, this engagement presupposes the wounding of the subject of theory or criticism. Indeed, to take the "responsible" role of that subject is also to inhabit the wound that for de la Campa is either coextensive with the life-world, or is its necessary condition.

Despite frequent allusions to the life-world, de la Campa never defines in detail what he means by the term. Sometimes he refers negatively to life-world as a form of culture that is not strictly literary (4). At other times he describes it more positively as "lived postmodernity" (4) or as the "living aspect of postmodern logic"(7), thus making of the act of "living" and a form of "culture" the two main attributes of the life-world. This sketchy definition resonates with aspects of the phenomenological concept of *Lebenswelt* (literally translated as "life-world") as defined by Edmund Husserl. In the lectures given in 1935, Husserl made a fundamental redefinition of phenomenology. He no longer took the transcendental ego to exist "absolutely." Instead, he took it to be correlative to *Lebenswelt,* the lived world, the world in which we live, the world as it is for an intersubjective community of individuals, as opposed to the world as known to science or to any transcendental individual (Schmitt 98). Rather than an empirical science, phenomenology was to be a reflective way to study the life-world, to contemplate not matters of fact but "the necessary conditions for coherence and adequacy of experience."

From such a phenomenological perspective, de la Campa distinguishes between a Latin American and a Western life-world, living culture or lived experience. He argues that "a concern with social, cultural, and ethnic hybridity speaks to internal changes within the Western life-world (19)" and he warns against constructing a Latin America strictly from such a perspective or from United States universities. More importantly, however, de la Campa does not understand these different life-worlds to be irreconcilable. Instead, with phenomenological emphasis on "life" and "intersubjectivity," he argues for the construction of Latin America from a "bridge" that "draws closer to the Latin American cultural life-world" (15). This bridge could be "Latin Americanism" (the transnational discursive community) or, more to the point, it could be intersubjective phenomenology or the study of the life-world without its Western or Latin American qualifiers. If the latter, this bridge would take us not only closer to the "Latin American cultural life-world" but more importantly it would take us to an alternative space that de la Campa describes as both "a distant future" and an "uncharted territory": "the possibility of a transnational dimension to the study of the Americas" (6).

If de la Campa's use of the metaphor of the bridge resonates with the pre-structuralist weight of Husserlian phenomenology and with phenomenology's references to the study of "the necessary conditions for coherence and adequacy of experience," de la Campa's simultaneous emphasis on the contradictions and the "founding catachresis" of this same space is a direct reference to Spivak's postcolonial mode of critique and textuality. Similarly, if de la Campa refers to the as-yet "uncharted territory" where this bridge will take us or to a future that in some ways we are already living, he also refers to that promised land as "an absence" (16) or as "a claim for which no adequate referent exists" (10), evoking in this way the puzzling image of the "undiscovered country from whose bourn no traveller returns" (Shakespeare 52).

De la Campa's emphasis on paradoxical figures of speech (catachresis), on absence, and on inexistence reveals a strong death drive struggling against an equally strong life-affirming intersubjective phenomenology. The death drive is belied by the melancholy spirit with which de la Campa emphasizes "concerns over the globalization of cultural forms as well as their tendency to absorb all spaces of contestation and resistance" (7). Similarly, if he "aims to find a framework able to examine the modern with the postmodern," he does so "with a vigilant eye to colonial residues" (27). De la Campa's "vigilance" about colonial loss and about the loss of spaces of resistance is also a self-conscious reference to Spivak, who calls on the intellectual to "leave the wound open" (18–19) in the struggle against an imperial tradition and to "say 'no'" to the luck "of having access to the culture of imperialism" while still recognizing that "she must inhabit it" (10).

Thus the death drive of *Latin Americanism* could be traced back to a similar impulse driving Spivak's essay, for whom "the narrow epistemic violence of imperialism gives us an imperfect allegory of the general violence that is the possibility of an episteme (Spivak 82)." Indeed, for Spivak, phallocentric and imperialist violence is but a version of a more general violence that, quoting Derrida, she calls writing. This "writing" is paradoxical. On the one hand, it produces the positions of and the violent struggles between the insurgent subaltern and the Subject of thinking and knowledge. On the other hand, for Spivak it holds the curious promise of producing a violence by the self on itself.

Significantly, writing for Spivak is a lost origin and an origin of loss in the face of which the historian who does not want to freeze insurgency into an "object of investigation" must "suspend (as far as possible) the clamor of his or her own consciousness" (82). In the face of this loss of origin, the postcolonial intellectual must "demote the Subject of thinking or knowledge as to say that 'thought is . . . the blank part of the text'" (89). This suspension or demotion of the Subject of thinking or knowledge is equivalent to consigning thought itself ("the place of the production of theory") to the subaltern or to "the Other of history." But according to Spivak, even this grammatological or deconstructive demotion, suspension, and consignment, even this critique of "the itinerary of the discourse of presence," does a violence and performs erasures of which one must be ever "vigilant." This all-important vigilance is an invocation, "an 'appeal to' or a 'call' to the 'quite-other'" in us rather than to the Other outside us (89). Indeed, not only is this 'quite-other' "in us" but it is that in us that is the very opposite of a self-consolidating other. Thus this vigilance is in the interest of a self-immolation that Spivak (quoting Derrida) describes as a delirium: "rendering delirious that interior voice that is the voice of the other in us" (89).

Both Spivak and de la Campa desire such a delirious, wounded, vigilant, disciplined, melancholy subjectivity for themselves as the means to gain access to the privileged state or as the way into what I've been calling the "third space," which functions as a threshold into the life-world (in the case of de la Campa) or the economic and/or material registers of experience (in the case of Spivak). Like the No of the ascetic priest in Nietzsche's *Genealogy of Morals,* this process of self-wounding, these negations of life, as if by magic bring to light "an abundance of tender Yeses" (Nietzsche 121).[3] Thus, like the actions of the ascetic priest who "[even] when he wounds himself . . . the very wound itself afterward compels him to live," the passage through this open "wound" or threshold is both a symptom and a remedy for a self-diagnosed condition. If on the surface this condition appears to be the exhaustion of postmodernism in the case of de la Campa, and the *huis clos* of Western thinking in the case of Spivak, closer inspection of their melancholy works might reveal a shared concern over the origin as loss of their own location or their dislocations as diasporic intellectuals.

The intensity of such acts of melancholy self-immolation makes the reader wonder what is at stake for these critics, what loss has been interiorized and then violently disposed of? One wonders whether what has been lost is the notion of language, discourse, or theory as offering, generosity, and goodwill. One wonders whether the melancholy gestures of these critics do not hide our complicity in the eradication of such a notion of language, discourse, and theory, as a proleptic act against the limit-events of our century that we have experienced and continue to experience, and that sometimes drive us into exile. One wonders whether another attitude is possible in front of those limit-events; an attitude that neither falls back on the disavowals and presumed transparency that Spivak is so right to criticize nor takes us to the degradation and self-violence that inevitably end in silence and death. But such meditation must be postponed to a later date in order to introduce similarly critical and sometimes melancholy attempts at reaching analogous spaces of hope in this collection of essays on Foucault and Latin America.

Foucault and Latin America is divided into four sections: Discourse, Government, Subjectivity, and Sexuality. The topic of each section is both an aspect of Latin America of interest to contemporary critical commentary and a central concept of the work of Foucault. Each section clusters a number of essays written by critics, theoreticians, and philosophers. Ten of these essays are original work written expressly for this collection. Five of the essays are reprints, and they were chosen for their lasting influence in contemporary critical thought about Latin America. Each one of the essays in the book is inspired by and puts emphasis on the topic of its respective section. Each essay bears on the topic as it appears in the writings of Foucault and as it materializes in Latin America.

The first section includes four essays on the topic of discourse. Foucault defines discourse variously and perhaps most famously as a practice of exclusion that includes but is not limited to language. The purpose of discourse, according to Foucault, is to establish a will to a specific truth. Chapter 1 focuses on discourse as analogic thought among the educated elites of Latin America. Rama argues that discourse is the ordering grid of a particular consciousness that lays the foundation for both their subjectivities and their cities. Chapter 2 diagnoses the influence of Foucault on Angel Rama. De la Campa suggests that Rama's limited exposure to Foucault's discursive analysis was nonetheless more productive than later appropriations by later critics of Latin American culture. Chapter 3 studies discourse as writing, specifically as it is conceived and practiced in and by the Latin American novel. González Echevarría claims that the simultaneously violent and liberating nature of writing in the Latin American novel holds the key to its structure, to the shifting nature of its will to truth, and to its paradoxical relation to history. Chapter 4 explores the remnants of a lucid madness in Hispanic literary tradition and in the wit of contemporary Mexican politics and Mexican American art. Inspired by Foucault's thoughts on the emergence of counterdiscursive practices at the points of exclusion, Ochoa argues that the tradition of lucid madness survives and engages the network of a medicoclinical discourse that paradoxically gives form to this tradition by seeking to erase it.

The second section addresses the Foucauldian notion of government, or the deployment of disciplining practices and discourse as technology to order and give form to what would otherwise be an unmanageable body or body politic. Chapter 5 is an insightful appropriation of Foucauldian concepts such as discipline and discourse in an attempt to think through the link between sexuality and government in Latin American culture. Sommer's essay has proven immensely popular and it has become a high-water mark of theoretical commentary on Latin American narrative. Chapter 6 follows Foucault's insights on the uncritical nature of the Enlightenment to diagnose its legacy of unresolved contradictions in Cuba's nationalistic discourse. Beaupied argues that while the Cuban revolution of 1959 represents a significant shift in the history of patriotic discourse, some of the contradictions reappear in the contemporary nationalistic discourse of Cubans living on the island or in exile. Chapter 7 focuses on the Foucauldian concept of pastoral power and uses it to study the case of Chile at the turn of the century. Poblete argues that a notion of power that combines the individualizing strategies of the Western Christian Church with the governing practices of the modern Western state is necessary to understand the national push in Chile for language improvement, civic formation, physical education, and hygiene. Chapter 8 profits from Foucault's understanding of the practices of clinical medicine in a study of the implications of the antianemia campaigns conducted in Puerto Rico between 1904 and 1911. Following Foucault, Feliú argues that such medical practices are but powerful deployments meant to govern collectivities through their medical management of specific and individual sites.

The third section contains essays that engage with Foucault's ideas about subjectivity. It is well known that in his work Foucault tried to separate himself from the notion of subjectivity generally attributed to Freudian psychoanalysis. His attempts, however, to articulate a notion of an epidermic subjectivity that eschews the concept of internal or deep psychic structures are rift with the same problems that haunted the Freudian project. Like Freud, Foucault had trouble distinguishing between subject and object, as well as between the constitutive principles of interiority and exteriority, sociality and organicity. All of these difficulties aside, however, like Freud's, Foucault's notion of subjectivity hinges on the spatial and temporal meeting of contradictory and powerful lines of force. In Chapter 9, I remark that the contradictions found in Foucault and Freud, as well as the manifestations of these contradictions in their respective notions of subjectivity, are resolved by recent appropriations of Foucault. In that chapter, I criticize this resolution as a foreclosure of the most promising aspect of Foucault's theory of subjectivity. Chapter 10 engages with the Foucauldian notion of a precarious modern subject informed by interiorized discourses and resisting counter-self-discourses. Unzueta traces the formation of this unstable subject in Pablo Olavide's representative sentimental novel written and published at the beginning of the nineteenth century. Chapter 11 leads Foucault's interrogation of the stable and coherent Western subject and author to a provocative assessment of Spanish-American testimonial narrative. Sklodowska revisits the controversy surrounding the testimonial text by Rigoberta Menchú and argues that Foucault's notion of the author function can be a way to gain insight sorely missed by Menchú's critics.

The last section of *Foucault and Latin America* is a topic deeply shaped by the same preoccupations that inform subjectivity, but its main focus is the construction of sexuality and the problem of sexual difference. Chapter 12 draws from Foucault's later writings on the care of the self to argue that references to the body in autobiographical writing in Latin America are neither merely metaphorical nor strictly corporeal. Sylvia Molloy uses Foucault's notion of self-writing to develop her dramatic and original notion of Presence as it emerges from the intersection of linguistic and corporeal registers in Victoria Ocampo's autobiography. Chapter 13 finds its point of departure in the Foucauldian notion of power as a field of relations and its accompanying notion of subjugated knowledges. Oliver argues that a genealogy of these subjugated knowledges is at the center of Julia Alvarez's novels. She further argues that genealogies such as this one are at the service of women's localized struggle against patriarchal domination. Chapter 14 mines Foucault's theories about state racism and uses them to advantage to discuss the complex interdependence of race and sexuality in the nationalistic discourse of Gabriela Mistral. In her essay, Fiol-Matta argues that one of this century's most important intellectuals from Latin America, Gabriela

Mistral, uses the markers of race and sex simultaneously to distinguish between the acceptable and the unacceptable in the construction of a Latin American identity. Chapter 15 revisits Foucault's reflections on subjection and in an intriguing turn links them with sexuality and more specifically with Freud's insights into sadomasochism. Sifuentes Jáuregui argues that the subjecting function of sexually charged controversies such as the one surrounding *Paradiso* (a twentieth-century novel by Cuban writer Lezama Lima) is evidence of the need to think the paradoxes of subjection through the impasse of sado-masochism.

Today a student of discourse in and about these different aspects of Latin America cannot afford to miss the growing interest in and deployment of Foucauldian methods of analysis. To date, however, there is not one source where students of Latin American critical thought can turn to find the landmark appropriations and deployments of Foucault's theories, a representative gathering of original essays likewise informed, as well as essays that reflect on those very appropriations. It is my sincere hope that *Foucault and Latin America* will begin to satisfy that need.

NOTES

1. Román de la Campa *Latin Americanism,* 1. All further references to this text will be within the body of the essay.

2. For a development of this interpretation of Foucauldian discourse, see Homi K. Bhabha *The Location of Culture,* 72.

3. I would like to thank Kelly Oliver for bringing my attention to this passage.

DISCOURSE

The Ordered City
From *The Lettered City*

ANGEL RAMA

Translated by John Charles Chasteen

From the remodeling of Tenochtitlán after its destruction by Hernán Cortés in 1521 to the 1960 inauguration of that most fabulous dream city of the Americas, Lúcio Costa's and Oscar Niemeyer's Brasília, Latin American cities have ever been creations of the human mind. The ideal of the city as the embodiment of social order corresponded to a moment in the development of Western civilization as a whole, but only the lands of the new continent afforded a propitious place for the dream of the "ordered city" to become a reality.

Over the course of the sixteenth century, the Spanish conquerors became aware of having left behind the distribution of space and the way of life characteristic of the medieval Iberian cities—"organic," rather than "ordered"—where they had been born and raised. Gradually and with difficulty, they adapted themselves to a frankly rationalizing vision of an urban future, one that ordained a planned and repetitive urban landscape and also required that its inhabitants be organized to meet increasingly stringent requirements of colonization, administration, commerce, defense, and religion.

Upon crossing the Atlantic Ocean they had passed from an old continent to a "new" one and had also entered a different era, animated by an expansive and ecumenical sort of capitalism still charged with a medieval sense of mission. The avenues toward this new era of Western culture had been opened by the Renaissance spirit of its sixteenth-century designers but would be perfected only later by the absolute monarchies. The absolutist European nation-states of the seventeenth and eighteenth centuries enjoyed the full support of religious institutions and focused their power at the royal court, seeking to impose from there a hierarchical discipline on the rest of society. The points of juncture between the ideal ordering impulse and the existing social reality produced an enduring urban model: the Baroque city.[1]

This ordering impulse could do relatively little to transform the old cities of Europe, where the stubbornly material sediments of the past encumbered the flight of a designer's fancy, but it found a unique opportunity in the virgin territory of an enormous continent. There, native urbanistic values were blindly erased by the Iberian conquerors to create a supposedly "blank slate," though the outright denial of impressive indigenous cultures would not, of course, prevent them from surviving quietly to infiltrate the conquering culture later.[2] Having cleared the ground, the city builders erected an edifice that, even when imagined as a mere transposition of European antecedents, in fact represented the urban dream of a new age. The cities of Spanish America were the first material realization of that dream, giving them a central role in the advent of world capitalism.[3]

Although the conquerors appended the adjective *new* to familiar regional names (New Spain, New Galicia, New Granada) in designating portions of their recently acquired territory, and though they vacillated initially under the lingering influence of Iberian cities like those from which they had originally set out, they did not reproduce those cities in America.[4] Gradually, through trial and error, they filtered the legacy of the past through the clarifying, rationalizing, and systematizing experience of colonization, in the "stripping down process" described by George M. Foster.[5] Thus the patterns of urbanization that they had known firsthand at home were superseded in America by ideal models implemented with routine uniformity in accordance with the vastness and systematic planning of the imperial enterprise.

The ideas of *The Republic,* revived by Renaissance humanism, arrived in America through the same Neoplatonist cultural channels that guided the advance of Iberian capitalism. And with Neoplatonic idealism came the influence of the quasi-mythical Hippodamus, Greek father of the ideal city—especially his "confidence that the processes of reason could impose measure and order on every human activity."[6] The imposition of these ideas in the sixteenth and seventeenth centuries corresponds to that crucial moment in Western culture when, as Michel Foucault has sagaciously perceived, words began to separate from things, and people's understanding of epistemology changed from one of triadic conjuncture to the binary relationship expressed in the *Logique* of Port Royal, published in 1662, theorizing the independence of the "order of signs."[7] The cities of Spanish America, the societies that were to inhabit them, and the "lettered" interpreters of them developed together in a time when signs became no longer "direct representations of the world, linked to it by secret, solid ties of likeness or affinity with what they represent," and began instead "to signify from within a body of knowledge" and "to take from it their probability or certainty."[8]

From that flow of knowledge sprang forth the ideal cities of the Iberian empire's American vastness. Their ordering principle revealed itself as a hierarchical society transposed by analogy into a hierarchical design of urban space. It was not the real society that was transposed, of course, but its organized form, and not into the fabric of the living city but merely into its ideal layout, so that in the geometrical distribution we can read the social morphology of the planners. This conversion was made possible by the advancing project of rationalization. The untrammeled rationalizing urge demanded similar flexibility in the order of signs. Rationalization also required a concentration of power to implement the directives of the rationalizers. That power was already visibly temporal and human, although it cloaked and legitimated itself ideologically in celestial absolutes, as power will do. Such legitimation had long been provided by religion, but when the religious masks of power were shattered, stately secular ideologies soon substituted them. In a like manner, efforts to legitimate existing power relations have always been the great source of new ideologies.

The lexical key to the entire imperial system was the Janus-faced word *order,* symptomatically ambiguous in grammatical gender (*el orden* or *la orden*), a concept pursued equally by the Church, the army, and the administrative bureaucracy of the Iberian empires. According to the received definitions of the day, order meant: "putting things in their places; concert and harmonious disposition among things; the rule or mode to be observed in producing things." Pursuit of order lay at the heart of the systems of classification (such as natural history, architecture, and geometry) that then loomed so large in the corpus of knowledge. The word *order* recurs obsessively in the instructions imparted in 1513 by the king, or rather by his council of advisers, to Pedrarias Dávila, leader of a Spanish expedition that pushed beyond the conquistadors' original foothold in the Caribbean once accommodation to the New World environment had readied them for further violent expansion and colonization. It is worthy of emphasis, though hardly surprising, that the instructions framed the entire enterprise in terms of Spanish colonial interests, establishing from the very first a coastal orientation and a string of port cities that would, centuries later, undermine attempts at national integration in not a few independent states. Point number seven of the instructions fixed the following guidelines for cities to be founded on the new continent:

> Having ascertained what things are necessary for the settlements and having chosen the site most advantageous and abundantly provided with all things necessary to those who will settle therein, distribute town lots for the construction of houses, in *orderly* fashion, according to the quality of the recipients, so that, once constructed, the town will appear well-*ordered* as regards the space designated for the central plaza, the location of the church, and the placement of the streets; because where such *orders* are given from the outset, *orderly* results will follow without undue cost and effort, and in other places *order* will never be achieved.[9]

Thus, beyond the immediate needs of urban planning, rationalized cities reflected a vision of the future. The transference of an idealized social order into the physical reality of the newly founded cities required the previous cultural elaboration of rationalizing symbolic languages. The royal directives sought quite explicitly to program eventual social development in accord with the vision of the rationalizers, and they were aided in this endeavor by the period's most abstract symbolic language: mathematics. The methods of analytical geometry had recently been extended to all areas of human endeavor by Descartes, who regarded them as the only valid—unerring and uncontaminated—tools of reason. When applied to urban planning in Spanish America, the result was the ubiquitous checkerboard grid that has endured practically until the present day.

Other geometric designs might have affected the same transference of social ideal into urban reality. Circular plans constituted a frequent option in Renaissance thinking, derived from the teaching of Vitruvio and visible in the works of Leon Batista Alberti, Jacopo Barozzi Vignola, Antonio Arvelino Filareta, and Andrea Pallacio, among others.[10] The circular layout responded to the same regulating principles as the checkerboard: unity, planning, and rigorous order reflecting a social hierarchy. Circular plans perhaps conveyed even more precisely than square ones the social hierarchy desired by the planners, with governing authority located at the center and the living spaces assigned to respective social strata radiating from the center in concentric circles. Both designs were simply variations of the same conception, in which the application of reason imposed a specific order on social reality through the engineer's "taut line and rule," as the royal instructions to the advancing conquerors frequently specified verbatim.

As Michel Foucault observed, "what made the classical episteme possible as a whole, of course, was its relationship to a knowledge of order."[11] In the case of cities, that indispensable knowledge resulted in the principle of urban planning. The Enlightenment, that epoch of faith in rational operations, further strengthened and institutionalized the planning impulse, and concern over the outcomes of urban planning elicited spirited commentary on its designs, its procedures, and, above all, its guiding philosophies.[12]

More important than the much-discussed grid design are the general principles behind it, directing a whole series of transmitted directives (from Spain to America, from the governing head to the physical body of the city) so that the distribution of urban space would reproduce and confirm the desired social order. But even more important is the principle postulated in the quoted directives of the king: before anything may be built, the city must be *imagined* in order to avoid circumstances that might interfere with its ordained norms. The notion that statutory order must be constituted at the outset to prevent future disorder alludes to the peculiar virtue of signs: to remain unalterable despite the passage of time and, at least hypothetically, to constrain changing reality in a changeless rational framework. Operating on these principles, the Iberian empires established rigid procedures for founding new cites and then extended them methodically across vast stretches of time and space.

Before their appearance as material entities, cities had to be constructed as symbolic representations. Therefore the permanence of the whole depended on the immutability of the signs themselves—on the words that transmitted the will to build the city in accordance with the stipulated norms—and also on the diagrams that translated the will into graphic terms. Without drawn plans, the mental image created by the written directives was more likely to suffer permutations owing to local conditions or to inexpert execution. *Thinking the city* was the function of these symbolic systems, and their growing autonomy suited them increasingly to the manipulations of absolute authority.

The conquerors still asserted territorial claims through rituals impregnated with magic, but now they required a writer of some sort (a scribe, a notary, a chronicler) to cast their foundational acts in the form of imperishable signs. The resulting scripture had the high function reserved to notarial documents, which according to the Spanish formula, give witness or "faith" to the acts they record. The prestige that could derive only from the written word thus began its portentous imperial career on the American continent.

In Latin America, the written word became the only binding one—in contradistinction to the spoken word, which belonged to the realm of things precarious and uncertain. It even seemed plausible that (contrary to Saussure) spoken language derived from written language rather than vice versa. Writing boasted a permanence, a kind of autonomy from the material world, which imitated eternity and appeared free from the vicissitudes and metamorphoses of history. Above all, writing consolidated the political order by giving it rigorously elaborated cultural expression. Over the framework provided by linguistic discourse, the planners stretched the canvas of graphic design. Not subject to the semantic multiplicity of words, this second layer of signs surpassed the virtue of the first as an instrument of urban planning. Drawn diagrams fused the thing represented (the city) with the representation (the drawing) in haughty independence from mundane realities, as period descriptions reveal. Of the 1535 founding of Lima by Pizarro (so criticized among thinkers of a later independent Peru), we learn that the city "was laid out and established according to the plan, and the drawing of it, which had been done on paper."

Drawn plans have always been the best examples of operative cultural models. Behind their ostensible function as neutral registers of reality lies an ideological framework that validates and organizes that reality, authorizing all sorts of intellectual extrapolations on the model. Clifford Geertz makes recourse to this example to define ideology as a cultural system,[13] and it may be traced back to the seventeenth-century *Logique* of Port Royal, which sought to establish a difference between "the ideas pertaining to things and those pertaining to signs," thereby codifying the modern notion. The *Logique* also appealed to the model represented by maps and drawn plans, in which reality is somehow absorbed by the signs that stand for it:

> When one considers an object in and of itself, within its own being, without transferring the view of the spirit to that which it could represent, the idea one has is the idea of a thing, like the idea of the earth or the sun. But when one looks at a certain object as merely referring to another, one has the idea of a sign, and so it may be called. Ordinarily, this is the way one regards maps or tableaux. Thus, a sign contains two ideas—one, of the thing represented, and the other, of the thing doing the representing—and it is in the nature of signs that the first idea is evoked by the second.[14]

In order to sustain their argument, the *Logique*'s authors Arnauld and Nicole must first suppose that the object will be perceived as a sign, a basic thought operation that does not depend on the diagrams themselves. Furthermore, the authors do not admit the degree to which the diagrams—along with their function of representing something else—acquire a certain autonomy of their own. Among the principles they derive from the discussion, Arnauld and Nicole conclude that signs possess a permanence remote from the limited lives of things. As long as a sign exists, its immutability is guaranteed, even though the object represented may have been destroyed long since—hence the unalterability of the universe of signs, not subject to physical decay but only to the operations of hermeneutics. "One could conclude that the nature of signs consists in stimulating, within the mind, the image of the thing represented by the application of the thing doing the representing. As long as the effect continues, that is to say, as long as the double idea is evoked, the sign endures, even though the thing represented may itself have been destroyed."[15] From here, it is easy to invert the process: instead of representing things already existing, signs can be made to represent things as yet only imagined—the ardently desired objects of an age that displayed a special fondness for utopian dreams. Thus the manipulation of signs opened the way to a futurism characteristic of the modern era, an attitude that has attained an almost delirious apotheosis in our own day. The dreams of a future order served to perpetuate the regining political power and its attendant social, economic, and cultural structures. In addition, any discourse raised in opposition to the reigning power was required, henceforth, to establish credibility by presenting an alternative dream of the future.

Accordingly, from the time of their foundation the imperial cities of Latin America had to lead double lives: on one hand, a material life inescapably subject to the flux of construction and destruction, the contrary impulses of restoration and renovation, and the circumstantial intervention of human agency; on the other hand, a symbolic life, subject only to the rules governing the order of signs, which enjoy a stability impervious to the accidents of the physical world. Before becoming a material reality of houses, streets, and plazas, which could be constructed only gradually over decades or centuries, Latin American cities sprang forth in signs and plans, already complete, in the documents that laid their statutory foundations and in the charts and plans that established their ideal designs. These visions rarely escaped the pitfall of rationalized futures, the fatal principle of mechanical regularity that Thomas More exemplified and glorified in his own *Utopia* of 1516: "He who knows one of the cities will know them all, so exactly alike are they, except where the nature of the ground prevents."

The dreams of architects (Alberti, Filarete, and Vitruvio) and designers of utopias (More, Campanella) came to little in material terms, but they fortified the order of signs, extending the rhetorical capacity of this instrument of absolutism to impose hierarchical order on sprawling empires. Born of circumstances specific to the age, the influence of these urbanistic designs far outlasted it. Such is the nature of the order of signs that it privileges potentiality over reality, creating frameworks that, if not eternal, have lasted at least until the late twentieth century. Even more rooted has been the capacity of the order of signs, in moments when its old formulas appear exhausted, to rearticulate itself, preserving and even strengthening its central principle of hierarchy amid new historical circumstances.

This capacity of the order of signs to configure the future was complemented symmetrically by an ability to erase the past. The fifteenth and sixteenth cen turies, far from effecting a renaissance of classicism, transported it to the universe of pure form, and thus established the splendorous first cultural model of modernity, harbinger of the grander transubstantiation of the past that would be propagated by eighteenth- and nineteenth-century historicism. Renaissance palingenesis facilitated European seaborne expansion much as, a few hundred years later, Enlightenment palingenesis laid the foundation of European world domination. In their rewritings of the past, according to Peter Gay's sympathetic description, historians of the period contributed to a larger systematic effort "to secure rational control of the world, reliable knowledge of the past, freedom from the pervasive domination of myth."[16]

Modern historians, economists, and philosophers increasingly recognize the tremendous impact that the "discovery" and colonization of America had on the development of Europe—not merely in socioeconomic but also in cultural terms. One could say that the American continent became the experimental field for the formulation of a new Baroque culture. The first methodical application of Baroque ideas was carried out by absolute monarchies in their New World empires, applying rigid principles—abstraction, rationalization, and systematization—and opposing all local expressions of particularity, imagination, or invention. The overbearing power of the order of signs became most intense in those regions that much later received the name Latin America. Gathered together and cloaked by the absolute concept called "Spirit," the signs allowed their masters to disregard the objective constraints of practicality and assume a superior, self-legitimating position, where unfettered imagination could require reality to conform to abstract whimsy. This notion did not stem merely from the need to build cities, of course, although cities were its privileged settings, the artificial enclaves in which the autonomous system of symbolic knowledge could function most efficaciously. The planned urbanism of America was simply the most notable concrete application of Baroque cultural patterns that achieved their apogee under the absolutist monarchy of Spain and generally permeated the social life of its peninsular and American subjects.

The style of the Spanish Conquest contributed to the freestanding character of the resulting urban centers. In the words of Pierre Chaunu, the mainland was "opened, explored, and roughly seized during the three initial decades of the sixteenth century at an insane rhythm, never equaled."[17] Quite contrary to the pattern of an incrementally advancing frontier of settlement (as in the early colonization of Brazil or in the expansion of the United States[18]) the Spanish Conquest was a frenetic gallop across continental immensities—along nearly ten thousand kilometers of mountains, rivers, and tropical forests—leaving in its wake a scattering of cities, isolated and practically out of communication from one another, while the territory between the new urban centers continued to be inhabited almost solely by the dismayed indigenous populations. A mere thirty years elapsed between the founding of Panama City by Pedrarias Dávila and the founding of the city of Concepción (in the south of Chile) by Pedro Valdivia. In the mechanism of military domination, the urban network functioned to provide, first, bases for successive forays of conquering forces, and then, relay stations for the transmission of subsequent imperial directives. By 1550, colonial governments centered in Mexico and Peru had already begun to implement the orders of their respective viceroys, charged with the duty to "preserve in the New World the charismatic character of royal authority, based on the belief that the king ruled by the grace of God."[19]

The conquest triumphantly imposed its cities on a vast and unknown hinterland, certifying and reiterating the Greek conception that contrasted the civilized inhabitants of the polis to the barbarous denizens of the countryside.[20] The urbanization of Spanish America did not recapitulate the process that had constituted the European norm, however. Instead, that process had been precisely inverted. Rather than stemming from agrarian growth that gradually created an urban market and trade center, rural development here followed the creation of the city, which, though initially tiny, was often situated in a fertile, well-watered valley with a view to encouraging agriculture. "I admit my fascination," declared Fernand Braudel, "with the history of these [Spanish] American towns settled before the countryside or at least simultaneously with it."[21] Having instituted these towns and cities according to preestablished norms, Spanish imperial designs frequently resulted in the forced urbanization of settlers who in their Iberian homeland had been rural people, many of them never more to return to agrarian occupations. From the outset, then, urban life was the Spanish American ideal, no matter how insignificant the settlement where one lived. All now aspired to be *hidalgos*—minor nobility with the title *don* attached to their names—disdaining manual labor and lording it over their slaves and over the indigenous inhabitants who had been entrusted to them by the crown. These urban dwellers had the responsibility of organizing the agricultural production of the surrounding countryside, and they sought to generate wealth as quickly as possible through merciless exploitation of their coerced labor force. Urbanization and *nouveaux riches* went together, and smaller centers (especially mining towns), too, had more than their share of conspicuous consumption. Viceregal edicts officially restricting the use of carriages, horses, and silken garments failed to check the raging appetite for luxuries that, once set as a cultural model by the opulent conquistadors themselves, continued to be imitated by the whole society, including the poorest among the city dwellers, as colorfully described by seventeenth-century traveler Thomas Gage.[22]

The Baroque cities created by this inopportune expansion did not, of course, function in a total vacuum. Fernand Braudel points out in his notable work outlining the early development of world capitalism that "capitalism and economy marched together and interpenetrated one another, yet remained distinct."[23] Similarly, these "unreal" cities, more than slightly detached from the surrounding landscape, nevertheless took advantage of indigenous social networks—their agricultural zones, their market centers, and, above all, their labor power. By abruptly inserting their new possessions into a capitalist economy, the Spanish did not completely obliterate the preexisting indigenous market economy, which continued to function in the background for centuries, withering only gradually. Indeed, that economy was to be the source of the Spaniards' most aggressive accumulations of wealth and resources, revealing the extent of the extractive violence introduced into indigenous communities by the conquest.

The priority of urbanism within the colonizing project can be gauged by the durability of the Latin American urban ideal. Three centuries after the conquest, in the early years of the region's independent nations, Domingo Faustino Sarmiento's *Facundo* (1845) continued to present cities as civilizing nodes in a countryside capable of engendering only barbarism. To Sarmiento, cities were the only receptacles capable of accommodating the culture which he wished to import from its European wellsprings (now those of Paris, rather than Madrid) in order to construct a civilized society in America. In order to achieve their civilizing mission, the cities founded by the Spanish and the Portuguese had to dominate and impose certain norms on their savage surroundings. The first of these norms was an education centered on literacy—a true obsession of Sarmiento, who devoted much of his life to seeing it instituted in his native Argentina. It was only half a century later, in the midst of urban Brazil's frontal assault on the culture of the countryside, that Euclides da Cunha began to question the Eurocentric premises that he had previously shared with the Argentine thinker. The result was *Os Sertões* (1902), da Cunha's pessimistic account of the butchery at the millenarian settlement called Canudos in the Brazilian backlands, where military force that relied on imported European technology barely prevailed over the settlement's rustic but determined defenders. The other side of city-led "modernization" had revealed itself nakedly and disagreeably.

Far from being mere trading posts, then, the cities created by the unbridled sixteenth-century conquest aspired to become focal points of ongoing colonization. At first, they functioned—more defensively than offensively—as fortresses, walled precincts where the spirit of the polis could be distilled, protected, ideologically elaborated, and prepared to undertake the superior civilizing responsibilities that it was destined to fulfill. Not infrequently, literary texts transported cities to a "divine" plane. The sixteenth-century Mexican priest Fernán González de Eslava provides an example in his *Coloquios espirituales y sacramentales* when he describes the seven forts linking Mexico City to the Zacatecas silver mines (thus securing the safe transport of mineral wealth to the viceregal capital) in terms that transform them into nothing less than the seven sacraments of the Catholic faith.

Isolated amid vast, alien, and hostile spaces, the cities nevertheless under-took first to "evangelize," and later to "educate" their rural hinterlands. Although the first of these verbs was conjugated through religious energies and the sec-ond by a secular and agnostic spirit, both referred to essentially the same enter-prise of Eurocentric transculturation. In order to accomplish these ends, Latin American cities became the residences of viceroys, governors, and archbishops, the seats of universities, high courts, and inquisitional tribunals, before becom-ing home to the presidents and legislatures of independent countries. Such institutions were obligatory instruments for the creation and conservation of *order,* above all after two further etymological derivations of that word—subor-dinate and insubordinate—gained currency in the eighteenth century, accord-ing to the philology of Pere Corominas.

By definition, all order implies a perfectly disciplined hierarchy, so Latin American cities emerged in stratified categories that, notwithstanding the vicis-situdes of the passing centuries, continued rigidly keyed to each city's greater or lesser links to the transoceanic sources of power. At the highest level were the viceregal capitals—Lima, Mexico City, and Rio de Janeiro chief among them; at the next level, the port cities visited regularly by the fleets that provided com-munication with Europe; then the cities where the high courts called *Audiencias* were located. Finally, all of the other towns and villages of the empire followed in descending order, forming a sort of pyramid. Each city was subordinated to the higher-ranking urban centers that lay nearby, and each extracted wealth from, and provided norms of social behavior for, the rank below. Everyone knew that Madrid, Lisbon, and Seville were located above the apex of this structure, but practically no one ruminated that, at least in eco-nomic terms, other European cities like Genoa or Amsterdam might stand higher still.

Incessant conflicts over the geographical jurisdiction exercised by the author-ities of one city or another were merely symptoms of struggles to establish or rearrange the pecking order among urban centers. If, as Stanley and Barbara Stein have provocatively asserted, Spain had already begun its decline by the time of the 1492 encounter, so that an Iberian capital like Madrid already func-tioned as an economic periphery of metropolitan centers in other parts of Europe, then the cities of Latin America constituted the periphery of a periph-ery.[24] A more rarified situation is difficult to imagine: a huge urban network branching out from transatlantic roots that jealously reserve all political power to themselves but exercise it, apparently, in the service of higher powers, only dimly glimpsed. Our chief interest is the urban culture of Latin America itself, but because it necessarily rested on material foundations we must not overlook economic relationships of dependency. Cultural production was affected at every turn—often decisively—by forces imperfectly understood by people in

Latin America, even people in positions of authority, charged with executing orders of obscure logic and distant origin. Local authorities must often have appeared actors in a phantasmagoric shadow play, disconnected from the immediate realities of material life, responding, and appealing for justification, solely to the dictates of the order of signs. Speaking of something as concrete as slavery and other forms of servitude, Braudel has pointed out that they are "inherent in the reduction of a continent to the condition of *periphery,* imposed by a faraway force, indifferent to the sacrifice of men, that moves according to the nearly mechanical logic of a world-economy."[25]

The cultural structures of Latin America floated above this economy, reproducing it in subtle ways. The most lucid minds of the Iberian colonies tried to unveil the hidden workings of the system by seeking its ultimate origins beyond the colonizing metropolis, though their efforts were often condemned by institutional dictates masquerading as public opinion. In his 1624 prologue, Creole author Bernardo de Balbuena shows that his life's work, *El Bernardo,* had an Italian model despite its Spanish subject. Two centuries later, another Mexican, Justo Sierra, suggested avoiding the figurative waters of the "Spanish aqueduct" to draw inspiration instead from French literary sources (the fountainhead not only of modernism but of modernity itself).

Like the huge majority of Latin American intellectuals, both Balbuena and Sierra were men of urban vocation. Both produced the sort of literary texts that served as tacit plans for urban development in an impeccable universe of signs where the ideal city could be imagined into existence—a model of the order that the urban citizenry should strive to incarnate.

NOTES

1. See J. H. Parry; Quintero; Scobie; Hardoy; Hardoy and Schaedel; José Luis Romero.
2. Robert Ricard; Silvio Zavala.
3. See Immanuel Wallerstein.
4. Hardoy, *El modelo clásico.*
5. George Foster.
6. Lewis Mumford pointed out that Hippodamus's "true innovation consisted in realizing that the form of the city was the form of its social order," 172.
7. Michel Foucault, *Les mots et les choses,* 92–136.
8. Foucault, *Las palabras,* 64–65.
9. *Colección de documentos inéditos,* 34: 280, emphasis added.
10. Giulio Argan.
11. Foucault, *Les mots,* 78.
12. Marios Camhis.

13. Clifford Geertz, "Ideology as a Cultural System," and *The Interpretation of Cultures.*

14. Antoine Arnauld, 53.

15. Ibid., 54.

16. Peter Gay, 36.

17. Pierre Chaunu, 12.

18. Nevertheless, see the work by Alistair Hennessy, a disciple of Frederick Jackson Turner, applying the thesis to Latin America.

19. Richard Konetzke, 119.

20. On the adaptation of the Greek urban ethos to the new conditions of the New World, see Richard Morse.

21. Braudel, 343.

22. Thomas Gage.

23. Braudel, 25.

24. Stanley and Barbara Stein.

25. Braudel, 338.

2

The Lettered City:
Power and Writing in Latin America
From *Latin Americanism*

ROMÁN DE LA CAMPA

A lasting work is always responsible for an infinitely plastic ambiguity; it is everything for everyone, like the Apostle; it is a mirror that traces the features of the reader; it is also a map of the world.

—Jorge Luis Borges, *Other Inquisitions*

Never have violence, inequality, exclusion, famine, and thus economic oppression affected as many human beings in the history of the Earth and humanity.

—Jacques Derrida, *Spectres of Marx*

Although Angel Rama is best known for his contribution to Latin American transculturation theory, most Latin Americanists would agree that he does not require an introduction. His earlier work on Latin American modernism charted the field for Latin America's literary specialists in the sixties and seventies, and his entire oeuvre, which includes two books published posthumously (he died in an airplane crash in Spain in 1984), continues to accrue value today as point of reference in debates over cultural studies and postcolonialism. Yet even as his stature continues to grow in Latin America, Rama's work remains for the most part unavailable in English and beyond the reach of the English-speaking world of contemporary criticism. There are many reasons for this neglect. The renowned Peruvian novelist Mario Vargas Llosa has written that Rama "belonged to a lineage of critics who were truly influential, those who turned criticism into an artistic form comparable to other genres: a Sainte-Beuve, an Ortega y Gasset, an Arnold Bennett, an Edmund Wilson."[1] It is important to note, however, that Vargas Llosa's praise is intended to date Rama: it is a burial of sorts, an attempt to place the Uruguayan critic among the ranks of figures whose time has passed. Rama's critical acumen always ran counter to Vargas Llosa's theories of creative passion and daemonic inspiration. For Rama, literature spoke from and to a broad spectrum of cultural and social articulations. More important, however, one should note that Vargas Llosa's critical obituary is based largely on Rama's early work on Latin American modernism and the novelistic boom of the sixties. It does not take into account Rama's posthumous texts, a key body of work published after 1983 and consisting of two books and many essays that bear considerably on contemporary poststructural theoretical debates and their application to Latin American cultural studies.[2] Thus Rama entered many contemporary theoretical debates posthumously. If his work still speaks to us, it is not as a newly crowned figure in Latin America's literary pantheon, but as a challenging, contradictory, and far-reaching critical corpus. This chapter attempts to read him precisely in that light.

Of Rama's posthumous texts, none is more important in its complexity and reach than *La ciudad letrada* (*The Lettered City,* published in Spanish in 1984). A look at its reception among academic critics reveals a notable paradox: a decade and a half after its first Spanish edition, one finds hardly more than half a dozen published studies of this thick, risky essay.[3] Yet at the same time, *The Lettered City* may well be the most frequently mentioned text in contemporary Latin American cultural studies. Always present in journalistic notes and bibliographies, it has become a benchmark of sorts, a legitimizing stopping point that is always mentioned, often glossed, but hardly ever scrutinized, on the way to other topics. As with Vargas Llosa's casual observation, one finds many citations of *The Lettered City* that simply aim to mark its presence as a key point in one's critical compass, often to leave it behind in passing praise of Rama's extensive oeuvre. It is also often cited for its intriguing title, largely taken as a self-referential signifier or as a metaphor for a writerly horizon that does not require explanation in today's theoretical scene, and even less so in the world of Latin American contemporary fiction, which is often cited as the quintessential site of postmodern writing.

It may well be that *The Lettered City* has become a title that lives fully outside the body of the work it attempts to articulate. Needless to say, such forms of reading through citation and brief quotation often fail to ask if the notion of a "lettered city" could not indicate the sense of a constraining grid as much as a liberating space. Indeed, as we will see, Rama's text encompasses both meanings, thereby allowing us to understand the relationship between power and writing as always prone to constriction as much as deconstruction. Yet an even more striking set of contradictions is found if one takes into consideration published criticism of this book. Those few instances that provide a detailed analysis of *The Lettered City* reveal that it has been simultaneously understood as a prototype of colonial, modern, postmodern, and postcolonial Latin American textuality—all at once. It could be argued that such a heterogeneous reception from academic critics derives from the complex singularity of Rama's text as well as testifying to the importance it still holds for contemporary Latin American cultural studies. On the other hand, one could also ask if the mixed, if not contradictory, nature of critical assessments surrounding *The Lettered City* does not invite a more general discussion regarding the state of contemporary theory. Is the convergence of such different discourses on this text a testimony to its theoretical value, or is it a symptom of theoretical self-generation, a state in which marketability of critical discourses is directly proportional to imprecision? It is my aim in this chapter to attempt an exploration of *The Lettered City* that takes both sides of this question into consideration, that is, the proliferation of theoretical discourses as well as the growing number of discursive communities within Latin Americanism. One hastens to add that the 1996 publication of the first English edition of *The Lettered City* will undoubtedly evoke many more new readings of this book, particularly from within postcolonial and cultural studies frameworks that are now revising the postmodern schools of criticism that flourished in the United States and Britain during the 1970s and 1980s. Needless to say, this new, transnational context will more than likely contribute its own set of ambiguities. On one hand, it will provide an occasion to place Rama's text alongside others that now form a provisional critical canon in the study of postcolonialism and postnationalism. I have in mind particularly Edward Said's *Orientalism* (1978) and Benedict Anderson's *Imagined Communities* (1983), whose proximity to *La ciudad letrada* (1984) in topical range, formal aspirations, date of composition, and Foucauldian lineage deserves some attention. On the other hand, such an empowerment, available largely, if not only, through the English-speaking world, deserves particular attention for its capacity to codify new Latin American discursive markets far removed from the literary and cultural logic of Latin America itself.

Rama's text, like Anderson's and Said's, bespeaks a discursive universe somewhere between epistemology and aesthetics, an "episthetics" or middle ground that encompasses a broad range of new methods of humanistic writing and scholarship that have emerged since the early 1970s. Indeed, in this globalizing context, Rama's book is less well known, but not only because of its unavailability in English. As noted earlier, even in Spanish there has been a dearth of careful readings. This may be explained, in part, by the difficulty of his texts, which are challenging hybrid constructs of humanistic and social science theory, a dense combination of cultural criticism and historical research, and an extensive bibliographical reach that challenges a readership perhaps too accustomed to the new transnational codification of Latin Americanism. Moreover, *The Lettered City* is also constituted by a performative ambition. Its pages attempt a writing aware of its own commitment to form, though not an entirely ludic expression willing to abandon conceptual territory but, rather, a project combining historical understanding with writerly pleasure in a constant double movement.

In many ways, *The Lettered City* returns to basic themes and methods found in Rama's earlier research on the two great Latin American literary periods: the poetry of modernism between 1870 and 1920 and the extraordinary corpus of contemporary novels. Such would be his mode of tracing literary history through a rich Latin American intertextuality often understood as transculturation. But Rama's posthumous work also provides evidence of important contrasts with his earlier work. Of these, the most striking would be his examination of Latin America's writerly history as a colonial residue largely informed by Michel Foucault's notion of epistemic breaks in *The Order of Things*. This is less a direct application of Foucault's early principles than a simultaneous deploying and problematizing of his discursive epistemology. In so doing, Rama shows a willingness to alter, if not endanger, his own previous modes of reading Latin America's modern culture. His main interest now becomes the extraordinary— one should say determining—weight of the lettered class in Latin America's colonial and postcolonial history. Rama takes this history on board as a direct relation between writing and colonial power, and sets out to examine it not in its contents but through its written forms. He understands the Foucauldian concept of episteme as a structuring map for our understanding of colonial relations. More than just looking at history as a text or underlining the importance that texts acquire in our understanding of epistemic organization, Rama becomes fascinated with the notion that a new understanding of history as discourse could also allow us to examine how writing and the explosion of signs ensuing from the onset of European modernity endow the imaginary of colonial power in Latin America. Rama's focus on discourse simultaneously suggests its potential for empowerment and its constitution of prison house. His new emphasis on the colonial residue as a persistent epistemic configuration entails a radical departure from his earlier work on Latin American modernity as a clearly demarcated, autonomous period.

One ventures to say that *The Lettered City* is a true essay—in the double sense of providing a test as well as a rehearsal—of many theoretical aspects that have fueled debates in the years since it was published, many of which are central to Foucault's own work. It is now well understood that *The History of Sexuality* or *Technologies of the Self*, for example, constitute profound revisions of the discursive epistemology that was central to *The Order of Things* or The *Archaeology of Knowledge*.[4] It is important, therefore, to look at Rama's book as a mode of theoretical experimentation. His most careful readers to date have tended to look at other key aspects and problems or touched on the question of colonial discourse as a structuring episteme only tangentially. Mabel Moraña, for example, makes a careful critique of the need to make more and greater distinctions in Rama's new history of Latin American culture as the product of a "lettered" class. She also calls for a more nuanced approach to the "autonomous nature of cultural practice" and of the independent role that writers assume in Rama's book.[5] Rolena Adorno provides a different critique. She praises Rama's attempt to study colonialism as a set of relations between language and power as well as his reach beyond "the frontiers that separate literary or intellectual histories of Latin America from political and social history."[6] Yet, Adorno also reminds us that colonial writing constitutes a more extensive space—indeed, a "labyrinth of ideological rivalries"—that transcends the concept of the "enclosed lettered city" she sees in Rama's essay.[7] In a very different register, Carlos J. Alonso provides the only reading that takes Rama's Foucauldian debt as the starting point. It is his contention, however, that Rama's bid to take up the autonomy and self-referentiality of writing as a central tenet in understanding history is both equivocal and insufficient, even though it constitutes the key contribution of his book. Alonso maintains that, though profoundly flawed and ultimately dispensable, Rama's approach constitutes a symptom of the need for a truly postmodern final sweep of Latin America's penchant for sociohistorical critical methods.[8]

The underlying common thread one gathers from these widely differing views is that Rama's text has a way of provoking a richer dialogue about how one deploys discursive paradigms, all the more so when approaching Latin America's colonial order as a lingering presence during modern and postmodern periods. This does not necessarily mean that we can now assert, uncritically, Rama's place as a precursor of postcolonial studies. That would be an important trace that has so far been explored only by Josaphat Kubayanda, who has argued that Rama, as well as other Latin American writers such as Augusto Roa Bastos, should be read alongside Frantz Fanon.[9] My specific interest at this point, however, lies in the conditions of possibility for such a postcolonial appropriation; hence it has more to do with the links between globalizing postmodernism and the production of critical discourses around Latin American literature.

I will argue that *The Lettered City* contains an early but distinct and important reading of the difficulties inherent in poststructural theorizing. Obviously, in so doing, this text also reveals its own contradictions, which one would expect of any attempt to transcribe, critically and creatively, a major strand of European theory in the context of Latin American studies. Rama's posthumously published research comes directly at the main questions that inform poststructural theory, armed with perhaps the most extensive understanding of Latin American literary and cultural modern traditions of any published critic at the time. This encounter, I believe, is centered on two central sets of questions: (1) If we understand discourse as the new core of historical knowledge that is largely constituted by textuality, how will we determine whether, when, and for whom writing may constitute a liberating transgression? and (2) If we understand the discursive, or "lettered," Latin American colonial order as a special moment of textual gestation that marks all of Latin American literature since the colonial period, how does one account for the widely divergent, if not opposed, ways of understanding such a transhistorical mode of periodization?

THEORY AS LEGACY

All through Rama's text there is a constant presence of what could be defined as *episthetic* play, that is, a theoretical performance simultaneously imbued by aesthetics and epistemology. *The Lettered City* not only traces how words and signs gain autonomy in colonial Latin America; it is also an attempt to enact, if not dramatize, that very process as a contemporary strategy. The book's pulse is marked by the constant iteration of the term *lettered city,* a term that moves from the initial title to signify a more general description of an epochal epistemic construct that Rama continuously articulates, defines, and exemplifies, almost as if to meet the immensity of a reified colonial order with an utterance never satisfied with its own capacity to refer. This also explains the morphological strategy of deriving chapter subtitles from his key term—lettered city, ordered city, writerly city, modernized city, politicized city, revolutionized city—as if to show how nimbly a shifting signifier can operate even while under the hold of a given epistemic order. All of these mutations of the Latin American city-as-history respond to one logic: the intensification of the world of signs that Rama traces from the moment of the conquest through the formation of the Baroque period, or city, culminating in the modernized city, but signaling all the way through to even postmodern times.

> It is already evident in *El Bernardo* that design occupies the entire life of Bernardo de Balbuena. This is even more explicit in the 1624 prologue, in which he cites the Italian source (Boyardo, Ariosto). The same occurs two cen-

turies later, in Justo Sierra's proposal to obviate the "Spanish aqueduct" and continue designing from French literary sources.

> Both [Bernardo de Balbuena and Justo Sierra] were urban planners by vocation, as were the overwhelming majority of Latin American intellectuals. Both worked as city planners who followed closely prodigious models laid out in literary texts, in the impeccable universe of signs that allowed them to think and dream the city, in order to claim that an ideal order would be embodied in its citizens.[10]

The question of the materiality of words, of their capacity to constitute their own reality, a reality that went beyond the representation of a previous given order, is obviously a central concern for Rama. This was not a new theme for him, even though it now intensifies considerably. He had already worked on and through this key topic in previous texts, notably in his *Transculturación narrativa en América Latina,* where Ferdinand de Saussure, Claude Lévi-Strauss, Theodor Adorno, and Max Horkheimer are discussed in the context of a contemporary understanding of the relation between signification and mythology.[11] What strikes Rama at this point is the intensity of this problem in Foucault's notion of epochal discourse as epistemic ordering. Thus he begins to understand the Hispanic Baroque or the French classical period of the sixteenth and seventeenth centuries as a moment in which "words began to separate from things," giving way to "the independence of the signs."[12]

> From this moment on, through this new conduit of knowledge, the immense Latin American extension of ideal cities will flow from here. They will be governed by an ordering reason that reveals itself in a hierarchical social order transposed to a geometric distributive order. . . . Thus society and city do not connect, but their respective forms do; indeed, they are perceived as equivalent, allowing us to read society when we are reading a city map. To make this conversion possible, it was first necessary to work through a previous rational project, which was what magnified and made the order of signs indispensable, allowing it to claim the greatest operational freedom it could marshal.[13]

Here we can clearly observe a shift in Rama's previous understanding of history, which up to then had been primarily concerned with links between Latin American literary modernism and the specific features of modernity in societies that remained somewhat peripheral to its First World definitions. The theoretical groundwork of *The Lettered City* was laid at the end of the 1970s and the beginning of the 1980s, a period that in Latin American literary criticism still belongs to an in-between moment of late structuralism and its later strands, which include, particularly in U.S. Latin Americanism, early forms of decon-struction. This transitional moment is roughly present, in different ways, in the work of Foucault himself, as well as in Said's *Orientalism*, which, like Rama's text, is itself informed by early readings of Foucauldian epistemics. Like Rama, Said takes on board this newly formed way of theorizing the arbitrariness of the sign, the so-called abyss between language and world, but never quite accepting unconditionally, nor failing to see it as an opportunity to continue to theorize colonialism, imperialism, and agency, as would be perhaps the case with much of the literary deconstructionism of this moment.

Said would eventually write books that continued to problematize this theo-retical legacy, as is evident from *The World, the Text, and the Critic,* and even more from *Culture and Imperialism.* It would be hazardous to guess what Rama would have written had he continued to live, but the early parallels with Said's work are not fortuitous. There are many ways of historicizing the Saussurean theoretical legacy and its subsequent evolution in literary studies, all the way into what I have called its contemporary episthetic moment. I would, however, hazard to sketch three general moments or tendencies that are often found in overviews: (1) the construction of epistemes, aggregates, and totalities prone to structuralist configuration and analysis; (2) the ensuing modes of deconstruction of such constructs, some strictly from the singularity of key or canonical texts, others with a more extensive model of how textuality and dispersal challenge his-tory as well as literary studies; (3) the post-1989 moment in which humanistic studies are confronted as never before with globalization, the privatization of all academic and social spheres, and the advent of cultural studies as a full-blown academic specialization in the United States. These are obviously not fixed cat-egories, nor do they denote firm temporal boundaries.[14] My fundamental inter-est here is to complicate any attempt that fails to account for the points of contact and contrast that contaminate these moments in rather unsettled ways.

To some readers, *The Lettered City* might correspond strictly to the set of con-cerns associated with a late-structuralist moment, but it is a bit more compli-cated than that. As stated earlier, its central preoccupation is the advent of a more arbitrary order of signification, or at least a more transparent way of under-standing the pretenses of a representational order that was taken to constitute "the real" in Latin American intellectual history. This allows disciplinary knowl-edge to come under scrutiny as a series of heuristic structures or totalizations configured by archives, grammars, literary genres, city plans, and other forms of organizing the production and reception of the social imaginary. Textuality, here understood as not just literature but all forms of writing and sign production, thus assumes a privileged role for unpacking and at the same time constituting a new totality out of the colonial order. Again, Rama's concern clearly parallels Foucault's "archaeological" moment regarding the classificatory power of disciplines or Said's demarcation of how orientalism forms a particular kind of knowledge that brings a certain lettered order to its practitioners by producing the very object it purports to describe.[15]

The second, or deconstructionist, moment began to manifest itself in Latin American criticism toward the end of the 1970s in some American universities. It came precisely at a time when the Latin American novelistic boom was becoming a world-class corpus in the United States. It was also much more skilled than previous paradigms at working with the experimental nature of writers such as Jorge Luis Borges, Gabriel García Márquez, Carlos Fuentes, Mario Vargas Llosa, and others who would eventually constitute a considerable part of the postmodern canon. Today this is still a predominant paradigm, even as it becomes absorbed by more recent articulations of literary postmodernism, postcolonialism, or high-end cultural studies. It has achieved a significant degree of sophistication and institutional recognition, particularly through work published primarily in English. Texts such as *Myth and Archive* by Roberto González Echevarría and *Inventing America* by José Rabasa continue to shape an already impressive bibliography. Interestingly, this mode of criticism also stems from a privileged sense of discursivity, now termed "writing," but it moves in a somewhat different direction from the work produced in the first moment. Rather than formulating objects of study as totalized aggregates that encompass history as discursive epistemes, it posits historical understanding and literary appreciation, often without distinguishing between the two, as an ongoing process of designification, particularly available when applied to major literary and philosophical texts. Its attention moves toward intensifying the practice of close reading as the ideal method for disinterring contradictions always present in discourse. The familiar regime of words or the epistemic grid of high structuralism now moves toward a liberating model implicit in the transgressive potential of deconstruction, particularly when drawn from the elaborate discursive patterns of literature and philosophy, an always-already polysemic presence that is said to exceed or subvert any representational bond between words and things.

What is generally assumed by this critical approach, particularly through literary deconstruction and metanarrative critique, is that the internal dynamics of specialized texts are equally inherent in all texts, or that model texts can be made to encompass the entire social realm.[16] This is the epistemological leap more prevalent among critical paradigms in the 1980s and early 1990s that Rama was already unwilling to take in *The Lettered City*. Today that leap may be considerably more difficult or open to debate. But what is important to note is how Rama already straddles the line between the two moments of the discursive legacy presented thus far, challenging each in different ways. At one level, based on his reading of Foucault, he undoubtedly assimilates an understanding of Latin American culture as a great archive of textuality, but he also confronts that totality with collective forms of popular and class culture that threaten to break the epistemic monolith. At another level, he fully apprehends the notion of semiotic excess internal to literary writing, but he also moves in an opposite direction by positing a way of looking at Latin American culture as a lettered order more than capable of absorbing individual acts of transgression, without failing to account for their artistic excellence.

Globalization, a term that lacks genuine specificity, can nonetheless serve provisionally to define a third moment in theoretical work. It is intended here to refer to the launching of a neoliberal market logic upon the blithe and ludic energies that dominated postmodern imaginaries up to 1989. With the end of the Cold War and the disappearance of the weaker side of an East/West, First World/Second World set of binaries, Western triumphalism began to manifest itself as globalization in the name of the end, whether of history, modernity, or ideology. It is now evident, however, that this vacuum is beginning to call forth more concrete approaches to questions of ethics and politics in theoretical work, as is apparent in the angst expressed in Derrida's *Spectres of Marx*. Needless to say, it remains to be seen how far the liberatory or transgressive understanding of postmodern academic practice will be tested from within by this latest capitalist expansion. We can now observe much more clearly, for example, that earlier moments of poststructuralist understanding also had their own utopian, if not identitarian, longings. This is what Christopher Norris calls a tendency to give language and writing "nearly anthropomorphic attributes."[17] Indeed, the need to clarify or sort out what I have called our contemporary legacy has also been felt by Latin American critics and theorists, particularly those who work outside the U.S. academy. Carlos Rincón, one of the most prolific theorists of Latin America's postmodern literary scene, stipulates that it is high time for an "indispensable differentiation" regarding the "multiple interconnections among postmodernism, postcolonialism, and Latin Americanism, not only in terms of analytic-descriptive terminology, but also in terms of what constitutes contemporaneity."[18] My argument here is not that the rich theoretical legacy of the past three decades has suddenly been rendered redundant, nor that its value has receded to what it was in a blissful epoch when theory was much less significant. I do want to suggest, however, that theory is now a rather muddled terrain in constant need of reassessment and clarification. Moreover, I would like to argue that certain early theoretical texts such as *The Lettered City*, which straddle the line between colonial and postcolonial subject matters, already contain many ambiguities that have of late become more evident in theoretical work. In short, it is my contention that Rama's attempt to engage Foucault's conceptual archaeology in the context of a nonsynchronous Latin American colonial legacy turns into a telling, albeit aporetic, confrontation between that very theory and its object.

Other attempts to theorize Latin American literature as an intricate part of the Western discursive legacy could serve as a pertinent background. One important example would be "neo-Baroque" theory, particularly as seen in the work of Severo Sarduy, which incorporates both structural and poststructural semiological precepts that first circulated in Latin American literary circles in unison with the advent of the novelistic boom period in the sixties and early seventies.[19] Rama's work, though chronologically close to that period, already affords significant contrasts: he studies literature as part of a cultural period composed of an array of texts that defies strict literary enclosure; he understands the links between literature and markets of reception, and he sees the great novels of the Latin American boom period as metatextual attempts to encompass an inexhaustible difference available only through multiple discourses and asynchronic constellations. It should not surprise us, therefore, that Rama becomes the first Latin American critic to engage Foucault—rather than Roland Barthes or Paul de Man—systematically, in a full-length study that afforded Rama a broader, more historical approach to the new discursive horizon. During the mid-1980s to early 1990s, other critics would attempt to incorporate Foucauldian categories into methods of deconstructionist close readings that had otherwise failed to render any workable sense of literary or cultural history. A key example mentioned earlier would be Roberto González Echevarría's *Myth and Archive*. Today this emphasis has assumed an even greater importance in the growing awareness that postmodern methods of reading, particularly those canonized by literary criticism, are at once necessary and insufficient. Texts such as Walter Mignolo's *The Darker Side of the Renaissance* and Rincón's already-cited *La no simultaneidad de lo simultáneo* constitute new attempts to map the territory of Latin American literary/cultural studies. But it is important to probe further how this contemporary problematic is already present in Rama's text as an embryonic set of symptoms and contradictions.

One problem that nearly all of Rama's readers observe is his unwillingness to take stock of the ways in which a given text can subvert hegemonic logic or the order sustained by Latin America's lettered class through various centuries. Actually, as one can see in the following quotation, Rama does on occasion distinguish the exceptional quality of certain texts and writers, even if he appears unwilling to render them individually capable of countervailing official history:

> Sor Juana's original (brilliant) move consists in having turned the dislocation between literary discourse and the world of affect into the central theme of her poetics. She managed to render suspect (hence the oneiric irruption of the *First Dream*) the belief that truth could only stem from the hemisphere of the occult, thus disrupting, if not destroying, rational discourse, which, while claiming autonomy and self-sufficiency, only managed to gather obscure impulses.[20]

Rama's critics will rightfully observe that his intellectual history does not quite allow for the promise of textual irruption to come through in seminal texts because he is much less concerned with exceptions than with a structured totality. Indeed, Rama looks for a representational field of force that functions almost as a pact between colonial power and organic intellectuals armed with the power to signify in ever more imaginative ways. He fails to see—or, more accurately, resists—the notion that specific texts or authors can be said to alter this relationship between power and signification, or that we can reconstruct the epistemic period solely based on the transgressive qualities of a given text. Put in different ways, he seems to challenge us to show how our newfound appreciation of rhetorical liminality is able to dent in any significant way the larger historical totality he creates out of this extraordinary lettered order of the colonial imaginary. One hastens to add, however, that Rama's approach also discards, radically, many other forms of Latin American criticism that were prevalent at the time and that continue to populate the critical landscape in the United States as well as in Latin America. I am referring not only to various forms of sociological content analysis often found in dependency theory, but also to literary histories bound by generational theory, author-bound models of literary hagiography, impressionism, and various other forms of unbridled aesthetic humanism. These methods, constituting modes of totalizing in their own right that are often absorbed by postmodern eclecticism, could not be more at loggerheads with Rama's work.

In *The Lettered City,* but even more so in *Las máscaras democráticas del modernismo* (a series of essays collected for book publication by friends and colleagues after Rama's death), he incorporates all of his earlier research in a new matrix that not only includes experimentation with notions of history as discourse, but also attempts to study how the language of desire and the erotic affect our understanding of history. At this stage, for the first time in his prolific career, Rama sees the crucial role of women and women's writing in any attempt to configure the Latin American modernist imaginary. There are some differences between these two books, because the latter begins to move away from the concept of a "lettered culture" toward the possibility of a more "democratized culture" that stems from a more nuanced understanding of eroticism, desire, and women's writing. But both books are still bound by a theory of orality that constitutes the only really transgressive space conceived by Rama, and both reiterate a central skepticism regarding the role of lettered intellectuals: "the doctrinal discourse they imposed on poetry": "the intellectual heroism of a few superior spirits, and the failure that awaited the majority of them."[21] Moreover, both texts respond to the new elaboration in Rama's work prior to his death: bringing literary intertextuality to a transcultural understanding of Latin American cultural forms and epistemic configuration from colonial times to the advent of postmodernity.

A key moment in this new casting would be Rama's approach to political discourse, particularly the model he offers to study Latin American revolutions during the twentieth century. He writes that these recurrent historical events should be evaluated by placing a greater value on "deep social change" rather than on "violent rupture."[22] This distinction disrupts many mythical moments of a revolutionary narrative. It also brings Rama to sense the advent of a new historical era by concluding that the 1970s mark the end of modern Latin American revolutions, "an epoch that has continued since 1911 in which the debates and protagonists look pretty much alike and their fight with universal circumstances varies only to the degree that it worsens."[23] Rama's critics have thus far failed to notice this new periodization of the almost sacred popular terrain of Latin American revolutions from a new historical schema that takes on board colonial and neocolonial intellectual residues. Notice how he approaches the difference between social change and lettered representation in what is incontestably the most marked chapter of Latin America's contemporary revolutionary legacy:

> The direct consequence of the politicization of the city will be a new functional conception of the political party, with the development of a new democratic base and other side effects that were never known to nineteenth-century political parties. This trend will continue during the twentieth century until the latter decades, when the old regime of Freemason lodges will reappear as new militarized nuclei (*focos*) that will require a new legitimizing theory to adjust well-entrenched customs: this is the well-known pamphlet by Regis Debray, *Revolution in the Revolution* (1969), which transcribes the Cuban revolutionary conception at the time, a conception that no longer does justice to the revolutionary movement that was indeed able to involve ample sectors of society, a conception that already began to become mystified with that little book by Franqui, *The Twelve*.[24]

One can also observe here how Rama leans on the distinction between a revolution and its discursive representation in order to exonerate deep social change from verbal mystifications of violent rupture. This is obviously a complex and controversial reading of revolution, undoubtedly an alternative to contemporary critiques of modern master narratives that tend simply to dismiss Latin American revolutionary movements without further ado, as if they were just a forgettable or misguided episode in history. It is also important to place Rama's complex critique in light of his personal story at the time of his death, the short period he spent living and working in the United States. During the early 1980s, Rama's work profited tremendously from the time afforded him by a Woodrow Wilson fellowship and University of Maryland visiting appointments, but it should also be noted that he suffered intense political harassment and personal denigration during those years from those who sought to deny him a work visa to continue working in the United States.[25] At the heart of Rama's exploration of the intertextual relations between literature and cultural studies lies a very Gramscian set of concerns and categories: most prominently, the function of intellectuals and the production of social-symbolic capital. This approach yields a different understanding of subversion that is not strictly bound to major texts and literary moments but involves what Rama calls the "real city." By this term, he does not mean a return to realism; rather, he intends an apprehension of the social text as a transcultural pivot of conflicting forces. This is why Rama attempts to configure a countercanon that expands our sense of colonial and premodern Latin American textuality. The main elements of such a canon would include: orality as a social formation, graffiti as collective writing, unorthodox grammars such as Simón Rodríguez's writing experiments, reread-ings of texts such as the picaresque novel *El Periquillo Sarniento,* and, above all, the idea of popular speech. Hence Rama's notion of transgression and resistance looks toward a multiplicity of conflictive voices and cultural forms that goes beyond the reach of narrative heteroglossia and the privileging of writing as the only site of difference and otherness.

THE OTHER CITY

It is difficult to find critical texts informed by deconstruction that are willing to encompass the social realm without neutralizing it or turning it into a literary trope that immediately reduces the social to an undifferentiated coefficient of writerly polysemy. This could well constitute one of the specific challenges for literary Latin Americanism and its postmodern metafictions, particularly as they turn into a paradigm for otherness as rhetorical space in figures such as Menard, Bustrófedon, and Melquíades. One needs to ask what is gained and lost as Latin American literature turns into a prototype of postmodern writing or is seen as the exotic source of a magic realism marketable on a worldwide scale. Nonetheless, signs of a more complex and heterogeneous criticism are already present in the work of Beatriz Sarlo, Néstor García Canclini, Roberto Schwarz, and Nelly Richard, among others.[26] That they generally write, work, and produce theory in Latin America itself is a telling, though not a singularly determining, factor in their more nuanced approach. What differentiates their writing is not simply that they operate from a different locus of enunciation, a concept that is quite capable of reintroducing a weak but celebrated sense of inchoate pluralism in which all loci claim truth and beauty at once. The problem has more to do with how sites of legitimation constitute markets that govern the production and reception of influential critical discourses. Like Rama, these Latin American critics approach contemporary developments in literary theory as an ongoing instability that also encompasses the social realm. They work in settings in which the institutional structure of their disciplines is not a stable, autonomous constellation of research universities. Hence their work tends to take episthetic work beyond its customary hermeneutical interplay to another terrain that can extend to the deconstruction of dominant postmodern aesthetics. In the last few paragraphs of Néstor García Canclini's *Consumidores y ciudadanos* (*Consumers and Citizens*), for example, one finds the call for new forms of urban subject formation and the public sphere in Latin American cities:

> Any realistic look at our contemporary societies will not find it difficult to conclude there are few reasons to be in favor of the excluded and the exploited. Walter Benjamin used to say that only because of our love for the downtrodden do we manage to conserve hope. I will add that it is still possible to justify solidarity, as artists, writers, and scientists, to the extent that we enjoy a certain degree of emancipation, or at least that we have an interest in keeping emancipation and renovation of the real—indeed, a certain utopian sense—as part of the social realm. During the seventies and eighties, postmodern thought taught us to liberate ourselves from the illusions implicit in metanarratives that promised totalizing and totalitarian emancipations. Perhaps it is time to emancipate ourselves from our disenchantment.[27]

But perhaps the most elaborate attempt to articulate a detailed deconstruction of society as a discursive category is found in Ernesto Laclau's *New Reflections on the Revolution of Our Time.*[28] Indeed, Laclau's text may well constitute a test case of the interesting contradictions that ensue when one transposes Derridean epistemology from the literary to the social. In the chapter titled "The Impossibility of Society," for instance, one finds a set of distinctions that may be usefully juxtaposed to Rama's notion of the "real city." For example, though Laclau underlines the centrality of the term *discourse,* he warns that such a term must be "liberated from its restrictive meaning as writing or speech."[29] He also assigns a special role to the "infinite play of differences," but he insists that it does not derive so much from the internal dynamism of specific texts as from the social space:

> The great advance carried out by structuralism was the recognition of the relational character of any social identity; its limit was its transformation of those relations into a system, into an identifiable and intelligible object (i.e., into an essence). But if we maintain the relational character of any identity and if, at the same time, we renounce the fixation of those identities in a system, then the social must be identified with the infinite play of differences, that is, with what in

the strictest sense of the term we can call *discourse*—on the condition, of course, that we liberate the concept of discourse from its restrictive meaning as speech and writing. . . . The social always exceeds the limits of the attempts to constitute society. At the same time, however, that "totality" does not disappear: if the suture it attempts is ultimately impossible, it is nevertheless possible to proceed to a relative fixation of the social through the institution of nodal points.[30]

Laclau assigns the key notion of "excess in meaning" to the sphere of the social, or what he terms "the infinitude of the social," whose contours always exceed the limits of representational order or any unitary concept of society. An understanding of "excess" as an interplay pertaining to the social sphere constitutes an interesting contrast with literary deconstructionism that tends to locate this phenomenon only in writing or relies heavily on a standard binary between language and the social, whereby the former is inherently excessive and the latter enclosing. Laclau disturbs that handy binary by introducing a different set of oppositions: the distinction between the social and society, as well as the distinction between the social and both speech and writing. Laclau's conceptualization of discourse allow us to redraw those boundaries, not only in a closer reading of his own book, but also as a propaedeutic for understanding *The Lettered City*. Moreover, a social grounding of excess enables us to open a space of discursive negotiation and contestation that goes beyond literary heteroglossia. This in turn augments the notion of textuality in significant ways: (1) the realm of the social includes ongoing political and economic conflicts that destabilize a critical practice whose radical claims seldom dare go beyond the shelter of distant texts and the inner sanctum of academic institutions; (2) it disrupts the conceptual slide that neutralizes pertinent differences between signifiers such as literature, writing, epistemology, and finally the social. As Laclau maneuvers around these theoretical turns, he arrives at a paradoxical juncture also present in Rama's text: the constant dissemination within the social makes it impossible to articulate society as a totality, yet that totality does not disappear, because the social is never reducible to "the constant interplay of differences" but instead can also respond to attempts to limit that interplay, that is, the forces that seek to "contain it within the confines of a given order." Inasmuch as it is a totality, society is unattainable; but it is possible to proceed toward a relative construction of the social through nodal points that are "subject to different determinations and overdeterminations."[31]

Laclau's articulation typifies how inherently flexible Saussurean metalanguage can be, and how immanently transferable its central conduits have become. It could be said that the historic *langue/parole* split that informs Derrida's center/margin opposition, or Homi Bhabha's pedagogy/performance divide is here transferred to a different terrain, as Laclau attempts to examine the society/the social interplay. This reorientation of the Saussurean binary is also evident in Rama's earlier attempt to demarcate the lettered city from the real city. Needless to say, it remains to be seen whether any poststructural artic- ulation that leans on a binary opposition or split is finally able to escape its struc- tural limitations. Flirting with binaries leaves it unclear if they are ever really abandoned, rather than just momentarily submerged to be reinstated once again. What Laclau and Rama introduce into this persistent problematic is a specific attempt to extend the play of differences and semiotic excess to the broadly social and cultural domains. More important, for Rama, society is represented by the complicity between social order and writing in the lettered cities during the colonial period. Both are breached only by the social as represented by the excesses of meaning found in Amerindian orality, in the marginal spaces of colo- nial everyday life, and in the hybrid chaos of urban centers attempting to mod- ernize: "with their leagues of unknown people, their constant waves of construction and demolition, their accelerated rhythms, and the mutations introduced by their new customs."[32] Rama's real city is therefore not stably demarcated, innocent, unitary. It is instead a relational matrix stemming from a representational crisis that composes the interplay of excesses inherent in a far- reaching set of social nodes that organize Latin America's epistemic horizon: city/countryside, elite/popular, resistance/complicity, Americanism/Eurocen- trism, writing/orality, among others. Rama's real/lettered city dyad could thus be understood as an attempt to grasp social forms and contents that tend to escape more stable demarcations of the binary model:

> Seen from the ardent infiltration of our everyday experiences, and from a past that we transport secretly within us, and inside the texture of our dreams, it is possible to suspect that the ideal city did not copy a precise European model over the Western shore of the Atlantic, as it has been often said of our always mimetic upper classes. But those cities were also an invention made with an appreciable margin of originality; they were daughters of a desire that is freer than all the real models, and even more frenzied. Moreover, given their aspira- tion to become *real-izable,* they would enter into a murky amalgam with the sur- rounding reality.[33]

Such a reading of colonial desire entails a double movement: it discards the simple idea of representational mimesis or governing conventional accounts of the relations between writing and the social, while claiming a space somewhere between the real and the real-izable. The latter aspect can only be understood through Rama's concept of orality as transculturation, that is, as the aggregate of multiple languages that converge on Latin America's popular culture: alternative modes of writing, undecidable gestures, and marginal, resistant modes of signifying that include a historical understanding of graffiti and musical forms such as *corridos* and tangos. He observes, for example, that the popular novel *El Periquillo Sarniento,* published in 1816 by the Mexican writer José Joaquín Fernández de Lizardi, "is much more of a threat to the lettered city than to the Spanish monarchy, or even the Catholic church."[34]

It should be emphasized that Rama is concerned with a form of orality that deviates substantially from Derrida's notion of speech as "presence." In his critique of the Western philosophical tradition, Derrida carefully deconstructs presence as the presumed authority of oral speech, behind which there always lies an arch-writing of sorts. For Rama, however, orality does not constitute a cult of originary presence; rather, it names an internal gaze directed at the colonial and neocolonial forms of epistemic excess, an attempt to delve into the discursive resources of the Creole verbal order from the colonial epoch to our times. A key moment in this order appears in the problem of linguistic transmission of American words to the narrative structures of Spanish language, a topic that Rama traces through various important writers over a period of three centuries. It is found in the reconversion of legal codes of Carlos de Sigüenza y Góngora, as well as the *costumbrista* novel filled with glossaries, and is later turned into theories of the Latin American Baroque by the contemporary Cuban novelist Alejo Carpentier. Here we see another instance of a colonial residue, for, according to Rama, Carpentier remains caught in this lingering problem of American linguistic reconversion inasmuch as he manages only to substitute for previous glossaries a new code of metalinguistic explication.[35] Reconversion, the process of translating Latin American languages and cultures into Spanish narrative forms, becomes a preoccupation among Latin American writers whom Rama also attempts to deconstruct, in his profoundly alternative ways, through his own understanding of radical transculturation. Perhaps the most elaborate example he gives is the social thought of Simón Rodríguez, which "is situated in a pre-Saussurean, anti-Derridean line, and which recognizes in language an oral tradition independent of writing that is formed in a rather different way."[36] It should be noted here that Rama's work exhibits frequent traces of engagement with continental critics and philosophers such as Adorno, Lévi-Strauss, Gilles Deleuze, Félix Guattari, and Foucault, particularly in his last books. It is not evident how much of an opportunity he had to study Derrida before he died, but it is clear he is aware of how the latter structures his critique of orality and Western logocentrism in *De la grammatologie* (1967).[37] Rama even makes an allusion to Jean-Jacques Rousseau's *Essay on the Origin of Languages* by way of a quotation from Simón Rodríguez that is both subtle and complex in its possible reading of Derrida's critique. The mystical force often ascribed to Rousseau's sense of oral speech, a self-sufficient medium that organizes society as an organic totality, is not Rama's interest. He understands orality as a site where the difficult crisscrossing of chronologies and discourses becomes history. This is best illustrated in his bid to locate historical change in oral traditions that are otherwise unavailable to the notion of myth proposed by Lévi-Strauss:

> Orality modulates itself within a cultural flow that is in permanent composition and transformation. Lévi-Strauss's observation that all variants compose the same myth is still pertinent to this matter. But orality allows us to recognize how the adaptation of different concrete circumstances takes place. It also allows us to introduce what amounts to a historical factor that is often difficult to measure from within the myths of aboriginal cultures, but which is more attainable through the verbal inventiveness of rural cultures. Through that historical factor we can ascertain new variants within traditional flows that generally seem atemporal, thereby illustrating how historical circumstances are adapted.[38]

Rama's critiques of structuralism and poststructuralism make clear how his work is situated in a significant chapter of Latin America's own encounter with the theoretical legacy that runs through Foucault and Derrida. It is also clear that even if Rama does not offer a close reading of these key European sources, he brings them to a pivotal give-and-take with his previous essays and research projects, themselves in constant theoretical and thematic movement. It could further be said that, like Derrida, Rama understands orality as a sort of arch-writing that constitutes a historical order sustained by norms, hierarchies, and verbal oppositions, even if he differs with Derrida over whether writing can be opposed to orality on a universal plane. The reason for that quibble emerges when Rama's own casting of orality diverges from the Saussurean legacy of structuralist and poststructuralist signification. As the passage cited earlier illustrates, Rama finds a central example of subaltern orality in some Latin American rural cultures. Another instance would be found in the multiple transcultural relationships he sees between writing and orality, a nonsynchronous text that springs from Latin America as a multilingual, multiethnic, and multinational construct. Rama's linguistic model—also underscored in the work of linguists and anthropologists such as Eugenio Coseriu and Martin Lienhard—is more hybrid in its appropriation of alphabetic forms and colonial models of writing different from those available to Western metaphysics and its more contemporary revisions.

There is ample room to disagree over how Rama's work may be understood today, but it seems clear that the main set of concerns guiding it is increasingly evident. *The Lettered City* endeavors to bring the social text and colonial residues within the range of poststructural theory. The former is obviously the central concern of cultural studies, the latter of postcolonialism. Furthermore, it could be argued that both aspects constitute an index of the shortcomings implicit in the poststructural methods that Rama somehow managed to detect fifteen years earlier. Perhaps I can illustrate this point by appealing to a text mentioned earlier—Walter Mignolo's *The Darker Side of the Renaissance*— which sets forth a political history of orality and the different writerly systems that were prevalent during Latin America's colonial period. The pivotal moment in this book, notwithstanding the author's unsuccessful attempts to downplay its implications, is an extensive examination of Derridean presuppositions in the contexts of colonial philology and semiotics. Mignolo, an Argentine critic originally trained as a philologist and semiotician, attempts to provide a comparative linguistic history of orality, which he sees as the basis for a potential school of Latin American postcolonial studies. What follows is an enumeration of the most important propositions that Mignolo finds wanting in Derrida's work. Together they provide not only a different accent on orality, but also an attempt to underscore the role of orality in the history of imperialism that reveals striking parallels with Rama's main postulates.

- Derrida's crucial insights do not transcend a certain evolutionary prejudice. They presuppose that with the invention of the alphabet, the history of writing takes a road that overcomes all alternative forms.

- There are nonalphabetical forms of writing as well as alternative forms to the Greco-Roman alphabet.

- One could begin with the grammars of Antonio de Nebrija instead of Rousseau: for Nebrija, the letter did not represent the voice but the domestication of voice, a crucial step in the constitution of contemporary imperial states as well as in the colonization of non-Western languages.

- During the colonial expansion, certain systems of writing sustained a different relationship between writing and the sounds of language that complicates the evolutionary history of letters in the Western tradition.

- Western logocentrism shows its limits when it confronts forms of knowledge and meaning that are based on alternative forms of speech and writing.

- The deconstruction of Western metaphysics is not preoccupied with the structure of power that allowed alphabetic writing to establish a hierarchy of cultures that in turn allowed the extension of its image of superiority.[39]

Horst Ruthrof argues in his *Semantics and the Body* that linguistically dominated literary theories have failed to include the "re-emergence of the corporeal in the linguistic structures which they emphasize,"[40] thereby echoing Édouard Glissant's *Caribbean Discourse* in the call for a new postcolonial understanding of the ways in which orality and the body unhinge the reification of writing. By "corporeal," Ruthrof means a realm of language that defies the predominantly syntactical enclosure inherent in theories derived from Saussurean epistemology. Although he finds Derrida's work slightly less driven to that enclosure (in comparison to, say, Jean Baudrillard, Paul de Man, or Jean-François Lyotard), he insists that "the discrepancy of reference and speech modalities" must be dealt with through an intersemiotic and heterosemiotic engagement that the theories based on the linguistic turn are unlikely to offer, particularly for multicultural societies, which "can only be enriched by the inevitable modification of standard meaning events by alternative representations."[41]

DISSEMINATION AND REORDERING

The Lettered City has a wayward quality about it, perhaps the only appropriate manner for an essay that takes so many risks and dares so much. As I have argued, this text constitutes a pronounced shift from Rama's previous essays on Latin American modernism and contemporary narrative that is best viewed in the continuum of contemporary theoretical work, itself filled with trials and errors during the past three decades. Only in that sense of accumulated dispersal could one see Rama's text peeping from his Latin American outpost into the contemporary postmodern sense of chaos. We may ask, however, if the 1990s did not shift that sense of dispersal toward a reordering of sorts, to a logic of privatization and the market often misread as just academic wars over the fate of print culture. This has no doubt led to a certain urgency in the work of theory, evident, for example, in such otherwise different texts as Derrida's *Spectres of Marx* and Aijaz Ahmad's *In Theory*. Each struggles, in distinct but analogous ways, to register the drama of this particular moment, to see how our present is a legacy filled with attainment as well as contradictions, revisions, and misplaced bets. Rama's work should not be exempt from that urgency. His work affords the possibility of grasping margins, supplements, and residues from Latin American cultural history to question that privilege generally reserved for literary masters as the only story worth retelling or deconstructing. That wayward articulation takes us to an alternative reading of Latin America's discursive dispersal, that is, to Rama's categories of colonial residue discussed earlier: subaltern social thought, subversive orthography, the social realm as epistemic excess, peripheral modernity as real-izable cities, unlettered revolutions, and the languages of graffiti, tangos, and *corridos.*

The questions raised by Rama have an undeniably contemporary tenor. They can be correlated within the contradictory sense in which today's cultural studies and postcolonial thought simultaneously attempt to challenge and invoke the same theoretical legacy of the past three decades. I would add that Rama's work leads to an appraisal of the conflictive impact of global capitalism and market forces on cultural formation that currently confounds theoretical work. I am referring to the voices that now seek to contain and reorder discursive dispersal from within the bosom of Western art and philosophy. An emblematic instance is Harold Bloom's *The Western Canon*. Bloom warns that we have lost a sense of values in literary study, and that the primacy of great Western literature has come under siege from a new gendered, multicultural context. It is important to ask here, I believe, how one of the most influential figures in U.S. literary criticism comes to terms not so much with contemporary theory but with the social text surrounding it. It could be said, following Rama's critical categories, that Bloom has identified the postmodern "real city" as consigned by an indifferentiated catalog of alternative cultural studies textuality threatening to claim too big a space in U.S. universities. Bloom labors to expose the contemporary academy, but his main philippic is aimed at the absence of aesthetic sensibility in today's social realm.

How might we take Bloom's charge seriously, and to what extent is Rama's work relevant here? Bloom seems to be asking us if we have not witnessed or perhaps even abetted the process of debasing academic disciplines and their object of study. But who is to blame for this degradation? New generations of assistant professors insufficiently refined? Universities restructured by privatizing globalization? The enlarged domain of mass media? Greater access to education on the part of women and racial minorities? Interdisciplinary cultural studies? New genres of autobiographical narcissism? These have admittedly produced extraordinary tensions, but the question of contemporary aesthetics and sensibility requires a more nuanced reading of the social text than is given by Bloom. Consider Néstor García Canclini's description of a new Latin American urban citizenry:

> Forty years after the electronic media took over the public sphere and became the principal formative agent of the collective imaginary, the ministries of culture continue to be fully committed to the fine arts. In the best of cases, they also concern themselves a bit with traditional popular cultures, but they almost never have anything to say or do about modern urban cultures such as rock, tabloid narratives, photonarratives, videos, in short, the media that move the thought and sensibilities of the masses. They are therefore disengaged from the scenarios of consumption that constitute what we could perhaps call the aesthetic basis of citizenship.[42]

Is it possible to reconcile the theoretical work of the past three decades, a process that originally included an enthusiastic younger Bloom, with the dynamic marketing of contemporary cultural forms and imaginaries? Are spaces for critique and contestation still available? Three responses are typically given:

(1) make the university a pillar of resistance for the lettered values in force prior to postmodern dispersion and cultural studies; (2) redraw the boundaries of critical and artistic values originally promulgated by poststructural theory to accommodate the neoliberal reordering of the academy through market logic and cultural studies; (3) configure a new set of critical and aesthetic relations out of diverse cultural forms, critical theories, and market strategies. Rama, in my view, speaks to the third alternative, even though his frame of reference remains largely literary. Bloom, on the other hand, appears to long for the autonomous space afforded to good taste implicit in the first response.

But Bloom's agenda is arguably more complex and could be said to approximate the second position in certain ways. His aim is not quite to reestablish the exclusivity of traditional humanistic order, but rather to reorder literary studies on the basis of a new canon of world literature capable of including a few non-European authors that could be organically translated into English. This program implies the possibility of a global hermeneutic based on a somewhat expanded corpus, a community of readers guarded by well-trained professionals, and enough well-funded, or at least sustainable, libraries and university presses. Global, though still largely Western, literature would then reach a higher level of universality than was known to the modernist paradigm, while at the same time it would depend less on the exigencies of localized cultural distinctions still spawned by global marketing. The constitution of a world literary canon, produced through English translations, would then be able to return value to literary studies, reaffirming at the same time the institutional space of tradition in the face of the mass-mediatic dispersion of academic disciplines. Such would be a deeper account of Bloom's alternative reordering: a post-postmodern realignment of theoretical dispersal inspired by a previous order, a move to transcend the most transgressive elements of the poststructuralist legacy.

It is not clear, however, if Bloom's literary sensibility could absorb the pressures of a modified canon sufficiently expanded to cover the world in any meaningful way. It is also not clear that one language can bear the weight of literary hierarchy and simultaneously serve as the currency of exchange through translation. A monolingual concept of comparative literature could well sustain a "world literature," but even though English provides the prism through which transnational literary valuation is refracted, it is quite likely that this more catholic form of literariness will be transformed by cultural forces and new readings it cannot really dissipate. Indeed, as the *lingua franca* of globalization, English may already be compromised as a true conduit of Western canon formation, for the House of English is now filled with permanent guests for whom the distinction between a native and a second language has been permanently transformed.

These same disjunctions are even clearer in the work of Richard Rorty, a prominent figure in contemporary American philosophy. His latest books and essays seek to define more concretely the confrontation between postmodern theory, the old lettered order, and global cultural dispersion.[43] He argues that Derridean deconstruction and Foucauldian critique of metanarratives should be understood more as a continuation of rather than a rupture within Western hermeneutics. Furthermore, he claims that they are meaningful only in the space of literature, philosophy, and the fine arts. Hence a profoundly equivocal dispersion of values takes place when these theories are taken to the space of popular culture, politics, or the social. In such transferrals, they become displacements prone to take too seriously the liberationist projections implicit in those discourses, as if one could really create a utopian moment from them or the social radicalism of modern metanarratives could be preserved through them. Somewhat analogously to the end-of-history theories proposed by Francis Fukuyama, Rorty insists that postmodernity has no need to aspire to new horizons; it needs only to consolidate the values and institutions of what he calls the "North Atlantic Postmodern Bourgeois Democracies," taking into consideration that these constitute the truly postmodern model because they have been able to "take privacy to the highest degree known to history, encompassing an unequaled margin of individual gratification, opinions, lifestyles, and means of selfpromotion."[44] The new subject of these communities, like its philosophers, participates in a self-sufficient internal dialogue that has no need for a new theoretical universality. Thus the attendant critiques of its metanarratives by this hermeneutical tradition respond only to its own immanent adjustments, and the problematics of difference derived therefrom do not imply a reduction of the space between public and private morality, but rather the knowledge that there is nothing beyond of any consequence. Only a reflexive writerly exploration of these traditions is valuable or necessary.[45]

Many readers of Foucault, Derrida, or de Man, including an entire generation of Latin American critics trained in U.S. universities formed by their work, may be somewhat surprised by Bloom's and Rorty's alternative reordering. Up to now, there was always the thought that attendant upon the deconstruction of modernity there remained a breath of liberationist spirit, an impulse or a flutter conjured by a new epistemology that would reinvent or rewrite history, even if it meant a more localized sense of justice and a less ambitious recipe for collective well-being. But the self-sufficiency of that promise has lost some of its force, as is evident in Derrida's own attempt to recast it by reverting to the emancipatory specters of Marx's different sense of promise.[46] More than a surprise, Bloom's and Rorty's proposals suggest an index or a symptom of how theoretical work scrambles to respond to a threatening dislocation it had not suspected. García Canclini's call for a new concept of citizenry is undoubtedly informed by a different response to the same challenge. In this context, one can see that Rama's essay provides an early sign of these very symptoms. He sets out to split the high/low cultural binary that is typically preserved in even the most radical theoretical work. More important, the radical force of capitalism's ceaseless revolutionizing, which is deeply inscribed in Latin America's cultural history, assumes a central role in his theoretical categories.

How will humanist and posthumanist theory draw lessons from its invaluable past while producing at the same time a more dynamic critique of a social text in which the private ambitions of all subjects, including those with few resources, are constantly stimulated through fandom, consumerism, and other attempts to market imaginaries? If that inventory is a significant part of aesthetic experience in contemporary societies, it is not clear how a monolingual world literary canon will respond to it. It is also doubtful that the aggregate of North Atlantic Postmodern Bourgeois Democracies provides even a pragmatic register of that inventory of excess, much less a critical one. Rama's work commands our attention in this context. Notwithstanding the totalizing impulse of *The Lettered City*'s archaeological reach, some of its premises remain powerful and provocative. Rama recognized that cultural forms, like words, are profoundly transformative but can hardly constitute autonomous forms of resistance. What is required, according to Rama, would be a more complex understanding of how human desires and the excesses of meaning are continuously drafted by both the discourses of culture and market forces. Without this engagement, which Rama approached with the conviction of a theoretical heretic, the work of theory remains trapped inside the "lettered cities"; at best, it can only return to them in calculated gestures of lamentation and nostalgia, a strategy that will prove inadequate to revitalize the dynamic elements of the Western tradition at this particular moment of global capitalism. In any contest between market forces and cultural nostalgia, the latter must perforce become the tool, however unwittingly, of the former.

NOTES

1. Mario Vargas Llosa, prologue to Angel Rama, *La ciudad letrada*, viii. It is indeed striking that this prologue makes no mention of Rama's text. It is more of a tribute to Rama after his death.

2. Rama's other posthumous book, *Las máscaras democráticas del modernismo*, was published in 1985. Unlike *The Lettered City*, its composition was not completely designed by Rama but by colleagues and editors. It is, nonetheless, a collection of Rama's late essays, which are discussed in this chapter.

3. Among the published studies of this chapter are the following: Rolena Adorno, "*La ciudad letrada* y los discursos coloniales"; Mabel Moraña, "De la ciudad letrada al imaginario nacionalista: contribuciones de Angel Rama a la invención de América"; Josaphat Kubayanda, "Order and Conflict: *Yo el Supremo* in Light of Rama's *ciudad letrada* Theory"; and Carlos J. Alonso, "Rama y sus retoños: Figuring the Nineteenth Century Spanish

America." See also Julio Ramos, *Desencuentros,* a book that includes many valuable insights on Rama's work.

4. For a comprehensive and comparative critique of Foucault's work, see Peter Boyne, *Foucault and Derrida: The Other Side of Reason;* and Christopher Norris, *Truth and the Ethics of Criticism.*

5. Moraña, *"De la ciudad letrada* al imaginario nacionalista," 47.

6. Adorno, *"La ciudad letrada* y los discursos coloniales," 4.

7. Ibid., p. 5.

8. Alonso, "Rama y sus retoños," 286–287.

9. Kubayanda, "Order and Conflict," 130.

10. Rama, *La ciudad letrada,* 34.

11. A more detailed discussion of *Tranculturación narrativa en América Latina* is found in chapter 3 of Román de la Campa's *Latin Americanism.*

12. Rama, *La ciudad letrada,* 4.

13. Ibid.

14. See Manfred Fran's *What Is Neostructuralism?* for a novel critique of the unsuspected links between structuralism and poststructuralism as well as an attempt to provide a dialogue between German and French theoretical approaches to these strands.

15. Boyne, *Foucault and Derrida,* provides an important critique of how Foucault moved beyond this stage and what aspects remained in his later work.

16. José Rabasa's *Inventing America* contains an elaborate illustration of this epistemology.

17. Norris, *Truth and the Ethics of Criticism,* 126.

18. Carlos Rincón, *La no simultaneidad de lo simultáneo,* 222.

19. Sarduy's *Escrito sobre un cuerpo* and Barroco are representative articulations.

20. Rama, *La ciudad letrada,* 34.

21. Rama, *Las máscaras democráticas del modernismo,* 166, 167.

22. Rama, *La ciudad letrada,* 137.

23. Ibid., 140.

24. Ibid., 144. Rama's reference here is to Carlos Franqui's book, *Cuba: el libro de los doce.*

25. See the author's comments in the book's acknowledgments, as well as Hugo Achugar's prologue to *La ciudad letrada.*

26. Beatriz Sarlo, *Escenas de la vida posmoderna;* Néstor García Canclini, *Consumidores y ciudadanos;* Roberto Schwarz, "Brazilian Culture: Nationalism by Elimination"; Nelly Richard, *La estratificaión de los márgenes.*

27. García Canclini, *Consumidores y ciudadanos,* 197–198.

28. Ernesto Laclau, *New Reflections on the Revolution of Our Time,* 91.

29. Ibid., 90.

30. Ibid.

31. Ibid., 91.

32. Rama, *La ciudad letrada,* 123.

33. Ibid., 116.

34. Ibid., 59.

35. Ibid., 53–54.

36. Ibid., 47.

37. See Christopher Norris's detailed analysis of this particular aspect in *Paul de Man, Deconstruction and the Critique of Aesthetic Ideology*, 153.

38. Rama, *La ciudad letrada*, 88.

39. Walter Mignolo, *The Darker Side of the Renaissance*, 318–322.

40. Horst Ruthrof, *Semantics and the Body*, 261.

41. Ibid.

42. García Canclini, *Consumidores y ciudadanos*, 185.

43. Richard Rorty, "Tales of Two Disciplines."

44. Richard Rorty, *Objectivity, Relativism, and Truth*, 198.

45. For a broad discussion of these problems, see Christopher Norris, *The Truth about Postmodernism*.

46. A more detailed discussion of Derrida's book on Marx, *Spectres of Marx*, and the current state of deconstruction is taken up in chapter 6 of *Latin Americanism*.

A Clearing in the Jungle:
From Santa Mónica to Macondo
From *Myth and Archive*

ROBERTO GONZÁLEZ ECHEVARRÍA

The Roman legalistic tradition is one of the strongest components in Latin American culture: from Cortés to Zapata, we only believe in what is written down and codified.

—Carlos Fuentes[1]

1

After a painful journey away from the modern world, the protagonist of Alejo Carpentier's *Los pasos perdidos* (1953) reaches Santa Mónica de los Venados, the town founded by the Adelantado, one of his traveling companions.[2] Santa Mónica is but a clearing in the South American jungle on which a few huts have been built.[3] The nameless protagonist has arrived, or so he wishes to believe, at the Valley-Where-Time-Has-Stopped, a place outside the flow of history. Here, purged of civilization, he hopes to rekindle his creative energies, to return to his earlier life as a composer; in short, to be true to himself. The narrator-protagonist plans to write a threnody, a musical poem based on the text of the

Odyssey. Musical ideas rush to his mind, as if he had been able at last to tap a deep well of creativity within him. He asks the Adelantado, or Founder of Cities, for paper to write all this down. The latter reluctantly—for he needs them to set down the laws of his new society—gives him a notebook. The narrator fills it very quickly in a frenzy of creativity and begs for another. Annoyed, the Adelantado gives it to him with the admonition that it will be the last one. He is forced to write very small, packing every available space, even creating a kind of personal shorthand, to be able to continue his work. Later, feeling sorry for him, the Adelantado relinquishes yet another notebook, but the narrator-protagonist is still reduced to erasing and rewriting what he has composed, for he lacks the space to move forward. Writing, erasing, rewriting, the narrator-protagonist's belabored manuscript already prefigures the economy of gain and loss of the Archive, the origin unveiled, the mode of current Latin American fiction made possible by Carpentier's novel. Many other such manuscripts will appear in the works of Gabriel García Márquez, Carlos Fuentes, and Mario Vargas Llosa as emblems of the very text of the Latin American novel.

When the narrator decides to go back to civilization temporarily, he does so with the intention of procuring enough paper and ink to continue his composition once he returns to Santa Mónica. He does neither. Instead of finishing his threnody, the narrator-protagonist writes a series of articles about his adventures, which he tries to sell to various publications. These may be, within the fiction, the fragments that lead up to the writing of the text we read, *Los pasos perdidos* (as in other modern novels, an unfinished manuscript represents, within the fiction, the novel in which it appears). The return to Santa Mónica is never accomplished either, for the rising waters of the river cover the inscription on the trunk of a tree that marked the channel to the town. There is writing everywhere in the jungle, but it is as unintelligible as that of the city from which he wishes to escape. The protagonist is caught between two cities, in one of which he must live. What he cannot do is live outside the city, outside writing.

Two events related to the need for paper occur at the same time that the narrator-protagonist is pestering the Adelantado for notebooks. The first is when Fray Pedro, another traveling companion, insists that the protagonist marry Rosario, the native woman with whom he has paired off during his journey upriver. The second is the execution of Nicasio, the leper who raped a girl in the town. The narrator, who has a wife back in the modern world, does not want to subject Rosario to a hollow ceremony and cannot bear the thought of her treasuring a piece of paper from one of the notebooks that he so desires, on which the marriage certificate would no doubt be written. But Rosario, it turns out, has no urge to seal their union according to laws that would tie her down and make her subservient to him. Nicasio, killed by another character (Marcos) when the narrator-protagonist is unable to pull the trigger, is said to suffer from the leprosy of Leviticus, that is to say, from the malady that led nomadic tribes to draw up laws excluding those infected with the disease as they settled down in a given place. Marriage and the execution of Nicasio are events that stand at the beginning of the need to write, like the creative impulse of the narrator-protagonist. All three will find their way into the notebooks hoarded by the founder of cities. Writing begins in the city with the need to order society and to discipline in the punitive sense. The narrator-protagonist recognizes that the clearing he seeks is already occupied by civilization:

> No sólo ha fundado una ciudad el Adelantado, sino que, sin sospecharlo, está creando, día a día, una *polis,* que acabará por apoyarse en un código asentado solemnemente en el *Cuaderno de . . . Perteneciente a. . . .* Y un momento llegará en que tenga que castigar severamente a quien mate la bestia vedada, y bien veo que entonces ese hombrecito de hablar pausado, que nunca alza la voz, no vacilará en condenar al culpable a ser expulsado de la comunidad y a morir de hambre en la selva. . . . (p. 268)

> Not only had the Adelantado founded a city, but, without realizing it, he was creating day by day a *polis* that would eventually rest on a code of laws solemnly entered in *Notebook . . . Property of. . . .* And the moment would come when severe punishment would have to be imposed on anyone killing an animal in the closed season, and it was apparent that this little, soft-spoken man would not hesitate to sentence the violator to being driven from the community to die of hunger in the forest. . . . (p. 209)

Writing is bound to the founding of cities and to punishment.[4] The origin of the modern novel is to be found in this relationship, thematic traces of which appear throughout its history, from *Lazarillo* and *El coloquio de los perros* to *Les Misérables, Der Prozess,* and *El beso de la mujer araña.*

The reader of contemporary Latin American fiction will no doubt recognize in Santa Mónica de los Venados and the story about the unfinished manuscript—both of the threnody and the novel—prefigurations of Macondo and of Melquíades's writings in *Cien años de soledad* (1967). Carpentier's *Los pasos perdidos* is a turning point in the history of Latin American narrative, the founding archival fiction. It is a book in which all the important narrative modalities in Latin America, up to the time when it was published, are contained and analyzed as in a kind of active memory; it is a repository of narrative possibilities, some obsolete, others leading up to García Márquez. *Los pasos perdidos* is an archive of stories and a storehouse of the master-stories produced to narrate from Latin America. Just as the narrator-protagonist of the novel discovers that he is unable to wipe the slate clean to make a fresh start, so the book, in searching for a new, original narrative, must contain all previous ones, and in becoming an Archive return to the most original of those modalities.

Los pasos perdidos brings us back to the beginnings of writing, looking for an empty present wherein to make a first inscription. What is found instead is a variety of beginnings at the origin, the most powerful being the language of the law. Thus *Los pasos perdidos* dismantles the central enabling delusion of Latin American writing: the notion that in the New World a new start can be made, unfettered by history. The new start is always already history; writing in the city. Because of his anxiety about origins, the narrator-protagonist's is the quintessential Latin American story and its critical undoing; hence its foundational quality both in terms of Latin American history and the history of the novel. By foundational, I mean that it is a story about the prolegomena of telling a Latin American story. For instead of being relieved of history's freight, the narrator-protagonist discovers that he is burdened by the memory of the repeated attempts to discover or found the newness of the New World.[5] *Los pasos perdidos* is the story of this defeat that turns into a victory. In loosening the central constitutive idealization of Latin American narrative from its moorings, Carpentier's novel opens up the possibility of a critical reading of the Latin American tradition; one that would make manifest the stories, including the one of which the narrator is the protagonist, that constitute the Latin American narrative imagination. It is in the process of baring the consciousness of his narrator-protagonist that Carpentier lays out the ruins of that construct as a map for his fresh narrative project. But what are the fragments, the analecta in those ruins, and what do they have to do with the notebooks that the narrator-protagonist seeks from the Adelantado in Santa Mónica de los Venados?

The answer, as a kind of counterpoint, is found in García Márquez's *Cien años de soledad*, a text in which those master-stories are again told and the vestiges of the origin found by Carpentier examined in greater detail. *Cien años de soledad* contains, as in a blowup, a map of the narrative possibilities or potentialities of Latin American fiction. If Carpentier's novel is the founding archival fiction, García Márquez's is the archetypical one. This is the reason why the Archive as myth constitutes its core.

2

This man had in his possession a leaden box which, so he said, he had found among the ruined foundations of an ancient hermitage, that was being rebuilt. In this box he had found some parchments written in the Gothic script but in Castilian verse, which contained many of the knight's exploits and dwelt upon the beauty of Dulcinea del Toboso, the shape of Rocinante, the fidelity of Sancho Panza, and the burial of this same Don Quixote, together with various epitaphs and eulogies of his life and habits. Such of these as could be read and understood the trustworthy author of this original and matchless history has set down here, and he asks no recompense from his readers for the immense labours it has cost him to search and ransack all the archives of La Mancha in order to drag it into the light. *Don Quixote*, I, 52[6]

To most readers, the Latin American novel must appear to be obsessed with Latin American history and myth. Carlos Fuentes's *Terra nostra* (1976), for instance, retells much of sixteenth-century Spanish history, including the conquest of Mexico, while also incorporating pre-Columbian myths prophesying that momentous event. Carpentier's *El siglo de las luces* (1962) narrates Latin America's transition from the eighteenth century to the nineteenth, focusing on the impact of the French Revolution in the Caribbean. Carpentier also delves into Afro-Cuban lore to show how blacks interpreted the changes brought about by these political upheavals. Mario Vargas Llosa's monumental *La guerra del fin del mundo* (1980) tells again the history of Canudos, the rebellion of religous fanatics in the backlands of Brazil, which had already been the subject of Euclides da Cunha's classic *Os Sertões* (1902). Vargas Llosa's ambitious work also examines in painstaking detail the recreation of a Christian mythology in the New World. The list of Latin American novels dealing with Latin American history and myth is very long indeed, and it includes the work of many lesser-known younger writers. Abel Posse's *Daimón* (1978) retells the story of Lope de Aguirre, the sixteenth-century rebel who declared himself free from the Spanish Crown and founded his own independent country in South America. As the title of the book suggests, Posse's fiction centers on the myth of the Devil and his reputed preference for the New World as residence and field of operations, a theme that had been important in two earlier Latin American masterpieces, Carpentier's *El reino de este mundo* (1949) and João Guimarães Rosa's *Grande sertão: veredas* (1956).

Given that myths are stories whose main concern is with origins, the interest of Latin American fiction in Latin American history and myth is understandable. On the one hand, Latin American history has always held the promise of being not only new but different, of being, as it were, the only *new* history, preserving the force of the oxymoron. On the other hand, the novel, which appears to have emerged in the sixteenth century at the same time as Latin American history, is the only modern genre, the only literary form that is modern not only in the chronological sense, but also because it has persisted for centuries without a poetics, always in defiance of the very notion of genre. Is it possible, then, to make of Latin American history a story as enduring as the old myths? Can Latin American history be as resilient and as useful a hermeneutical tool for probing human nature as the classical myths, and can the novel be the vehicle for the transmission of these new myths? Is it at all conceivable, in the modern, post-oral period, to create myths? Are the coeval births of the novel and the history of Latin America related beyond chronology? Can a new myth make the New World intelligible? More importantly for our purposes, can a novelistic myth be inscribed in the clearing that the narrator of *Los pasos perdidos* seeks, and is such a myth the archival fiction this novel and others following it turn out to be? Because it is the repository of stories about the beginnings of modern Latin America, history is crucial in the creation of this myth. Latin American history is to the Latin American narrative what the epic themes are to Spanish literature: a constant whose mode of appearance may vary, but which is rarely absent. A book like Ramón Menéndez Pidal's *La epopeya castellana a través de la literatura española*[7] could be written about the presence of Latin American history in the Latin American narrative. The question is, of course: How can myth and history coexist in the novel? How can founding stories be told in this most ironic and self-reflexive of genres? The enormous and deserved success of García Márquez's masterpiece *Cien años de soledad* is due to the unrelenting way in which these forms of storytelling are interwoven in the novel, which thereby unveils the past of the narrative process in Latin America and leads to a consideration of the novel as genre.

It is an uncritical reflex of philologically inspired literary history to think of the evolution of the novel in the same terms as that of other literary genres. This is a vestige of a kind of primitive historicism that is modeled on the natural sciences and which, in the case of the history of conventional literary forms, has yielded impressive results. I do not think that the same can be said of studies on the novel. I am not convinced by theories that attempt to make the novel evolve solely or even chiefly from the epic, or any other literary form. The most persistent characteristic of books that have been called novels in the modern era is that they always pretend not to be literature. The desire not to be literary, to break with *belles-lettres,* is the most tenacious element in the novel. *Don Quixote* is supposed to be the translation of a history written in Arabic, or of documents extracted from the archives of La Mancha; *La vida de Lazarillo de Tormes* is a deposition written for a judge, *The Pickwick Papers* are *The Posthumous Papers of the Pickwick Club, Being a Faithful record of the Perambulations, Perils, Travels, Adventures, and Sporting transactions of the Corresponding Members: Edited by Boz.* Other novels are or pretend to be autobiographies, a series of letters, a manuscript found in a trunk, and so forth. Carpentier once exclaimed that most modern novels were received by criticism with the complaint that they were not novels at all, making it seem that, to be successful, the novel must fulfill its desire not to be literature.[8] He cited as examples *À la recherche du temps perdu* and *Ulysses.* A number of years ago Ralph Freedman made a useful suggestion concerning the origins of the novel:

Instead of separating genres or subgenres artificially and then accounting for exceptions by stipulating mixtures and compounds, it is simpler to view all of prose fiction as a unity and to trace particular strands to different origins, strands which would include not only the English novel of manners, or the post-medieval romance, or the Gothic novel, but also medieval allegory, the German *Bildungsroman,* or the picaresque. Some of these strands may be close to folk material or to classical epics, others may have modeled themselves on travelogues and journalistic descriptions of events, and others again suggest drawing-room comedies and even lyrical prose poetry, yet all, to varying degrees, seem to mirror life in aesthetically defined worlds (life as myth, as structure of reality, as worlds of feeling or quotidian reality). . . .[9]

I wish to retain from Freedman the notion of multiple origins and add that the origin of the novel is repeated over and over again, retaining only the mimetic act *vis-à-vis* a nonliterary form, not directly as a mirror of life. The novel's origin is multiple not only in space but also in time. Its history is not, however, a linear succession or evolution but a series of new starts in different places. The only common denominator is the novel's mimetic quality, not of a given reality but of a given discourse that has already "mirrored" reality.

It is my hypothesis that the novel, having no fixed form of its own, often assumes that of a given kind of document endowed with truth-bearing power by society at specific moments in time. The novel, or what is called the novel at various points in history, mimics such documents to show their conventionality, their subjection to strategies of textual engenderment similar to those governing literature, which in turn reflect those of language itself. It is through this simulacrum of legitimacy that the novel makes its contradictory and veiled claim to literariness. The power to endow a text with the capacity to bear the truth is shown to lie outside the text by narratives that we call novelistic; it is an exogenous agent that bestows authority upon a certain kind of document owing to the ideological power structure of the period, not to any inherent quality of the document or even of the outside agent. The novel, therefore, is part of the discursive totality of a given epoch, occupying a place opposite its ideologically authoritative core. Its conception is itself a story about an escape from authority, which is often its subplot. Needless to say this flight to a form of freedom is imaginary, a simulacrum predicated on textual mimetism that appears to be embedded in narrativity itself, as if it were the *ur*-story, the irreducible master-story underlying all storytelling. This is perhaps the reason why the law figures prominently in the first of the master-stories the novel tells through texts like *La vida de Lazarillo de Tormes,* Cervantes's: *Novelas ejemplares,* and the *Crónicas de Indias.* The novel will retain from this origin its relation to punishment and the control of the state, which determines its mimetic penchant from then on. When the modern Latin American novel returns to that origin, it does so through the figure of the Archive, the legal repository of knowledge and power from which it sprung, as we observed in *Los pasos perdidos.*

Although I have learned a good deal from the theories of Mikhail Bakhtin, as should be obvious, my approach here differs considerably from his. In the first place, because I like to see the novel as part of the textual economy of a given epoch, not simply or even primarily that part considered literary. In the second, I place more emphasis on texts that are part of official culture in the formation of the novel. In addition, I will include in my purview texts such as *Facundo* which are not considered novels in the conventional sense. My departure from Bakhtin may be due to the nature of my object of study—the Latin American narrative—which is created under circumstances that are considerably different from the European novel that interests him. I believe that Bakhtin dismisses too easily the role of official texts, which to my mind are fundamental in the formation of the modern novel. Bakhtin writes that "Carnival is the people's second life, organized on the basis of laughter. It is a festive life. Festivity is a peculiar quality of all comic rituals and spectacles of the Middle Ages."[10] He also writes: "This is why the tone of the official feast was monolithically serious and why the element of laughter was alien to it" (p. 9). Bakhtin conceives of the offical as something alien to society, as if officialdom were something extraterrestrial, imposed on humanity by some foreign invader. But what he calls official is as much a part of society as laughter and carnival; in fact, one could not exist without the other.

Having said this, however, I should make clear that I do share certain assumptions with Bakhtin; for instance, that humankind is a producer of texts, that these texts never exist individually but in relation to others, and that there is no possible metatext, but always an intertext.[11] That is to say, that I believe that my text is part of the economy of texts that it attempts to describe and classify, that my book is necessarily also an archival fiction. To my mind, the problem with Bakhtin is that he is still within the sphere of influence of classical anthropology, in the sense that he feels that the folk are some sort of privileged element of humankind, as the non-Europeans were to anthropologists, where something true, which can be betrayed by another part of humankind, survives. This is why he has trouble with the written. Writing is precisely part and parcel of officialdom. Here is where I choose to follow Michel Foucault. For Foucault, mediation is the very process of constraining, denying, limiting, invented by humanity itself; these hegemonic discourses which oppress, watch, control, and furnish the models parodied later, models without which parody itself could not exist. Cutting, slicing, locking up, writing, authority, are as much a contrivance of humankind as their antidotes. This is what I do not see present in Bakhtin's theories, and this is why he idealizes the folk. Intertextuality is not a quiet dialogue of texts—a pluralistic utopia perhaps born of the monolithic hell Bakhtin lived through—but a clash of texts, an imbalance among texts, some of which have a *molding and modeling* power over others.

The object of my study, then, is not simply the Latin American novel, but more broadly the Latin American narrative, and within that narrative an evolving core whose chief concern, particularly since the nineteenth century, is with the issue of the uniqueness of Latin America as a cultural, social, and political space from which to narrate. The search for uniqueness and identity is the form the question of legitimacy takes after the colonial period. The very first narrative of Latin America is determined by the issue of legitimacy as granted by the documents through which the first modern state—Habsburg Spain—dealt with the issue of enfranchisement.

In sixteenth-century Spain, the documents imitated by the incipient novel were legal ones. (I use incipient only to signal a beginning, not to suggest that as the structure was established, it first yielded a kernel; the whole structure is assumed to have been present in *Lazarillo,* the very "first" novel.) The form assumed by the picaresque was that of a *relación* (report, deposition, letter bearing witness to something), because this kind of written report belonged to the huge imperial bureaucracy through which power was administered in Spain and its possessions. The early history of Latin America, as well as the first fictions of and about Latin America, is told in the rhetorical molds furnished by the notarial arts. These *cartas de relación* were not simply letters or maps, but were also *charters* of the newly discovered territories. Both the writer and the territory were enfranchised through the power of this document which, like Lazarillo's text, is addressed to a higher authority, as in the case of Hernán Cortés, who wrote to Emperor Charles V. The pervasiveness of legal rhetoric in early American historiography can hardly be exaggerated. Officially appointed historians (with the title of *Cronista Mayor de Indias*) were assigned a set of rules by the Crown and the Royal Council of the Indies which included ways of subsuming these *relaciones* into their compendious works. Latin American history and fiction, the narrative of Latin America, were first created within the language of the law, a secular totality that guaranteed truth and made its circulation possible. It is within this totality that Garcilaso de la Vega, el Inca, wrote his *Comentarios reales de los incas* (1609), for, as will be seen in greater detail, the mestizo's book is an appeal to exonerate his father. Like Lázaro, Garcilaso addresses a letter to a higher authority to gain enfranchisement.

Since the eighteenth century, all forms of narrative, but particularly the novel, have had to compete with those created or adapted first by the natural and later by the social sciences. These were the true stories. Balzac, Galdós, and Dickens were the social analysts and theoreticians of their time, as was, even more forthrightly, Zola. A study of the relationship of the European novel to scientific forms of hegemonic discourse has yet to be written, as far as I know. Our study is concerned with the strand of the narrative that takes us to Latin America, where the mediating force of science was such that the most significant narratives did not even pretend to be novels, but various kinds of scientific reportage. Consequently, in Latin America in the nineteenth century (until the teens of our century) the narrative assumes the form of a new hegemonic discourse: science, and more specifically the scientific consciousness that expresses itself in the language of travelers who journeyed across the continent, writing about its nature and about themselves. Scientific exploration brought about the second European discovery of America, and the traveling naturalists were the new chroniclers. Traces of their writings are present in the journey the narrator-protagonist undertakes in *Los pasos perdidos* (the diary form of parts of the novel is also derived from this kind of writing) and in those by Melquíades in *Cien años de soledad*. Comparatively little attention has been paid to this vast process of exploration and reportage whose dimensions can be glimpsed by looking at the recent *Travel Accounts and Descriptions of Latin America and the Caribbean 1800–1920: A Selected Bibliography*, compiled by Thomas L. Welch and Myriam Figueras, and published by the Organization of American States (1982).[12] Though selective, this volume contains nearly three hundred pages of tightly packed entries. The names of these scientific travelers are quite impressive, ranging from Alexander von Humboldt to Charles Darwin, and including the likes of Robert and Richard Schomburgk, Charles-Marie de la Condamine, Captain Richard Burton, and many others. Their fictional counterpart is Professor Challenger in Sir Arthur Conan Doyle's *The Lost World* (1912), whose voyage to the origins of nature takes him to South America.

A consciousness that expresses itself in the language of the scientific travelogue mediates the writing of Latin American narratives in the nineteenth century. I am aware that the canon of Latin American literary history places conventional novels such as *Amalia* and *María* at the centre of the evolution of Latin American narrative. This is an uncritical copy of European literary history which veils the fact that the most significant narratives, the ones that had a powerful impact on those that followed in the twentieth century, were not novels copied from European models, as Mármol's and Isaacs's texts were, but issue from the relationship with the hegemonic discourse of the period, which was not literary, but scientific. This is so, even, of course, in the case of some conventional Latin American novels, such as Cirilo Villaverde's *Cecilia Valdés* (Cuba, 1880), which owed much to reports on slavery in Cuba that were cast in a scientific mold. Domingo Faustino Sarmiento's *Facundo* (1845), Anselmo Suárez y Romero's *Francisco* (1880), and Euclides da Cunha's *Os Sertões* (1902) describe Latin American nature and society through the conceptual grid of nineteenth-century science. Like the chronicles of the discovery and conquest, which were

often legal documents, these are books whose original role lies outside of literature. *Francisco* was originally part of a report sent to the British authorities doc-
umenting the horrors of slavery in Cuba. Latin America's history and the stories
of adventurers who sought to discover the innermost secrets of the New World,
that is to say, its newness and difference, are narrated through the mind of a
writer qualified by science to search for the truth. That truth is found in an evolutionary conception of nature that profoundly affects all narratives about the
New World. Both the self and science that make this conception possible are
reflections of the power of the new European commercial empires. The capacity to find the truth is due not so much to the cogency of the scientific method
as to the ideological construct that supports them, a construct whose source of
strength lies outside the text. The "mind" that analyzes and classifies is made
present through the rhetorical conventions of the travelogue. Sarmiento ranges
over the Argentine landscape in a process of self-discovery and self-affirmation.
In his book he dons the mask of the traveling savant, distanced from the reality
he interprets and classifies according to the intervening tenets of scientific
inquiry.

This particular mediation prevails until the crisis of the 1920s and the so-
called *novela de la tierra* or telluric novels.[13] This modern novel avails itself of a
different kind of mediation: anthropology. Now the promise of knowledge is to
be found in a scientific discourse whose object is not nature but essentially language and myth. The truth-bearing document the novel imitates is the anthropological or ethnographic report. The object of such studies is to discover the
origin and source of a culture's own version of its values, beliefs, and history
through a culling and retelling of its myths. Readers of anthropology are aware
that in order to understand another culture, the anthropologist has to know his
own to the point where he can distance himself from it and, in a sense, disappear in the discourse of method. Distancing, a process whose counterpart can
be found only in modern literature, involves a kind of self-effacement. This dramatic process has been beautifully expounded by Lévi-Strauss in *Tristes
tropiques,* a book in which he devotes a good deal of space to his stay in Brazil.
John Freccero and Eduardo González have studied how much this book has in
common with Carpentier's *Los pasos perdidos,* and today Clifford Geertz and
others are studying, from the point of view of anthropology, the relationship
between the discourse of anthropology and that of literature in a way that is prefigured in the Latin American novels that I shall be dealing with here.[14]

Anthropology is the mediating element in the modern Latin American narrative because of the place this discipline occupies in the articulation of founding
myths by Latin American states. But of course anthropology also assumes such
mediating power because of the role anthropology plays in Western thought and
the place Latin America occupies in the history of that discipline. Anthropology

is a way through which Western culture indirectly affixes its own cultural identity. This identity, which the anthropologist struggles to shed, is one that masters nonhistorical cultures through knowledge, by making them the object of its
study. Anthropology translates into the language of the West the cultures of the
others and in the process establishes its own form of self-knowledge through a
kind of annihilation of the self. Existential philosophy, as in Heidegger, Ortega
y Gasset, and Sartre, is akin to this process, because it is only through an awareness of the other that Western thought can pretend to wind back to the origin of
being. The natives, that is to say, Latin Americans or in general those who could
be politely called the inhabitants of the postcolonial world, provide the model
for this reduction and beginning. The native has timeless stories to explain his
changeless society. These stories, these myths, are like those of the West in the
distant past, before they became a mythology instead of a theogony. Freud,
Frazer, Jung, and Heidegger sketch a return to or a retention of these origins.
Anthropology finds them in the contemporary world of the native. The modern
Latin American novel is written through the model of such anthropological
studies. In the same way that the nineteenth-century novel turned Latin
America into the object of scientific study, the modern Latin American novel
transforms Latin American history into an originary myth in order to see itself as
other. The theogonic Buendía family in *Cien años de soledad* owes its organization to this phenomenon, as does the very concept of Macondo, which recalls
the village studies common in ethnography.

The historical data behind my hypothesis concerning the modern novel and
its relation to an anthropological model are extensive, and I shall return to it in
the last chapter. Suffice it to say that Miguel Angel Asturias studied ethnology
in Paris under Georges Raynaud, an experience that produced in 1930 his influential *Leyendas de Guatemala*. One of the Asturias's classmates at the Sorbonne
was none other than Alejo Carpentier, who was then writing *¡Ecué-Yamba-O!*
(1933), a novel which is, in many ways, an ethnological study of Cuban Blacks.
Carpentier's interest in anthropology never abated. For instance, at the time he
was writing *Los pasos perdidos* in the late 1940s, he followed the Griaule expedition closely, as well as the activities and writings of the group of anthropologists
who took refuge in New York during World War II.[15] Another Cuban writer was
also preparing herself in Paris in those years: Lydia Cabrera, whose pioneering
studies of Afro-Cuban lore would culminate in her classic *El monte* (1954). In
more recent times, Severo Sarduy has been a student of Roger Bastide, and his
De donde son los cantantes (1967) is, amongst several other things, an anthropological study of Cuban culture, seen as the synthesis of the three main ethnic
groups inhabiting the island: the Spanish, the African, and the Chinese.
Borges's 1933 essay "El arte narrativo y la magia," where the art of storytelling is
compared to two kinds of primitive cures outlined in *The Golden Bough*, is but

one indication of the widespread impact of Frazer on Latin America. Traces of this influence are visible in Octavio Paz, Carpentier, Carlos Fuentes, as well as in many others.

Lydia Cabrera is perhaps the most significant author here because she stands for a very important kind of Latin American writer who sits astride both literature and anthropology. Cabrera is a first-rate short-story writer, just as she is a first-rate anthropologist. Her teacher, Fernando Ortiz, was also claimed by literature and his influence on modern Cuban letters is vast. Examples of writers straddling literature and anthropology are plentiful. The most notorious in recent years is Miguel Barnet, whose *Biografía de un cimarrón* (1966) not only contains all the perplexing dualities and contradictions of that relationship, but is also the perfect example of a book whose form is given by anthropology yet winds up in the field of the novel. The Peruvian José María Arguedas is without a doubt the most poignant figure among these anthropologist-writers: a novelist and anthropologist, Arguedas was brought up by Indians, and his first language was Quechua, not Spanish. He felt within himself the contradictions and the tragedy inherent in the relationship between anthropology and literature with an intensity that in 1969 led him to choose suicide.

Arguedas's extreme solution is a literal version of the reduction of the self inherent in the process of rewriting Latin American history in the context of the anthropological mediation. Method, discourse, writing, take the place of life. Arguedas's gesture has its literary counterpart in *Los pasos perdidos* and *Cien años de soledad*. Arguedas's radical effacement of self, like the one practiced by Barnet as he turns, or pretends to turn, himself into Esteban Montejo, is part of the "unwriting" involved in the modern Latin American narrative. For the most recent Latin American narrative is an "unwriting" as much as it is a rewriting of Latin American history from the anthropological perspective mentioned. The previous writings of history are undone as the new one is attempted; this is why the chronicles and the nineteenth-century scientific travelogues are present in what I call the Archive in modern fiction, the mode beyond anthropology, inaugurated by *Los pasos perdidos*. The new narrative unwinds the history told in the old chronicles by showing that history was made up of a series of conventional topics, whose coherence and authority depend on the codified beliefs of a period whose ideological structure is no longer current. Those codified beliefs of the origin were literally the law. Like the Spanish galleon crumbling in the jungle in *Cien años de soledad,* the legal discourse in the chronicles is a voided presence. Likewise, modern novels disassemble the powerful scientific construct through which nineteenth-century Latin America was narrated by demonstrating the relativity of its most cherished concepts or by rendering literal the metaphors on which such knowledge is based. The power of genealogy is literalized in *Cien años de soledad* by, among other devices, the stream of blood that flows from José

Arcadio's wound to Ursula. The presence of the European naturalists Robertson and Bonplant in Augusto Roa Bastos's *Yo el Supremo* attests to this second voided presence, as do the obsolete and partially magical scientific instruments that Melquíades brings to Macondo, soon to be replaced by the machinery of the banana company which comes to exploit the area.

But the paradigmatic text among these unwritings is Carpentier's *Los pasos perdidos.* This is no accident. Carpentier was associated from the beginning of his career with avant-garde artists, particularly the Surrealists, who were intimately associated with anthropological pursuits. It is clear that in Caracas, when he was writing *Los pasos perdidos,* he kept a close eye on developments in anthropology, especially French anthropology. Carpentier was interested in a group of anthropologists (among them Lévi-Strauss and Leiris), who took refuge in New York during the war, and suggested that the musicologist Schaeffner may have been the model for the narrator-protagonist of the novel, but there were others who were in Venezuela at the time, actually journeying to the sources of the Orinoco.[16] Essentially, the journey the narrator-protagonist makes is that of an anthropologist, and the whole novel is so much like *Tristes tropiques* because it could very well be taken as the personal account of an anthropologist formed in the avant-garde years and surveying the state of his discipline and of himself at a time when ethnography was going through a crisis which severely undermined its discourse. But what he brings back is an archaeology of Latin American narrative forms.

As the narrator-protagonist of the novel travels upriver—clearly the river in which Melquíades dies many years later—he writes about his voyage as if it were a journey back not only through time but through recorded history. Hence he passes through various epochs, the two most significant of which are the nineteenth century, with its traveling European scientists, who provide him with a way of interpreting nature and time; and the colonial period of Latin American history, characterized by activities such as the founding of cities; in short, the beginning of history in the New World as set down by the charters of those institutions—the *cartas de relación.* There are other epochs, reaching all the way back to prehistoric times, but the above are the most important ones, because they are present not only thematically or allusively but through mediating texts themselves, through the very substantiality of their voided forms. The era of the petroglyphs, for instance, is narrated in the language of the naturalists, and the founding of cities in that of the legalist chronicles. At various points in the novel, the narrator-protagonist plays the roles of conquistador, naturalist, and also anthropological expert in myth, comparing stories he hears in the jungle to those of classical times, looking, in short, for the founding structure of storytelling. He plays these roles because none is current any longer, none provides him with the ideological underpinning to reach a truth, a beginning, an origin. His own story is the only one that he can authenticate, that is, his story about looking for stories, telling past stories, repeating their form. The narrator-protagonist's text is organized according to a set of rhetorical conventions—hollowed out, obsolete, extinct—that reveal themselves as such in the process of reading. In the fiction of the novel, the narrator-protagonist cannot remain in what he termed the Valley-Where-Time-Has-Stopped, the origin of time and history, for, as we saw, he needs to secure enough paper to set down the music he has begun to compose. In the fiction, the quest for that degree zero of time and history on which to inscribe a rewriting of Latin American history has not been found; the protagonist escapes from one city to find another city. But in the writing of the novel a clearing has been reached, a metafictional space, a razing that becomes a starting point for the new Latin American narrative; the clearing for the building of Comala, Macondo, Coronel Vallejos, for the founding of the imaginary city containing all previous forms of Latin American narrative as well as the origins of the novel; a space for the Archive.

That razing involves the various mediations through which Latin America was narrated, the systems from which fiction borrowed the truth-bearing forms, erased to assume the new mediation that requires this level ground of self and history. This clearing is the point at which *Cien años de soledad* begins, and the reason why the world is so recent: "que muchas cosas carecían de nombre, y para mencionarlas había que señalarlas con el dedo" (p. 71); ("that many things lacked names, and in order to indicate them it was necessary to point" [p. 1]).[17] It is also the place that the last Aureliano seeks at the very end when he discovers how to translate Melquíades's manuscripts. He reads in a frenzy "descubriendo los primeros indicios de su ser, en un abuelo concupiscente que se dejaba arrastrar por la frivolidad a través de un páramo alucinado, en busca de una mujer hermosa a quien no haría feliz" (p. 492); ("discovering the first indications of his own being in a lascivious grandfather who let himself be frivolously dragged across a hallucinated plateau in search of a beautiful woman whom he would not make happy" [p. 421]).[18] What is left for the novel after *Los pasos perdidos* and *Cien años de soledad*? Clearly, only fiction. But novels are never content with fiction; they must pretend to deal with the truth, a truth that lies behind the discourse of the ideology that gives them form. So, paradoxically enough, the truth with which they deal is fiction itself; that is to say, the fictions Latin American culture has created to understand itself. What is left is the opening up of the Archive or perhaps only the story about the opening of the Archive—the story I hope to be telling here.

The Archive is a modern myth based on an old form, a form of the beginning. The modern myth unveils the relationship between knowledge and power as contained in all previous fictions about Latin America, the ideological construct that props up the legitimacy of power from the chronicles to the current novels. This is why a kind of archive, usually containing an unfinished manuscript and an archivist-writer, appears with such frequency in modern novels. The Archive keeps, culls, retains, accumulates, and classifies, like its institutional counterpart. It mounts up, amounts to the law, the law of fiction. Fictions are contained in an enclosure, a prison house of narrative that is at the same time the origin of the novel. It is not by chance that Cervantes began to write the *Quijote* in jail, nor that the narrator-author of *Historia de Mayta* (1984) should seek the ultimate truth about his character in a prison. The Archive goes back to the origins of Latin American narrative because it returns to the language of the law, the language that the protagonist of *Los pasos perdidos* will find in the innermost recesses of the jungle, where a city awaits him. That city, which the Adelantado had called Santa Mónica de los Venados, becomes Macondo, the story of which is the myth of the Archive. Let us read in detail the contradictory origin and nature of that myth in *Cien años de soledad,* the archetypal archival fiction.

3

The importance of myth in *Cien años de soledad* was noticed by the first commentators of the novel, and later studies have again taken up the topic.[19] It seems clear that myth appears in the novel in the following guises: (1) there are stories that resemble classical or biblical myths, most notably the Flood, but also Paradise, the Seven Plagues, the Apocalypse, and the proliferation of the family, which with its complicated genealogy, has an Old Testament ring to it; (2) there are characters who are reminiscent of mythical heroes: José Arcadio Buendía, who is a sort of Moses; Rebeca, who is like a female Perseus; Remedios, who ascends in a flutter of white sheets in a scene that is suggestive not just of the Ascension of the Virgin but more specifically of the popular renditions of that event in religious prints; (3) certain stories have a general mythic character in that they contain supernatural elements, as in the case just mentioned, and also when José Arcadio's blood returns to Ursula; (4) the beginning of the whole story which is found, as in myth, in a tale of violence and incest. All four, of course, commingle, and because *Cien años de soledad* tells a story of foundations or origins, the entire novel has a mythic air about it. No single myth or mythology prevails. Instead, the various ways in which myth appears give the novel a mythical character without it being a distinct version of any one myth in particular.

At the same time, there is lurking in the background of the story the overall pattern of Latin American history, both as a general design made up of various key events and eras, and in the presence of specific characters and incidents that seem to refer to real people and happenings. Thus there is a period of discovery and conquest when José Arcadio and the original families settle Macondo. There is in this part of the book little sense that Macondo belongs to a larger political unit, but such isolation was in fact typical of Latin American towns in the colonial period.

Even the viceroyalties lived in virtual isolation from the metropolitan government. The sense of beginning one has when reading about Macondo was shared by some of the conquistadors, who, for instance, when encouraging Gonzalo Pizarro to rebel against the Crown, urged him to declare himself king of Peru, thinking that the deeds he had accomplished with his brothers were of the kind to merit the establishment of a new monarchy. The appearance in Macondo of Apolinar Moscoso and his barefoot soldiers is the beginning of the republican era, which is immediately followed by the outbreak of the civil wars in which Colonel Aureliano Buendía distinguishes himself. Though Colombia is the most obvious model for this period, nearly the entire continent suffered from civil strife during the nineteenth century, a process that led to the emergence of *caudillos*. Argentina, with Facundo Quiroga and Juan Manuel Rosas, could just as well be the model for this era in Macondo's history.

This period is followed by the era of neocolonial domination by the United States and the struggles against it in most Latin American countries. These culminate in the novel with the general strike and the massacre of the workers. There are, unfortunately, countless models for this last, clearly defined period in the novel. After the flood, there is a time of decay before the apocalyptic wind razes the town at the end. The liberal priest and the various military types who surround Colonel Aureliano Buendía are among the characters with counterparts in Latin American history. Lucila I. Mena has already demonstrated that some of the historical incidents in the novel can be documented, and a sedulous critic with time and the proper library can probably document many others.[20] But to carry this sort of research much further than Mena has would be a rather gratuitous critical exercise. Set against the global, totalizing thrust of the novel are these historical details which, without being specific, are nonetheless true in a general sense. Each of the above-mentioned epochs is evoked not only through major historical events but also through allusions to specific minor incidents and characters. For instance, early Macondo is inhabited by a *de jure* aristocracy made up of the founding families, which is analogous to towns in colonial Latin America where the first conquistadors and their descendants enjoyed certain privileges and exemptions, a situation which, in some measure, provoked the civil wars of Peru.

The blend of mythic elements and Latin American history in *Cien años de soledad* reveals a desire to found a Latin American myth as well as the voiding of the anthropological mediation. Latin American history is set on the same level as mythic stories; therefore it too becomes a sort of myth. The lack of specificity of the various incidents, which appear to represent several related or similar events, points in that direction. The Latin American myth is this story of foundation, articulated through independence, civil war, struggle against United States imperialism, all cast within a genealogical line that weaves in and out, repeating names and characters. There is a Whitmanesque thrust to the brash declaration of the existence of a literary language that underlies this mixture of historical fact and mythic story in *Cien años de soledad*. The novel is in fact intimately related to similar efforts in poetry, such as the ones by Neruda in his *Canto general,* Nicolás Guillén in his *El diario que a diario,* and Octavio Paz in his *Piedra de sol. Canto general* in particular is one of the most important sources of García Márquez's novel. Framed by Genesis and Revelation, fraught with incest and violence, the story of the Buendía family thus stands as Latin American history cast in the language of myth, an unresolved mixture that both beckons and bewilders the reader. Latin America's irreducible historicity—its discovery creates an awareness of transitoriness and change that propels Western consciousness into modernity, self-questioning, and relativity—constantly undermines the language of myth.

This duality—history/myth—is present throughout *Cien años de soledad,* separating the world of writing from the atemporal world of myth. But the play of contradictions issuing from this duality reaches a precarious synthesis that is perhaps the most important feature of the novel. Myth represents the origin. Latin American history is narrated in the language of myth because it is always conceived as the history of the other, a history fraught with incest, taboo, and the founding act of naming. Latin American history must be like myth to comply with this conception, which issues from the authority of the anthropological mediation. The novel's persistent preoccupation with genealogy and supernatural acts performed by various characters belongs to this mythic realm.[21] History, on the other hand, is critical, temporal, and dwells in a special place: Melquíades' room in the Buendía house, which I have chosen to call the Archive. The room is full of books and manuscripts and has a time of its own. It is here that a succession of characters attempt to decipher Melquíades's parchments, and the last Aureliano, in an epiphanic inspiration, orally translates nearly the whole manuscript and dies. What occurs here, the text of the novel suggests, is unrepeatable. In the fiction of the novel, on the other hand, there are many repetitions. Ursula, for instance, twice feels that time is going around in circles and that members of the family follow one or two patterns of behavior indicated by their names. Time is circular in the fiction but not in Melquíades's room. The Archive appears to be successive and teleological, while the plot of the novel itself is repetitive and mythical. *Cien años de soledad* is made up of two main stories: one has to do with the family, and culminates in the birth of the child with the pig's tail; while the other is concerned with the interpretation of Melquíades's manuscript, a linear suspense story that culminates in Aureliano's final discovery of the key to the translation of the parchments. The product of incest and revelation is the same: Does it stand for truth? And if the truth of the novel is like the child with the pig's tail, what are we to conclude about the nature of novelistic discourse?

That there should be a special abode for manuscripts and books in *Cien años de soledad* should come as no surprise to readers of modern Latin American fiction. There are analogous enclosures in *Aura, Yo el Supremo, El arpa y la sombra, Crónica de una muerte anunciada,* and *Oppiano Licario,* to mention a few of the novels in which the figure plays a prominent role. One could also say that this enclosure is prefigured in the box where the narrator-protagonist of *Los pasos perdidos* keeps the manuscript of his threnody. What is characteristic of the Archive is: (1) the presence not only of history but of previous mediating elements through which it was narrated, be it the legal documents of colonial times or the scientific ones of the nineteenth century; (2) the existence of an inner historian who reads the texts, interprets, and writes them; and finally (3) the presence of an unfinished manuscript that the inner historian is trying to complete. In *Cien años de soledad* the most tenuous presence is that of the legal texts, but one can infer it from the allusions to the chronicles that were in fact *relaciones,* and particularly in the founding of Macondo, for the founding of cities, primordial activity of conquistadors, was closely connected to the writing of history. The vagueness of this presence is only so in relation to the others, for at least two critics have convincingly argued in favor of the overwhelming influence of the chronicles in *Cien años de soledad.*[22] The presence of nineteenth-century travel books is evident in the descriptions of the jungle and at a crucial moment when José Arcadio Segundo hears Melquíades mumble something in his room. José Arcadio leans over and hears the gypsy mention the name of none other than Alexander von Humboldt and the word *equinoccio,* which comes from the title of the latter's book, which in Spanish is *Viaje a las regiones equinocciales del Nuevo Continente.* In Macondo's Archive there are in addition two key works: the so-called *English Encyclopedia* and *The Thousand and One Nights.* These two books play an important role in Melquíades's writing, and the *Encyclopedia* is instrumental in the decoding of his manuscripts. The existence in Melquíades's fiction of precisely these two books adds a peculiar twist to the Archive, one that points to its own literary lineage.

I do not think it would be too far-fetched to say that *The Thousand and One Nights* and the so-called *English Encyclopedia* together are allusions to that master of fictions: Borges. In fact, Melquíades is a figure of the Argentine writer. Old beyond age, enigmatic, blind, entirely devoted to writing, Melquíades stands for Borges, the librarian and keeper of the Archive. There is something whimsical in García Márquez's inclusion of such a figure in the novel, but there is a good deal more. It is not difficult to fathom what this Borgesian figure means. Planted in the middle of the special abode of books and manuscripts, a reader of one of the oldest and most influential collections of stories in the history of literature, Melquíades and his Archive stand for literature; more specifically, for Borges's kind of literature: ironic, critical, a demolisher of all delusions, the sort of thing encountered at the end of the novel when Aureliano finishes translating Melquíades' manuscript. There are in that ending further allusions to several stories by Borges: to "Tlön, Uqbar, Orbis Tertius," for Macondo is a verbal construct; to "El milagro secreto," in that Aureliano, like the condemned poet, perishes the moment he finishes his work; to *El Aleph,* for Aureliano Babilonia's glimpse of the history of Macondo is instantaneous and all-encompassing; and particularly to "La muerte y la brújula," for the moment of anagnorisis is linked to death. Like Lönnrot, Aureliano understands the workings of his fate only at the moment of his death.

The Archive, then, is like Borges's study. It stands for writing, for literature, for an accumulation of texts that is no mere heap but an *arché,* a relentless memory that disassembles the fictions of myth, literature and even history. The master-books in the Archive are, as indicated, the *Encyclopedia* and *The Thousand and One Nights.* The *Encyclopedia,* which Aureliano has read, according to the narrator, from A to Z as if it were a novel, is in itself a figure of the totality of knowledge as conceived by the West. But how is it knowledge, and how has Aureliano read it? The moment we consider the order of knowledge in the *Encyclopedia* and the way in which Aureliano reads it, we realize the paradoxes inherent in the Archive as repository of history. The *Encyclopedia* is organized, of course, in alphabetical order, without the order of the entries being affected by any chronological or evaluative consideration: Napoleon appears before Zeus and Charles V before God. The beginning is provided arbitrarily by the alphabet as well as by the sequence: apocalypse must appear in the first volume. *The Thousand and One Nights,* on the other hand, stands for a beginning in fiction, or beginning as fiction, as well as for a series of individual, disconnected stories linked only by the narrator's fear of death. Aureliano is like Scheherazade, who tells her stories on the verge of death. Neither book seems to have a priority over the other. Both have a prominent place within the Archive, providing their own form of pastness, of documentary, textual material. The order that prevails in the Archive, then, is not that of mere chronology but that of writing; the rigorous process of inscribing and decoding to which Melquíades and the last Aureliano give themselves over, a linear process of cancellations and substitutions, of gaps.

Writing and reading have an order of their own, which is preserved within the Archive. It might be remembered that in Melquíades's room it is always Monday and March for some characters, while for others his study is the room of the chamber pots, where decay and temporality have their own end, embodied in the essence of eschatology. The combination of feces and writing in the Archive is significant enough. Writing appears as an eschatological activity in that it deals with the end. Yet writing is also the beginning insofar as nothing is in the text until it is written. Hence the prevalence of Monday and March in the secret abode of Melquíades, the beginning of the week and of spring respectively

(March, not April, is the "cruelest month" in García Márquez). Melquíades is both young and old, depending, of course, on whether or not he wears his dentures; he presides over the beginning and the end. The Archive, then, is not so much an accumulation of texts as the process whereby texts are written; a process of repeated combinations, of shufflings and reshufflings ruled by heterogeneity and difference. It is not strictly linear, as both continuity and discontinuity are held together in uneasy allegiance. This fictional archive, of course, is a turning inside out of the Archive in its political manifestation, a turn that unveils the inner workings of the accumulation of power; accumulation and power are a rhetorical effect in this archive of archives. This is the reason why the previous mediations through which Latin Americans narrated are contained in the Archive as voided presences. They are both erased and, at the same time, a memory of their own demise. They are keys to filing systems now abandoned, but they retain their archival quality, their power to differentiate, to space. They are not archetypes, but an *arché* of types.

This process is manifest in the way in which Melquíades's manuscript is written and translated. Throughout the novel we are told that Melquíades writes indecipherable manuscripts, that his handwriting produces something that looks more like musical notation than script, that his writing resembles clothes hung on a line. Eventually José Arcadio Segundo discovers, with the aid of the *Encyclopedia,* that the writing is in Sanskrit. When Aureliano begins to translate from the Sanskrit, he comes up with coded Spanish verses. These verses have different codes, depending on whether they are even or odd numbered. Aureliano is finally illuminated when he sees the dead newborn being carried away by the ants and remembers the epigraph of the manuscript, which is supposed to read: *"El primero de la estirpe está amarrado en un árbol y al último se lo están comiendo las hormigas"* (p. 490); (*"The first of the line is tied to a tree and the last is being eaten by the ants"* [p. 420]) (emphasis in the original). He realizes then that the manuscript contains the story of his family and hurries on to translate it to discover his own fate and the date and circumstances of his death. I shall return to the significance of all this, but not before I complete the description of the manuscript and its translation, for it is very easy to leap to false conclusions about Melquíades's writing.

Aureliano begins to translate the text out loud, jumping ahead twice to arrive at the present faster. Once he reaches the present he has a second illumination: that he would die in the room where the manuscript is kept once he finished translating the last line of poetry ("el último verso"). Is this the text of Melquíades's version of the history of Macondo, and is this version *Cien años de soledad?* Even if in fact it is Aureliano's translation that we read, then some changes have been made. The text is neither finished nor definitive, like that of the narrator-protagonist of *Los pasos perdidos.* To begin with, the epigraph has been omitted. In addition, either Aureliano's leaps to get to the present have not been accounted for in this version, or the holes they left have been restored. But when and by whom? The only solution to this enigma is to say that our reading—that each reading—of the text is the text, that is to say, yet another version added to the Archive. Each of these readings corrects the others, and each is unrepeatable insofar as it is a distinct act caught in the reader's own temporality. In this sense, we, like Aureliano, read the instant we live, cognizant that it may very well be our last. This is the eschatological sense announced in various ways by the Archive: the chronicle of a death foretold.

The radical historicity to which the Archive condemns us belies its apparent atemporality and the bizarre order that the masterbooks within it have. It is a historicity that is very much like the one to which the narrator-protagonist of *Los pasos perdidos* is condemned at the end of that novel. In fact, Aureliano's reading of the manuscript in search of his origins and of an understanding of his being in the present is analogous to the reading performed by Carpentier's character in search of the origins of history and of his own beginnings. Such dearly achieved historicity in spite of the circularity and repetition of the family's history is somewhat ironic, given the sense of ahistoricalness with which many readers, intoxicated by the similarity of names and by Ursula's notion that time is going round and round, leave the novel. Such historicity, however, is needed to represent, within the anthropological mediation posited, the "lucid" consciousness of the West, able to understand itself by posturing as the Other, but unable to abandon the sense of history to which writing sentences it. This is a sentence from which we can gain acquittal by means of a willful act of delusion, but one that *Cien años de soledad,* for all its fictive force, does not allow the reader.

There is a significant fact that few readers of *Cien años de soledad* remark upon: even though the novel begins with Colonel Aureliano Buendía facing the firing squad, the one who dies at the end is not Aureliano the soldier, but Aureliano the reader. This displacement, plus the fact that Aureliano's moments of vision are flashes of insight parallel to the rebel's, seem to suggest a most significant connection between the realms of history and myth, one that constitutes a common denominator of the repetitions of the family history and the disassembling mechanisms of the Archive. In the Archive, the presence of Melquíades and Aureliano (and in *Aura,* Felipe Montero, in *Yo el Supremo,* Patiño, and so on) is an insurance that the individual consciousness of a historian-writer will filter the ahistorical pretense of myth by subjecting events to the temporality of writing. But in *Cien años de soledad* the death of these figures is indicative of a mythic power that lurks within the realm of writing, a story that makes the Archive possible. In *Yo el Supremo* this is clearly indicated by Patiño's being a "swollen foot," that is, an Oedipus who pays a high price for his knowledge. In *Cien años de soledad* Aureliano suffers a similar fate. He commits incest with his aunt, engenders a monster with her, and dies the moment he has a glimpse of his fate. Aureliano is the propitiatory victim necessary for us to be able to read the text, for us to acquire the arcane knowledge we need to decode it. He (we) is/are no Oedipus but more likely the Minotaur, which brings us back to Borges (and also to Cortázar). The ritualistic death—which prefigures *Crónica de una muerte anunciada*-is necessary because of the incest committed both at the genealogical and the textual level. In both cases, what has been gained is a forbidden knowledge of the other as oneself, or vice versa.

The most salient characteristic of the text we read is its heterogeneity. However, this heterogeneity is made up of differences within similarity. The various versions of the story are all related yet differ in each instance. Their difference as well as their relation is akin—*valga la palabra*—to the relationship between the incestuous characters and the broader confrontation between writer and a primitive Other who produces myth. Put differently, the self-reflexiveness of the novel is implicitly compared to incest, a self-knowledge that somehow lies beyond knowledge. A plausible argument can be made that the end results of both are similar in the most tangible sense, or at least related. When the ants carry away the carcass of the monstrous child engendered by Amaranta Ursula and Aureliano, its skin is described in terms that are very reminiscent of Melquíades's parchments. The English translation blurs that similarity. It reads: "And then he saw the child. It was a dry and bloated bag of skin that all the ants in the world were dragging. . . ." (p. 420). The Spanish reads: "Era un pellejo [it was a skin] hinchado y reseco, que todas las hormigas del mundo iban arrastrando . . ." (p. 349). I need not go into the etymological and historical kinship uniting skin and parchment because the novel itself provides that link. The parchments are once described as "parecían fabricados en una materia árida que se resquebrajaba como hojaldres" (p. 68), and the books in the Archive are bound "en una materia acartonada y pálida como la piel humana curtida" (p. 160). The English reads: "The parchments that he had brought with him and that seemed to have been made out of some dry material that crumpled like puff paste" (p. 73), and "the books were bound in a cardboard-like material, pale, like tanned human skin" (p. 188).

The monster and the manuscript, the monster and the text, are the product of the turning in on oneself implicit in incest and self-reflexivity. Both are heterogeneous within a given set of characteristics, the most conspicuous of which is their supplementarity: the pig's tail, which exceeds the normal contours of the human body, and the text, whose mode of being is each added reading and interpretation. The plotline that narrates the decipherment of the manuscripts underscores our falling into this trap. Like Aureliano, we follow along in search of the meaning of the manuscripts, constantly teased by scenes where Melquíades appears scratching his incomprehensible handwriting onto rough parchment, by scenes where José Arcadio Segundo or Aureliano make preliminary discoveries that eventually lead them to unravel the mystery. But like Lönnrot in "La muerte y la brújula," and like Aureliano himself, we do not discover until the very end what the manuscripts contain. Our own anagnorisis as readers is saved for the last page, when the novel concludes and we close the book to cease being as readers, to be, as it were, slain in that role. We are placed back at the beginning, a beginning that is also already the end, a discontinuous, independent instant where everything commingles without any possibility of extending the insight, an intimation of death. This independent instant is not the novel; it is the point to which the novel has led us. By means of an unreading, the text has reduced us, like Aureliano, to a ground zero, where death and birth are joined as correlative moments of incommunicable plenitude. The text is that which is added to this moment. Archive and myth are conjoined as instances of discontinuity rather than continuity; knowledge and death are given equivalent value. Death, as we shall see, is the trope for the Archive's structuring principle.

It is a commonplace, almost an uncritical fetish, to say that the novel always includes the story of how it is written, that it is a self-reflexive genre. The question is why and how it is so at specific moments. Clearly, *Cien años de soledad* is self-reflexive not merely to provoke laughter or to declare itself literary and thus disconnected from reality or history. In García Márquez, and I dare say in all major Latin American novelists, self-reflexivity is a way of disassembling the mediation through which Latin America is narrated, a mediation that constitutes a pre-text of the novel itself. It is also a way of showing that the act of writing is caught up in a deeply rooted mythic struggle that constantly denies it the authority to generate and contain knowledge about the other without at the same time generating a perilous sort of knowledge about itself and about one's mortality and capacity to know oneself.

What do we learn about Latin American history in *Cien años de soledad*? We learn that while its writing may be mired in myth, it cannot be turned into myth, that its newness makes it impervious to timelessness, circularity, or any such delusion. New and therefore historical, what occurs in Latin America is marked by change; it is change. García Márquez has expressed this by tantalizing the reader with various forms of history as writing, of history as Archive. He has also achieved it by making Borges the keeper of the Archive, for the figure of the Argentine ensures that no delusions about literature be entertained. In a sense, what García Márquez has done is to punch through the anthropological mediation and substitute the anthropologist for a historian, and to turn the object of attention away from myth as an expression of so-called primitive cultures to the myths of modern society: the book, writing, reading, instruments of a quest for self-knowledge that lie beyond the solace mythic interpretations of the world usually afford. We can always use *Cien años de soledad* to escape temporality, but only if we willfully misread it to blind ourselves to its warnings against that. Latin American history can only become myth enmeshed in this very modern problematic that so enriches its most enduring fictions.

It is not toward a high-pitched rationality that *Cien años de soledad* moves, but toward a vision of its own creation dominated by the forces that generate myth. This is perhaps most evident if we consider that the Archive may very well be the most powerful of cultural retentions and the origin of the novel. The Archive is, first of all, a repository for the legal documents wherein the origins of Latin American history are contained, as well as a specifically Hispanic institution created at the same time as the New World was being settled. As is known, the great archive at Simancas, begun by Charles V but finished by the king-bureaucrat Philip II, is the first and possibly the most voluminous of such storehouses in Europe. The same Herrera who designed the Escorial had a hand in planning the archive, that is to say, in turning a castle that was originally a prison into the archive. Simancas became the Archive in 1539; *La vida de Lazarillo de Tormes, y de sus fortunas y adversidades* was published in 1554. The Archive and the novel appear at the same time and are part of the same discourse of the modern state. Latin America became a historical entity as a result of the development of the printing press, not merely by being "discovered" by Columbus. Latin America, like the novel, was created in the Archive. It may very well have been Carlos Fuentes in his *Terra nostra* who most clearly saw the connection, making Cervantes the inner historian in that novel. In terms of the novel's ability to retain and pass on cultural values, the message contained in books such as Fuentes's and *Cien años de soledad* is indeed disturbing, for they tell us that it is impossible to create new myths, yet bring us back to that moment where our desire for meaning can only be satisfied by myth.

4

Ferdinand and Isabella, Charles I and Philip II can truly be called—all four, not only the last one—papermonger kings, for they all indeed were, each in his or her own way. And the most seasoned fruit of their tenacious and intelligent archival policies was the world-famous Simancas Archive, near Valladolid, which was then a true capital. Philip II's shrewd foresight, aided by Juan de Herrera's solid technical knowledge, turned a fifteenth-century castle into the first fireproof Archive known to Europe and, crowning the efforts of his predecessors, he managed to gather there the central Archive of the State.

—José María de la Peña y Cámara,
Archivo General de Indias de Sevilla. Guía del Visitante.[23]

And the temple of God was opened in heaven, and there was seen in his temple the ark of his testament; and there were lightnings, and voices, and thun-
derings, and an earthquake, and a great hail.

—Revelation, 11:19

I am interested in the cluster of connections between secrecy (or privacy of
knowledge), origin, and power encrypted in the concept of Archive. This is so,
perhaps, because like the modern novel, my own discourse tends to mythify the
Archive, to use it as a heuristic device to investigate, conjure, or invent its own
foundations. By heuristic device I mean, in the best of cases, that the Archive is
a hypostasis for method—for my method in this book; in the worst, it is a wild
card or joker around which to build a system to read the history of the Latin
American narrative and the origins of the novel. If my apprehensions about the
contamination of my discourse by that of the novel turn out to be justified, then
Archive is a sort of liturgical object that I invest with the faculty of calling forth
the innermost secrets of the narratives—the hidden, secret origin. Whichever of
these it is, the term is derived from the reading of *Los pasos perdidos* and *Cien
años de soledad* offered above. Though my theoretical debts should be obvious, I
fancy to read this new history of the Latin American narrative, and its origin, by
activating a self-interpreting discourse latent within it. That is, I wish to legit-
imize my theory by drawing it from within my very field of study. I am conscious
of the circularity of this approach, but circling around a point (like the plane that
comes to rescue the protagonist of *Los pasos perdidos*) may be revealing, may
allow one to see or at least make one think he or she sees it from many perspectives. The reader will decide on the usefulness of my approach and whether by
circling I am not really spiraling into the ground or mistaking dizziness for
insight.

Etymologically, "archive" has a suggestive background that supports, I hope,
the work that it is made to perform here. Corominas writes:

Archivo, 1490, Tomado del latín tardío *archivum,* y éste del griego *archeion* "resi-
dencia de los magistrados," "archivo," derivado de *arkhe* "mando," "magistratura."
(Taken from late Latin *archivum,* and this from the Greek *archeion,* "residence of
the magistrates," "archive," derived from *arkhe* "command," "magistracy.")[24]

The dictionary of the Spanish Academy reads:

Archivo (Del lat. *archivum,* y éste del griego . . . principio, origen) m. Local en
que se custodian documentos públicos o particulares. 2. Conjunto de estos
documentos. 3. fig. Persona en quien se confia un secreto o recónditas intimi-

dades y sabe guardarlas./fig. Persona que posee en grado sumo una perfección o conjunto de perfecciones. *Archivo* de cortesía, de la lealtad. (From the Latin *archivum,* and this from the Greek . . . beginnings or origin.) Masculine. Building in which public or private documents are placed for safekeeping. 2. The sum total of these documents. 3. Figurative. A person to whom is entrusted a secret or very private knowledge and knows how to guard them/ Figurative. A person who is endowed with the highest degree of perfection or sum of perfections. To be an *archive* of courtesy or of loyalty.

Power, secrecy, and law stand at the origin of the Archive; it was, in its most concrete form, the structure that actually housed the dispensers of the law, its readers, the magistrates; it was the building that encrypted the power to command. In philosophy *arche* is the primordial stuff in the beginning, the first principle. In Anaximander and the earlier Greek philosophers it was a substance or primal element, and with later philosophers, especially Aristotle, an actuating principle, a cause. It is this word *arche* which appears in the first verse of the Fourth Gospel: "In the *beginning* was the word." All observable regularities were viewed as reflections of the *arché's* enduring presence in the cosmos.[25] So *arch,* as in *monarch,* denotes power, to rule, but also the beginning, that which is chief, eminent, greatest, principal; it denotes primitive, original. Through the *arche,* in addition, *archive* is related to "arcane" and "arcanum" (Webster: "*arcanum,* A secret, a mystery, esp. one of the great secrets that the alchemists sought to discover; hence, a sovereign remedy"). So *Archive* suggests not only something that is kept but that which is secret, encrypted, enclosed, and also the common though old-fashioned Spanish word for chest, for safe, for trunk, like the trunk found in *Lazarillo de Tormes* and *Aura.*[26] Trunk, *arca,* according to the Academy:

> Caja, comunmente sin forrar y con una tapa llana que aseguran varios goznes o bisagras por uno de los lados, y uno o más candados o cerraduras por el opuesto. Especie de nave o embarcación (Noé). Ant. sepulcro o ataúd. (Box, commonly without a lining, which has a flat lid secured by several hinges on one side and one or more locks on the other. A kind of ship or boat (Noah). Old Spanish, sepulcher, tomb.)

Power encrypts knowledge of the origin, the principles, kept in a building or enclosure that safeguards the law, the beginning of writing; it also kept the body after death, like a relic of life, possessor still of its darkest secrets, abandoned abode of the soul. It is no accident that the word *archivo,* according to Corominas, appears to have entered Spanish in 1490, during the reign of the Catholic kings, two years before the discovery of America; it was in that period that modern archival practices began, organized by the new state created by Ferdinand and Isabella. The mystery of the object, its prestige, is made a functional part in the foundation of the modern state and a key figure in the narratives therein generated.

Like the Archive, the novel hoards knowledge. Like the Archive's, that knowledge is of the origin, meaning that it is about the link of its own writing with the power that makes it possible, hence with the possibility of knowledge. In the beginning that power was the law, but later other origins replaced it, though preserving the seal of that initial pact between power and writing. The modern novel retains those origins and the structure that made them possible. While the knowledge kept there is difficult to plumb, hence its secretiveness, it is not private but, on the contrary, common property. It can be read, and it is indeed read. The very act of reading and sharing that knowledge assumes the form of ritual, of celebrating the common knowledge, the transpersonal history. Archives keep the secrets of the state; novels keep the secrets of culture and the secret of those secrets.

It should be evident that the archaeology of narrative forms that I seek to describe owes much to Foucault's theories about discursive regularities and their relation to power in society. I am interested in the place of narrative within discursive practices overdetermined by power structures that either base or project their authority through them. The novel's contamination with nonliterary forms of discourse justifies the association I propose here with the language of the law, of natural science, and anthropology. But, most of all, at the point of departure and arrival of the project, it is the Archive that seeks our attention. I am also inspired by Foucault's version of the Archive, though mine has somewhat different characteristics because, in spite of the novel's pull away from literature, it is ultimately in that ambiguous and shifting space called literature that my Archive is lodged. I wish to retain from Foucault, above all, the negative, proscriptive element of his Archive, because interdiction, that is negation, is at the beginning of the law, hence of writing and of the novel. Foucault writes in *The Archaeology of Knowledge:*

> The Archive is first the law of what can be said, the system that governs the appearance of statements and unique events. But the Archive is also that which determines that all these things said do not accumulate endlessly in an amorphous mass, nor are they inscribed in an unbroken linearity, nor do they disappear at the mercy of chance external accidents; but they are grouped together in distinct figures, composed together in accordance with specific regularities; that which determines that they do not withdraw at the same pace in time, but shine, as it were, like stars, some that seem close to us are already growing pale. The Archive is not that which, despite its immediate escape, safeguards the event of the statement, and preserves, for future memories, its status as

escapee; it is that which, at the very root of the statement-event, and in that which embodies it, defines at the outset *the system of enunciability* . . . far from being only that which ensures that we exist in the midst of preserved discourse, it is that which differentiates discourses in their multiple existence and specifies them in their own duration.[27]

Narrative in general, the novel in particular, may be the way in which the statement's status as escapee is preserved, the Counter-Archive for the ephemeral and wayward. The novel endows the negativity of the Archive, the proscription of the Archive, with a phantasmagoric form of being, embodying only, particularly in the modern period, the Archive's very power to differentiate. The following, from Foucault again, would be an apt description of the modern novel, one that, as we shall see, has already taken shape in another text by Carpentier, though these lines could also be about Melquíades' room in *Cien años de soledad*:

The description of the Archive deploys its possibilities (and the mastery of its possibilities) on the basis of the very discourses that have just ceased to be ours; its threshold of existence is established by the discontinuity that separates us from what we can no longer say, and from that which falls outside our discursive practices; it begins with the outside of our own language (*langage*); its locus is the gap between our own discursive practices . . . it deprives us of our continuities; it dissipates that temporal identity in which we are pleased to look at ourselves when we wish to exorcise the discontinuities of history; it snaps the thread of transcendental teleologies; and where anthropological thought once questioned man's being or subjectivity, it now bursts open the other and the outside. In this sense, the diagnosis does not establish the fact of our identity by the play of distinctions. It establishes that we are difference, that our reason is the difference of discourses, our history the difference of times, our selves the difference of masks. That difference, far from being the forgotten and discovered origin, is this dispersion that we are not make.[28]

The dispersive quality of this Archive is found in the modern novel's apparent grab-bag approach to history, its endemic power to negate previous narrative forms from which it takes texts rather than continuities; the power, in short, to question received knowledge and its ideological coagulations as identity, culture, educational institutions, even language, or perhaps better, ultimately, language itself. By letting loose the arcana, by breaking open the safe, the novel-Archive unleashes a ghostly procession of figures of negation, inhabitants of the fissures and cracks which hover around the covenant of writing and the law.

Carpentier's last novel, *El arpa y la sombra* (1979), deployed and displayed the inner workings of this Archive in a way that is most instructive. The protagonist of Carpentier's novel is Columbus; not Columbus in his role as discoverer of the New World as much as Columbus the first writer of the New World, Columbus as origin of the Latin American narrative record. In one strand of the narrative the Discoverer appears on his deathbed in Valladolid. He is reviewing his life to prepare for the visit of the priest who will confess him and administer extreme unction. Technically, as he remembers his life, Columbus is performing an act of contrition, a sort of inner narrative atonement. He is also rereading and commenting upon some of the texts that he wrote about his most famous deed, the ones that we all read in the opening chapter of all anthologies of Latin American literature. Carpentier finished *El arpa y la sombra* when he knew that he had terminal cancer, in a sense also on his deathbed and as a kind of final audit of his life as novelist. Since Carpentier's texts often, almost obsessively, deal with the origin of Latin American history, with the beginning of the Latin American narrative tradition, Carpentier's identification in his role as writer with Columbus is evident. In the conventional scheme of Latin American literary history Columbus's texts constitute the origin, the beginning of the narrative tradition, the foundational writing. Columbus was the first to name things in the New World, like Blake's Adam, a gesture that in Carpentier's Neo-Romantic ideology signals the start of Latin American literature.

But Columbus is not the only projection of Carpentier in *El arpa y la sombra*: there is also Mastai Ferreti, that is to say, Pope Pius IX, who is described, in the opening scene of the novel, with his pen suspended over a sheet of paper, hesitating over whether he should sign the documents that will set in motion Columbus's beatification process. This would constitute the first step toward an eventual canonization of the Admiral of the Ocean Sea. Like Columbus and Carpentier, Mastai is both a reader and a writer: he has gathered as many documents as possible about the Discoverer to prepare the dossier that must be presented at the trial in which, once read and examined in detail, sentence will be passed in the case. Columbus's authority as narrator, of course, rests on his being at the beginning: his is the prestige of the origin. Mastai's authority rests on his erudition and, needless to say, on his office. Carpentier's identification with Pius IX is clear and ironic. Like Carpentier, Mastai was a man of two worlds: Europe and Latin America. Having once gone on a mission to Latin America, he identified with the New World, where he became an avid reader of Latin American and Spanish texts. Mastai is the compiler of the dossier, the researcher for facts and documents, the curator of the file, the Archivist *par excellence.* By means of that signature that he delays in scribbling, his sacred presence will endow with authority the texts that he has gathered: Mastai, creator of the canon, canonizer of the Latin American narrative tradition from Columbus to Carpentier, alfa and omega. Columbus, because he occupies the origin, and Mastai, because of his investiture, are capable of making the texts sacred; they are texts outside the flow of history, hence possessors of an irreducible truth about history, texts containing a story of mythic proportions, the stories that make possible all other stories. They are the key to the Archive.

Mastai and Columbus are figures of the Archive, hoarders of secrets, owners of the first, most *archaic* rule, emblems of authority and power. Columbus jealously keeps his texts under the pillow, from where he pulls them out to read and reread them. He later hides them under the bed. The Archive keeps and hides, it guards the secrets, which is the first law. Mastai keeps his papers in a portfolio which, one assumes, is part of the Vatican Archive. This Archive is evoked in the novel through yet another repository: the Vatican's stockpile of saints' bones, the *ostea sacra* kept and classified to be distributed around the world to constitute the relics each church requires. This is the *lipsanateca*. The Archive safeguards, retains, orders dissemination, both commands it and organizes its regularities as a discourse. The Archive keeps the arcanum, the secret. It keeps the secret of Columbus's texts, their foundational arch-texture, from which, like the bones in the Vatican dispensing sacredness, issue the Latin American texts; origin as death, as cut, as void, as proscription, as negation. The secret is the negation, the prohibition, the origin of law. It is the proscriptions that Fray Pedro will have to write in the notebooks that the narrator wants in *Los pasos perdidos*. Columbus, his texts, is the modern myth that Mastai wishes to sacralize, compiling the documents at the origin and of the origin, submitting those documents to the Archive's *arche*. Mastai signs the document and sets in motion the judicial process.

The judgment goes against Columbus. He is not beatified, hence he cannot be canonized. The canon that the Keeper of the Archive seeks to establish is not sanctioned. This Archive's origin is not a library, volumes here float unbound, without pagination; this is its true secret, the negation in the origin. The Archive contains essentially nothing. This is the contradictory force that constitutes the Archive, the cut, the loss whose image is the eschatology of Melquíades' abode, the bones signifying death in Carpentier's. Death's dark perimeter encircles the Archive and at the same time inhabits its center. This secret is also revealed in the part of *El arpa y la sombra* where Columbus the reader comments on his own texts and declares them to be false, a tissue of lies:

> Y la constancia de tales trampas está aquí, en estos borradores de mis relaciones de viajes, que tengo bajo la almohada, y que ahora saco con mano temblorosa— asustada de sí misma—para releer lo que, en estos postreros momentos, tengo por un Vasto Repertorio de Embustes. (And the proof of such tricks is here, in these drafts of my travel accounts that I keep under my pillow, and that I now pull out with a trembling hand, afraid of itself, to reread what in these final moments I consider a Vast Repertory of Lies.)[29]

The Archive does not canonize, because the first law of the Archive is a denial, a cut that organizes and disperses. This negation is represented by the phantasmic figure of Columbus present as a ghost at his own trial, present and absent at the very moment when his sacralization is denied. That afterlife of Columbus's is the escape from the Archive, the thrust to freedom forever present in the narrative, only that it is a fictive supplement, a fake afterlife. This is the profound statement made by Carpentier about the novel, himself on the verge of death; that it is that cut, one of whose representations is extinction itself, that rules the Archive and constitutes the ultimate form of knowledge. The truth of the Archive, the secret of its secret, is that it contains no truth but that "dispersion that we are and make," as Foucault put it, the image of which in *El arpa y la sombra* is the *lipsanateca,* the collection of bones to be disseminated throughout the world, relics of an order that exists only in the dissembling memory of the Archive or in our desire to project our fictive capacity upon it.

It is this dissembling quality, this empty space where the novel's capacity for retention and loss balance out, that leads to the series of breaks in history, breaks where the novel's mimetic desire leads it to choose a different form in reaction to changes in the textual field in which it is inscribed. A new nonliterary document will acquire the legitimating powers lost by the previous model, and the novel will follow that form as it had done originally in relation to the legal documents of the Archive. This mimetic displacement is more important than superficial, aesthetic changes, such as those that novels outside the core of the tradition will undergo. Texts like that will not be remembered except in conventional literary histories; they will be forgotten, and this is what is important, by the new novels that will look always outside literature to implement a radical change. This is why the history of the Latin American novel proves to be so deficient, except when told by the internal process of reading and rewriting that I have been sketching here; that is to say, when that history is told by the Latin American novel itself.

The history of the Latin American novel has been variously told. For the most part, however, no matter what method the historian employs, the blueprint of evolution and change continues to be that of European literary or artistic historiography. Whether he or she be a thematic historian of the novel or of Latin American literature in general, or one whose approach purports to be sociopolitical and hence Marxist-inspired, ordinary categories like romanticism, naturalism, realism, the avant-garde surface sooner or later. If it is questionable that this historiographic grid is applicable to European literature, it is even more so regarding the literature of Latin America. What undermines this approach is, to begin with, the inclusion of the narrative within the broader concept of literature, or *belles-lettres.* As I have suggested, what is most significant about the novel, or even about prose narrative in general, is that its point of departure is to deny that it is literature. The novel, as we have seen, continues to exist without a poetics because the main tenet of its poetics is to have none. The novel dons a disguise to appear as something else; the novel is always something else. That something else includes a desire to preserve secrets about the origin and history of a culture, and in this it may be related to the epic (as Lukács suggested, and others, like Bakhtin, continued to accept),[30] but also its protean ability to change and to disavow the knowledge/power equation lodged in those secrets. For reasons about which one can only speculate, this phenomenon seems to be particularly prevalent in Latin America, where the greatest narratives are not novels (but appear to be so), or are novels pretending to be something else. I have in mind, of course, Columbus's diaries and letters about the discovery, Sarmiento's *Facundo,* Euclides da Cunha's *Os Sertões,* Lydia Cabrera's *El monte,* Martín Luis Guzmán's *El águila y la serpiente,* Miguel Barnet's *Biografía de un cimarrón,* and many others. This is the reason for including in my discussion books such as *Facundo* and *Os Sertões,* which do not claim to be novels, but in not doing so, appeal to the most basic conceit of novelistic discourse; not to be literature. It is a hopeless task to force texts such as these into a conventional history of the Latin American novel, and a blatant error to leave them out. It is clear that they are the very core of that tradition.

I seek to produce a history of the Latin American narrative that goes beyond the surface differences determined by artistic trends, looking for the subtext determined by the phoenixlike quality of novelistic discourse, a subtext that takes into account the synchronicity between the picaresque and the first narratives of and about Latin America, and delves into the relationship between novelistic discourse and nonliterary forms of hegemonic discourse. The novel razes all previous constructs to create itself anew in the image of another text, a text which, as I suggest, is endowed with specific power to bear the truth at a given moment in history, owing to a given set of socioeconomic circumstances. That truth, in the case of the narratives being discussed here, is about Latin America itself as a cultural entity, as a context or archive from which to narrate. The first issue is, precisely, one of legitimation, as the trial to decide upon the canonization of Columbus clearly reminds us. Archival fictions like *El arpa y la sombra* bear the indelible imprint of the law, the form of writing that was generated by the initial political circumstances that made Latin American narrative possible.

The first and defining set of circumstances that determined the emergence of such narrative was the development in Spain and its colonies of a modern state and the fashioning of a legal system to sustain it by controlling individuals. The evolution of narrative prose prior to 1554, when *Lazarillo* was published, is of interest but of minor relevance when compared to the importance of the state bureaucracy and the emergence of texts, based on models provided by the bureaucracy, to allow individuals, often criminals or otherwise marginal people, to obtain exculpation or enfranchisement. There are fabliaux, oral and written tales, Petronius, Boccaccio, Don Juan Manuel, Chaucer, *Il Novellino,* Juan Ruiz and the novelistic elements of Dante's *Commedia,* but all these are absorbed into a large quilt with a radically new pattern when Lazarillo "writes": "Pues sepa Vuestra Merced que me míllaman Lázaro de Tormes. . . ." ("May Your Worship know that I am called Lázaro de Tormes. . . .") A different mimetic contract is established by that enunciation, which has the form of a legal act. The object of that mimetic contract will be violated as the novel or the narrative takes on different forms, but not its basic structure.

This version of the history of the Latin American narrative wishes, then, to find, analyze, and describe those breaks and renewals, believing that the central strand in that narrative obeys such an underlying structure and tells the same story about constraint, mimesis, and escape. I do not believe, of course, that every Latin American narrative within a given period is dependent on each of the models offered here; but I do argue that the major ones are and that is the structure that defines the tradition, the canon, or the key to the canon, as it were. Hence I do not maintain that the psychological novels of Eduardo Barrios, for instance, are as crucial as *La vorágine,* or that any servile imitation of *Paul et Virginie* can compare with *Facundo,* or that the last echo of the *nouveau roman* stands next to *Biografía de un cimarrón.* What determines the centrality of these works is their rewriting or their being rewritten. *Terra nostra* takes up Cervantes, the chronicles of the conquest of Mexico, *Cien años de soledad, Tres tristes tigres,* but not *María,* or *Santa.* Novels like these last two do fit in the conventional European historiographic scheme, precisely because they are mere echoes. It is important to determine if Gamboa's novel is naturalistic or not, and how romantic Isaacs was. Not so with narratives at the core of the tradition, which are redeployed violently as they insert the new form assumed by the narrative. Hence the chronicles of the exploration accounts are turned into part of the new Archive or passed off as mythic, foundational stories.

In my book *Myth and Archive* I analyze the main forms that the Latin American narrative has assumed in relation to three kinds of hegemonic discourse, the first of which is foundational both for the novel and for the Latin American narrative in general: legal discourse during the colonial period; the scientific, during the nineteenth century until the crisis of the 1920s; the anthropological, during the twentieth century, up to *Los pasos perdidos* and *Cien años de soledad.* At the end of the book, of which this essay is the first chapter, I return to the Archive, to the current mode, perhaps beyond the anthropological mediation, the locus on which my own text is situated. It would be aseptically formalistic not to recognize that the law, nineteenth-century science, and anthropology are powerful *cultural,* not merely narrative, constructs. Latin America continues to be a culture of lawyers, as well as one whose beliefs about itself are strongly colored by science and anthropology: the absorbing preoccupation with the issue of cultural identity, the ever-present belief in the uniqueness of Latin American nature and its influence on everything. It is because of the weight of these forms of discourse within the culture that I believe them to play such an important role in the narrative, not the other way around. There is no doubt, either, that both anthropology and science, as they existed then, have been present in Latin American narratives since the colonial period. Ramón Pané, and many of the friars and missionaries that followed him, embarked on activities and wrote reports that were precursors of modern anthropology. The same can be said of science. From Columbus on, and particularly in writers such as Fernández de Oviedo and José de Acosta, there was a curiosity about American reality and an effort at description and classification. But neither anthropology nor science became disciplines *per se* until later, nor did they acquire until much later a hegemonic position in relation to the discovery and dissemination of the truth. No matter. Their embryonic presence surely facilitated their acquiring such a status in Latin American culture and narratives, as well as the possibility of remaining as strong memories in modern narratives such as those by Carpentier and García Márquez.

By hegemonic discourse, I mean one backed by a discipline or embodying a system that offers the most commonly accepted description of humanity and accounts for the most widely held beliefs of the intelligentsia. Within such a discourse, the individual finds stories about himself and the world that he or she finds acceptable and in some ways obeys. Prestige and sociopolitical power give these forms of discourse currency. When they are abandoned, they are merely stories or myths, voided of power in the present, in the way in which we read about Melquíades's scientific prowess in the early chapters of *Cien años de soledad*. It does not escape me that the hegemonic discourse described here comes from "outside" Latin America; therefore Latin America appears to be constantly explaining itself in "foreign" terms, the helpless victim of a colonialist's language and image-making. There is a level at which this is true and deplorable. However, in Latin America in every realm, from the economic to the intellectual, the outside is also always inside; García Márquez and Vargas Llosa hardly think like *llaneros* or *campesinos*. This duality, which is for the most part a stance or in the worst of cases a posture, is present from the start, for instance, in Garcilaso de la Vega, el Inca. Latin America is part of the Western world, not a colonized other, except in founding fictions and constitutive idealizations. In addition the internalization of these forms of discourse is not a passive process nor a celebration, but a dialectical struggle with no victor and no satisfactory synthesis, save through fiction; if our individual subconscious is not made up of nice stories about mommy and daddy, neither is our history composed of epic tales leading to independence and cultural identity, yet both are irreducibly ours and part of our stories. The Latin American narrative, both in the stories it tells and in the structure of those stories, reflects a struggle to free the imagination of all mediation, to reach a knowledge of self and collectivity that is liberating and easily shared; a clearing in the current jungle of discourses of power, emblematized in the one the narrator of *Los pasos perdidos* seeks or in the remote and foundational Macondo created by the Buendías. But since this foundation has not yet occurred in reality and is unlikely to occur in the foreseeable future, the stories told here, which I think are master-stories, are about a process toward liberation, not the story of its accomplishment. Nor is one naïvely to suppose that similar stories culled from the European tradition could be substantially closer to such a desideratum. Pollyanna exists only in Eleanor Porter's novel and in the naïve doctrines of dull ideologues and bad novelists.

I have chosen the most representative works, at the risk of covering territories better charted by others. Here I begin with the law and I end *Myth and Archive* with a return to the law in the Archive.

NOTES

1. Fuentes *The New York Times*.

2. Varner defines "Adelantado" as: "Title given a man who was sent out to explore and govern new lands." In the "Glossary of Spanish and Quechuan Words," appended to his *El Inca*, 387.

3. All references are to Alejo Carpentier, *Los pasos perdidos*, 252; *The Lost Steps*, 189–190.

4. Although my debt to Michel Foucault's *Surveiller et punir* should be obvious (more on this later in the text), my study of the relationship between the novel and the law has been enriched by the current movement in the U.S. academy generally called "the law-literature enterprise," which appears to have culminated with the foundation of the *Yale Journal of Law and the Humanities* (on whose editorial advisory board I am honored to serve). The first issue of that journal is recommended as an entry into this already vast field of enquiry and debate. I have also learned much from the special issue "Law and Literature" of the *Texas Law Review*, 60, 3 (1982), which contains a lively exchange capped by a lucid piece by Stanley Fish. A recent book by judge Richard Posner, though somewhat belligerent and shortsighted, contains a useful overview of the issues as well as ample bibliographical information in the footnotes. The "law-literature enterprise" has been dominated, not surprisingly, by the issue of interpretation. Deconstruction and other schools of literary criticism have invaded the law with their claims about the arbitrariness of the sign, hence questioning the validity of interpretations and the truth-value of monumental texts such as constitutions and legal codes. Fish shows that the pluralism that emerges is itself a position, allied to a conception of literature tied to a liberal ideology for the past two centuries. My position is that the shifting shape of what is called narrative or the novel is determined by outside forces that determine it in a given moment, and that these changes take place initially in the rhetoric of the law. In the U.S. the issue of rhetoric and its relationship to the law, both as a matter of instituting power (persuasion) and as a historical phenomenon (the evolution of modern legal practices in Renaissance Bologna) has not been given enough attention.

5. I have studied in great detail this process in my *Alejo Carpentier.*

6. Cervantes, *The Adventures of Don Quixote,* 457–458.

7. Of course, Menéndez Pidal's monumental enterprise is based on philology, so for him the *epopeya* is an origin that persists in Spanish literature. I would invert the perspective and say that, in many ways, the *epopeya* is an invented origin, as is the history of Latin America for Latin American literature.

8. Carpentier, *Tientos y diferencias,* 7.

9. Ralph Freedman, 65. It is obvious now that Mikhail Bakhtin had made a similar proposal years earlier, but this was not known when Freedman wrote his piece.

10. Bakhtin, *Rabelais and His World,* 8. Henceforth all quotes, indicated in the text, are taken from this edition.

11. The most reliable summary of Bakhtin's ideas on these issues is Tzevetan Todorov's *Michail Bakhtine.* I have also profited from my friendship with my colleague and great Bakhtin scholar Michael Holquist.

12. See also Goodman; Jean Franco. Goodman's book contains an excellent bibliography on exploration in Latin America.

13. On the *novela de la tierra,* the most advanced work is Carlos J. Alonso's *The Spanish American Regional Novel.*

14. Freccero; Eduardo G. González, Geertz *Works and Lives.*

15. Carpentier corresponded with André Schaeffner, a musicologist who participated in the Griaule expedition (see note 27, 89–90, in my edition of *Los pasos perdidos*). While in New York, a group of anthropologists closely associated with the avant-garde and which included Claude Lévi-Strauss, published a journal called *VVV,* the cypher giving access to Santa Mónica de los Venados in *Los pasos perdidos.* It is quite possible that the narrator-protagonist of the novel was modeled on these anthropologists. See James Clifford, 117–185. Clifford's excellent book is a must-read for anyone interested in Carpentier. The Cuban novelist was in intimate intellectual contact with the world described by Clifford, from the writings of Michel Leiris, a potential model for the narrator-protagonist of *Los pasos perdidos,* to Lévi-Strauss. The relationship between this group and Carpentier deserves more detailed study and reflection. Carpentier mentions the group of artists and anthropologists and the magazine *VVV* in one of his last novels, *La consagración de la primavera,* 273.

16. See Lichy, *Yakú.* This expedition, which also included Marc de Civrieux, took place in 1951.

17. All references are to Gabriel García Márquez, *Cien años de soledad* and to *One Hundred Years of Solitude.* I have also consulted the two critical editions extant by Joaquín Marco (Madrid, Espasa Calpe, 1984) and Jacques Joset (Madrid, Cátedra, 1984).

18. I have had to change the translation, for this is one of the very few places where Gregory Rabassa made a mistake.

19. See, for example, Gullón; and Arnau. There have been many studies since along these lines. The most convincing is by Palencia Roth, whose splendid piece argues in favor of the biblical myth of Apocalypse as the principal one in the organization of the novel and insists on the influence of Borges on García Márquez. As I will argue below, however, no single myth controls the novel, and no transcendence is allowed by the constantly undermined and undermining world of writing, of the Archive. Only if we could escape the ver-

bal would the sort of simultaneity and atemporality of which Palencia Roth speaks so persuasively, and which are characteristic of myth, be possible. On the influence of Borges on García Márquez, see Roberto González Echevarría, "With Borges in Macondo"; and Emir Rodríguez Monegal *"One Hundred Years of Solitude."* I have learned a good deal from this article, in which the author singles out Melquíades's room as an important feature of the novel, and insists on the notion of the Book as key to an understanding of the text.

20. Mena.

21. Patricia Tobin has written an illuminating chapter on genealogy in *Cien años de soledad* Another excellent study, written by someone trained in anthropology, is López-Baralt.

22. Iris Zavala; Calasans Rodrigues. García Márquez's interest in the *Crónicas de Indias,* established beyond doubt in Zavala's article, was made evident again in his speech accepting the Nobel Prize: "Los cronistas de Indias nos legaron otros incontables [testimonies of astonishing events and things in the New World]. En busca de la fuente de la eterna juventud, el mítico Alvar Núñez Cabeza de Vaca exploró durante ocho años el norte de México [*sic*], en una expedición venática cuyos miembros se comieron unos a otros, y sólo llegaron cinco de los 600 que la emprendieron." *El Mundo* 12. An English translation of this address appears in McGuirk's *Gabriel García Márquez.* In a long interview published as a book, García Márquez said: "Yo había leído con mucho interés a Cristóbal Colón, a Pigafetta, y a los cronistas de Indias. . . ." *El olór de la guayaba,* 32. The early history of Macondo furnished in "Los funerales de la Mamá Grande" links the origins of the town to colonial Latin America through legal documents setting down the proprietary rights of the Matriarch: "Reducido a sus proporciones reales, el patrimonio físico [de la Mamá Grande] se reducía a tres encomiendas adjudicadas por Cédula real durante la Colonia, y que con el transcurso del tiempo, en virtud de intrincados matrimonios de conveniencia, se habían acumulado bajo el domino de la Mamá Grande. En ese territorio ocioso, sin límites definidos, que abarcaba cinco municipios y en el cual no se sembró nunca un solo grano por cuarenta de los propietarios, vivían a título de arrendatarias 352 familias," *Los funerales* 134–135.

23. Peña y Cámara, 35. For a thorough and official description and history of the Archive at Simancas, see Romero de Castilla y Perosso. In mid-October, 1785, 253 trunks full of documents arrived at Seville in two expeditions consisting of thirteen and eleven carts respectively. These papers, drawn from the Archive at Simancas, would constitute the Archivo de Indias in Seville, whose organization was due to the enlightened Bourbon Spanish monarch Charles III.

24. Corominas, 59.

25. Edwards, *The Encyclopedia of Philosophy,* 145.

26. I am referring to the box in chapter 2 of *Lazarillo* in which the priest hides the bread, and the trunk in *Aura* where Consuelo keeps the manuscripts left by her dead husband. There is a more thorough discussion of this in the last chapter of my book *Myth and Archive.*

27. Michel Foucault, *Archaeology,* 129.

28. Ibid., 130–131.

29. Alejo Carpentier, *El arpa y la sombra,* 112. My translation.

30. Georg Lukács, *The Theory of the Novel* (original German publication, 1920); Bakhtin, *Dialogic Imagination.*

4

Bordering on Madness:
The *Licenciado Vidriera*,
Guillermo Gómez-Peña and
the Performance of Liminality

JOHN OCHOA

We can trace the literary lineage of Miguel de Cervantes's *El licenci-ado Vidriera* (1613), a story about a madman who thinks he is made of glass, in several directions within the Hispanic tradition. Issuing from the margins are echoes of the voice of this holy fool, who criticizes both his society and his own ponderous voice. We hear these echoes in J. Joaquín Fernández de Lizardi's *El Periquillo Sarniento* (1816), in José Rodó's *Ariel* (1900) as well as in José Vasconcelos's bizarre, séancelike pronouncements which defy logic in *La raza cósmica* (1926). Given postmodernity's penchant for ironic dissociation, the paradoxical, self-reflexive voice of the mad *licenciado* is particularly resonant in late-modernity and postmodernity. A recent "Vidriera" madman is the Mexican Zapatista guerrilla leader Subcomandante Marcos, who broadcasts his disembodied, self-ironic pronouncements from the jungle via the Internet. Another contemporary "Vidriera" madman is the performance artist Guillermo Gómez-Peña, a "Mexican in the process of Chicanization" (*New World Border* 102). This essay will examine the work of Gómez-Peña through the filter of the *licenciado* Vidriera's peculiar brand of madness.

The *licenciado* Vidriera is a very particular kind of holy fool. Other famous fools—Shakespeare's Fool in *King Lear,* Rabelais's Panurge, even Cervantes's own Sancho Panza—use their position as mad oracle to offer witty, topical wisdom, the significance of which seems either lost or immaterial to the fool himself but is received by his hearers with wonder. Vidriera, on the other hand, seems to be keenly aware of the nature of his folly, and in a way his nonwisdom offers to society a parody of what insights it expects to receive from its madmen. Gómez-Peña, like Vidriera, is a master rhetorician who appears to offer pointed social and political criticism but who also critiques the privilege of offering advice; by calling attention to the spectacle of wisdom, he at once exploits and questions the place of wisdom itself.

CROSSING THE BORDER INTO MADNESS

The plot of *El licenciado Vidriera* places it within the tradition of the picaresque. The story begins on the banks of the River Tormes—at the same place where the *Lazarillo* begins—and also starts with a rootless young boy who is taken in and apprenticed by strangers. Since these strangers happen to be students on their way to Salamanca, he is apprenticed into scholarship. Tomás Rodaja excels at book-learning, for as Tomás says, he has heard that men can become bishops through learning. We thus perceive one of the central themes of the story: awareness about the power of knowledge. Tomás's search for knowledge gains a new dimension when he is given the opportunity to travel abroad with a soldier, a captain going abroad on a military expedition. Tomás agrees to go, for, as the narrator states, "long pilgrimages increase men's knowledge and discretion" (2: 107).[1] But he agrees only under the condition that "he would bow to no flag" except the flag of learning. His wish for bookish detachment goes far. As Ruth El-Saffar notes, we barely see or hear the main character in this section, and the narrative flattens into a panoramic *Guide bleu* of Italy, listing wines, places to visit, and sights to see, in an engaging if impersonal style (54). The main character becomes almost insignificant if not outright irrelevant to this travelogue. He dimishes in stature and presence, and is already showing the symptoms of his future madness. When he returns from his travels, a would-be lover makes a desperate attempt to capture his attentions with a poisoned quince. After a protracted illness from this spell, he awakens with the conviction that he is made of glass. This delusion frees him from all materiality and is in direct response to his ultimate goal of reaching pure knowledge. In his madness, he begins spouting wit, criticism, and assorted facts to anyone who will listen. It seems that the vast amounts of information that for years collected inside him have broken loose.

As Foucault notes in *Madness and Civilization,* during the Renaissance madness was intricately tied to arcane knowledge: "Madness fascinates because it is knowledge. It is knowledge, first, because all these absurd figures are in reality elements of a difficult, hermetic, esoteric learning" (21). The imagery of the *licenciado's* madness is related also to other Renaissance devices with which the community can learn about itself in a Theater of the World: glass, mirrors, transparent and reflective surfaces.[2] The *licenciado* seems to be both a reflective prism and a holy fool, a wise madman. Madness during the Renaissance, according to Foucault, had a recognizable place and shape within society; culture had contingencies in place to accept and to learn from the fool. This made the fool a twilight figure, a liminal entity invested with a certain expectation from society: he was different; he was wise; and he had access to information unavailable to the sane still within society.

Liminality is an in-between, ritual stage when the rules of society are suspended, either for the whole society (for instance during certain festivals such as Carnival) or for individuals (during certain rites of passage such as funerals, coronations, and puberty rites). Participants are deliberately marginalized, placed on the threshold between the mainstream and the margin. It is important to note an aspect about liminality: it occurs by the grace and venue of the mainstream. Despite the countercultural Carnival Bakhtin describes so compellingly, liminality is not revolutionary. Liminality is hardwired into culture and is in fact meant to preserve culture by allowing it to renovate. Liminality is a contingency of culture. "Edgemen," as Victor Turner calls liminal beings, are "betwixt and between" the dictates of "law, custom, convention and ceremonial" (95). While this is true, "edgemen" are marginalized from within. Culture has ways of acknowledging and utilizing them. Likewise, as Foucault explains, madness existed as a recognizable and often useful fixture within European culture, as a kind of permanent liminality, at least until European culture itself changed. Foucault argues that after the rise of reason and empiricism around the seventeenth century, madness was banished as "unreasonable" and hidden away in madhouses and prisons; society's contingencies for dealing with its madmen were thus repressed. But until this change, the madman was in a certain way privileged: "his exclusion must enclose him; if he cannot and must not have another prison than the threshold itself, he is capped at the point of passage" (*Madness* 11). The madman, then, was the consummate, liminal outsider, and society knew exactly what he was and where he belonged, "at the point of passage." Poor Tomás, by being poisoned, has gone through the looking glass and has been trapped in such a liminal state, in the "threshold itself."[3] Or so it would seem.

There is something not quite right with the liminal *licenciado*'s madness. Vidriera's insanity, like Don Quixote's, stems from an excess of knowledge. But the worlds conjured by their respective madnesses are opposites. In his fantasy, Don Quixote bookishly resurrects a world of dead chivalry out of necessity, since his humdrum existence as a country squire simply would not contain him. The mad world Don Quixote creates is internally coherent; perhaps more so than the messy "real" world into which he crashes headlong. This unforgiving "real" world is full of ignoramuses, petty thieves, and escaped convicts—and the clash of Quixote's madness with the brutality of this "real" world generates real pathos. His world is one out of step with reality.

The *licenciado*'s mad world, on the other hand, is almost overwhelmingly synchronous with the real world. Despite Cervantes's clear identification of the *licenciado* with the devices of the holy fool and of reflective surfaces and the privileged insight of "outsiderhood," the "wisdom" the *licenciado* begins to spout once he "liminizes" seems rather banal. His sententious "insights" are indeed funny and topical, but they are often either mean-spirited extremely local to the point of irrelevance, or playful without being truly wise. Expecting earthshaking maxims, we slowly become aware that what he says is not really wisdom. It is *too* current and *too* topical to resonate in any universal way.[4] Indeed a large portion of the second half of the story is devoted to listing apothegma which seem patched together and placed arbitrarily in the mouth of the *licenciado*. Juan Bautista Avalle-Arce speculates that Cervantes wrote the section with a hefty reference book on his desk (2: 24). The *licenciado*'s comments fall into time-tested satirical categories: anecdotes or puns poking fun at social fixtures such as the vain or at ethnic groups; jokes at the expense of a professional pursuit or type, usually echoing classical models (like his fairly conventional discourse praising poetry but damning poets, or his pun on bankers); "folk" or ribald "wisdom" (as with the washerwoman and her decked-out daughter), and attacks on easy targets such as prostitutes. Luis Rosales remarks that the *licenciado*'s humor lacks the "gaiety and generosity of understanding of Cervantes's great humor" (in Forcione 269). Instead of the Bakhtinian "lower body" humor of *Don Quixote,* we get an aloof and distant wit bordering on the commonplace, a humor which is somehow damaged or "diseased" (Forcione 269). The narrow topical allusions to a particular idiosyncrasy of the weather in Valladolid or throwaway jokes about loose women are hardly the oracular truths that the *licenciado*'s condition would lead us to expect. At one point, he recoils when he is bitten by a wasp, and is asked why he feels pain if he is made of glass. He responds quickly that the wasp must have been a gossip (2: 140). There is the faint sense that this is something of a put-on or an act: in short, that the Licenciado is *per-forming* having crossed into madness, rather than actually having undergone the change itself.

It is possible to read *El licenciado Vidriera* as a primer in performance art. Tomás's passage into "madness" is one doubly born from knowledge: it is what Gómez-Peña would call an "intervention," in which a performer, in this case Tomás, goes out into the "field" and performs an act that explodes one of soci-ety's convictions by offering an exaggerated example of its effects. In a sense, Tomás has indeed become the knowledgeable, reflective vessel he anounces himself to be. If his audience looks closely enough at his performance, they can see into themselves and their system of beliefs. They are not informed about mundane things like prostitutes, or the plight of poets, or about the weather in Valladolid; rather, they are told about the function of liminality itself, and its relationship to "wisdom." The *"licenciado" appropriates* the trappings of madness and announces himself to society as a certifiable and recognizable fool, and then waits to see what happens. His true revelation consists of laying bare the mechanics of "wisdom." He earns the rubric "wise fool" because his audience has fashioned him that way and has chosen to believe in him in that way. While he may not be Foucault's madman as otherworldly clairvoyant, as instrument through which men can see some abstract piece of information, Tomás Rodaja is a holy fool, if in reverse.

Vidriera reverses the function of the holy fool ironically: instead of an other-worldly voice from the wilderness speaking in oracular tones about things that make sense, he is a ridiculously corporeal voice, claiming to make sense while issuing nonsense, yet still attracting the attention normally given to wise fools. The *licenciado* draws crowds not because of the content of his utterances but rather because of his spectacular condition resulting from his position as pur-portedly liminal. His voice is validated by his supposed glassiness, by the sheer "spectacle" of something to see, or to see through. We see confirmation of this when he returns to court finally "cured," no longer claiming to be mad but still issuing "wisdom." He asks the crowd "instead of things it is said that I said and did while mad, consider the things I will say and do while sane" (2: 143). Instantly the crowd loses interest. The brilliant young man's newfound body is an extension of the emperor's new clothes. Now that the invisible wise man is visible, the crowds scatter because there is nothing to see.

GÓMEZ-PEÑA, DOCUMENTED MADMAN AND MACARTHUR-CERTIFIED GENIUS

Guillermo Gómez-Peña, like the *licenciado* Vidriera, is a self-conscious border-crosser. Most of his major artistic projects of the latter 1980s and the first half of the 1990s—works such as *Border Brujo* (1988–92), or *1992* (1992), as well as his collaborative work with Coco Fusco in *The Guatinaui World Tour* (1992–1993) and with Roberto Sifuentes in *The Temple of Confessions* (1994)—cross generic borders.[5] They combine theater, visual arts, poetry, and technological media with political activism. Gómez-Peña's performances, usually presented in public spaces such as museums and city streets, are generally documented in "performance notes," journals, or videos, and collected in published volumes along with photographs, CDs, manifestos, critical essays, and "performance poetry."

These performances and texts often include autobiographical reference to Gómez-Peña's beginnings as a performance artist. Although he occasionally refers to his education and artistic formation in Mexico City, Gómez-Peña claims that the primal scene of his transformation into performer ("my American birth rite") takes place on the border between Mexico and the United States: "I crossed the border in 1978 and something broke inside of me, forever . . . [this] abrupt confrontation with otherness, triggered many processes inside of me, the most significant being the exploration of the conflictive relationship between my Mexican past and my U.S. present" (*Warrior* 20). His early solo performances ruminate on the "the pain of departure and the indescribable loneliness of the immigrant" (20). Despite arguments and performances to the contrary, Gómez-Peña's border-crossing is not necessarily traumatic in any fundamental way. Rather, his act of immigration itself can be seen as an inaugural act of self-conscious performance.[6] One of his carefully limited references to his artistic expression before his "borderization," the poem "My First Performance Ever (Morelia, 1974)" presents particularly unmomentous beginnings in a deadpan fashion:

> *I entered church.*
> *I hide behind the pulpit.*
> *Three days pass by.*
> *No one discovers me.*
> *I get bored.*
> *I return to the hotel.*
> *I try to commit suicide.*
> *I receive no phone calls.*
> *I get bored.*
> *I go out to the plaza.*
> *I buy 10 avocados.*
> *I throw them to the cops.*
> *They don't seem to mind.*
> *I get bored.*
> *[The journalists ignore*
> *The importance of my actions.]* (*Warrior* 143)

The actions—throwing avocados, hiding in a church—are almost arbitrary and meaningless, like the *licenciado* Vidriera's "wisdom." It seems that the "importance" of his actions is determined by the specific context, by the crowd's reaction to them, and not by any transcendent meaning. His first performance in the United States was structurally similar to his "first performance." It involved "hiding," wrapped in a cloth, not behind the solitary pulpit of a church but rather inside a busy elevator in Los Angeles for twenty-four hours. This time he received attention. "My total anonymity and vulnerability seemed to grant people the freedom to confess intimate things to me . . . to verbally abuse me, and to kick me. I overheard two adolescents discuss the possibility of setting me on fire, a dog peed on me . . ." (*New World Border* 82). The biggest thing that happened to Gómez-Peña when he crossed the border is that his yen for an audience ("the journalists ignore/ The importance of my actions") was fulfilled, another echo of the *licenciado* Vidriera's "long pilgrimage" into notorious "invisibility."

Gómez-Peña's "border" is quite different from the border of many of the Chicano artists, activists, and theorists with whom he has aligned himself politically and aesthetically. For the poet and essayist Gloria Anzaldúa, the border is traumatic, static, and atavistic, and in many ways a trap:

> The U.S.-Mexican border es una *herida abierta* where the Third World grates against the first and bleeds. . . . Borders are set up to define the places that are safe and unsafe, and to distinguish *us* from *them*. A border is a dividing line, a narrow strip along a steep edge. (3)

This kind of traumatic division for Anzaldúa has resulted in a despotic duality ("what we are suffering from is an absolute despot duality that says we're able to be only one or the other" [19]), a tyranny which must be fought against. Its opposite—synthesis, *mestizaje,* "merging to form a third country"—is the one potentially redeeming outcome of the trauma. For Anzaldúa, as for many other Chicano artists and thinkers, the tentatively positive aspect of the border (both literal and metaphoric) is that it is a place of hybridity; it is where plural realities can conjoin into a richly multiple, articulated reality, into what the Mexican politician and philosopher José Vasconcelos called "the cosmic race." For a theorist like Alfred Arteaga, border-crossing and racial hybridization result in a new and positive subjectivity, a "xicano," defined by the sign of the x, which is more than the sum total of any of its origins: "xicano is the subject of Aztlán the cultural nation but not the state and not subject to capricious borderlines. . . . Hybridity is a fundamental physical reality of chicanismo" (155, 11). The crossing, in other words, means—or can mean—fusion.[7]

In contrast, Gómez-Peña's border, unlike Anzaldúa's, relies on the binarism the border provides, on the double (and multiple) articulation it offers. Gómez-

Peña's work rages against essentialisms: "terms like Hispanic, Latino, ethnic, minority, marginal, alternative, and Third World, among others, are inaccurate and loaded with ideological implications. They create categories and hierarchies that promote political dependence and cultural underestimation" ["Multicultural Paradigm" 18]). But his work seeks to *preserve* the various realities meeting head to head in the border, and the dualities which juxtapose them; the categories, he implies, are still vital: "We have no choice but to utilize them, but with extreme care" ("Paradigm" 19).[8] From *Documented/Undocumented* (1987):

> *I stand out in front of an academic*
> *audience linguists, sociologists, anthropologists*
> *surveilling my "authenticity" los muy cabrones*
> MEROLICO & PACHUCO VOICES
> *[Alternating]:*
> *me dicen el half & half*
> *half-Indian/half-Spaniard*
> *half-Mexican/half-Chicano*
> *half-son/half-father*
> *half-artist/half-writer*
> *half-wolf/half-eagle*
> *half-always/half-never (Warrior 115)*

Gómez-Peña's border is always a dialogic, binary articulation. Unlike Gustavo Pérez-Firmat's "life on the hyphen" or Arteaga's sign of the "x," his sign seems to be the slash ("/"), the sign of doubleness and juxtaposition. It is the sign of dissimilars which are still categorically close enough to meet at a common border ("half-artist/half-writer . . . half-wolf/half-eagle"). Gómez-Peña, influenced by Deleuze's and Guattari's notions of "deterritorialization" and cultural schizophrenia, sees split existences everywhere. This penchant for duality is different from Anzaldúa's oppressive *herida abierta,* which needs to heal, to scarify and soften into new skin. Gómez-Peña's dialectic of difference is predicated on its two moving parts retaining some distinction, some aspect of their original, unhyphenated beginning. The somewhat unsettling juxtapositions are not incompatibilities; rather, they are the somewhat awkward meetings of dissimilar relatives from either side of the border; the voices, for example, of the "Merolico" the Mexican snake-oil salesman, and the "Pachuco," the street-smart urban Chicano, *alternate.* Gómez-Peña's dualisms are meant to raise the consciousness of the individuals on either side but they are not designed for those individuals to lose their individuality, to lose the sense of different sides altogether.

In his 'bilingual performance poem' "Califas" (1987), Gómez-Peña offers a kind of Californiad, weaving together several archetypal immigrant and Chicano experiences into epic form. In canto 5, a young Chicano, Johnny, just busted by the "ethnopolice" simply for "cruising low/ from Aztlán to Tenochtitlán/ & back," begins to yell at the "gringos" in frustration:

> "... *what if 200,000 Anglosaxicans*
> *were to cross the border each month*
> *to work as gardeners, waiters*
> *musicians, movie extras*
> *bouncers, babysitters, chauffeurs,*
> *syndicated cartoons, featherweight*
> *boxers, fruit-pickers & anonymous poets?*
> *what if they were called waspanos, waspitos, wasperos or waspbacks?*
> *what if we were the top dogs?*
> *what if literature was life?*
> *what if yo were you*
> *& tú fueras I, Mister?"*
>
> *the Linguistic Patrol busted El Johnny again*
> *for speaking too loud in an unknown tongue. ...*
> *he left prison to become a poet*
> *but instead*
> *they sent him to Vietnam* (*Warrior* 69)

Understandably, this caged cruiser sings about a wish for inversion. His *cri de cœur* is for the ruling class to put itself in his shoes and live through the oppression he has faced. The police's treatment of Johnny drives him not just to anger but to speculation and to poetry. Yet there is a wistful sense of futility to this poetic wish for inversion, a kind of resignation to the knowledge that he is asking the impossible. At the heart of his cries for empathy lies an apparently insurmountable language border: "what if *yo* were you & *tu fueras* I, Mister." *Yo* and you are tantalizingly close, only one letter distant, but still they are worlds apart. The pathos of Johnny's dilemma comes from his futile appeal to resolve differences, which, in his world, cannot be resolved. The *yo* and you cannot transmute one for another. The scene leaves Johnny as a mad sage, yelling impotently at the street corner—a Vidriera-like figure, emblematic of Gómez-Peña himself. Such scenes of incomprehension, of incompatibility, make both the poem and the performance exist.

Where for Anzaldúa the binarisms are traumatic and must be fought and overcome in favor of a new understanding, for Gómez-Peña binarisms are a symmetrical performance tool, a way to capitalize on the mechanics of incompatibility. The many binarisms that pervade his work can be reduced to the one between the performer and the viewers. The fact remains that the staged encounters with the "other" are *staged;* the border is mobile, and what lies on either side of it is too. His "border," like the *licenciado's* liminal madness, is a performance fiction, an appropriation of a belief. The only "real" border, his play of dualisms suggests, is the one between Gómez-Peña himself, shaman/performer, and the audience.

An integral part of the manipulation of the viewer/reader of these performances comes from watching the theatrical display of the madman convincing himself of his own unusual condition (that he is made of glass, that he is a "savage" Guatinaui chieftain caged in a museum exhibit, that he is a "Mexican in the process of Chicanoization" [*New World Border* 102]) despite evidence to the contrary. In his introduction to a selection of bilingual "poetical texts" "Sin/translation (for Spanish to English and vice versa)" which were performed in various venues, Gómez-Peña soothes his readers into simply suspending their incomprehension and accepting linguistic difference, yet another of his dualisms: "note: I encourage my monolingual readers to attempt to read the texts and Spanish and Spanglish. I'm sure you will understand them" (*Warrior* 143). The representation of difference, which looks traumatic, is really didactic and rhetorical.[9]

The rhetorical hallmark of the *licenciado* Vidriera's brand of performance art is *parrhesia,* (a feigned reluctance at one's need to speak) taken to an extreme. It takes this feigned reluctance to the point of ironic self-effacement and to (supposed) transparency. When told a "great person of the court" wishes to see him, *Vidriera* answers that he is no good at flattery and would be out of place there (2: 121), but indeed he finally ends up at court, issuing his wisdom at great length. For Gómez-Peña, parrhesia is elevated to the point of beseeching the viewer to assist him in his put-on (Fig. 1).

Many of Gómez-Peña's characters and performances attempt to draw in his audiences in a carefully calculated way. In perhaps his most famous work, *The Guatinaui World Tour* (1992), a collaboration with Coco Fusco, he and Fusco parody the nineteenth-century practice of human exhibits *à la* Hottentot Venus. The couple, dressed as flamboyant "authentic primitives"—he as a "kind of Aztec wrestler from Las Vegas" and she as a "Taina straight out of *Gilligan's*

FIG.1. Gómez-Peña as the "Warrior for Gringostroika" during the performance of *Original Aboriginals*, Minneapolis Sculpture Garden (September 12, 1992). Photo courtesy Walker Art Center.

Island"—exhibited themselves in a cage in various genuine museums, were fed bananas, performed "indigenous rituals," and were photographed with tourists (*New World Border* 97). For a charge, the "male of the species" would show his genitals. The video recording of the performance, *The Couple in the Cage* (1993), is not so much a record of the performance as it is of the crowd's reactions (which were often mixed because many museum-goers did not realize the scene was ironic—they truly believed these were caged natives). The result, claim its creators, is "reverse ethnography," in which the ignorance of the crowds becomes the spectacle. Yet when Diana Taylor asked Gómez-Peña what his ideal spectator would have done, he replied "open the cage and let us out" [169].

In *Temple of Confessions* (1994), Gómez-Peña and Roberto Sifuentes set up a quasi-religious confessional and asked the crowd to confess, in written or recorded form, their "intercultural fears," snippets of which they incorporated into later performances. Gómez-Peña and Sifuentes took this trust in the audience a step further in *The Crucifiction Project* (1994), in which the two, dressed as "contemporary enemies of California," one as an "undocumented bandido" and the other a "generic gang member," crucified themselves in front of a crowd of three hundred at Rodeo Beach in San Francisco. Attendees received handouts asking them to "free us from our martyrdom as a gesture of political commitment" (*New World Border* 102).

FIG. 2. Coco Fusco and Gómez-Peña during the performance of *Original Aboriginals*, Minneapolis Sculpture Garden (September 12, 1992). Photo courtesy Walker Art Center.

There exists in Gómez-Peña's work, despite its attempts to challenge "people to reflect on their attitudes towards other cultures," deep complicity with the audience, a reliance on the goodness of strangers (*New World Border* 104). The duality of Gómez-Peña's own persona ("My activities as cultural commentator and my performance work have always influenced each other. My theoretical voice is more balanced and logical. . . . My performance voice is frantic and fractured" [*Warrior* 16]) hints at the paradox at the heart of Gómez-Peña's work: the impossible goal of

Fig. 3. Gómez-Peña as the "Undocumented Bandito" during the performance of the *Crucifiction Project*, San Francisco (April 10, 1994). Photo from Guillermo Gómez-Peña and Roberto Sifuentes, *Temple of Confessions: Mexican Beasts and Living Saints*. New York: powerHouse Books, 1996, 125. Reprinted by permission of powerHouse Books.

standardizing marginality, of inviting *everyone* into otherness. ("today, if there is a dominant culture, it is border culture. And those who still haven't crossed the border will do it very soon. . . . As you read this text, you're crossing a border yourself." [*Warrior* 19] he hurls at his readership/audience). The only way of doing this, of course, is through a carefully controlled environment.[10]

A scripted performance, *A Seminar on Museum Race Relations* (1995), has Gómez-Peña and Sifuentes, dressed in garish three-piece suits as "Bill" and "Bob," engaging a crowd in a mock motivational/sensitivity seminar. When it comes to the question-and-answer period, several plants in the audience ask the two some questions meant to elicit jokey answers:

Plant 3: Gwermo, can you say something in Nahuatl?

GP: Ggggua . . . camole. . . .

Plant 2: To the alien on the left: Do you have a green card?

GP: [Responds in tongues.]

Plant 3: Hey Roberto, can you please tell us what's the relationship between the Zapatistas, rap, L.A. gang culture, and the resurgence of Chicano nationalism?

RS: No.

Plant 1: Mr. Peña, I read in *Artforum* that you don't want to pay child support, and that you mistreat women artistic collaborators. Is that true?

GP: It must be true. Critics are always objective when they talk about my work. . . . *[At this point audience members feel compelled to begin to ask other insensitive questions. For some reason, it never fails.]*

RS: *[Slowly gets pissed.]* Come on, guys. What kind of questions are these? How about something more shocking? Let's tell some racist jokes. Would anyone like to share a racist joke? Come on, it's all part of the healing process. *[To Gómez-Peña]* Bill, you got any racist jokes? *[Gómez-Peña nods.]* Come on everybody. Let's encourage this man to be brave. *Órale vato,* give us some racist stuff!

GP: Alright, alright! What do you call a Chicano baptism? . . . A bean dip! [He laughs neurotically.]

RS: [Pissed.] That's not good enough. Come on, say something really offensive, motherfucker! Go on, say it!!

GP: *[Tries to speak, but is unable to. He laughs, cries, and falls on his knees. RS grabs a knife and stands behind him in a menacing manner. He brings the knife up as if getting ready to stab him.]*

RS: [Screaming.] What's the difference between a Mexican and a Cuban, eh?! [No answer.] How many Mexican artists does it take to fill up a the-ater like this, eh?! You pathetic stereotype! You stand-up comedian wannabe. . . . [Blackout.] (*New World Border* 158–159)

Performers, impersonating audience members, prompt the audience to imitate them in asking the "correct" kinds of funny, "insensitive" questions which cross the border of good taste. And just as this airy and lighthearted spectacle is given to the uncertainty of the crowd's response, control is taken back by the perform-ers. The tone breaks and the threat of conflict appears. But the conflict stops short of "crossing the line" into discomfort. Just at the moment where "Bob" starts becoming aggressive to the crowd, he deflects his aggression upon "Bill." It returns from potential real aggression to *staged* aggression. In a sense, the vio-lence that "Bob" was threatening to inflict on the crowd is turned to "Bill," and "Bill" becomes a stand-in for the crowd. We watch a scene of abuse, and the thin membrane between the crowd and the performance is preserved. Gómez-Peña puts marginal jokes and questions of poor taste in the mouths of audience mem-bers, thus making "liminized" Vidrieras of the attendees by making them spout nonsense; in doing so, he reinforces the division between himself—who is truly in command— and them.

When Gómez-Peña and Fusco put themselves on display at various institu-tional venues, they invite the complicity of the very institutions they critique. As with all liminal spaces, Gómez-Peña's anti-institutional performance is clearly bounded by its own institutionalization: he and Coco Fusco pretend to be long-lost Indians and cage themselves as a living display within the walls of an actual museum—with the museum's blessing. The mad wanderer may pretend to travel "under no flag," like the *licenciado* on his first trip to Italy, but he still travels by the good graces of the captain—or, in the case of Gómez-Peña, the Field Museum, in Minneapolis, or the Smithsonian. This kind of doubleness—which has been read as hypocrisy by some critics—can also be read as a genuine inquiry into arbitrary difference, with the purpose of displaying how it works.[11] The border, for both the *licenciado* and for Gómez-Peña, is rather imposing and seems to be fordable only by beings who are free-floating and translucent. But in fact it is fordable by beings who only *appear* to be free-floating and translucent, because the border itself, it turns out, is arbitrary and constructed for didactic purposes.

Gómez-Peña and the *licenciado* Vidriera offer two different possible outcomes to falsifying liminality and uncovering the myths of privileged knowledge and of invisibility to the public. The *licenciado* returns from his false liminality at the end of the story when he is "cured" by a Hieronimyte monk, an expert in making mutes speak but who instead silences the *licenciado*. Tomás Rodaja, no longer "Vidriera," now goes by the name of "Rueda," ["wheel" or "round"] and has indeed gone full circle. He repeats his trip to Italy but now fully committed to the world and to a flag. He dies abroad with honor and in silence. "He has found his way back to himself, to his community, and to his body . . . and his prudent death for his country is, oddly enough, the first wise act of his life" (Cascardi 316). This return might indeed be wise in the conventional sense, but it is not wise in the foolish, liminal way. Gómez-Peña, on the other hand, has no plans to return to the anonymity and silence of the church pulpit of his first performance, for, as he says: "I firmly believe that . . . the role that art and education can perform is crucial and irreplaceable" (*New World Border* 109).

We can read the story of the *licenciado* Vidriera's ironic, un-wise madman—with his unfunny jabs, his mean-spirited or obscure jokes—as a curious variant of the picaresque tradition. The story reads like a picaresque tale with a surprise ending: instead of confessing unapologetically for his life, like the *Lazarillo de Tormes*, the *licenciado* comes back to the fold, where he dies without accounting for his life. This subaltern truly cannot speak anymore, unlike his picaresque brethren who confess in the first person and in full color. Yet like the *Lazarillo* or *Guzmán de Alfarache*, Tomás is also a traveler and a huckster. And his final confidence job is the role of holy fool. When he is "cured" of his madness, his only recourse is to engage with the world, become legitimate, and die a socially redeeming death in battle. There is a real danger to leaving this liminal, picaresque world of the con-job, of the performance put-on, and returning to the real world, because one can end up in the middle of a very real war, just like the cruiser Johnny who "left prison to become a poet/but instead/ they sent him to Vietnam."

Thus we can also see the mock–holy fool *licenciado* as the discoverer, perhaps by accident, of one of the last spaces in which a holy fool—the critic—can exist within the rationalist modernity Foucault describes as so hostile to the wisdom of the mad: the space of self-conscious performance. Madness no longer has a place, so it must be invented and counterfeited.

This inverted madness has evolved in one important way between Vidriera and Gómez-Peña. Vidriera's madness ends in tragedy and silence. When he chooses step away from his performance, Vidriera retreats into conventionality and dies with honor but in oblivion, since no one will listen to the sane. This tragic ending is why Vidriera's inheritor Gómez-Peña chooses instead to collude with his audience. Gómez-Peña constantly invites his viewers into the frame narrative of his performance, under the guise of a challenge. Unlike Vidriera, however, Gómez-Peña will not return but rather he will invite all who watch to cross over with him, or at least to assist him in his crossing. The finale of one of his performances is a direct address to the audience, which appropriately recalls the *envoi* at the end of a fanciful baroque masque:

> *I go back to the city*
> *to think of a better text*
> *to put into practice thank you, my other selves, my other voices*
> *for traveling with me tonight.*
> *[I blow out the candles.]* (*Warrior* 123)

> > > FIN

This is Gómez-Peña's alternative to the *licenciado*'s sad reentry into society from his false liminality. Gómez-Peña instead thanks his audience for having allowed him *his* false liminality, for colluding with him and allowing him to remain in this space by remaining his accomplices.

NOTES

I would like to thank Stacy Andersen for her constant and invaluable help.

1. All translations from the Spanish are mine.

2. The mirror, doubling, and the artificial frame of the mirror resonate the theme of theater-as-life, all familiar fixtures of the Baroque. As Peter Skrine writes: "Glass can be used both as a mirror and as a window pane; it can open up new prospects and reveal a cosmos or a minute microcosm—or it can reveal us to ourselves with startling exactness, and capture a reflection even more fragile and ephemeral than it is itself" (147). Foucault relates this imagery to madness, noting that somewhere from the middle to the end of the sixteenth

century (when the *licenciado* Vidriera appears): "the symbol of madness will henceforth be that mirror which, without reflecting anything real, will secretly offer the man who observes himself in it the dream of his own presumption. Madness deals not so much with truth and the world, as with man and whatever truth about himself he is able to perceive" (*Madness and Civilization,* 27).

3. In his study of folly and the development of the figure of the fool in sixteenth-century literature, Walter Kaiser notes that the fool speaks in hyperhuman terms; his madness is a condensed reality which, as Aristotle suggested, is the "most human of all" (Kaiser, 11). The fool, inseparable from his culture, if it listens to its fools, can correct its course and reaffirm a community's very existence. Both Kaiser and Foucault locate the incidence of fools in transitional times, during what Northrop Frye, echoing Vico, would call the "myth of winter," the reflexive moment late in the evolution of a culture, a time ripe for irony and fools.

4. Instead of being like Don Quixote or King Lear, the figure of the *licenciado* has all the markers of a more traditional—medieval, to use Foucault's chronology—fool, a mere mouthpiece for opprobrium, like Erasmus's Stultitia in his *Praise of Folly* (1511), who is simply a satirical tool, and not yet the cultural barometer of unstable times which the fool would become in the later sixteenth century. Indeed the structure of the *licenciado*'s unprovoked diatribes resemble Stultitia's prudish invectives against the professions, issued out of fairly conventional morality, and not out of cosmic and ontological uncertainty as they are for Don Quixote.

5. Most of Gómez-Peña's performance pieces are presented several times and in numerous venues, with script variations between each performance. The dates given are for the span of time during which the pieces were performed. Performances are codified after the fact in "performance notes"—transcriptions accompanied by descriptions and photographs— or on video recordings, as follows: "Califas" and *Documented/Undocumented* in *Warrior for Gringostroika* (1993); *Border Brujo* as a videorecording of the same name (1990); *Guatinaui World Tour* as the video recording *The Couple in The Cage* (1993); *A Seminar on Museum Race Relations* in *New World Border* (1996); *Crucifiction Project* in both *New World Border* (1996) and in *Temple of Confessions* (1996); and *Temple of Confessions* in *Temple of Confessions* (1996).

6. Gómez-Peña's own crossing is further complicated by its class implications. A member of the educated class, he came north to study performance at Cal Arts, but he claims to dramatize the plight of the working poor. There exists a staged 1979 photo of a bare-chested Gómez-Peña smoking a cigarette in a detention center of the INS, in character as "El mojado peligroso" (*Warrior,* 70). As José Saldívar has noted about *Border Brujo,* "My own sense is that . . . Gómez-Peña's experimental videotext is probably 'about' cultural reconversion . . . a polysemic visual-oral collage in which a number of hybrid, low-tech/hi-tech signals coexist (*norteño* vs. opera, Gregorian chants vs. the pelado's signifyings made famous by Cantinflas, about avant-garde vs. *rasquachi*), all with an unmistakable class message: High versus mass culture" (157).

7. Fusion, hybridity, and mestizaje are themes of much recent U.S. Latino literature, theory and criticism, for instance in Cherríe Moraga's "identity that dissolves borders" or Gustavo Perez-Firmat's notion of "life on the hyphen." Ilan Stavans claims that Chicanos' early cultural and political awareness—which fostered resistance and awareness of difference— has given way, roughly in the last twenty-five years, to "notions of transcreation and transculturation" (13). This syncretic vision—whose patron theorists are the Cuban anthro-

pologist Fernando Ortiz and the Mexican thinker José Vasconcelos, have found their way
into the language of other U.S. ethnic discourses, for instance, in Eric Liu's *The
Accidental Asian,* (where Vasconcelos is invoked [190, 202]).

8. Gómez-Peña's attempt's to de-essentialize nationality, race, and language opens itself to
   an obvious critique: that once the artist as committed social commentator pulls out the
   rug from all situational alliances, all "belongingness," nothing is left but depoliticized
   glassiness. Critics often cite his departure from "site-specific," community-performance
   art (like his work during the 1980s with Poyesis Genética and with Border Arts Workshop/
   Taller de Arte Fronteriza, most notably *The End of The Line* (October 12, 1986) in which
   performers set up a dinner table on the beach where the Mexico-U.S. borderline runs into
   the Pacific, passing food across the table/border, and occasionally changing seats and thus
   crossing the border, illegally, several times during the performance) in favor of high-
   concept and individual performance as an abdication, a "universalization" of a very specific border. As Claire Fox puts it: "The idea of alternation among personae, spaces, and
   languages is so integral to the performance that it raises the issue of whether Gómez-Peña
   would really like to see borders eliminated, or whether his work is indeed dependent upon
   borders to uphold the oppositions that he critiques" (125). Jill Kuhnheim expresses a similar opinion: "there is a deceptive hybridity in this text; attempts to multiply personae do
   not fragment into difference but reproduce like echoes or mirrors. The speaker's identity
   depends upon an opposition between multiculturalism and a monoculture that he has
   asserted no longer exists, but that he must reinforce so that he can position himself as a
   hero destroying it" (29)

9. In some of their proscenium pieces, Gómez-Peña and Fusco "segregated" the audience as
   it entered the theater. "Sometimes 'ethnic minorities,' immigrants, and bilingual audience
   members would be allowed to enter the theater first and to take the best seats. . . . In
   doing so, we made the 'others'—the monolingual 'Anglos'—feel 'excluded' or marginalized. The idea was to . . . [force] monolingual/monocultural Americans to feel like out-
   siders and 'minorities' in their own country. . . . At the end of each performance we would
   have a discussion." (*New World Border* 95–96).

10. Diana Taylor finds this impulse to incorporate the audience understandably disquieting:
    "So what do we do? Play along as a 'good' audience? And what would that mean,
    exactly. . . . There is no appropriate reaction, no 'true' or 'false' response to this perfor-
    mance that, as Fusco writes, 'falls between truth and fiction'" (169).

11. Grant Kester criticizes Gómez-Peña and other performance artists like Karen Finley for
    engaging in what Kester calls "rant" performance, cravenly invading the subject positions
    and "speaking for" the oppressed to further their own, performative agenda, without "hav-
    ing to account for their own cultural position, and privilege" (15). Kuhnheim similarly
    argues that although Gómez-Peña pretends to aim for generic and political pluralism, his
    range of narrative "languages," displays no "social heteroglossia, but one authoritative
    voice" (28).

GOVERNMENT

5

Love and Country:

An Allegorical Speculation

From *Foundational Fictions:*

The National Romances of

Latin America

DORIS SOMMER

*I*t is worth asking why the national novels of Latin America—the ones that governments institutionalized in the schools and that are by now indistinguishable from patriotic histories—are all love stories. An easy answer, of course, is that nineteenth-century novels were all love stories in Latin America; but it just begs the question of what love has to do with the requirements of civic education. The novels weren't immediately taught in public schools, except perhaps in the Dominican Republic, where *Enriquillo* appeared rather late and where the number of students may have been limited enough for an adequate production of books.[1] In other cases, serialized or sentimental novels were at first hardly academic or even proper literature, to judge by their exclusion from the first national literary histories. Written at the same mid-century moment as the novels and with largely the same legitimating impulse, authors of literary histories had comparable political credentials but more classical criteria than the novelists. Literary historians selected a kind of elite prehistory for the "progressive conservative" consolidations that were stabilizing the new states,[2] but they omitted perhaps the most useful renderings of those oxymoronic consolidations: the romances that celebrated or predicted an identification between the nation and its state.[3] The programmatic centrality of novels came generations later; precisely when and under which particular circumstances in each country are questions that merit a different study.[4] But in general, one can surmise that after renewed internal oppositions pulled the image of an ideal nation away from the existing state, like a mask pulled from the masquerader, after nationalism could be understood as a political movement against the state,[5] nineteenth-century novels apparently promised the ministries of education a way of covering over the gap between power and desire. The books, so immediately seductive for elite readers whose private desires overlapped with public institutions, might reinscribe for each future citizen the (natural and irresistible) foundational desires for/of the government in power.

My musing here about why erotics and politics come together—in school no less—begins by noting that it happened practically everywhere in Latin America. A particular novel may be celebrated in its national tradition as autochthonous, characteristic, and somehow inimitable; yet we have seen that each romance shares far more than its institutional status with others. The resemblances may be symptomatic of nationalism's general paradox; that is, cultural features that seem unique and worthy of patriotic (self-)celebration are often typical of other nations too and even patterned after foreign models.[6] Almost like sexual intimacy, that which seems most private turns out to be embarrassingly public knowledge.[7] In this essay I would like first to consider *why* eroticism and nationalism become figures for each other in modernizing fictions and then to notice *how* the rhetorical relationship between heterosexual passion and hegemonic states functions as a mutual allegory, as if each discourse were grounded in the allegedly stable other. For examples of the perhaps constitutive connection between private and political passions, one can certainly turn to any of the chapters in my book *Foundational Fictions*. Here I want to speculate on what may account for the generic coherence that individual readings will necessarily miss.

From our historical distance, both romantic love and patriotism can be mistaken for natural givens, although we know them to be produced, perhaps, by the very novels that seem merely to represent them. To acknowledge this possibility is also to ask whether what may have passed for effects of the greater culture in the novel (for instance, the representation of romantic love or of conciliatory nationalism) may indeed be partial causes of that culture. If heroes and heroines in mid-nineteenth-century Latin American novels were passionately desiring one another across traditional lines and desiring the new state that would join them, they were hardly representing timeless or essential affections. Those passions might not have prospered a generation earlier. In fact, modernizing lovers were learning how to dream their erotic fantasies by reading the European romances they hoped to realize.

The appropriateness of European fiction for Latin American founders may perhaps be read backward too (in a reflex learned from Benedict Anderson),[8] meaning that the appropriateness suggests a cultural overlapping that should be as easily identifiable from Latin America as from Europe. Therefore my rather local observations about a particular moment and genre in Latin America tempt me to hazard some conjectures about more general implications. Is it possible, for example, that outside of Latin America, too, political passion was being grounded in erotics? Had sexual desire as the shorthand for human association become "the explanation for everything," as Foucault said it had?[9] The claim is hardly hyperbolic or even original. By 1865 in England, John McLean's influential *Primitive Marriage* considered "sexual attraction the underlying principle of all social formations," thus agreeing with other early texts of cultural anthropology including those by Herbert Spencer which would be so popular among Latin American positivists.[10] Alternatively, if there were no erotic or sentimental investment in the state, if our identities as modern sexually defined subjects did not take the state to be a primary object and therefore the partner on whom our identity depends, what could explain our passion for *"la patria?"*[11] Is it also possible that the romances are themselves synecdoches of the marriage between Eros and Polis that was taking place under the broad canopy of Western culture? I hesitate to say "bourgeois culture," because it may be as much the child as the maker of the match. Nancy Armstrong's provocative work on England, *Desire and the Domestic Fiction: A Political History of the Novel,* is wonderfully suggestive here: "Rather than see the rise of the new middle class in terms of the economic changes that solidified its hold over the culture," her reading "shows that the formation of the modern political state—in England at least—was accomplished largely through cultural hegemony," primarily through the domestic novel.[12] This is possibly true for Latin America as well, where, along with constitutions and civil codes, novels helped to legislate modern mores. But unlike the English books that empowered the language of feminine domesticity by "disentangling" it from masculine politics, Latin American novels took advantage of the tangle to produce a secure knot of sentimentalized men.

The broad possibilities I am suggesting for readings of these novels are not (merely) an effort to suggest that Latin Americans may have general lessons to teach. The possibilities also derive from a suggestive coincidence between two significant books—one about desire, the other about nationalism—that have no apparent investment in each other's project. They are Michel Foucault's *The History of Sexuality* and Benedict Anderson's *Imagined Communities*. Together they will help to map out a context for passionate patriotism. Despite the books' different points of departure, their lines of inquiry intersect at two evident places. One is on the matter of timing: the end of the eighteenth century, when the fundamental discourse originates (sex for Foucault and patriotism for Anderson).[13] The other coincidence is a denial: each historically marked discourse claims to be timeless and essential to the human condition (Foucault *History* (a), 105; Anderson *Imagined,* 14). However paradoxical and provocative their obsevations (respectively that sexuality is a function of the power structure that appears to repress it, and that nationalism is always a modeled but not inauthentic phenomenon), Anderson's and Foucault's timing is rather conventional and unlikely to arouse skepticism.[14] Could there be some mutual significance to the overlap? To find out, Anderson and Foucault might be invited to a tête-à-tête, or a heart to heart, that would begin with their respective quandaries.

For Foucault the problem is why we so endlessly discuss what we say is repressed, which leads him to show how the "prohibition" against discussing sexual "irregularities" has spawned an array of institutional discourses for its control. The pathologies didn't exist before the authorities invented and deployed them. Perhaps for his own strategic purpose of foregrounding "marginal" sexualities and arguing, no doubt correctly, that they have been both the motive and the effect of juridical and clinical power, Foucault tends to elide what we could call the "other" sexuality and the "other" discourse. He seems almost indifferent to the most obvious deployment of bourgeois sexuality, the legitimate conjugal variety without which there could be no perverse difference, as indifferent as he was to the best-selling genre of bourgeois discourse, the novels that did so much to construct the heterosexual hegemony in bourgeois culture.[15]

Foucault defends this relative silence on the majority phenomenon by saying that it was itself discreet and decorous: "The discursive explosion of the eighteenth and nineteenth centuries caused this system centered on legitimate alliance to undergo two modifications. First, . . . heterosexual monogamy . . . was spoken of less and less. . . . It tended to function as a norm, one that was stricter, perhaps, but quieter. On the other hand, what came under scrutiny was the sexuality of children, madmen and women, and criminals" (Foucault *History* (a), 38). Yet we know that heterosexual love was being scandalously exhibitionistic from the concern caused by masses of young women who read sentimental novels. The absence of an *ars erotica* in the West does not necessarily signal discursive boredom with heterosexuality, as Foucault assumes, since we can boast an incredibly voluminous literature of courtship and titillation. Romantic novels seldom invite us into the bedroom, it is true, but they succeed very well at inciting our desire to be there. Because Foucault limits his range of discourses to the medicojuridical systems that exercised power rather directly, he understands desire to be the product of a power network that appears repressive. Had he included the novel, desire would also have been seen as the effect of a less paradoxical kind of training, something like an apprenticeship to republican parenthood. The exclusion helps to explain why his almost defensive insistence that power can be experienced in positive terms lacks really convincing illustrations. The "spirals of pleasure and power" that professionals and wards derived from each other (Foucault *History* (a), 44–45) could not have had the broad appeal of the power that enthralled readers who wanted to possess or be possessed by the heroes and heroines of novels.

To stand Foucault's observation on its head, we could say that alongside the ubiquity of "perversion" in Western Europe there is a more obvious and public discourse of "normal" conjugal love. It must have had an enormous appeal to have kept all the other discourses in business—not so much an emotional appeal (without minimizing that) but more importantly a legitimating appeal, which is Foucault's point. But what monumental body needed legitimation so desperately as to account for the kind of public sex appeal that the novel evidently had? What was the defensive impulse that generated the spirals of power and pleasure in other discourses? I can think of only one body inclusive and insecure enough: the tenuously constructed antimonarchical state that needed a self-legitimating discourse, and found one in erotic desire. Sexual love was *the* trope for associative behavior, unfettered market relationships, and for Nature in general. If the traditional hierarchies were to be legitimately deposed, the ideological ground had to shift; and the natural ground as it was redefined was not only humanity's intrinsic acquisitiveness but also its productive desire, the socially harnessable urge for heterosexual companionship and family. For some reason, Foucault writes off the republican pursuit of legitimacy by making bourgeois states curiously continuous with monarchies. Although not exactly silent on the construction of modern states, he shifts gear after describing the rupture in the history of sexuality and accounts for republics with a rather seamless genealogy (Foucault *History* (a), 115). The modern state, he argues, is not qualitatively different from the monarchy; one inherited a juridical system practically intact from the other: "At bottom, despite the differences in epochs and objectives, the representation of power has remained under the spell of monarchy. In political thought and analysis, we still have not cut off the head of the king" (Foucault *History* (a), 88). Objections to monarchs were basically objections to their abuse of perfectly reasonable laws. Why, then, does Foucault insist that the new (universal) class invented a new (universal) language?

> The bourgeoisie made [sex] identical with its body, or at least subordinated the latter to the former by attributing to it a mysterious and undefined power; it

staked its life and its death on sex by making it responsible for its future wel-
fare; it placed its hopes for the future in sex by imagining it to have ineluctable
effects on generations to come; it subordinated its soul to sex by conceiving of
it as what constituted the soul's most secret and determinant part. (Foucault
History (a), 124)

The guidebooks to that inner sanctum were largely the novels that Foucault
ignores. They tended to banish alternative sexualities and construct legitimate
models. Even so, an erotic education—whether natural or no—was officially
off-limits for young girls, not because it taught perversion, but evidently because
it made even legitimate sex seem like fun. Novelists tried to insist that their work
was "history" not fiction; and therefore not idle or fuel for fantasies.[16] But the
protestations of innocence became as much a rhetorical come-on as the sentimental plots. Foucault's readers can already guess what this "repression" did for
sales. In the nineteenth century everyone was reading the forbidden texts, which
is one reason the Mexican Ignacio Altamirano, among many others, was using
them for patriotic projects. "Novels are undoubtedly the genre that the public
likes best," he wrote in 1868; "they are the artifice through which today's best
thinkers are reaching the masses with doctrines and ideas that would otherwise
be difficult to impart."[17]

Thanks to Foucault, some homophobic ground has been cleared away in discussions of sexuality; and now we can afford to notice how strategically laconic
he was about heterosexuality and the novel. What remains curious, though, is
the way he seems to take for granted the concept of "state power" on which he
grounds so many arguments about policing sexuality and controlling populations
(e.g., Foucault *History* (a), 25). Is it conceivable that the state derived some of its
power from its positive attractions as the guarantor (or promisor) of rights, ser-
vices, and national pride, and that, like some jealous lover, the state punished
disloyal affections? Yet Foucault's hypothesis doesn't really acknowledge a
seductive moment in state-celebrated sexuality (as the motivation both for
engendering more patriots and for securing their embrace), as if all institutional
stimulations were indirect or repressive.[18] To sum up, Foucault's love of paradox, his arguably eccentric focus, and the seductive rhythm of his own powerful
discourse cannot but produce pleasures for the reader. But these as well as his
important insights are generated around a cluster of blind spots, including heterosexual exhibitionism, the novel, and the invention of modern states.

Some of these are what Benedict Anderson sees best. One organizing question
of his book is precisely how nation-states were constructed, and his speculations
take him directly to the "fictive" discourse of newspapers and novels. Specifically,
he asks how we can account for the passionate charge of nationalism even, or
most especially today, in Marxist regimes that should have gone beyond the lim-

its of national bourgeois culture. In part it is because nationalism is not "aligned" to abstract ideologies such as liberalism or Marxism but is mystically inflected from the religious cultural systems "out of which—as well as against which—it came into being" (Anderson *Imagined*, 19). A certain spiritual investment in Christendom was deflected to a limited territory and therefore intensified, once the hegemony of Latin fragmented along the borders of secular administrative vernaculars. The fissures deepened after the local bourgeoisies developed vernacular print capitalism.[19] The imagined community of a nation, he suggests, inherits or appropriates a spirit of sacrifice that would be unimaginable from the kind of cost-benefit calculations that self-conscious ideologies assume, and that Foucault apparently assumes when he wonders at the insanity of masses of people dying to save the "people" (Foucault *History* (a), 137). Nationalism makes it possible for "so many millions of people, not so much to kill, as willingly to die for such limited imaginings" (Anderson *Imagined*, 16). Limited, because the modern state is "fully, flatly, and evenly operative over each square centimetre of a legally demarcated territory," very different from monarchies which "were defined by centers" and where "borders were porous and indistinct" (26).

The fullness and uncompromising visibility of these new states—which were at the same time particular and universally proliferated in the West—brings to mind a different kind of body being constructed simultaneously. While nations were being embodied, their borders meticulously drawn and their resources territorialized, so too were the sexual bodies that attract Foucault's attention. For the early period of bourgeois consolidation Foucault notes that sex was forced into a productive economy that distinguished a legitimate realm of sexuality inside a clearly demarcated conjugal relationship and "banished" the casual pleasures of polymorphous sexuality (Foucault *History* (a), 36). At the borders "the isolation, intensification, and consolidation of peripheral sexualities . . . *measured the body,* and penetrated modes of conduct" (Foucault *History* (a), 48, my emphasis).

Therefore Foucault understands his project to be a "history of bodies" (Foucault *History* (a), 152)—ungendered bodies that don't betray the long-standing convention that makes territory female—much as Anderson's project is a study of national bodies. As if they assumed that the other's discourse were their own stable grounding, Foucault charts sexual bodies as sites of national production and governmental surveillance, while Anderson wonders at the libidinal attachment we have to bodies politic. The eighteenth century is not only remembered for the rationalizing of sex (Foucault *History* (a), 23–24) but also for drawing maps as the logos (locus too?) of desire. In a double paradox, repression was producing desire while diffuse empires were spawning patriotic passion for the local territory.[20] Yet Foucault doesn't wonder about how the nation is engendered, and Anderson doesn't mention that the definite contours of the new (national) bodies were making them the objects of possessive bourgeois desire.

Because of the relevance for Latin American national romances, I should point to the very different values Foucault and Anderson can imagine for territorialization. For Foucault it is always constraining, as when he makes the link between state-supervised sexuality and racism: "The works, published in great numbers at the end of the eighteenth century, books on hygiene, etc., improving the lineage bear witness to . . . the correlation of this concern with the body and sex to a type of 'racism'" (Foucault *History* (a), 125; cf. 26). But Anderson notices the redemptive potential attributed to the national body and contemplates a map of interlocking bodies far beyond Foucault's Western Europe. He remarks that state-supervised sexuality had been seen as the "solution" to racism, sometimes with similarly nefarious results. His striking example, typical for Latin America, is Pedro Fermín de Vargas's suggestion that the way to *exterminate* the lazy degenerate Indians of his early nineteenth-century Colombia was to intermarry with them and grant them property through land (Anderson *Imagined,* 21). Miscegenation was the road to racial perdition in Europe, but it was the way of redemption in Latin America, a way of annihilating difference and constructing a deeply horizontal, fraternal dream of national identity. It was a way of imagining the nation through a future history, like a desire that works through time and yet derives its irresistible power from *feeling* natural and ahistorical. "The fact of the matter is that nationalism thinks in terms of historical destinies, while racism dreams of eternal contaminations, transmitted from the origins of time through an endless sequence of loathsome copulations: outside history" (Anderson *Imagined,* 136).

Unlike Foucault's dour tracing of sexuality to a priesthood of moralizers and pseudoscientists, Anderson locates the production of nationalism precisely in the space of our democratically shared imagination, the private space of novels that links us serially and horizontally through a "print community." Newspapers, of course, were the hub of market and political information for an ascending bourgeoisie, but they would have been inconceivable, Anderson suggests, without the preparation of a print community through books, specifically novels. Novels pioneered what Walter Benjamin called "homogeneous, empty time," measured for everyone on the same calendar so that it linked an entire society through simultaneity. This is radically different from figural or "messianic" time, in which there is no "meanwhile" but only a paratactic relationship to revealed truth.[21] So, instead of considering novels (often published serially alongside the news) to be a function of newspapers, Anderson argues that newspapers derived from novels, that in the profound "fictiveness" of their kaleidoscopic juxtapositions among people and events newspapers were in effect "one-day best-sellers" (Anderson *Imagined,* 39). And the imagined communities of readers produced by these fictive juxtapositions became modern nations. It was a process that Anderson brilliantly argues took shape first among the linguistically homogeneous elites of the New World who became practical models—in nationalism's loopy trajectory—for the Europe that first imagined modern nations (Anderson *Imagined,* 49, 78–79). It may therefore not be too presumptuous to maintain here that Latin American novels seem to be "correcting" European romance, or at least putting them to good, perhaps exemplary, use by realizing their frustrated desires.

But those desires are precisely the issue on which Anderson is strangely silent. He values the novel, like the newspaper, for its synchronicity, its *horizontal* and democratizing commonality of time, rather than for its dynamism through time, which he leaves fundamentally "empty." Therefore the overview of colonial Mexican society in Fernández de Lizardi's picaresque *Periquillo sarniento* (1816) seems ideologically indistinguishable from the romantic novels that would soon take over the newspaper columns (Anderson *Imagined,* 35). Those novels were trying to pull calendar time forward by spacing the readings in consecutive issues of the paper, but mostly by constructing a desire for certain narrative developments. We can read out of Anderson's observations that in addition to sharing news items, print communities were being consolidated because everyone who read the paper was either laughing or (usually) panting and crying over the same installment of the serialized novel. Yet he doesn't discuss the passions constructed by reading novels, or their ideal gender models that were teaching future republicans to be passionate in a rational and seductively horizontal way.

This is where Foucault comes in. He points to the locus of modern social investments as the sexual body, which can be interpreted perhaps to be a national body as well. It is also where Anderson himself makes a suggestive aside while discussing the passion of patriotic feeling. After he accounts for it through the analogy with religion, Anderson mentions the equal centrality of our sexual identities (almost parenthetically and without development) in an observation about how universal both nationality and discrete genders are today: "[I]n the modern world everyone can, should, will 'have' a nationality, as he or she 'has' a gender" (Anderson *Imagined,* 14). Said inversely, everyone not only "has" a nationality and gender in the same imagined way, but these imaginings constitute us as modern subjects. Unlike the competitive comparison between nationalism and religion, the interchangeability between nation and sex here is mutually reinforcing. And it is possible, through their overlapping analogies to religion, to see sex and nation helping each other to displace earlier attachments. At least this mutual incitement of love and country is felt in the Latin American novels that helped to train generations of patriots in the appropriately productive passions of liberal intercourse.

By assuming a certain kind of translatability between romantic and republican desires, writers and readers of Latin America's canon of national novels have in fact been assuming what amounts to an allegorical relationship between personal and political narratives, a relationship that my reading is bound to repeat. Allegory is a vexed term but unavoidable to describe how one discourse consistently represents the other and invites a double reading of narrative events. So if I shuttle back and forth from reading romantic intrigues to considering political designs, it is because everyone else was doing the same.

The difficulty with the term *allegory* here is that the shuttling is not a simple matter of round-trips to the same two points or lines but is more loomlike in that the thread of the story doubles back and builds on a previous loop. Love plots and political plotting keep overlapping with each other. Instead of the metaphoric parallelism, say between passion and patriotism, that readers may expect from allegory, we will see here a metonymic association between romantic love that needs the state's blessing and political legitimacy that needs to be founded on love. Walter Benjamin provides a lead out of this terminological impasse through his unorthodox matchmaking between allegory and dialectic, a lead that detours back from Fredric Jameson's rather conventional and Paul de Man's acetic allegories.[22]

Not long ago, Jameson discovered the possible charms of contemporary "third-world literature," thanks to allegory: "All third-world texts are necessarily, I want to argue, allegorical, and in a very specific way: they are to be read as what I will call *national allegories*."[23] We will miss the interest of Third World literature, Jameson says, by missing the allegory, "a form long discredited in the west and the specific target of the Romantic revolution of Wordsworth and Coleridge, yet a linguistic structure which also seems to be experiencing a remarkable reawakening of interest in contemporary literary theory" (Jameson, 73). With this gesture, Jameson joined a number of critics who bemoan allegory's fall from favor and who individually attempt to redeem and appropriate the term, as if there were a "repressive hypothesis" about allegory that insures it as the topic of our critical interest.[24] If we would but learn how, Jameson exhorts us, we could get beyond the rather unremarkable surface narrative to "an unveiling or deconcealment of the nightmarish reality of things, a stripping away of our conventional illusions or rationalizations about daily life" (Jameson, 70). This reading lesson is a gratifying acknowledgment for some of us and a welcome reminder for others about the way many people still read and write, so that it will not do to simply dismiss the relationship between nation and allegory.[25] But Jameson both affirms too much by it (since clearly some "third-world" texts are not "national allegories") and too little (since "national allegories" are still written in the First World, by say Pynchon and Grass among others). I also wonder if Jameson's assumption that these allegories "reveal" truth in an apparently transparent way, rather than construct it with all the epistemological messiness that using language implies, doesn't already prepare him to distinguish too clearly between Third and First World literatures. Even he strains at the borders by including Dostoyevsky with Proust and Joyce as a purveyor of First World literary satisfactions.

In any case, the texts that concern me here date from a period before that vexed geoliterary breakdown, before Jameson's guilt-ridden worry over our readerly disappointments with "underdeveloped" literature (Jameson, 65). When Latin America's national novels were being written, there were no First and Third Worlds but only an Old World that was producing model texts and a New World where those texts were grist for the nation-making mill. Perhaps this choice of novels accounts for my admittedly unorthodox but not wholly original appropriation of the term *allegory*. Following Walter Benjamin, when he identified baroque allegory as the vehicle for time and dialectics, I take allegory to mean a narrative structure in which one line is a trace of the other, in which each helps to write the other, much as I took Anderson and Foucault to imply traces of each other's discourse. A more standard interpretation describes allegory as a narrative with two parallel levels of signification. These are temporally differentiated, with one revealing or "repeating" the anterior level of meaning (either trying desperately to become the other or looking on from a metanarrative distance at the futility of any desire for stable meaning). Jameson's sense that the personal level reveals the priority of the political seems safely within this interpretation. But he ventures beyond it with the observation that the static structure could be "set in motion and complexified were we willing to entertain the more alarming notion that such equivalences are themselves in constant change and transformation at each perpetual present of the text" (Jameson, 73). Had he wanted to track the change from one moment to the next, Jameson might well have taken Benjamin's clue, as my working definition tries to do when I describe the allegory in Latin America's national novels as an interlocking, not parallel, relationship between erotics and politics.

The combination of allegory and dialectic will no doubt be oxymoronic for readers who begin with standard definitions, but it was the basis for Benjamin's effort to salvage allegory for historical writing, and probably to salvage history itself from the late-Romantic love of immediacy so dear to Nazi culture. Benjamin's essay on "Allegory and Trauerspiel," in *The Origin of German Tragic Drama* (1928),[26] is a polemic against the Romantic critics who preferred symbol over allegory. This was the same as preferring a "resplendent but ultimately noncommittal knowledge of an absolute" over the consciousness that language, like allegory, functions in time as a system of conventions (Benjamin *The Origin*, 159–160). He explains in a protopostmodern way that allegory is alive to the dialectic between expression and meaning because it is "a form of expression, just as speech is expression, and, indeed, just as writing is" (Benjamin *The Origin*, 162). Allegory works through the gaps, whereas "organic" symbols sacrifice the distance between sign and referent and resist critical thinking in order to produce more awe than irony.

Benjamin was apparently impatient with what he considered the Romantics' philosophical laziness. With the symbol they had short-circuited the apotheosis of the beautiful, even sacred, individual: "In contrast the baroque apotheosis is a dialectical one," because its subject could not stop at the individual but had to include a politicoreligious dimension, "that worldly, historical breadth," which is "dialectical in character" (Benjamin *The Origin,* 160, 166). His prime example of the allegorical dialectic is the relationship between human history and nature, which was of course the Romantics' favorite instance of symbolic correspondences. But Benjamin takes care to point out a strategic difference between the figures: in symbol, nature is a hint of eternity and seems independent of culture; in allegory it is a record of human history and decay (Benjamin *The Origin,* 167). This dialectical record is what distinguishes modern secular allegory, initiated with baroque literature, from the medieval variety in which nature is the immutable background for the history it contains (Benjamin *The Origin,* 171). Yet Benjamin evidently had difficulty maintaining the distinction by 1938, when he wrote notes for an essay on "Baudelaire as Allegorist"; there he identifies the poet as a straggler of the seventeenth-century "allegorical way of thinking," yet adds that Baudelaire had excluded (baroque) dialectics from this notion of history.[27]

Benjamin's distinction between medieval and baroque allegories may therefore have seemed negligible to Paul de Man, or he may deliberately have omitted the historical difference, along with Benjamin's respect for dialectics, for his own "new critical" purposes.[28] If I pause to mention de Man, it is to clear some theoretical space, because his version of allegory as the inevitable failure of words to attain meaning (surprisingly conventional in its strictly parallel structure and ironically reminiscent of Romantic enchanted timelessness) has become so general as to practically cancel Benjamin's dialectical departure.[29] Years after the *Trauerspiel* essay, de Man would begin "The Rhetoric of Temporality" (1969)[30] by apparently reviving Benjamin's preference for allegory's pause over symbol's rush. Yet de Man was declaring a polemic from his very title, which makes disappear the historical temporality Benjamin associated with allegory as a fiction of rhetoric. The battle cry is time, but the stakes are dialectics.

Curiously, though, Benjamin had never made his dialectic count for anything constructive. It moves only downward and backward into an infinite regression in which "history does not assume the form of the process of an eternal life so much as that of irresistible decay. . . . Allegories are, in the realm of thoughts, what ruins are in the realm of things" (Benjamin *The Origin,* 177–178).[31] Irresistible, too, would be the corollary tragic sense of life for those of us who tend to suffer more from allegorical double vision than from symbolic ex/implosions. But before we are overcome by comforting pessimism, we might consider the possibility that it depends on Benjamin's ambivalent farewell to theological allegory when he claims that human, historical time is only an opportunity for distance from nature, for decay. In Benjamin's essay (as in de Man's), allegory is the trajectory of a philosophically felicitous failure, the recurrent waking from an endless dream of absolute presence.

If, however, we care to misread Benjamin willfully in order to sustain the possibility of mutually constructing terms without looking back at the crumbling structure of bad fits, we may get a sense of how the foundational fictions work. My reading consciously delays the ultimate questions of meaning, because I am more concerned to suggest *how* these books achieved their persuasive power than to determine *if* they had any right to do so. The foundational fictions are philosophically modest, even sloppy. Lacking the rigor that would either keep levels of meaning discrete or show how that was impossible, these novels hypostatize desire as truth and then slide easily between them. With the exception, perhaps, of *María,* these novels are not trapped in unproductive impasses. They do not actively worry about any incommensurability between Truth and Justice, the aporia that de Man locates in Pascal,[32] because they know themselves to be performing and seducing.[33] Their object is to win at love and at politics, not to anchor the narrative or to reckon the cost of winning. Content to construct personal and public discourses "upon each other in a circle without end," as Pascal had described his own mundane allegorizing,[34] with no stable philosophical ground either to violate or to desire, foundational novels are precisely those fictions that try to pass for truth and to become the ground for political association.

If the novelists had closely followed a popular model such as Rousseau, they might have worried about what they were doing. Rousseau had fretted over the "referential error" of the word "love." He sensed that love was not the cause of desire but desire's effect: "Love is a mere illusion: it fashions, so to speak, another Universe for itself; it surrounds itself with objects that do not exist or that have received their being from love alone; and since it states all its feelings by means of images, its language is always figural."[35] And figure masquerades as reality once: "Pathos is hypostatized as a blind power . . . , it stabilizes the semantics of the figure by making it 'mean' the pathos of its undoing . . . the figurality of the language of love implies that pathos is itself no longer a figure but a substance" (de Man *Allegories,* 198–199). But the nation-building novelists didn't fret. The possibility that hypostatized passion would be taken for empirical reality was hardly a "danger" at all but precisely their opportunity to construct a legitimating national culture. Whereas Rousseau's *Julie* counterpoises passion to piety in a way that must have seemed too classical to Latin American writers from the middle of the nineteenth century on, they were making a virtue of love.

For Rousseau erotic passion may well have been pathological; for them it was the cure to the pathology of social sterility.

Despite their admiration for fashionable French and English styles, we noted that Latin Americans dared to adjust imported patterns. Balzac's Chilean disciple explicitly accommodates the master to local material in *Martín Rivas:* "The French . . . say: l'amour fait rage et l'argent fait mariage, but here love makes both: rage et mariage."[36] This "improvement" does not mean that the national novels represent any literary advance over a work like *Julie;* on the contrary, they are far more conventional. The genre has all "the stock characters in a situation of sentimental tragedy, persecuted by the social inequities of wealth and class and by the caprices of a tyrannical father" that *Julie* puts into question. They are closer in spirit to what de Man said about *"Werther* or the Mignon chapter in *Wilhelm Meister* or *Sylvie,"* than to *La nouvelle Héloise,* which "would be a very different (and a much shorter) text . . . if the narrative had been allowed to stabilize" (de Man *Allegories,* 215). More predictable, and understandably less challenging to read, these novels set up a dialectic between love and the state—as does *Julie* in the first part—but never stop, as *Julie* does, to turn around (in the Augustinian sense of converting)[37] and look back.

They look relentlessly forward, like the mortals Benedict Anderson leaves with their backs to Benjamin's nostalgic Angel of History (Anderson *Imagined,* 147) and so do not draw desire into the regress of loss that seems inevitable in allegory.[38] Instead, they set desire into a spiral or zigzagging motion inside a double structure that keeps projecting the narrative into the future as eroticism and patriotism pull each other along. Rather than rue their artificiality, these novels celebrate their own handiwork as revolutionary departures. There is no crisis associated with the loss/castration that triggers the telling. Instead the loss opens a space because it is the father who has been castrated, not the hero of the piece. I am suggesting that some allegories, such as the ones in national novels, may have no preexisting and eternal level of referentiality, but—like Nietzsche's point about the fiction of empirical moorings—make themselves up, all the while attempting to produce an illusion of stability.

If I read a double and corresponding structure between personal romance and political desiderata, it is not with any priority of either register. I am suggesting that Eros and Polis are the effects of each other's performance, something like the Marquis de Sade's explanation of sexual desire as the effect of another's commotion (although the analogy would certainly have scandalized the Latin American founders).[39] Erotic interest in these novels owes its intensity to the very prohibitions against the lovers' union across racial or regional lines. And political conciliations, or deals, are transparently urgent because the lovers "naturally" desire the kind of state that would unite them. For example, histories still debate the political portrayal of Juan Manuel de Rosas. Was he a bloodthirsty and vindictive barbarian who singled out Argentina's intelligentsia for terror and torture? Or was he a sophisticated defender of Argentine cultural and economic autonomy, no more bloody than his equally extravagant opponents who wanted to Europeanize the country as soon as possible? If we "know" from reading *Amalia* that Rosas was an unscrupulous dictator, our knowledge is to a considerable degree a political articulation of the erotic frustration we share with Amalia and Eduardo. And we feel the intensity of their frustration because we know that their obstacle is the horrible dictator.

In national romance, one level represents the other and also fuels it, which is to say that both are unstable. The unrequited passion of the love story produces a surplus of energy, just as Rousseau suggested it would,[40] a surplus that can hope to overcome the political interference between the lovers. At the same time, the enormity of the social abuse, the unethical power of the obstacle, invests the love story with an almost sublime sense of transcendent purpose. As the story progresses, the pitch of sentiment rises along with the cry of commitment, so that the din makes it ever more difficult to distinguish between our erotic and political fantasies for an ideal ending.

What I find ingenious, indeed brilliant, about this novel productivity is that one libidinal investment ups the ante for the other. And every obstacle that the lovers encounter heightens more than their mutual desire to (be a) couple, more than our voyeuristic but keenly felt passion; it also heightens their/our love for the possible nation in which the affair could be consummated. The two levels of desire are different, which allows us to remark on an allegorical structure; but they are not discrete.[41] Desire weaves between the individual and the public family in a way that shows the terms to be contiguous, coextensive as opposed to merely analogous. And the desire keeps weaving, or simply doubling itself at personal and political levels, because the obstacles it encounters threaten both levels of happiness.

These obstacles are almost always a social convention or a political impasse; that is, they are public and interpersonal rather than some intimate and particular differences between the lovers. The fact that the lovers almost never quarrel probably has something to do with the vestigial aristocratic character of these romances; its heroes and heroines appear on the scene full blown, immutable, and easily distinguished from the masses of servants and supporters. Romantic heroes don't develop in the way we expect from the heroes of novels; instead they move the narrative as a magnet moves unanchored metals, selectively and at the center. When novels were imported by Latin Americans, the genre suffered some sea changes, along with its companion ideology of liberal democracy.[42] The Latin American elite wanted to modernize and to prosper, yes; but it wanted at the same time to retain the practically feudal privilege it had inherited from colonial times. Logically, a functioning aristocracy by any name might prefer to represent itself in the incorruptibly ideal terms that Northrop Frye finds characteristic of romance, "the structural core of all fiction."[43] In Latin America's newly won bourgeois excess, Frye's heroic heroes, villainous villains, and beautiful heroines of romance are dislodged, unfixed. They cross class, gender, and racial stereotypes in ways unspeakable for European romance. Yet Frye's observations about masculine and feminine ideals are to the point here; they point backward to medieval quest-romances where victory meant restored fertility, the union of male and female heroes.[44]

One might say that modernizing romances, too, are written backward, progressing like religious or mythical discourse from a sacred given and reconstructing a trajectory toward it. The narrative begins conceptually from a resolution of conflict, whether that resolution is realized or not, and serves as a vehicle for love and country that seem, after the fact, to have preexisted the writing. For some evidently cautious and controlling reason, its heroes are not the self-reflexive, naïve, and developing protagonists that European theorists expect in the novel. Instead, they are unerringly noble, by birth and talent. Nonwhite lovers are more often than not indigenous or imported princes, like Sab's mother, Alencar's Guaraní, Enriquillo, Tabaré, and the African lovers in *María*.

To mention the "aristocratic" quality of Latin America's bourgeois heroes is meant to reinforce an observation about a particular narrative lack in their stories. It is the lack of personal antagonism or intimate arguments between lovers (except perhaps for the erotic power struggle in *Martín Rivas*), the stuff that sentimental romance is apparently made of. The only problems here seem external to the couple. That they can thwart the romance fuels our desire to see it flourish. So it is not only desire that doubles itself on public and private levels here; it is also the public obstacle that deters (and goads) the erotic and national projects. Once the couple confronts the obstacle, desire is reinforced along with the need to overcome the obstacle and to consolidate the nation. That promise of consolidation constitutes another level of desire and underscores the erotic goal, which is also a microcosmic expression of nationhood. This zigzagging movement describes a kind of allegory that works primarily through metonymic associations between the family and the state rather than through the parallelism of metaphoric analogy which seems so standard for allegory.[45]

There is no insistence here on translating from one discourse to another, say from the Good Shepherd in standard Christian allegory to God himself. In these sentimental epics, one meaning doesn't merely point to another, unreachably sublime register; it *depends* on the other. The romantic affair *needs* the nation, and erotic frustrations *are* challenges to national development. By the same token, requited love already *is* the foundational moment in these dialectical romances. This is one reason for my not including here Alberdi's far more conventional allegory *Peregrinación de luz del día o viajes y aventuras de la verdad en el nuevo mundo* (1871), with its standard translatability already visible in the title. The main reason, though, may be a result of the first: the book was simply not so popular nor (therefore) so institutionally promising as to help reinforce love of country. Alberdi may have borrowed his title from Eugenio María de Hostos's *La peregrinacíon de Bayoán* (Puerto Rico, 1863), an intriguing attempt at pan-Caribbean (amorous) alliance which is hardly as schematic as Alberdi's "travails of truth." Yet *Bayoán* is rather heavy-handed about announcing distinct allegorical registers, and its contradictory affairs with politics and passion founder in the rather un-American competition between erotics and duty. Whether or not the conventionally allegorical and puritanical features of Hostos's sentimental and political peregrinations kept *Bayoán* off the canonical list of national romances I take up here, it can hardly have had a similar career. Which country would it celebrate or project? Which existing government could it have supported, when Bayoán's dream was precisely international, beyond the future institutions that might have required it?[46]

Of course the allegories will appeal rhetorically to some legitimating *a priori* principle. Being a justification for modern and antiauthoritarian projects, that principle is often Nature that has been conveniently redefined since the days of enlightened Independence as interactive rather than hierarchical. If erotic desire seemed to be the natural and therefore eternal grounding for happy and productive marriages (including national families by extension), it was thanks to these redefinitions. Nature was no longer the classical realm of predictable law but the realm of flux where energy could meet obstacles and turn frustration into excess. It was a world that produced angels and monsters, not clockwork. The allegories will strain at points against these redefinitions. For one thing the writing elite was loathe to give up its hierarchical privilege to conciliatory projects, and for another compelling characters may exceed or somehow miss an ideally assigned meaning.

But the observation I am making is far more fundamental than any demonstration of the allegory's partial failures. I am simply registering the incredible measure of its success. In many cases, the double-dealing romance actually helped to give a cognitive expression and an emotive mooring to the social and political formations it articulates. The historical romances became national novels in their respective countries, a term that refers not so much to their market popularity, although to be sure many of these novels were immediately popular, but to the fact that they became required reading by the first decades of the twentieth century. Perhaps their promise of a nationalizing embrace was particularly appealing after massive immigration in some countries seemed to threaten a cultural core, and after Latin American regimes decided on patriotic programs for economic and civic development as responses to the Depression and to competing "foreign" ideologies. These states, in other words, tacitly accepted the nineteenth-century potboilers as founding fictions that cooked up the desire for authoritative government from the apparently raw material of erotic love.

NOTES

1. Franklin J. Franco tells us that *Enriquillo* was "elevated since the past century to the level of required reading in the public school system." *Trujillismo: Génesis y rehabilitación, 67.* But other national novels became required reading later, after governments had resources for massive publication of anything but textbooks (often of natural law, philosophy, literature, through selections of Latin classics, and later history). As in the United States, American literature didn't have immediate academic legitimacy. The first documented "Programa de literatura española y de los estados hispano-americanos" in Argentina is the 1884 course by Prof. Calixto Oyuela for the fourth year at the Colegio Nacional de la Capital. On p. 16, *Amalia* figures along with *La Cautiva* and gauchesca poetry. But literature as part of patriotic education was still being argued for by Ricardo Rojas in *La restauración nacionalista.* In Mexico the first university courses in literature were instituted in 1912, with the beginning of the (antipositivist) Revolution. See Reyes, 214. By 1933, required readings had for some time included Altamirano along with Fernández de Lizardi, Payno, Sierra, and others. See *Programas detallados para las escuelas secundarias,* 54.

   The example of Chile has a documented analog in teaching national history. It is the delayed cult of Arturo Prat, the 1879 hero of the War of the Pacific. Iván Jaksic speculated for me that *Martín Rivas* was probably required by the same nationalist leaders and educators who responded to civic demands during the Depression—and in the face of "alien" ideologies—by institutionalizing Prat's heroism, turning it into a model of hard work and national reconciliation. See Sater.

2. See González Stephan, esp. 193 and 159. Most of the literary historians had rigorous religious training, and some studied to be priests. They borrowed esthetic criteria from Aristotle, Boileau, and Luzán, and worked in party politics as lawyers, university professors, or deans; most were senators, deputies, ministers, and diplomats. Often the project was more a desideratum than a record, since new countries, so resistant to their colonial past, had little literature to report on, Brazil being an exception.

3. Also excluded from first literary histories were indigenous literatures, oral hispanic literature, many chronicles, and various hybrid forms. González Stephan, 191–192.

4. In anticipation of such a sociology of literature, one way to read the history of institutionalization is symptomatically, from the record of publications. I am grateful to Antonio Cornejo Polar for this suggestion, and to Ludwig Lauerhaus of the library at UCLA for assenting. That record is often thin until the 1920s or 1930s, when large editions would follow one another almost yearly. In the admittedly spotty entries of *The National Union Catalog Pre-1956 Imprints,* several editions of *Amalia* appear before the 1930s (more in Europe than in Buenos Aires, and two editions for American students, with notes and exercises). But from 1930, Sopena—first in Barcelona then in Buenos Aires—begins to repeat printings every two or three years even in this incomplete list. Simultaneous publishers of *Amalia* are Espasa-Calpe in Madrid and Buenos Aires, and Estrada. Altamirano's *El Zarco* (another favorite of American Spanish teachers, as indeed were almost all of these national novels) appeared in 1901 and shows three printings in this list until 1940. In the following decade, Espasa-Calpe of Buenos Aires and Mexico reissued it four times, joined by Mexico's Editora Nacional in 1951. *Tabaré,* by Zorrilla de San Martín, to give just one last example from the *Catalog,* has had a remarkable number of printings and editions over time, especially since the 1920s (two full pages of the catalog for this one work). And Blest Gana's *Martín Rivas* seems to have been standard reading early (for Chileans as well as for American students through the D. C. Heath edition).

Román-Lagunas informs that during the last century the novel had five printings; in this one, by 1980, it has already had thirty.

5. This is John Breuilly's general definition.

6. See Breuilly, 342. "The demand for a nation-state with many of the features of other nation-states seems hard to reconcile with the justification that a unique nation needs its own special form of independence."

7. González Stephan repeatedly notes (e.g., 184) that this was one of the contradictions faced by elite nation-builders in the nineteenth century. Because they were elite, they imitated Europe; and because they were American nation-builders, they celebrated their premodern surroundings.

8. Benedict Anderson, *Imagined Communities*. Subsequent page references will appear parenthetically.

9. Michel Foucault, *The History of Sexuality* (a), 78. Subsequent page references will appear in the text.

10. Quoted in Levy, 75.

11. Patriotic passion evidently has a long history, which Kantorowicz masterfully traced as a progressive reconquest of classical patriotism. Very schematically one can summarize the progression as follows: the early Middle Ages denied an earthly patria; then made it (France is his prime example) parallel to Jerusalem; shifted the mystical body of the Church to the corporate body of the state; understood corporation as the nation's body with the king at its head; and finally left the king behind. But in this return, the ancient *patria* (city, *polis*) is substituted by the idea of inclusive nation as it developed during the Middle Ages.

12. Armstrong, 9.

13. Regarding timing, Foucault prefers to highlight the Victorian age rather than the seventeenth century, which would coincide with—and be explained by—the rise of capital.

14. A recent example of the consensus is Abelove, who argues that a cult of bourgeois productivity coincided with an increased taste for reproductive love that redefined other sexual practices as mere foreplay.

15. D. A. Miller notes that "perhaps the most notable reticence in Foucault's work concerns precisely the reading of literary texts and literary institutions," as if they couldn't amount to objects of analysis. (viii, n.1.)

16. Davitt Bell, xii.

17. Altamirano, 17.

18. George L. Mosse also takes the position that sexuality is repressed or deformed, not constructed, by the state.

19. Pratt offers some cautionary remarks on Anderson's assumption of community through national languages; they can be exclusionary and caste-coding in an internal map of dialectical differences. See her "Linguistic Utopias."

20. In a recent paper, Benedict Anderson comes to a similar observation for Southeast Asia: "The official nationalist model was drawn from Europe. But I am now increasingly convinced that the colonial state was more significant." It may have been violently *anti*nationalist, but below the rhetoric is a "grammar," a mapping grid, of territorial specificity that nationalists inherited. "Census, Map, Museum: Notes on the Origins of Official Nationalism in Southeast Asia."

21. "Messianic" as against "homogeneous, empty time" (on which, Anderson suggests, "every essential modern conception is based," 30) are concepts borrowed from Benjamin's "Theses on the Philosophy of History." Bhabha argues that Anderson's utopian misreading of homogeneous time misses Benjamin's warnings about our incommensurate differences in experiencing time. "Introduction," *Nation and Narration*.

22. I develop this in "Allegory and Dialectics."

23. Jameson, 69. "Third-world texts, even those which are seemingly private and invested with a properly libidinal dynamic—necessarily project a political dimension in the form of national allegory: *the story of the private individual destiny is always an allegory of the embattled situation of the public third-world culture and society.* Need I add that it is precisely this very different ratio of the political to the personal which makes such texts alien to us at first approach, and consequently, resistant to our conventional western habits of reading?" Following page references to this essay will appear parenthetically.

24. See Melville. This is a "response to a series of essays recently published in *October*." They include: Crimp, "Pictures" "On the Museum's Ruins," Fineman," and Owens,"*Einstein on the Beach* and "The Allegorical Impulse."

25. This is what Ahmad does in his otherwise apt response, "Jameson's Rhetoric."

26. Published originally as *Ursprung des deutschen Trauerspiels.* I will refer to the English translation by John Osborne.

27. Benjamin, "Central Park," 47–48. "The correspondence between antiquity and the modern is the only constructive conception of history to be found in Baudelaire. It excluded a dialectical conception rather than contained it." Despite Baudelaire's rage against the system of commodity production, his allegory is a record of decay as strangely alienated from process as the (other) commodities produced around him.

28. Jonathan Arac notes a "powerful pattern of omission" in de Man's adaption of Foucault and Benjamin for "The Rhetoric of Temporality," the omission of genealogy or periodization that had "placed" Foucault's Mallarmé in the postclassical episteme and Benjamin's Baudelaire at a formal and contextual distance from baroque allegorists. Arac, 351.

29. Other readers, of course, can and have interpreted this intervention as de Man's elucidation of the impossibility that Benjamin prepares. They may be entirely justified; but from my interested position something has been lost. It is the promise that Benjamin's unorthodox matchmaking will contribute to a critical vocabulary for describing a commonplace and canonical but little understood genre.

   One such reader is Hartman, who applauds de Man's reading of allegory as freeing the term from Benjamin's tragic overtones (which are erroneously cast here as independent of history), 8–9. In the same volume, Kevin Newmark explains in "Paul de Man's History," 121–135, that de Man's apparent impatience with history was with "organic," nonlinguistic, and empirical history. An alternative, one that began from tropological relationships and from reading history through, not as, metaphors, was far more promising to him.

   And Waters offers a sustained comparative reading in his introductory essay, "Paul de Man: Life and Works." His periodization places "The Rhetoric of Temporality" at the turning point to his last and most rigorous stage of academic writing; it augurs a deliberate emphasis on rhetoric and language.

   Lloyd Spencer, the translator and commentator of "Central Park," apparently reads Benjamin back from the use de Man would make of him, 63: "Allegories, even those which proclaim the stability and fullness of meaning in the (hierarchized) universe can thus be seen as deconstructing themselves, as revealing the opposite of that which they seek to imply." And Stephen Melville's "Notes on the Reemergence of Allegory" explicitly begins with a reference to de Man as the most important figure for the reemergence in literary criticism. See n. 24.

In another effort to redeem allegory, Dimock makes it a functional development of personification. She begins from de Man's reduction of time to an effect of allegorical rhetoric, assuming that Benjamin's backward view over time's ruins amounts to the same, and concludes that the "timeless order of allegory" is the space that governs both Melville's self-governing narratives and the social governance in antebellum America.

30. Originally published in Singleton, ed., and then in de Man's *Blindness and Insight.*

31. See Jennings. He is careful to point out the ambivalent use Benjamin makes of allegory. It was not simply the record of self-alienation, the ruinous result of totalizing efforts, but also a frame for "living images," once historical projects are read back from the ruins. (172–173.)

32. de Man, "Pascal's Allegory of Persuasion," 23.

33. Thanks to Richard Rorty, I can call these moves pragmatic and "postphilosophical" (having given up the stable ground of human nature) rather than sloppy. "If we come to see the novel rather than the theological or scientific or philosophical treatise as the paradigmatic repository of wisdom we shall not be inclined to say . . . that 'philosophy and democracy were born in the same time and in the same place.' We shall be more inclined to say that *fiction* and democracy are connate." See his "Comments on Castoriadis's 'The End of Philosophy,'" 28.

34. de Man, "Pascal's Allegory of Persuasion," 17.

35. From the Second Preface to *Julie,* quoted by Paul de Man, *Allegories of Reading,* 198. Page references to *Allegories* will appear parenthetically.

36. Blest Gana, 249.

37. Kenneth Burke, 51.

38. Joel Fineman, 46.

39. See Bersani. He describes the "Sadean view of sexual excitement as a shared commotion . . . we do not have sex with others *because* they excite us; excitement is the consequence of sex rather than its motive. . . . Sexual excitement must be represented before it can be felt; or, more exactly, it *is* the representation of an alienated commotion," 145.

40. I owe this provocative comment to a conversation with Jean Bethke Elshtain.

41. Gallagher develops a similar double reading. I am grateful to Marshall Brown for pointing the book out to me.

42. See Schwarz, "Misplaced Ideas: Literature and Society in Late Nineteenth-Century Brazil."

43. Northrop Frye, *The Secular Scripture: A Study of the Structure of Romance,* 15, 38.

44. Northrop Frye, *Anatomy of Criticism,* 193–195.

45. Fineman, 32. After a review of the scholarship, he concludes that allegory works in two possible ways: perpendicularly, in which case metaphor organizes it (like the great chain of being and other visual, hardly narrative models), and horizontally, organized by metonymy that produces narrative. Jakobson, he says, sees metaphor, however, as central in either case: "It is always the structure of metaphor that is projected onto the sequence

of metonymy, not the other way around, which is why allegory is always a hierarchicizing mode, indicative of timeless order, however subversively intended its contents might be . . . an *inherently political and therefore religious* trope, not because it flatters tactfully, but because in deferring to structure it insinuates the power of structure, giving off what we can call the structural effect" (my emphasis). From my vantage point, this seems to be arguing tautologically. Why does the political level necessarily look sacred?

46. In the 1873 Prologue, de Hostos emphasized the book's combative intention against Spain's continuing despotism in the Antilles. To insure an allegorical reading, de Hostos introduces the letters of this epistolary novel with a *clave,* or key. It explains that the protagonists Bayoán, Marián, and Guarionex are also Puerto Rico, Cuba (his beloved), and Hispaniola (her father). See de Hostos, 37. On page 251 the protagonist repeats his characteristic lament: "Glory and love! . . . The former conquered by the latter!" I thank Julio Ramos and Rubén Ríos for their suggestions about de Hostos's special case. See also Ramos's *Desencuentros,* 52–57.

6

From Liberty to Fatherland:
Sacrifice and Dead Certainties in the
Critical Discourses of Cuba

AÍDA BEAUPIED

> We must try to proceed with the analysis of ourselves
> as beings who are historically determined, to a cer-
> tain extent, by the Enlightenment.
>
> —M. Foucault, "What Is Enlightenment?"

*F*oucault's views on the Enlightenment can be readily used in any analysis of Spanish America, especially if such analysis is an attempt to understand the impact of an ideology that, in the nineteenth century, contributed to the birth of the Spanish American republics. It is a well-known fact that the spark which ignited the Spanish American wars of independence was the Napoleonic invasion of Spain in 1808. Although it is true that the economic, political, and racial components that instigated those wars were different in different parts of the region, it is also true that the liberal ideology of the Enlightenment—which had been disseminated throughout the continent long before the Napoleonic invasion—was a common denominator among the new

Spanish American republics. As we know, that ideology was an important ingredient in the construction of the new national identities, and even today it continues to be a determinant factor in Spanish American history, particularly in its discourses of freedom and justice.

Anyone familiar with Cuban history is aware that the genealogy of that island's nationalism can be traced to the influx of liberal ideas from Europe. An inevitable element present in those inherited ideas was the lack of self-criticism among Cuba's men of letters. By alluding to the "blindness" or insufficient self-criticism among Cuba's *"letrados,"* I do not imply that there was uniformity of thinking among them. As Rafael Rojas has recently observed, there were different and often antithetical discourses among Cuban thinkers. Rojas describes a tension between two ideologies in nineteenth-century Cuba which he defined as two antagonistic discourses. One represented a "modern will" and it inscribed an "instrumental meta-narrative of richness and progress" whose first articulation appeared in 1792, in Arango y Parreño's discourse in favor of the means to foment agriculture in Havana (Rafael Rojas, 19). According to Rojas, the other discourse signals an "antimodern will," responsible for articulating Cuba's "meta-narrative of morality, emancipation and justice" (19). The representatives of this antimodern discourse were among the most revered Cuban men of letters—Félix Varela, José Agustín Caballero, and a considerable number of intellectuals including José Martí. Rojas is quick to point out that an avatar of this antimodern discourse can be observed in the Cuba after the 1959 revolution (17–18).

A legacy of bourgeois morality colors, to this day, the antimodern discourses of many Cubans of both democratic ideals and Marxist ideology. This apparent contradiction can be understood by considering the connection between bourgeois respectability and nationalism and by recognizing this connection as a common and important element that is at the core of Cuba's moralizing discourses. As George Mosse has observed, nationalism, "the most powerful and effective ideology of modern times" (1), was inevitably linked to the bourgeois notions of respectability which were disseminated throughout Europe, and later the Americas, during the eighteenth and nineteenth centuries:

> In its long career, [nationalism] attempted to co-opt most of the important movements of the age, to absorb all that men thought meaningful and held dear even while holding fast to certain unchanging myths and symbols. It reached out to liberalism, conservatism, and socialism; it advocated both tolerance and repression, peace and war—whatever served its purpose. Through its claim to immutability, it endowed all that it touched with a 'slice of eternity.' But however flexible, nationalism hardly wavered in its advocacy of respectability. (9)

The precepts and restrictions of bourgeois morality can be traced to the origins of the Judeo-Christian tradition. However, the belief in progress that is at the core of modernity helped shape those old antimodern precepts into the totems and taboos of nationalism. It can be said that the unresolved tensions that plagued many of the projects of the Enlightenment have a curious emblem in Cuba, a land of masters and slaves whose war of independence was fought under the banner of universal freedom and justice for all. Slowly in the nineteenth century, the bourgeois precepts of respectability began to penetrate some of the most "uncivilized" places in the New World at that time: Cuba's sugar mill plantations:

> I believe that in the decade of the 1830s the learned Creoles . . . perceived the sadism and the sexual desire of the masters towards the slaves as a typical aberration of slave society; that is to say, as a social malady. The planters had managed to move the Church to a distance from the sugar mill, thus the plantation remained outside the limits of sin. However, during that period, a fever of bourgeois decency was penetrating the world with the Victorian era. Today we know that this was due to the demands of industrial capitalism but in those days no one spoke of it in these terms [instead, the bourgeois fever was seen] as moral, civic and religious duties, which the civilized world should exercise for itself as well as for others. (Benítez Rojo, 117)

The economic factor was responsible for bringing and spreading throughout Cuba the antimodern "fever of decency"; however, although the economy—particularly the economy of plantations—played a crucial role in determining how the liberal ideals of justice and emancipation were, and often were not, embraced by nineteenth-century Cubans, it is important to keep in mind that those ideas often took a life of their own. Besides the market, there were other reasons that compelled so many people to dedicate and often sacrifice their lives at the service of the fatherland. Along with the economic motivations, there was also nationalism; a nationalism that was acting from the trenches of culture through the vehicles of language, poetry, fiction, and so forth. I refer here to the nationalist story of triumph and tragedy that has been shaping the individual's national identity and which—as in the case of Cuba—has too often demanded sacrifices that are not always rational nor economically motivated.

Paradoxically, modernity is found at the center of the antimodern will. As Rafael Rojas indicated, the liberal ideals of the Enlightenment gave way to a discourse of richness and progress that Rojas correlates with a "modern will," but, the moralizing *letrados,* whose religious notions of respectability and decency compelled them to choose the antimodern path, were modern men themselves. They confronted the problem of freedom in the same way many others did all over the Western world: by opting for a future solution which, as they saw it, could be achieved in time, with the right ideology. Their choice was emblematic not only of the search for a future but also of the quest for "recovery and appropriation of the foundation-origin" which characterized modern philosophies (Vattimo, 2). Their teleological notion of progress lead them to typically modern contradictions and eventually compelled them to choose the "antimodern will" that conceives freedom as an imperative to be achieved by humanity in a uniform and timely fashion. This conception of freedom was the origin of what has been defined as Cuba's most recurrent metanarrative, often conceived as an "insular teleology."[1]

One of the Cuban thinkers who illustrates the contradictions inherent in the legacy of modernity to the antimodern will is Jorge Mañach. Mañach suggests how the Cuban version of the crisis associated with modernity was still experienced during the republican era—which encompassed the first half of the twentieth century. In an essay published in 1932, Mañach speaks of the crisis that followed the war of independence and of its contribution to "the tyrannical essence of our republican fiction. . . . The confrontation with the officious way of thinking brought about, at different levels, a radicalization of ideas and historical materialism offered a doctrine and a program to those convinced that public conduct is determined by economic conditions" (89).[2]

In spite of his anti-Marxist remarks, Mañach's nationalism is sustained by a Hegelian, totalizing vision that eventually leads him to an ideological transformation. In an essay entitled "El estilo de la revolución" ("excerpted in Mañach's *Historia y Estilo*"), written in 1935, Mañach alludes to the ideological transformation that he underwent when he became critical of his previous involvement with the avant-garde movement. In this essay, Mañach describes his departure from the rebel style that characterized his past writings and prescribes a different and more engaging style—not just for himself but for all artists and thinkers. Renouncing his previous tolerance "for the artist who keeps himself at the margin of public endeavors" (93), Mañach now proclaims the need for a different freedom, one that would entail a civic compromise on the part of writers. Mañach here is not advocating a negative kind of freedom that would remove the obstacles which would guarantee individual expression.[3] He is prescribing a freedom that demands active involvement on the part of the artist and the intellectual in order to facilitate the arrival of "The true Revolution, the one that does have a capital R and is still in the making" (99). For Mañach, the style capable of heralding the advent of that "true Revolution" would use a language that could never be for intellectual minorities (99–100). Some thirty years later, the functionaries of the Cuban Revolution would make similar demands. Both Mañach and the functionaries of the Cuban Revolution share an antimodern moralizing metanarrative and demand sacrifice: the sacrifice of the individual who loses his or her identity to the identity of the nation. Not surprisingly in Cuba's recent history, this antimodern discourse has systematically brought to the fore the rhetoric of imminent danger to the nation and, with it, the demands of self-sacrifice as the norm for civic duty.

An aspect of Cuban culture that has been present throughout the past two hundred years is its—explicitly or tacitly violent—patriotic discourse. With this statement I do not want to imply that other countries have neglected their attention to patriotic themes, but I believe that Cuba, comparatively speaking, stands out by the intensity with which the discourse of patriotism appears in its every day life. For instance, for the last four decades, only Cubans among Latin Americans wake up to the dramatic slogan of "Fatherland or Death!" (*"Patria o muerte!"*), disseminated throughout the island. Today's ubiquitous *Patria o muerte!* is an echo of the nineteenth-century *"Libertad o muerte"* that instigated the battles of Cuba's independence. It is true that the legacy of these exalted slogans goes hand in hand with a long history of struggles to defend and protect national freedom, but the fact remains that, throughout these two centuries, the contradictions and failures of Cuba's patriotic discourse—its uses of division and violence at the same time that it claims to be an instrument for national unity, justice, and freedom—has not been sufficiently investigated. This persistent and at times fanatic rhetoric of freedom is not only a symptom of the actual lack of freedom suffered by Cubans throughout most of the past two centuries but, with its power to disseminate the beliefs of an unyielding value system, is one of its most significant foundations. Underneath those loud demands for national liberty there are two contradictory impulses: a desire for individual self-expression, and the sacrifice or renunciation of that compelling desire. This deep-rooted vocation for sacrifice has been the result of moralizing ideas associated with the antimodern impulse. While those moralizing ideas can be traced back to the religious teachings of Christianity, modern brands of nationalism have appropriated the old spiritual need for transcendence and its concomitant surrender of the individual identity, now for the sake of the nation's freedom.[4]

There is an aspect of the Enlightenment analyzed by Foucault that could be very useful to anyone interested in Cuban studies: its role as instigator of a critical attitude towards time and the manner in which that attitude relates to the concept of freedom. Foucault associated that attitude towards time with modernity, which for him was not so much a historical period as a disposition intimately linked to the exercise of freedom. According to him, modern man, like Baudelaire, exercised his freedom by fashioning himself as he assumed an aesthetic interpretation of the world:

> The deliberate attitude of modernity is tied to an indispensable asceticism. To
> be modern is not to accept oneself as one is in the flux of the passing moments;

it is to take oneself as object of a complex and difficult elaboration: what Baudelaire, in the vocabulary of his day, calls dandyism. . . . Modern man, for Baudelaire, is not the man who goes off to discover himself, his secrets and his hidden truth; he is the man who tries to invent himself. This modernity does not "liberate man in his own being," it compels him to face the task of producing himself. (Foucault *Ethics; Subjectivity and Truth,* 311–312)

On the other end of the spectrum is man's immaturity as it is revealed in his will to be governed: a condition that, according to Kant, the Enlightenment would help eliminate.[5] Foucault associated the will to be governed described by Kant with an antimodern or countermodern attitude and, at times, with a humanist impulse that often appears in tension with the critical attitude of modernity.[6] For Kant, the meaning of the Enlightenment was the force behind a moral desire to best govern a free society. Unlike Kant, Foucault was more concerned with a personal, rather than a collective, responsibility. Foucault described the Enlightenment as a moment when there was an opportunity to choose between two very different paths: one would lead to a modern attitude towards time and to the exercise of personal freedom, the other he envisioned as a dead end, as a lost opportunity in the care of the self. For him, the antimodern pursuit of transcendental truths leads to the dead end of an anticritical attitude:

Could we not try to take this road again—but in the other direction? And if we have to raise the question of knowledge and its relation to domination, this would be due first and foremost to a decisive will not to be governed, the decisive will—an attitude both individual and at the same time collective—to get out, as Kant says, of one's immaturity. (Foucault *The History of Sexuality* (c), 53)

Since the end of the eighteenth century and throughout the last two hundred years, Cubans have written unceasingly on the topics of national independence and civil rights. In their writings, they too have described Cuban society as "immature" and in need of the guidance that would guarantee national as well as individual freedom. However, most of Cuba's learned thinkers have chosen to glorify the surrender of personal freedom for the moral imperatives that inspired them. Thus an important aspect of Cuba's master narrative of nationalism is the glorification of sacrifice, at the core of which is found an old longing for transcendence—culturally and religiously transmitted. The notion of sacrifice associated with this transcendental desire is ill-fated and it has played a foundational role in the ideas of national freedom throughout most of last two centuries of Cuban history.

Despite the different ideologies sustaining Cuba's nationalistic discourses, they nevertheless contain a common nationalist antimodern narrative whose internal contradictions must now be discussed. These contradictions take the form of two aims which are not only believed to be compatible but are also believed to be capable of enhancing each other. One is the goal of securing national unity through the "right" ideology. The other is the achievement of freedom conceived as the by-product of national unity. Often in recent decades, national unity—whether under democracy or socialism—has been not only compatible but even productive of the notion of freedom for all. This recurrent master narrative aims at achieving its goals by giving a face, a voice, and often a heroic destiny, to the imaginary Subject whose story is taken as emblematic of the nation's history. Appearing in such different discourses as the political, the sociohistorical, and the literary, the recurrent nationalist narrative of unity and freedom has been identified as Cuba's "insular teleology." Its protagonist is a collective national Subject. According to that traditional master narrative, a "true Cuban" is willing to sacrifice his or her individuality to become a fragment of the transcendental national Subject.[7] Although there is a prescribed happy ending for the story of the Cuban Subject whose destiny is to fulfill, in time, the nation's glorious destiny of freedom and justice for all, from the point of view of the individual who sacrifices freedom, the plot is always tragic. Cuban history, long before José Martí's death in the battle of Dos Ríos, has been plagued with examples of that inevitably tragic end.

The surrender of individual freedom is at the core of any institutionalizing discourse. In the case of Cuba, the impasse in its struggle for freedom is intimately linked to that ever-present motif, easily observed in the nationalist narrative known as the "insular teleology." This recurrent motif is the description—which is also a prescription—of the indispensable moral attribute for the imaginary national Subject: the willingness to sacrifice everything for the fatherland. Taking José Martí's life as an emblem to which all true Cubans should aspire, the attribute of absolute obedience exhibited by the imaginary national Subject could be described as a vocation for sacrifice; that is to say, as a willingness to feed a fatherland's insatiable hunger for human wills. This constant demand for the surrender of wills by Cuba's master narrative of freedom is at once a symptom and a cause of the impasse in the island's struggle for freedom.[8]

One could speak of the modernity of the Cuban revolution of 1959 if one were to agree that the critical attitude associated with modernity breaks with a past identity in order to construct a new one. This modern rupture could be easily identified with the Cuban revolution's goal to break with the past in order to create a new kind of citizen—*"el hombre nuevo"*—whose most prominent role models include José Martí, Ernesto (Che) Guevara and Fidel Castro. It could also be said that such a modern rupture is the culmination of a path inspired by the Enlightenment. However, one could also argue that, for the majority of Cubans, the path did not lead to the creative exercise of personal freedom but to an even more "immature" willingness to be governed. Anyone familiar with recent works of Cuban literature would be inclined to notice the antimodern aspects of those texts, particularly in their portrayal of the effects of the revolution and of the way in which those effects have over determined how Cubans construct their identities. The testimonies of the modern and the antimodern discourses that have surfaced since the Cuban revolution are not limited to literary texts. In order to have a better understanding of these discourses, I offer two quotes. The first is by the Cuban leader Fidel Castro and it appeared in a collection of interviews edited by Frei Beto. The second is by a character in a recent work of fiction by Leonardo Padura Fuentes:[9]

> How do you destroy that entanglement of lies, all those myths, how do you destroy them? I remember that the masses were ignorant but they suffered; the masses were confused and also desperate. They were capable of fighting, of moving in a given direction. The masses had to be guided in the path of the revolution in stages, step by step, until they were ready to achieve total political awareness and total confidence of their destiny. (Beto, 151)

> As you know, we are a generation of followers and such is our sin and our crime. First we were lead by our parents, so that we would be good students and good people. Then, in school, we were also led in order to be very good. There they ordered us to work, and because we were so good, they were able to command us to work. But it never occurred to anyone to ask us what we wanted to do. They ordered us to study in the school that we were assigned to attend, to pursue the career that we had been prescribed to follow, to work in the job designated for us, and they kept ordering us around without asking us even one fucking time in this screwed-up life if that was what we wanted to do. . . . For us everything has been prearranged, hasn't it? From the nursery to the cemetery plot that has been assigned to us, they've chosen everything without even asking us what malady we want to die from. That is why we are the shit that we are, and why we don't even have dreams. . . . (Padura Fuentes, 199)

Before attempting an analysis of these quotes, I should alert the reader by saying that my objective is to be very free in my treatment of them. I have ordered them chronologically, according to the dates of publication, to suggest that there is a relation of cause and effect between the two. The use of the first person plural in the second text invites a comparative reading, since it offers the point of view of the "confused masses," years after the speaker in the first quote led them into the path of the revolution. Castro's text could be seen as an example of the critical attitude of the modern man as he exercises the freedom to reinvent himself. The only moment in that text when the "I" openly appears is when he distances himself from his environment by virtue of his critical attitude towards time: "I remember that the masses were ignorant." Although the "I" is suspiciously absent throughout the rest of the text, I would contend that the use of the indefinite subject is a stylistic device which attempts to diminish, and perhaps even hide, the overpowering presence of the narrator's "I." Anyone informed of Castro's role as agent of transformation in Cuban history would have no problem identifying his tacit presence in this paragraph as the force capable of exercising absolute freedom to reinvent himself as maker of his own destiny and as the leader in charged of the destiny of several generations of Cubans. Also implicit in his words is the idea of a bad and a good destiny. The willful leader has chosen for his people—the confused and desperate masses— a way out of the myths and lies of the past. He—presumably the only one capable of envisioning the good destiny—has chosen a path that would lead the masses towards the Promised Land of justice.

In contrast with that willfulness, the quote by the character in Padura's novel suggests a sense of desolation, nihilism, and also a surrender of the individual's will to freedom that betrays a deterministic view of the world. If one were to believe that the speaker of the first quote represents a modern man whose self-discovery grants him the freedom to reinvent himself, one could assume that he is the perfect model for the weak and confused masses of the second paragraph. However, the modernity of that first speaker is given up when he reproduces Cuba's teleological master narrative and with it the notion of a destiny to be achieved through the personal sacrifice of enduring a revolution. He is yet another spokesman for the belief in a collective destiny whose glorious end justifies any means, particularly the sacrifice of personal freedom—as it is evident in the idea that "the masses had to be guided . . . in stages, step by step." Just as the modernity of the speaker in Castro's text is contradicted by his antimodern vision of history, the second speaker's willingness to be governed is also superficial. In spite of his defeatist attitude, his will to power is very strong. It is true that the perspective offered by that character in Padura's text illustrates the despair of a generation that seems to have lost faith in the traditional values and in the possibility of ever reaching freedom; however, although he represents the moral point of view of the slave, the articulation of his desire is in itself a way of participating in the struggle for power.

If one considers how readily the speaker in Castro's text assigned for himself the role of maker and protagonist of Cuban history, one could easily read him as an extreme example of the effect of allowing the imposition of a teleological master narrative like that of Cuba's national Subject. One could also see the speaker of the second text in the role of the enslaved Other. This is almost the role of a phantom: one who has experienced, if not a physical death, certainly the death of the will to dream, to plan, to assume the direction of his life; in short, the death of the will to live. A traditional historian—a believer in the force that gives a tele-ological direction to Cuba's struggle for freedom—would read the dialogue between the two speakers as allegorical of the struggle for recognition between lord and bondsman. According to this reading, the speakers in both texts are but fragments of the same national Subject, thus the inequality between them would inevitably be destined to find a culmination and a synthesis in time.[10] The defeatist tone in the second text could then be read as that moment when the national Subject achieves the self-recognition that motivates his search for free-dom;[11] a freedom that is not guaranteed by the typical instability of the relation-ship between lord and bondsman, but by the glorious moment when they will finally be united in time and space.[12] Needless to say, such a reading would rep-resent another version of Cuba's teleological master narrative.

I do not know if the seductive power of that narrative is so strong that it will survive days when disillusionment is rampant in Cuba. Pessimism is so wide-spread throughout the island that it is as if the nihilistic tendencies of what used to be a select group of Cuban writers—from Julián del Casal in the nineteenth century to Virgilio Piñera in more recent years—had disseminated to the point that it was now the spirit of the people. Behind that apparent nihilism I see a resistance to the surrender of personal freedom. This leads me to read today's disillusionment as symptomatic of a rejection of the traditional ideas that have sustained the master narrative of the national Cuban Subject, particularly the idea of a patriotism dependent on the individual's ability to surrender his or her personal dream—his or her difference—for the fatherland. I do not know if Cubans will ever abandon their attachment to the "insular teleology" and with it the notion that transcendence requires sacrifice; however, it is my hope that the positive aspect behind today's pessimism—the dismantling of traditional val-ues—will pave the way for the opportunity to choose another path: one in which the Cuban subjects—with small "s" and plural—will invent for themselves the role of protagonists in their endless battles for freedom.[13]

NOTES

1. Enrico Mario Santí and Rafael Rojas have made important contributions to the under-standing of Cuba's teleological vision of its history.

2. This translation and all the Spanish into English translations in this essay are mine.

3. See Ross Poole for a detailed explanation of today's political implications between positive and negative freedom (Poole, 83–113).

4. In communist Cuba, such acts of self-renunciation have not been presented as an indi-vidual choice but as way of life to be assumed by every citizen for the sake of national free-dom. Keeping this in mind, it could be useful to consider Ross Poole's insightful correlation between sacrifice, transcendence, and the role of culture in fomenting a national identity (69–70).

5. Throughout most of his essay Foucault alludes to Kant's newspaper essay of November 1784, "Was ist Aufklärung?"

6. Although Foucault is aware that the Enlightenment has been linked to humanism, he makes a clear distinction between the two and goes on to say that the Enlightenment and humanism are opposing rather than identical forces: ". . . it is a fact that, at least since the seventeenth century, what is called 'humanism' has always been obliged to lean on certain conceptions of man borrowed from religion, science, or politics. Humanism serves to color and to justify the conceptions of man to which it is, after all, obliged to take recourse. Now, in this connection, I believe that this thematic, which so often recurs, and always depends on humanism, can be opposed by the principle of a critique and a permanent creation of ourselves in our autonomy: that is, a principle at the heart of the historical consciousness that the Enlightenment has of itself. From this standpoint, I am inclined to see the Enlightenment and humanism in a state of tension rather than identity" (Foucault, *Ethics, Subjectivity and Truth* 314).

7. Throughout most of my essay I will often use the masculine gender to represent the national Cuban Subject. I have chosen this gender to avoid confusion and to call attention to the fact that, traditionally, the national subject is always male.

8. Before going any further, I should clarify that I speak of an "impasse" in the struggles for freedom and not of an "obstacle"; and that I do so in order to avoid the suggestion that any such struggle could have telos or a resolution at the end of history. I am, however, optimistic in the belief that the impasse—and not the struggle—is a challenge that each citizen should have the right and the opportunity to solve for himself or herself, even if that solution is always a temporary one.

9. If the reader keeps in mind that I am limiting the scope of my analysis to the scrutiny of an aspect in the narrative structure of a nationalist discourse, he or she will not mind the fact that I am mixing "reality" and "fiction."

10. "Since to begin with they are unequal and opposed, and their reflection into a unity has not been achieved, they exist as two opposed shapes of consciousness, one is the independent consciousness whose essential nature is to be for itself, the other is the dependent consciousness whose essential nature is simply to live or to be for another. The former is lord, the other is bondsman" (Hegel, *Phenomenology of Spirit* 189, 115).

11. "Self-consciousness is faced by another self-consciousness; it has come out of itself. This has a two-fold significance: first, it has lost itself, for it finds itself as an other being; secondly, in doing so it has superseded the other, for it does no see the other as an essential being, but in the other sees its own self" (Hegel, *Phenomenology of Spirit* 178, 111).

12. Judith Butler points out that Foucault agrees with Hegel in the instability of that union but not in the overcoming of the conflict (*Subjects of Desire,* 280). She also notices that the French reception of Hegel—Foucault included—has paid too much attention to Hegel's totalizing impulse without considering the dismantling effect of Hegel's irony (*Subjects of Desire,* xx, 7–8).

13. "Humanity does not gradually progress from combat to combat until it arrives at universal reciprocity, where the rule of law finally replaces warfare; humanity installs each of its violences in a system of rules and thus proceeds from domination to domination" (Foucault *Reader,* 85).

7

Governmentality and the
Social Question:
National Formation and Discipline

JUAN POBLETE

I will use the concept of governmentality and the so called "cuestión social" (social question) at the turn of the nineteenth century and beginning of the twentieth to analyze the Chilean case and show, I hope, the potential of a Foucauldian concept such as governmentality in the study of the Latin American elites' problems with the management of mass populations. Essentially the essay will analyze discourses that linked the needs of the Chilean state and those of the elites identified with it for the creation of a secular-pastoral power, that is, a power that connected the classic individualizing function of Christianity in the West to the totalizing function of political government under the aegis of law which the state is said to embody.

GOVERMENTALITY AND THE SOCIAL QUESTION

What is characteristic of Foucault's late interest on governmentality, or the arts of governing the state and the populations under its aegis, is how it displaces some of the basic problems that have come to define standard political theory.[1] For Foucault in fact, govermentality raises not the issues of the origins and nature of the social contract nor those of the legitimacy of authority and the exercise of power. Governmentality or governmental rationality deals thus not with "the legitimate foundations of political sovereignty and political obedience" but instead concerns itself with the "how-to-govern" problem.[2] It therefore consists not so much of state institutions as of practices and the multiple discourses informing those practices. It does not reflect a supposed essence of the state but instead defines the reality of the state in the continuity of practices that range from the control of mass populations and their problems to the government of the self that the subject learns to perform on itself. Power and its exercise manifest as objects of study within a continuity of macro- and microphysical domains.

In the sixteenth century in Europe, Foucault says, the general problem of government exploded, fueled by a series of social developments that made it the modern problem *par excellence*. To the government of oneself and the state that the prince was supposed to perform was added the government of souls and lives that defines the scope of Christian pastoral doctrine, the government of children, and the formulation of pedagogies.

What was needed, then, was a social space that could provide the transition between subject and society, between micro- and macrolevels. It was found in the family. Governmentality came to be seen as:

> essentially concerned with answering the question of how to introduce economy—that is to say the correct manner of managing individuals, goods and wealth within the family (which a good father is expected to do in relation to his wife, children and servants) and of making the family fortunes prosper—how to introduce this meticulous attention of the father towards his family into the management of the state. . . . This I believe is the essential issue in the establishment of the art of government: introduction of economy into political practice.[3]

The contribution of the European late eighteenth century to this problematic of governmentality was partially to displace the family as a model of the art of governing in favor of the specificity of the problems of mass population that the nascent application of statistics was highlighting. A range of problems specific to populations became relevant: rates of death and disease, cycles of scarcity, epidemics, regimes of labor and wealth, behavioral patterns, and so on. In the Latin American nineteenth century, it will be my contention here, the family model retained a stronger position as the privileged instrument of conceptualization of intervention by the discourses and practices composing governmental rationality, just as these discourses faced the emergence of mass populations.[4] In Latin America, and more specifically in Chile, this emergence was thought of as "the social question."

The social question was not a monolithic object posited by a monolithic agent (the state). It was instead a space where the boundary between civil society and the state became less clear and more of a continuous, porous connection. This is what Jacques Donzelot has called the social: "the social designates a field of governmental action operating always within and upon the discrepancies between economy and society"[5] Between civil society and the social as both a market and a security space, government of the social question in Chile became an issue of creating the best mechanisms of security for proper economic government in times of mass populations—not simply or so much an issue of control as a problem of rational administration.

Nevertheless, the state did aim at producing a pastoral economy of populations or an economically productive pastoral for the state's rationality. This is not to say, however, that the state developed a national "concientization" plan for the production of robotlike subjects. On the contrary, what needed to be produced were self-regulating freedom and the free self-regulated subject itself. For this task, governmental rationality deployed a number of discourses which came together on the space of the subject: language and literary education (Castellano), civic formation education, physical and hygienic education, urban and housing planning, domestic and moral economy, and so on.[6] What they all had in common was the stated goal of redirecting the material, intellectual, and physical energies of mass populations towards productive goals, defined as such by the parameters of governmental rationality. They attempted to produce subjects that were simultaneously totalized and individualized, to reach all and each one of them, *omnes et singulatim.*[7]

Already by 1850 two newspaper articles made evident the stakes the so-called social question was going to bring to the fore in the years to come in Chile. In the first, addressing the needs of the poor to which the mayor of Santiago needed to pay close attention, the author uses the term "police" with the same constitutive ambiguity which Foucault emphasized in the origins of governmentality:

> If the police [policía] were to watch closely over these neighborhoods [the poor ones] as it does those where the wealthy live, those winter mud puddles would not exist. . . . There could be a better and perhaps more economic policy [policía] that would avoid inspiring the most profound hate against the authorities. It is the authorities' duty to show the poor that their needs are being attended along with those of the rich.[8]

Policia is here both policy and police, prevention and control, physical and social security, urban policy and urban policing. The second article threatens rhetorically with the possibility of agitating the masses with revolutionary discourses, but chooses in fact to stress an alternative:

> It seems preferable to treat the people as the doctor treats the exhausted patients, without providing big dosages of heroic remedies. We do not want to upset them, we want to civilize them.[9]

The social question thus demanded a governmental effort to face the challenge of the poor, the challenge of the sheer number of pauperized subjects clogging the outskirts of the metropolitan centers but also the challenge of those organizing in labor associations, mutual societies, and later unions represented for the security and the economy of government. The nonalternative, at least from the elite and government viewpoints, was the revolutionary and subversive *remedios heroicos*.

PERIODIZING TWO EPOCHS OF GOVERMENTALITY

José Pedro Barrán has proposed, in order to understand what French historiography would call *"mentalités"* and he prefers to call *sensibilidades,* the following periodization for the Latin American nineteenth century. Essentially two moments: *la cultura bárbara* from 1800 to 1860, and *la cultura civilizada* from 1860 to 1920. The years 1860 to 1890 in particular are those in which, according to Barrán, the transition occurred and one culture conquered the other. Alluding to this transitional moment, Barrán states:

> New times were beginning. Physical punishment would be replaced by the almost imperceptible but more efficient repression of the soul, the effort to convince children, youngsters, mad people and popular sectors of their guilt and their necessary subjection. The unfettered body was followed by its restraining, uninhibited sexuality by a puritan one, the predominance of playfulness by an obsession with work and its total separation from the happy life; the shameless. I gave way to the build up of the walled castle of intimacy; finally, crowning all these changes and secretly connected to them, death open and close was replaced by a distant, negated and terrible death.[10]

In the Chilean context, following the lead of José Luis Romero, Luis Alberto Romero has proposed to distinguish two macroperiods in the history of urban identity in the nineteenth century. Towards 1875, the increasing process of urbanization and massification of the city of Santiago—and the problems of public health (*salubridad*) and control that this expansion represented for the dominant sectors of society—mark the shift from a patrician society "divided but integrated" (*"escindida pero integrada"*) to a Bourgeois society divided into classes. While the first was divided into two halves (the "decent half" and the "plebeian" one), it nonetheless had forms and spheres of sociability shared by the population as a whole. The bourgeois city substituted a more complex stratification in the form of social classes for the two divided but connected halves.[11]

José Luis Romero selects the year 1880 as marking this transition from the patrician to the bourgeois city and credits the change to the effects of the final integration of Latin America in the capitalist world economic system. This integration thus produces a heterogenizing of the urban and social landscape in Latin American societies.[12] This heterogenizing of the urban context and its concomitant security problems for both capital and the upper classes are what the elite would eventually come to call "the social question," a problem which demanded an immediate response.

Theretofore the Church and its pastoral care of Christian souls had sufficed to keep if not social harmony at least some kind of reproducible status quo. In that, the Church had been the perfect complement to the state's work. As José Hipólito Salas put it in 1843: "laws do not include but the arm, religion mends the heart; laws refer only to the citizen, religion encompasses the man."[13] But the massive increase in the size of the population of urban subjects to be disciplined would require some important alterations in that Church-state equation.[14] Thus, according to Barrán, one of the important changes that marks the transition from a barbarian to a civilized culture is the agent in charge of disciplining the national subjects:

> the only difference with the "civilized" men is that they were to attribute to the school the main role in the internalization of obedience, while the "barbarian" reformists believed instead more in the role of religion. Yet, when it came to the essence, i.e., that it was better to repress the soul than to punish the body, the accord between them was complete.[15]

Agreeing in general with the existence of this shift from church to school, I would rather posit however that disciplining then became not so much an issue of soul repression, although there was quite a bit of this too, as it was a matter of the production of a disciplined subjectivity which is different from a totally dominated one. The ambiguous past and present work of school practices, for example, is hardly thinkable if not enough attention is paid to this productive and not simply repressive side of governmentality.[16] Likewise, Barrán seems to oppose too drastically the work of the school to that of the Church and religion during the civilized moment. More than an opposition, as it was already stated, one should talk of an interpenetration of discursive spheres, of the discourses as practices and of the nondiscursive practices that characterize the disciplining work of the state and the Church.

Therefore the main feature separating those two epochs is the extent to which official culture is able to reach the social world at large in the process of state consolidation; that is to say, to what extent this source of governmentality can, wants to, and must extend its subject formation practices. At the start of the Chilean republican nineteenth century, educational and disciplining plans reflecting the state's limited capacity and resources attempted only to reach privileged upper-class subjects.

In a second stage, this disciplining extended itself to encompass a broader segment of the national population. The main stress was still on the formation of the elite, but it now included a specialized emphasis on the control and regulation of passions and on the production of trained and competent subjectivities. This shift reflected the incorporation of new popular sectors to the scope of what governmentality could and had to regiment.[17] In both cases though, the main process was that of formation of national citizens. Change was here a matter of differential emphasis and not a radical transformation in the nature of the process. What did actually change was the correlation of forces of the actors involved. The state and the Church developed throughout the Chilean nineteenth century a reciprocal attitude of collaboration, mistrust, and eventually formal separation with regards to the task of national education. At first, as already stated, due to limited resources and policy, the Chilean state concentrated its efforts in the preparation of elite cadres to satisfy the increasing needs of the bureaucratic and commercial Chilean machinery.[18] Insofar as the goal of its educational effort was not the transformation of the social order but its efficient and controlled reproduction, the state could afford, specially at the beginning, to delegate the task of primary education to the Church. Thus it allowed at that level a great degree of continuity between colonial and republican educational traditions.[19] The increasing political power of the liberals from 1861, the rift between state-centered modernizing and traditional conservatives, greater economic and political resources in favor of extending the power of the state to ever-widening aspects of civic life, the existence of new teachers formed in the state schools, are all factors of a gradual fracture in the unity that theretofore, at least in relation to education, state and Church had kept. The pastoral power and the power of governmentality seemed to have required at this point a redefinition of their spheres of competence that allowed an operative redistribution of roles for, among other things, the formation, control, and administration of national subjectivities. Eventually they would reach a new consensus whereby the Church ended up accepting the power of the state and the state, in its turn, came to acknowledge the right of the Church to sustain its specific educational institutions.[20]

This macroprocess (the two epochs Barrán and Romero talked about) should also be understood, I would like to emphasize, as the gradual configuration of a nationally unified marketplace for the circulation not only of goods but now also for the administration and circulation of power and its effects. The bourgeois paradox of this process is that such an integration of the national market occurs through its active stratification in what would eventually become social classes neatly differentiated. Only in a unified market is it possible to enjoy fully the benefits of distinction that the possession of a certain (cultural and economic) capital offers as symbolic profits.[21]

CREATING A NATIONAL SOCIABILITY

In a process whose causality is always reversible, the development of a national economy (in its dominant form) demands the optimized administration of the labor capacity of available subjects. This in turn calls for a certain degree of generalized disciplining, the acquisition of certain minimal forms of literacy and the development of a sociability in accord with this regimentation of life. Governmental discourses can be here classified by the realm of social life they attempted to regiment while trying to answer or solve the social question.

One such realm was the production of a national pedagogic discourse which attempted to regiment the functioning of school practices and institutions in the production of national(ized) subjectivities. Another was the implementation of physical education and hygiene, at both the urban social and personal levels. Yet another was the general reformation of customs and collective behavioral patterns. Finally, there was the discourse and practice of saving (money, time, energies.) In all of them, as already stated, the government of mass populations was the art of combining a pastoral individualizing with a political totalizing power to reach each and all of the citizens, producing a secularized, modern version of the good and obedient soul of the subject (súbdito) of colonial times.

The development of this sociability involved, as I said, a long process of subject formation of the citizenry, grounded on a rigid economy of the social which linked very directly private morality with a public one, politics with morality. Said development required also a transformation. It was a process that needed to be experienced in practice. The result would be, down the road, a disciplined subjectivity with full rights to political participation. For the vast majority of the population, located at a great distance from the social model used for the definition of the proper sociability of the proper citizen, such a form of subjectivity lay well in the future. The religious, educational, moralizing, and economic discourses of governmentality all shared this structural and very convenient degree of (potentially permanent) deferral. It can be seen if we compare the following quotes, from 1822 and 1888 respectively, by

Diego Portales, the authoritarian minister who has been credited with instituting the state in Chile, and by the liberal president (from 1881 to 1886) Domingo Santa María:

> Democracy, so lauded by the daydreamers, is absurd in countries such as the Americans, full of vices, where the citizens lack any virtue to establish a true Republic. Republicanism is the system we must adopt; but do you know how I conceive of it for these countries? A strong, centralizing government, whose men be true paradigms of virtue and patriotism in order to lead all citizens to the road of order and virtues. When they have become moral, let the free, liberal, idealistic government come with full participation for all citizens.[22]

> I have been called authoritarian. I understand the exercise of power as a strong, managerial will capable of creating order and citizenship duties. This citizenship is still unconscious to a high degree and needs to be lead with a stick. To give the franchise and universal right to vote to the needy and poverty-stricken would be the suicide of the ruler and I will not commit suicide for a chimera. I see perfectly clear and I will govern with the best possible means supporting any liberal law to prepare the road for a future democracy. Listen carefully: a future democracy.[23]

Without fears of self-contradiction, the same Santa María, but this time in his liberal and militantly anticlerical side, could develop this sharp analysis of the Church's participation in the formation of the Chilean national subjectivity:

> I have fought against the Church and even more, against the conservative sect, because in Chile they represent, as does the party of the pious and devout, the most significant obstacle for the country's progress. They have the wealth, the social standing and they are the enemies of culture. They call for it but they give it out orienting consciousness towards spiritual and soul slavery . . . they talk a subtle language of patriotism and responsibility but are capable of the worst treasons.[24]

Santa María's texts reflect both consensus and differences. The differences are apparent. The consensus is on the need for moralizing the masses before granting them any political participation. For conservatives as much as for liberals, it was a matter of producing the right subjectivity, that which had internalized a sociability that was deemed appropriate. To produce, in sum, what we could call the national subject aesthetically constituted, that in which the law functions internally and without coercion, that in which the national (*lo nacional*) functions like the aesthetic object: an embodied law which operates not as direct force but as law without a law—the full liberty of obedience and proper participation.[25] Or to put it in economic terms, the national subject constituted as the laissez-faire of the market: regulations which permit natural regulations to operate.[26]

The content of education was where the progressive separation of Church and state became more apparent and felt more needed. Secularization gradually produced an education oriented towards everyday life in the context of a socially constructed national reality.[27] Nevertheless, while it is true that the secularization of educational contents implied some substantial changes in the subject-object thus produced, it is no less true that said secularization appropriated many of the subject-producing techniques that Christianity had used for centuries. The mechanics of full transparency of consciousness for the now secularized but no less vigilant gaze of the instructor or preceptor; the abdication of private interests in favor of a collective overcoming of those particularities; the existence and encouragement of a set of secular national "saints" (from the war of Independence [1810–1818] to the War of the Pacific [1879–1883]); and above all, the imitative mechanism of exemplary behavior—all are elements of the Chilean educational system that bespeak a high degree of continuity between the Church's and school's work, if not so much in the direction of their orientation, at least in the definition and forms in which many of its objectives were accomplished. Change thus came along with some important degree of continuity in the formation of national subjects.

THE MORAL ECONOMY OF SOCIABILITY

It has always seemed obvious that the nineteenth-century national question polarized Chilean intellectuals and politician into two discernible sides. José Victorino Lastarria, on the liberal one, referring to the Chilean people's conservative spirit:

> Among these social conditions, it is important to keep in mind those which produce the conservative spirit so prevalent in the people of Chile. The work habit which gives them morality, sobriety and energy, inspires in them also a strong attachment to the status quo; and the regularity of agricultural and mining labor, which are Chile's main industries, fortify passive manners and assent. . . . Add to this the predominance of religion, based there as it is on and strengthened by superstition, and you will understand the reason why in Chile not only the owners [propietarios] but the proletarians are conservative.[28]

A Catholic journal, on the other hand, expressing with unsurpassed clarity and brevity the opposite, Catholic and conservative vision of the problem:

> The Conservative Party has as its defining mission that of reestablishing in
> Chile the civilization and sociability of the Spanish spirit in order to fight
> against the socialist spirit of French society.[29]

For Lastarria, the work of national education was to "dehispanicize" (*deses-pañolizar*) Chilean customs and traditions and to separate morality and religion. The conservative journalist instead proposed a rehispanicization of Chilean society; that is, a reuniting of morality and religion in the form of a Catholic sociability.

Nevertheless, going beyond this traditional opposition, let us remember that the ideological distances separating Lastarria and the conservative author were not in the least insurmountable when it came to the practice of subject formation. Just one page before the one quoted, Lastarria added:

> The people are convinced that there is no barrier preventing anybody access to
> a better social position. . . . Therefore, inequalities of fortune are not there an
> element of coercion, nor a cause of antagonism, but instead an incentive that
> bites the dignity of the poor, when he feels the difference, and that instead of
> overwhelming him, encourages him.[30]

This formulation captures well both a liberal-conservative consensus on the subjected poor and the work of sociability as its privileged operating mechanism in social and educational practices. Sociability is here defined as a mimetically acquired capacity to imitate the social behavior of the ruling elites.[31] The founding fiction is, of course, that the social space is homogeneous for all the actors functioning on it. Within this belief, the only factor that explains social inequalities is the degree of acquired education, which is in turn conceptualized as the degree of internalization of the proper and legitimate sociability. In this scenario it would suffice if the poor concentrated their efforts in the right direction, that is, if they channeled their social energies in the proper way, for all differences to become if not extinct at least relative. Socioeconomic inequalities were thus turned into cultural differences.

From this shared basic pattern derived both the liberal reformist and the conservative and/or Catholic responses to the Chilean "social question." In general, three types of cures were prescribed for the problem of redirecting the social energies of subaltern populations which were supposedly wasted or used improperly. They were sometimes combined, sometimes opposed. Namely, the moralization of popular sociability via work, savings, and/or education. As we have repeated throughout, the degree of discursive interpenetration between the liberal and conservative arguments was high. This often resulted in the presence of many conservative clichés in the midst of a liberal case. Fernando Santa María, in his "Ojeada sobre la condición del obrero y medios de mejorarla"

(1874) notes that ". . . the worker lives generally isolated, thinks alone, and gets together with others only for gambling or drinking."[32] That is to say, the worker develops a deviant or pathological sociability. His voluntary forms of association thus demand a rechanneling or total transformation according to the dictates of a less spontaneous rationality. The answer, for Santa María, is the school:

> The basis of reform is the freedom to act, believe, think and judge. The worker needs an atmosphere dominated by freedom. . . . In this field and only in this field of freedom grows and stands that sanctuary where the prayer is the murmur of those who learn, while the priest is the book. It is the school then, and the library, that save the worker, settle the family; it is the school that is the one destined to bring about the moral revolution, to consolidate freedom and give personality and independence to the worker. It is the school which by teaching duties brings frugality, unity, study, moralizing man, thus raising the woman and rescuing the children, because it makes moral and conscious human beings."[33]

One of the most remarkable aspects of this paragraph is Santa María's insistence on the need to foment a subjectivity which, precisely because it has learned its lesson, can be considered free and sovereign. This type of learned freedom is crucial:

> It is necessary to reform man by bringing him to the school, by teaching him to think freely, to believe and work all by himself, to believe because that is what his reason tells him, to fight and work because that is the law that brings men together, to live by love because that is also the law.[34]

It is the explicit manifestation of a mechanism to which we have had occasion to refer. The subject is always *subject of and to* itself; that is, subject of and to the socially produced subjectifying effects that come together to determine its identity. That precisely, Santa María seems to be saying, is the work of the school and not, at least not mainly, that of religion.

In 1877 Marcial González inverts the causality and proposes, instead of schools, a practical learning based on what he called "The Morality of Saving." For him it was not enough to learn a certain amount of abstract or abstruse knowledge:

> When in order to improve the lot of those forgotten by fortune education is recommended, very little is gained, . . . it is not enough to teach how to read or write nor to learn the catechism by rote: it is necessary to educate above all, the heart and the spirit of the common man and woman.[35]

This education of the heart refers to a moral economy of the subject's mental and physical energies, a morality exercised in the practice of daily life and not learned in ad hoc educational spaces:

> Instead of recommending elementary education and building schools destined to remain empty like those of the countryside, it seems much better to recommend economy for the poor, which constitutes their true moral education, because economy is really the best prevention against temptations of all kinds, which dissipate the worker and keep him apart from his duties.[36]

What is essential in this new kind of education within the laws of market economy—a type that supersedes or perfects the two previous models that González lists: religious and formal educational training—is how the *practice* of saving money and energies can become *"la base preciosa del orden doméstico"* ("the precious base of domestic order") and thus of society. In words that anticipate Freud's metapsychology and in fact reflect a long-standing Protestant and Catholic religious discourse, González closes his article by remarking:

> Let us always meditate on the holy morality of saving and let us try to preach and recommend it at all social levels and most importantly at the level of the poor. Let us not forget that a civilized man is only such when he is capable of imposing on himself the denial of certain immediate pleasures.[37]

Important also is how economical the mechanism for the internalization of control of the self and of external resources (money, time, energies) could be for the state and capitalists alike. Since "that majority of our fellow citizens [the poor], will not be independent nor free, and will be unable to properly exercise their political rights while they are not honest, frugal and sober,"[38] the state would do better to encourage the practice of savings than to build more schools. Capitalists, in their turn, would not squander the salaries paid to the workers as, González claimed, happened then: "we all know that a pay raise is more damaging than beneficial to them since the more they get the more they waste"[39]

Thus the morality of control for many conservatives was the morality of capital and savings for some liberals; for all of them, it was a morality of internalizing and economizing for the national subject: Internalizing in the mind and body a practical nationalized reason via everyday life *practices*,[40] and economizing some kind of energy supposedly being wasted without control by the popular sectors. The popular sectors were in this consensual vision, characterized by their "dissipation" and their inability to behave in all aspects of their lives with the propriety that only the internalized interest in one's own properties could generate. Therefore the model continued to be that of the upper classes, as if private property and social propriety had nothing to do with the exploitation of many by a few or were really within the reach of everyone. The problem, to sum up, was reduced to a transformation or reform of Chilean sociability. What was needed was a social activation of those who were many times referred to as *"vagos flojos y mal entretenidos"* ("idle and corrupted vagabonds"). Said activation would of course make sure that no undesired capabilities were unwillingly activated in the process. One radical solution, promoted by both conservative and liberal sectors in Latin America, to the problem of the proper national subject was state-sponsored massive European immigration. This was supposed to bring the right subjects, those already endowed with the right habits and thus capable of functioning as models for the local barbarians or, if need be, as their replacement.[41]

This moral economy of sociability also highlights some of the parameters within which Chilean dominant intellectuals begun to conceptualize the more-or-less massive distribution of printed materials which the press was increasingly making available to ever-widening sectors of Chilean society. Idleness, dissipation, libertinism, corruption, and the defense and transformation of customs, work, and recreation were some of the topics that framed the discussion of the national cultural field and which therefore began to occupy the imagination of elites immersed in the process of developing a national economy without losing control of the social order.

It is, finally, important to remember that this proliferation of governmental practices also meant a multiplication of those spaces where subjectivity and subjection were constructed. That is to say, if government was increasingly the administration of the subjects (to and of that government), it should also be noted that the possibilities for contestation of those subjectivities increased as well. Practice is never the space where one agent unilaterally imposes itself on others but is a space of often asymmetrical encounters of social forces which act in an effective and productive interrelation. In other words, both government and freedom are practices that must be exercised and to that extent are always in a constant albeit often limited process of transformation.

Thus Chilean artisans from the middle of the nineteenth century on, for example, began organizing, being appropriated by but also appropriating the discourse of and on sociability for their own ends. In their social and political practice, associating, discussing, learning, and participating became so many ways for popular political mobilization.[42]

NOTES

1. By governmentality Foucault means: "The ensemble formed by the institutions, procedures, analyses and reflections, the calculations and tactics that allow the exercise of this very specific albeit complex form of power, which has as its target population, as its principal form of knowledge political economy, and as its essential technical means appara-

tuses of security." Foucault's full definition of governmentality can be found in Burchell et al., *Foucault Effect,* 102–103.

2. See Gordon, Colin. "Governmental Rationality: An Introduction," in Burchell et al., *Foucault Effect,* 7.

3. Burchell et al., *Foucault Effect,* 92.

4. For an analysis of the importance of family networks and language in Chilean political practice and discourse, see Mary Lowenthal Festiner, "Family Metaphors" and "Kinship Politics."

5. As quoted by Gordon, "Governmental Rationality: An Introduction," 34.

6. I will refer here although only briefly to the last of these spaces of subject formation. For "Castellano" as nationalizing literary education, see Poblete, Juan, "El Castellano."

7. See Foucault, "Omnes et singulatim."

8. Anonymous, "Necesidades," 113–115.

9. Anonymous, "Condición."

10. Barrán, *Historia de la sensibilidad,* 234.

11. Romero, Luis Alberto, "Los Sectores Populares."

12. Romero, José Luis, *Latinoamerica,* 247.

13. Quoted by Serrano, 90.

14. Santiago's population in the nineteenth century grew as follows: in 1810 the population was 60,000; 1843, 80,000; 1875, 129,807; 1895, 256,403; 1907, 332,7724. See Ramón 221.

15. Barrán, *Historia de la sensibilidad,* 226.

16. See Foucault "The Subject and Power."

17. The state's expanding capacity is perceived in the growth of the national education budget in Chile, which grew 653 percent between 1842 and 1879. See Serrano, 96–97. While the budget for secondary education increased sevenfold, that of primary education grew at twice that rate (14 times higher by the end of that period) The number of students in state run schools went from 14,854 in 1855 to 171,182 in 1900. The biggest increase corresponded to the period from 1860 (20,485 students) to 1900. See Cariola and Sunkel, 143.

18. For the growth of Chilean bureaucracy, see Cariola and Sunkel, 141. The number of public sector employees went from 1,165 in 1845 to 13,119 in 1900. Most of the growth was concentrated between 1880 (3,048 employees) and 1900.

19. That continuity within change is one of the reasons why it is important to understand the Church's participation in the Chilean national development during the nineteenth century not simply as a remnant against which modernization fought (the view of classical liberal historiography), but as a part and an integral actor of the form which modernity and modernization take in Chile. This thesis, from a conservative viewpoint, has been proposed by Ricardo Krebs in his excellent study "El pensamiento de la iglesia frente a la laicización del estado en Chile."

20. At any rate, both actors were well aware of their need for each other and of the complementarity of their many disciplining efforts. The Catholic schools, centers of specialized formation, and the Catholic University (1888) itself can be seen simultaneously as the expression of the Church's counterattack and as the most visible manifestations of the hybridization of Catholic and political morality in the Chilean educational apparatus.

21. Ernest Gellner has highlighted the importance of massive and homogeneous educational processes as a condition for and at the same time a characteristic of modern industrial nationalism. For Gellner, though, the imposition of a common literacy is precisely the demonstration of an essential egalitarism typical of modern industrial societies (see Gellner). My fundamental disagreement with Gellner's book, important insofar it places education and the literacy needs of industrial development at the center of a theory of nationalism, is, to repeat, that for me the process of unification and homogenization of the economic and cultural markets, far from producing an egalitarian and distinctionless society, generates and in a certain sense makes distinctions possible to a much higher degree than before. This is not to deny that the educational space is in our modern societies one of the clearest forms of controlled social mobility.

22. Quoted by Collier, 315.

23. Quoted by Góngora, 59.

24. Santa María, in Góngora, 56–57.

25. On the political subject aesthetically constituted, see Eagleton.

26. See Gordon, "Governmental Rationality" in Burchell et al., 17. Or to put it in the Hegelian terms of the new relationship between the rights and the duties of the citizen (subject to and of the state) in the space of morality (or ethical life) within the state: "The right of individuals to be subjectively destined to freedom is fulfilled when they belong to an actual ethical order, because their conviction of their freedom finds its truth in such an objective order, and it is in an ethical order that they are actually in possession of their own essence or their own inner universality." Then Hegel adds: "When a father inquired about the best method of educating his son in ethical conduct, a Pythagorean replied: 'Make him a citizen of a state with good laws,'" *Philosophy of Right* 109.

27. See my "Castellano."

28. Lastarria, *Obras Completas*, 445.

29. Quoted by Donoso, 75.

30. Lastarria, *Obras Completas*, 443–444.

31. For a fuller account of this crucial concept, see my "Lectura."

32. Santa María, 249.

33. Santa María, 251.

34. Santa María, 253.

35. González, Marcial, 305.

36. González, Marcial, 305.

37. González, Marcial, 307.

38. González, Marcial, 300.

39. González, Marcial, 306.

40. For a fuller account of national sociability as embodied practical reason, see Poblete, "Lectura."

41. The paradigmatic case is here Juan Bautista Alberdi's work. See Alberdi's *Bases*.

42. The most comprehensive treatment of that process is Grez Toso, *De la "Regeneración del pueblo."*

Rendering the Invisible Visible and the Visible Invisible: The Colonizing Function of Bailey K. Ashford's Antianemia Campaigns

FERNANDO FELIÚ

Translated by María Elena Cepeda

*T*he observance of the one-hundred-year anniversary of the Spanish-American War has provoked numerous historical, literary, and sociological studies to examine the process of colonization that began with the transfer of power over Cuba, Puerto Rico, and the Philippines to the United States in 1898. Of particular note are the studies dedicated to investigating medicine's participation in the U.S. colonization of the tropics.[1] In thematic terms, these analyses study the colonizing role of medicine and demonstrate how medicine contributed to the consolidation of U.S. hegemony over the invaded populations while also highlighting the preventive function of the medical discourse that facilitated Anglo-Saxon adaptation to the Caribbean milieu.

These analyses tend to study rapid, mortal, epidemic diseases. Thus cholera, malaria, and yellow fever occupy a privileged role in revisions of medical history during the years immediately following 1898.

At the beginning of the twentieth century, yellow fever, malaria, and cholera manifested themselves through devastating epidemics; however, other diseases, such as uncinariasis, or "hookworm disease," popularly known as anemia, also wreaked havoc, particularly among the Puerto Rican population. According to Blanca Silvestrini, at the close of the nineteenth century the mortality rate for anemia reached nearly 90 percent, a figure higher than that of either malaria or yellow fever. Although by the final third of the nineteenth century, Salvador Brau, Francisco del Valle Atiles, and Manuel Zeno Gandía had made note of the endangered health of Puerto Rico's rural populations and the deplorable conditions in which they lived, anemia still had not received the necessary attention from health authorities. This attention was not given until 1904, when army doctor Bailey K. Ashford managed to convince health authorities of the need to design a plan for eradicating anemia. That same year, the U.S. War Department named Ashford as president of the Anemia Commission, a body subsidized by the state and charged with organizing and directing the hygiene campaigns in the coffee-growing towns of Puerto Rico's interior. My intention here is to examine the theoretical and practical strategies behind these campaigns.[2] I identify two principal mechanisms: the first, rendering the visible invisible; and the second, rendering the invisible visible. In addition to fighting the disease, the interaction of both mechanisms had a colonizing role: they helped to shape a health code vertically imposed upon the Puerto Ricans. The health code illustrates what Foucault calls the "microphysics of power," or measures that permit the state to exercise direct control over the body and conduct of the citizen (*Discipline* (b), 26–27). The interaction of these mechanisms produced a series of binaries, among them that of civilization versus barbarism, the racial contrast between black and white, and the tensions between the modernization of the island and the weight of a premodern tradition, all of which correspond to what Abdul Jan Mohamed calls the "Manichean allegory."[3] The production of this allegory was supported by the results of the scientific studies published in the medical reports of the Anemia Commission (Jan Mohamed, 61–63). In these reports, the Manichean allegory is created through the descriptions of direct interactions with Puerto Rican patients, as well as descriptions of the environment and topography, and their influence on anemia's spread. However, it is necessary to clarify that as the commission instituted a microphysics of power through public health campaigns widely accepted by the rural populations and by the elite minority alike, there were also examples of the practices employed by the *jíbaros* (Puerto Rican peasants) to reject the regulations imposed upon them.[4]

RENDERING THE INVISIBLE VISIBLE

Unlike yellow fever, whose transmitting agent is the *Anopheles* mosquito, the organism that produces hookworm disease is invisible to the naked eye. Intrigued by the numerous anemia cases in Ponce, Puerto Rico, Ashford discovered that in all of the examined fecal samples there appeared a high number of the worm *Necator americanus.* This 1899 discovery significantly altered anemia's etiology. From then on, anemia was no longer considered a disease in and of itself but, rather, one of the symptoms of what came to be known as "hookworm disease." Moreover, linking uncinariasis's origins with a pathogenic agent refuted the prevailing tendency to attribute the Puerto Rican peasant population's ill health to poor nutrition and excessive labor.[5] Similarly popular, though mistaken, notions also contributed to uncinariasis's longtime status as an "invisible" ailment whose symptoms were often confused with those of a head cold or, according to Ashford, with those of yellow fever or malaria. While the incubation period for yellow fever and malaria is short, with patients suffering from chills and dehydration, uncinariasis patients agonized in a slower and less dramatic way. The parasite slowly takes possession of the organism, nourishing itself through the food consumed by the victim. The parasite, which grows in manure, perforates the organism's skin and, traveling through the blood stream, establishes itself in the intestines, where it reproduces. Once afflicted, the patient gradually loses energy and spirit until he or she dies of inanition. This quality thus makes the *Necator americanus* one of the "invisible monsters" to which Georges Vigarello (15) refers: a silent killer that the *jíbaros* referred to as *la muerte natural* (a natural death).

The worm's invisibility demanded that the commission devise a strategy that would permit a better understanding of the worm's life cycle in hopes of designing a treatment and plan for eradicating uncinariasis altogether, hence the need to make the parasite perceptible. In other words, it was a question of rendering the invisible visible, or providing the *jíbaros'* natural assassin with form and content. The preoccupation with visually defining the etiology and pathology of a disease is clearly outlined in the opening pages of Ashford's autobiography, *A Soldier in Science:* "And so this afternoon, his research directed hither by his many days of examining blood, he was *staring* at a thin film of feces crushed between cover-glass and glass slide. It was his first *look* at the feces" (emphasis mine, 3).[6] Here the narrator emphasizes the "stare" and the "look," both terms related to visual perception and, more specifically, to the magnifying power of the microscope, the instrument that renders the worm's visibility a reality.

This reference to the microscope directly locates the reader in the laboratory, or in the space where the invisible is rendered visible. In order to examine blood and fecal samples, the commission furnished each of its treatment centers, or dispensaries, as Ashford called them, with laboratory equipment. Much like the nineteenth-century hospitals where, according to Foucault in *The Birth of the Clinic*, research and instruction were inextricably linked, the dispensaries simultaneously conducted medical research and restored health as primary objectives (107–123). Hence the blood and fecal analyses and fecal samples undertaken in the centers facilitated nosological knowledge of various diseases while informing the staff of patients' levels of infection. Thanks to the dispensaries' structure, by 1905, just one year after their creation, the fatalities attributed to uncinariasis were reduced from 17,009 to 414. By 1911, when the Anemia Commission ceased to exist, more than 300,000 patients had been treated. These figures demonstrate that the treatment devised by the Anemia Commission was a success. But the success of the dispensaries was not limited exclusively to the treatment of uncinariasis; they also contributed directly to improving the general health of the Puerto Rican peasants. Patients suffering from other diseases, such as malaria, yellow fever, and colds, were also treated at no cost. In fact, Ashford wrote in his autobiography that the success of the dispensary treatment lay in the ability to show the *jíbaros* "how to avoid death from preventable illnesses of all sorts" (88). And indeed, that was the case. Ironically, the success of the Anemia Commission made postmortem research far more difficult. The decrease in the death rate led Ashford to express concern about the difficulties of obtaining cadavers. The lack of corpses, ironically, made "complicated the study of the disease's pathology."[7] Rendering the invisible visible therefore reconfigured the meaning of death. Death was no longer just considered the end of life, but rather an anatomic state that enabled a gathering of knowledge related to the effects of uncinariasis on human organs. If *jíbaros* feared anemia as *la muerte natural*, Ashford valued death and used human remains in order to understand better the hookworm's effects.

Thus Ashford's work suggests a semantics of observation. Observation (in addition to its literal value in the physician's work, as he first employs observation to examine superficial symptoms such as pigmentation, frequency of pains, or the presence of fever) also serves as a methodological stereoscope or as a system for interpreting, analyzing, collecting, and, most importantly, ordering the Puerto Rican reality.[8] Aiming to catalog this reality and its inhabitants, medical discourse organized patients' records according to skin color (white, black, or mulatto), gender, and municipality. But more interesting than the racial nomenclature (which was typical of census terminology of the period) was the clinical taxonomy used to divide patients. Patients were labeled as either "cured," "partially cured," "improved," "unimproved," or "dead." This system of classification reveals the intimate relationship between the direct observation of the patient and the creation of the medical map of anemia in Puerto Rico. One defines what one can observe; consequently, the observable is classifiable, definable, and can be converted into statistical data. However, Ashford abandons the use of statistical data and instead emphasizes clinical observation of the *jíbaros,* which becomes an emblematic feature of his style: "we still have an unseen army of pale people hidden away in the mountains where coffee is grown. These are almost never observed by the tourist and casual visitor" (*Uncinariasis in Porto Rico,* 51). Hidden in the mountains, the peasant population remains an anonymous mass that acquires individuality only upon admission into the dispensaries. Not visiting the dispensaries meant remaining invisible. This invisibility was not due to the physical distance between the *jíbaros* and the dispensary (though in many cases this was considerable, since the commission's centers were often located on the outskirts of cities), but to the fact that the *jíbaros* took on a concrete and immediate form only as patients of the commission. The visit to the dispensaries gave the *jíbaros* a specificity relative to the anonymous masses. Upon arrival at a center, the subject assumed a clinical existence as he/she was examined by the physician's clinical eye, an eye that scrutinizes in hopes of diagnosing the patient's illness and of identifying its corresponding taxonomy. Observation allowed description, an act which in the Foucauldian sense made the invisible accessible (although it is doubtful that Ashford permitted his patients to examine their blood samples under the microscope) and produced a language that rendered visible and intelligible what was once a mystery to the *jíbaros.* One hoped that the patient could "see without looking" via the doctor's technical jargon (*Uncinariasis in Porto Rico,* 115).

Ashford's interest in giving visibility to the invisible is also present in his book's format, which includes numerous photographs. Of particular interest among these is the photo of Dr. Ashford taking a blood specimen. As its caption indicates, the photo shows Ashford extracting blood from the ear of a young boy. Ashford's location in the center of the photo underscores his

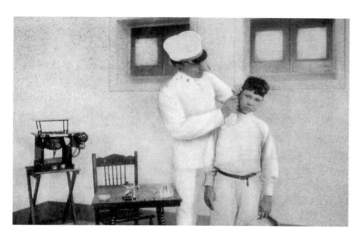

FIG. 1.
Dr. Ashford
taking a blood
specimen from
an anemic
Puerto Rican
boy.

authoritative position. Next to Ashford, the beakers and other instruments, all neatly placed on the table, suggest that the action depicted, taking a blood sample, is an action in progress, to be completed once the sample has been analyzed.

If, as Roland Barthes (195) claims, every photo shapes the historical moment in which it is inscribed, then this particular photograph captures the year 1904 as it establishes an important spatial and geographic distinction. Lacking references to the Puerto Rican populace, or even to the dispensary in which the photo was taken, the photo focuses instead on the internal space of the laboratory, a place that remains isolated from the social context in which it is inscribed. This omission stresses the importance of the action itself as well as the atemporality in which it seems to exist. The photo reveals a continuous, uninterrupted present in which the laboratory is presented as a place where the invisible is rendered visible, thanks to the technology housed within.

The role of the laboratory in the economy of the commission's campaigns takes on even more significance in the modernizing process that Ashford deemed the only possible means of improving the condition of the anemic *jíbaro*. "Better homes, better means of communication with towns, now becoming an accomplished fact, better food, education, in which remarkable progress has been made at this day, better habits of life, especially those relating to the modern prevention of disease, must form part of any plan adopted to improve his condition" (*Uncinariasis in Porto Rico,* 15). Thus sanitary management depends upon the development of a structure of power that regulates the transition from the premodern to the "modern." From this perspective, laboratory work was the foundation of Puerto Rico's scientific modernization. The photograph epitomizes the transition from the invisible to the visible and the passing from the superstitious, *la muerte natural,* to a supposedly objective analysis based on a series of facts. It is, in the end, an image that captures the physical and cultural encounter between colonizer and the colonized—an image governed by a clear hierarchy in which the doctor assumes an active role while the patient remains a mute spectator in the face of the changes to his physical identity and health care, or, in other words, to the changes to his way of life.

A close examination of the photo thus reveals a significant contrast between the visual and the audible. Ashford observes the ear while the child attentively gazes at the camera. The child's expression communicates his displeasure in the face of such pain and discomfort. However, what appears to be a gesture of contained rejection, which could easily represent the reaction of thousands of other patients, demonstrates, according to Ashford, the innate submissiveness and obedient nature of the *jíbaros.* "We have been agreeably surprised how readily they comprehend and how faithfully they obey our counsel in the matter."[9] However, perhaps this gesture of discomfort, with its distant gaze and subtle way of expressing resistance to the body's colonization, as minute a tactic as it may seem, reveals that the faith of the *jíbaro* in the counsel of the doctor was not as blind as Ashford perceived it to be. Instead, the *jíbaro's* gesture is a reaction that could well be attributed to the fear inspired by the deployment of such intimidating and power-ful technologies. Thus the child's resistance in the face of the medical treatment to which he is subjected hints at the possibility that within the nicely arranged order of the laboratory there is a fissure or a symptom of disorder.

Even though the photograph isolates the laboratory from the social context, Ashford was aware that in order for the commission's work to be successful, it was imperative to make the knowledge produced in the laboratories accessible to the patients and to other doctors. Ashford addresses this concern directly in his autobiography when he describes the first years of the campaigns: "That objective [eradication of uncinariasis] we had carried by centering the work in one place, and then by gradually and cautiously extending our front by throwing out sub-stations in the charge of men in whom we could trust" (*A Soldier in Science*, 81). By expanding and increasing the numbers of dispensaries or sub-stations, Ashford attempts to reach more patients in order to change the *jíbaros'* mentality: the *jíbaros* had to believe, first, that anemia was a disease and did not signify the presence of supernatural powers, and second, that anemia was in fact curable and preventable, given certain precautions. Instead of isolating himself within the laboratory and avoiding contact with his surroundings, Ashford labored, as Pasteur before him, to abolish the boundaries between the laboratory and society.[10] The knowledge produced in the laboratories had immediate and important social repercussions. As Ashford states, anemia "cripples industrial effort, limits mental expansion, weakens the body, and depresses the spirit, until laborers in a country where agriculture is the chief course of revenue are ener-vated, despondent, without the power to save themselves" (*Uncinariasis in Porto Rico,* 168). Improving the physical condition of the coffee workers was directly related to the economic situation of the new colony. The production of informa-tion in the laboratory made accessible to the public not only the treatment and prevention of uncinariasis, but also health and public hygiene themselves. The application of these discourses improved the overall economic development of the island. Furthermore, the success of the commission not only consolidated the prestige of its members, Ashford, Walter King, and Pedro Ingarávidez, but also contributed significantly to the creation of permanent regional laboratories. As P. Morales Otero, director of the Biological Laboratory of the Department of Health indicates, the overwhelming success of the anemia campaigns led the legislature to pass a law in 1909 that appointed "a physician for each of the sen-atorial districts where laboratories were to be established" (Morales Otero, 10). The institutionalization of these laboratories demonstrates that the moderniza-tion of the health infrastructure, a process Ashford had been clamoring for since the beginnings of his research, was significantly influenced by the effectiveness of the commission in dealing with the sick. But it also demonstrates that since its inclusion as part of the dispensaries, the laboratory was increasingly called on to authenticate knowledge.

As part of the microphysics of power enacted by the commission, treatment centers served as spaces in which to glorify the conquest, or in Ashford's words, the "scientific reconquest" of Puerto Rico. He declares in a military briefing that according to the peasants of Aibonito, the commission is "the best thing that has occurred since the age of age of sovereignty" (*A Medical Economical Problem*, 2), a comment that implicitly equates health with better quality of life and makes this improvement the direct contribution of the colonizer. Thus Ashford implies that the *jíbaro* should accept this intervention because it supposedly serves only to benefit him or her, as he indicated at an international medical conference in Providence, Rhode Island. At the Providence conference, Ashford exhibited a group of Puerto Ricans afflicted with uncinariasis. As Ashford declared, the members of this group were valuable precisely due to their role as objects on display: "They were useful to me not only as sources for a continuation of my study, but also as living examples of this new disease, on which I was asked to discourse at the Annual meeting of the Westchester County Medical Society" (*A Soldier in Science,* 49). The display of these Puerto Ricans as objects imparts a new meaning to the strategy of rendering the invisible visible. The staging turns observation into a theatrical act corresponding to what Warwick Anderson calls "the medical spectacle" ("Where Every Prospect Pleases," 519). Participation in the conference was considered a patriotic gesture: the peasants, adds Ashford, "had made their first contribution to their new Patria" (*A Soldier in Science,* 63). Although exposure of human subjects in scientific congresses might have been a common practice during the early years of the twentieth century, in this case the peasants' participation transcends the scientific and becomes and takes on a nationalist hue. But it is not the peasants who are expressing their patriotism, it is Ashford who imposes on their participation an ideological value. To be displayed is, then, a contribution to the new *patria*, that is, the United Sates, not Puerto Rico.

This capacity for manipulating nationalist discourse found support among bourgeois Puerto Ricans. During a visit to the Institute of Tropical Medicine of Utuado, a station of the Institute of Tropical Medicine created by Ashford, island doctors, accompanied by prominent island politicians, praised Ashford's work: "Due to their love for the land and their efforts in popular medical research, the American members of the Institute," states an anonymous writer, referring to Ashford and King, "are as Puerto Rican as the natives" (Anonymous "Una visita," 15).[11] In a second article, another anonymous author focuses on the necessity of establishing laws that regulate sanitation: "We are living in a climate of freedom where we, the people, make the laws and it is unfair for those who enhance them to be criticized." (Anonymous "Nuestra visita," 11) The author recognizes that "those who enhanced the law," a commentary that might refer to the health police the commission instituted, were being criticized. Although the author does not provide details about the source of the criticism, it becomes evident that despite the success of the Anemia Commission, the enactment of such laws was opposed.

In the commission's briefings, as in Ashford's autobiography, the *jíbaros'* are reduced to the status of laboratory specimen, but they appear in a more favorable light than do other sectors of the Puerto Rican population. Puerto Rican blacks suffered the most prejudice. According to Ashford, the African slaves who were brought to the island during the seventeenth century carried within them the *Necator americanus*. Ashford presents this as an historical fact from which he concludes that the blacks "infected the soil" and "cursed Puerto Rican history" (*Uncinariasis in Porto Rico,* 22). Over the years, blacks developed a natural immunity to the disease (*Uncinariasis in Porto Rico,* 23). The alleged black immunity to anemia is a construct that precedes Ashford. As Benigno Trigo ("Anemia and Vampires") has suggested, nineteenth-century intellectuals, immersed in a political struggle against Spanish authority, had equated blacks with a parasitic agent. In Ashford's work, proposing racial criteria as the root of genetic immunity amounts to a tautological move: race determines immunity as much as immunity defines race. Implicit in Ashford's work is the concept that races were fixed criteria, "pre-existing natural entities," as Nancy Stepan defines them. What seems to be a clearly racist approach to the study of races was a generalized tendency in American scientific discourse during the late nineteenth century and early twentieth century, as John Haller has demonstrated.[12] Ashford's racial construction partakes of this metanarrative. Furthermore, by establishing that African slaves brought the worm, Ashford is explicitly linking the black body with bodily fluids where the worm procreates. If rendering the invisible visible facilitated a physiological sketch of the hookworm, then the next step was to eradicate the worm, cleansing the topography of the "putrid" material. In the battle against anemia, the theoretical knowledge regarding uncinariasis's pathology led to the practical concealment of excrement. Thus we have before us the justification of the second strategy put into effect by the commission: rendering the visible invisible.

RENDERING THE VISIBLE INVISIBLE

While the first strategy is undertaken in the laboratory, rendering the visible invisible gathers meaning beyond that realm. If the first strategy facilitated the attainment of knowledge that could cure the sick, or rather, combat anemia, the second strategy was directed towards the elimination of hookworm as a practical problem. As such, these strategies should not be understood as opposing each other, nor as two phases of a long-range program, but rather as complementary expressions of the Anemia Commission's methodology. Two complementary fronts whose interaction depended on the success of the Anemia Commission's operations. First, the doctor researches, observes through the microscope, and counts the cells or corpuscles in order to later conceal, dispose of, and remove from sight the "excrement," all actions that cleanse the face of the nation, as Mary Louise Pratt states ("Scratches on the Face," 144).[13]

The methods adopted by the commission were principally aimed at avoiding physical contact with solid wastes. Rain scattered the larvae, thereby contaminating the soil and allowing the worm to multiply on mountain slopes or in bodies of standing water such as small ponds. Deodorization was not an option, since the danger lay in direct contact with the feces, not exposure to its odor.[14] By the same token, it was impossible to eliminate the parasite through the use of aerosols because the carrier was not a mosquito, as in the case of malaria and yellow fever. Considering these limitations, the commission stressed prevention, prescribing the use of footwear and the installation of latrines. Since the initiation of his research, Ashford had maintained that the use of footwear as well as the construction of latrines represented the most effective ways of minimizing exposure to the parasite; he even went as far as to consider mandating the use of shoes, a notion that he later abandoned.[15] In contrast, the construction of home latrines was obligatory from the very onset of the commission's campaigns, although in 1905 Ashford confessed that such a strategy "would work harm by creating opposition which would be hard to overcome, as it would appear to them as purely arbitrary and an unreasonable piece of nonsense."[16] However, the Puerto Ricans' resistance was gradually worn down, in part because affected patients understood that the latrines limited the possibility of contracting the disease and of suffering a relapse, and in part because the installation of latrines became law. Not having a latrine or keeping one in an unsanitary condition constituted a punishable offense. To ensure that these latrines were assiduously used, the commission formed a body of "health officials" whose duties, as defined by Ashford, involved overseeing the ingestion of required medicines and supervising the latrines' maintenance. In this way, the strategy of rendering the visible invisible was legalized and endorsed by the legal system. Health and hygiene were transformed from a body of knowledge designated for improving health, as in the illustrated pamphlets that the commission passed out to the sick, into a discourse that redefined criminality and validated the incipient social order that the colonial military authority was imposing on the country. Thus personal hygiene was subordinated to the collective will, and the biological act of defecating became a potentially criminal act, an affair of state that justified the interference in the private life of the citizen.

The explicit association of the *jíbaros* with the production of excrement contrasts with Ashford's interest in concealing the waste. Unlike the infirm, the commission's doctors take notes, measure, weigh, examine patients, crisscross the island's towns, and appear immersed in labors that transcend the natural necessities of the human body. In this fashion, Ashford's body is idealized, while that of the *jíbaro* embodies all that is filthy, vulgar, and scatological. As author, Ashford constructs an image of himself as an individual capable of evaluating the island's health, curing patients and directing complex campaigns at the national level without so much as hesitating or committing an error. This rhetoric promotes the briefings' appearance as a monolithic source of information, or a closed, self-sufficient universe, much like the laboratory space. Furthermore, the inclusion of data that supports evidence of a decline in anemia in all regions containing dispensaries simultaneously constructs an efficient image of the commission as an entity that controls (via health officials) the private lives of thousands of peasants, a type of Big Brother whose power rests in the conjunction of legal support and the voluntary complicity of the *jíbaros*. According to Ashford, upon embracing the norms, the Puerto Rican acquires an acceptable identity and is transformed into one who is "faithful and warm" (*Uncinariasis in Porto Rico,* 20). By the same token, rejection of the norms renders him or her "a violently prejudiced *jíbaro*" (*A Soldier in Science,* 73) This limits the complexity of power relations between the colonizer and the colonized to a reductionist, idealized binary. Ashford observes that Puerto Ricans accepted voluntarily the construction of latrines "without coercion or harsh compulsion," as if health officials or the fear of being fined did not influence the *jíbaros'* will.[17]

In a significant passage of his autobiography, Ashford convinces the mayor of the town of Utuado to install a latrine at his home. Some weeks later, Ashford returns to the neighborhood and finds the "*jíbaro alcalde* with the torn shirt and the bare feet at work in a tobacco patch" (*A Soldier in Science,* 71), who takes him to the recently built latrine located far from his home. Surprised, Ashford reprimands the mayor, who replies: "The law requires us to have one, and there it is, but neither my wife nor I believe in these things, as they produce constipation. And besides, it is a nasty thing to have near the house. But the law requires it, and everybody else has one, too" (*A Soldier in Science,* 72). The anecdote's presentation is noteworthy: words such as *jíbaro* and *alcalde* are included in italics as if their presence were contaminating the discourse. As narrator, Ashford places himself in a supposedly objective position from which he maintains some distance in relationship to the mayor, the Other, and from which he is able to register and transcribe the observed events. The description is suggestive of the writing of his briefings, where Ashford also deliberately attempts to remove himself from events in order to "report on" advances in the eradication of uncinariasis.

But perhaps more important than the presentation, the anecdote provides an example of the complexities of colonizer-colonized relationships. For Ashford, the incident is presented as proof of the ignorance that justifies the commission's intervention in Puerto Rican daily life. If we take the perspective of the mayor, however, we can interpret in his response a tactic of resistance in the face of the imposition of a sanitary economics. The mayor is complying with the law while simultaneously subverting Ashford's prophylaxis: he refuses to build the latrine near his house since it causes "constipation." The mayor's refusal "tricks" the law and affirms, in the process, his own beliefs about what is sanitary and what is not—a code of values that evidently rejects those promoted and sponsored by the American colonial authorities. Moreover, in light of the mayor's refusal, which could easily have represented the cases of thousands of Puerto Ricans, it is fitting to ask just what percentage of them fully accepted the prescribed use of latrines and just how many Puerto Ricans were fined for infringing on health regulations.[18] Ashford's anecdote downplays the tensions between the military and the islanders. Hence rendering the visible invisible transcends a purely sanitary practice (concealing excrement) and also works on a symbolic plane as a device that minimizes or even hides the everyday tactics of resistance articulated by the natives against the sanitation rules promoted by the commission.

Although rendering the visible invisible operates on a literal as well as on a symbolic level, its practicability depended upon the knowledge produced in the laboratory, that is, in making the invisible visible. If rendering the invisible visible provided the theory, the body of knowledge that enabled the physician to understand the *Necator americanus* life cycle, rendering the visible invisible translated this body of knowledge into practice. But even more important is that the interaction of these strategies comes into being in the context of the colonization of Puerto Rico. From this perspective, these strategies acquire in Ashford´s briefing and in his autobiography an ideological meaning as they construct a scientific discourse which in turn proposes a new pathology of the colonized body. In narrating this new pathology of the Puerto Rican, Ashford writes of the encounters with the Other in a way that erases the tensions between colonizer and colonized and treats the Puerto Rican subject as a monolithical entity. There is no racial or class distinction in the descriptions of the *jíbaro*. The little boy of the photograph is as much a *jíbaro* as the mayor of Utuado, although the latter holds a public office. Ignoring these important differences that contributed to the heterogeneity of the native population, Ashford reduces the Puerto Rican inland inhabitant to an infirm and ignorant patient waiting to be brought by science into modernity.

NOTES

1. Regarding the role of medicine in the consolidation of English colonial power, see David Arnold, *Colonizing the Body,* and Rajnarayan Chandravarkar, "Plague Panic and Epidemic." With respect to the repressive measures utilized by North American military authorities in the Philippines, see Warwick Anderson, "Where Every Prospect Pleases."

2. I use the term strategies in the Foucauldian sense. In the study of the microphysics of power, the power exercised on the body is conceived not as a property but instead as strategies or as the interplay of maneuvers, techniques, and actions by which institutions control and dominate the citizens (Michel Foucault, *Discipline and Punish* (b), 26).

3. Abdul Jan Mohamed responds to Homi Bhabha's discussion on the colonial subject and proposes the Manichean allegory "as an alternative definiton through analysis that maps its ideological function in relation to actual imperialist practices." Thus the Manichean allegory is conceived as "an economy based on the transformation of racial difference into moral and metaphysical difference" ("The Economy," 61).

4. According to Michel De Certeau, such "tactics" include those actions employed by the "Other" in order to manipulate events, and ultimately turn them into opportunities to undermine the actions emanating from the center of power (De Certeau, xix).

5. Brau, 9–75.

6. In this passage, appropriately included in the section entitled "Arms and the Microscope," Ashford refers to himself using the third person. By assuming the perspective of an outsider, a voyeur, Ahsford "observes" this historical moment, the discovery of the worm, from a distance, emphasizing the discovery itself. While establishing the identity of the narrator as a doctor, Ashford attempts to provide an "objective" account of the origin of the disease suffered by the *jíbaros.*

7. *Informe Parcial* 1904.

8. According to Kelvin Santiago, Americans perceived Puerto Rico as "wayward and unruly" (Santiago, 20).

9. *Informe Parcial* 1904.

10. See Latour.

11. Although the source of this quote is anonymous, Ashford states in his autobiography that Luis Muñoz Rivera (governor of Puerto Rico), as the result of a 1913 visit to the Utuado station of the Institute for Tropical Medicine, praised his leadership in the field of public health. The coinciding dates suggest that the anonymous article was written by the famous politician.

12. As John Haller argues, American physicians during the nineteenth century assumed the inferiority of the negro race as scientific fact. For them, particularly in the Southern United States, "segregation and disfranchisement were steps leading towards preparing the negro race for extinction" (Haller, 167).

13. In a study of *John Barrow's Account of Travels ino the Interior of Southern Africa in the years 1797 and 1798,* Pratt argues that Barrow's "narrative deals with the landscape while indigenous people are represented separately in descriptive portraits." In these accounts, Pratt adds, "The Bushmen searching for roots, scratched the surface." (Pratt, "Scratches on the Face," 123) These elements conform to a panoramic view that Barrow uses to incorporate a particular reality into different orders, geographical, botanical, and others.

Like Barrow, Ashford offers detailed descriptions of the landscape; however, the natives are not just presented separately. In fact, Ashford argues that the slaves contaminated the soil.

14. As Warwick Anderson has demonstrated, late in the nineteenth century bacteriology allowed a deeper understanding of the composition of excrement. Since then, Warwick Anderson argues, medical doctors have "discontinued the morbidity of stenches in favor of the dangers of germs; the dire consequences of feces derived more from physical contact than from olfactory action at a distance" ("Excremental Colonialism," 642). Ashford's research evidently partakes from this bacteriological frame of mind.

15. *Informe Parcial* 1905, 3.

16. *Informe Parcial* 1904, 4.

17. *Informe Parcial* 1906, 5.

18. With regard to this theme, Fernando Picó indicates that the latrine regulations motivated bitter controversies such as the conflict in Orocovis, where the mayor's refusal to construct latrines provoked his immediate dismissal (Picó, 187).

SUBJECTIVITY

9

Thinking Subjectivity in
Latin American Criticism

BENIGNO TRIGO

*I*t is well known that Michel Foucault tried to separate himself from the notion of subjectivity conceptualized by Freudian psychoanalysis and by earlier forms of psychology.[1] And yet both his early efforts to practice what he calls a phenomenological psychology and his later attempts to articulate a notion of an epidermal subjectivity that eschews the concept of internal or deep psychic structures are rift with the paradoxes that constitute the Freudian notion of subjectivity.

Like Sigmund Freud, Foucault found creative inspiration in the inability to integrate fully the object into the subject in a tightly conceived theory of primary narcissism, or to separate fully the subject from the object, or to differentiate between constitutive principles such as interiority and exteriority, sociality and organicity. Instead, Foucault developed a theory of subjectivity based on a modality of power that exceeds the boundaries of discreet units or disciplined organizations such as subject or object for which power is itself ultimately responsible. In other words, Foucault developed a notion of subjectivity that is based on the concept of excessive flows of energy that are not very different from the Freudian drives. These overflows or excessive forces are as much a part of disciplining and ordering power as they are resistant to it, as they always have the capacity (and they hold the promise) to go beyond and overcome the disciplining and ordering forces that Foucault called biopower.[2]

This notion of subjectivity as an overabundance or excess of force is perhaps best developed in Foucault's later works, but it can also be found throughout his earlier work. Appropriations of Foucault by prominent critics of Latin American culture, however, make no references to it. Instead, they cling to a notion of subjectivity and power that despite its coherence lacks dynamism and ultimately crystallizes in what appear to be either programmatic oppositions to dominating powers or violent visions of self-sacrifice.

In this essay, I will argue that the productive paradoxes found in Foucault, as well as the manifestation of these paradoxes in his account of the process of subjectivity, are resolved by a number of critical theorists in their works about Latin American culture. I will criticize this resolution as a foreclosure of the most promising aspect of Foucault's theory of subjectivity, which I claim is derived in part from Freud's theory of the drives. I will also diagnose this resolution and will explain its conditions of possibility. I will argue that these critics cling to an aspect of Foucault's theory that is reminiscent of Freud's own attempts to resolve the paradoxes of his account of subjectivity. Readers of both Foucault and Freud, these critics ultimately remain within Freud's account of subjectivity, which never fully escapes an anxious economy of scarcity. Instead, these critics walk away from Foucault's promise of an alternative account of subjectivity based on a generous economy of excess and overabundant forces. I will end by suggesting ways in which recent literary production by women writers in and about Latin America engages in a productive exchange with this line of critical thought. I will claim that, owing to an account of subjectivity close in spirit to Foucault's, these texts provide an alternative to the mortally wounded or disembodied subject that must emerge from contemporary critical appropriations of Foucault's account of subjectivity.

In "Instincts and Their Vicissitudes" (1915) Freud gives his first comprehensive version of a theory of the drives described as the release of a sustained force or energy comparable to the eruption of a volcano whose source is the body and whose aim is the return to a dormant state. Subjectivity, Freud suggests, is a process that begins with a primal violent eruption of drives: it is the asymmetrical result of the accumulated layers of lava from this erupting volcano (*General Psychological Theory*, 94–95). But subjectivity is also the violent process of mastery of these erupting drives. Subjectivity is not only a passive heterogeneous effect but also an active process of ordering subjection. The process of subjection begins the moment the subject emerges as a response principally to internal impulses (or drives). The paradoxical aim of the process of subjection is to return the subject to a primitive state devoid of any stimuli whatsoever: the inactive state of the dormant volcano.

In his later essay "The Economic Problem of Masochism" (1924), Freud would repeat many of the same moves but would also manifest a strange and strong resistance to the violent nature of his theory of subjectivity. In that essay, Freud says that he is "tempted" to compare the life drive to a "watchman" whose "job" it is to "subjugate" (to watch over and to punish) the death drive (*General Psychological Theory*, 190). This subjugation is compared to a "coalescence," a "fusion," or an "amalgamation" of the death and life drives, returning the reader to the earlier image for subjectivity as the petrification of layers of lava. In his later essay, Freud is most interested in masochism, which he calls an excess or residue of this subjugation process. Significantly, Freud compares primary masochism to "a witness and a survival," and he compares secondary masochism to a "classical piece of evidence for the existence" of "subjugation" (*General Psychological Theory*, 195, 201). Freud's metaphors for the life drive and masochism seem strangely at odds with their presumed contents and are based on a series of pointed Nietzschean inversions. On the one hand, he compares life to a policing and punishing agent that kills, castrates, or "blinds." On the other hand, masochism is described as the witness or the evidence that survives the crime of life (*General Psychological Theory*, 193).

Freud's redefinition of masochism as a remainder, as an excess, as a force that remains outside the self-enclosed and violent subjecting process hints at the failure of that very process of subject formation. The failure of this process is doubly significant. On the one hand, it fails because it is not resolved according to one force (life drive) or the other (death drive). On the other hand, it also fails because it is irreducible to the two terms that appear to originate it.

The failure of the process of subjection points in the direction of an ambivalence in Freud, perhaps felt as the result of perceiving a different account of subjectivity: one where the subject is always in the company of another and is always feeling the forces that link it to another. In this alternative account, Freud does not presuppose a clear distinction between autonomous entities such as subjects or objects, and instead underscores the preexisting forces that course through them and link them together.

Akin to this understanding of Freud's ambivalence, Foucault argues in *Mental*

Illness and Psychology that the study of mental illness calls for an intersubjective method of analysis based on intuition which presupposes the affinity of objective and subjective knowledge as well as the identity between the world of the mentally ill and the world of the analyst.[3] Indeed, Foucault's earliest account of subjectivity hinges on a spatial and temporal meeting of paradoxical and powerful lines of force that is not unlike the Freudian theory of drives.

But it is in his last works on ethics and subjectivity that Foucault focuses on the possibility of thinking subjectivity outside of a violent process of subjection. In his effort to renew the living body of his own philosophy, in his effort to rethink his central concepts of technique and technology as something other than an attempt to normalize a population and as something other than self-punishment, Foucault again turns to the notion of intersubjectivity, this time in the guise of the dialogues and exchanges of friendship.[4]

In his essay on "self-writing," Foucault studies the letters of the Stoics and suggests that their correspondence was reciprocal in a profound sense (Foucault *Ethics*, 216). Foucault writes that on the one hand, correspondence had a constitutive effect on the self. For the Stoics, the art of consolation in correspondence was a proleptic exercise. It was a preparation of the self (even in the sense of physical training) for the inevitable moment when the self would be in need of consolation himself. Thus to write such a letter was an exercise in subjection, in taking care of oneself by preparing oneself through the proleptic confrontation and struggle with one's mortality. On the other hand, Foucault suggests (more mysteriously) that the same act is "an objectification of the soul." By this objectification, Foucault means a profound transformation of the self caused by its inevitable fall under the other's gaze. Rather than describe this transformation as the cruel struggle of Christian confessional practices, however, Foucault describes it as "a self offering," or "a self opening" to a divine gaze that occupies the place of an inner god and plunges into the depths of the heart of the self (Foucault *Ethics*, 217).[5]

There are perhaps two principal implications of this notion of subjectivity. On the one hand, the "intersubjectivity" of Foucault's early essays on mental illness and his late essays on the care of the self resist a notion of subjectivity based on a primary narcissism that collapses the subject-object binary into a master subject. In so doing, they also resist a Hegelian account of subjectivity based on violent struggle over scarce resources which forever pits the subject against its object for their mastery. On the other hand, following Freud's theory of the bodily drives, Foucault's works also put into question the Cartesian identity of being and thinking.

In the diaries of the Stoics, Foucault finds a notion of subjectivity that is not the result of an autonomous consciousness thinking itself. For the Stoics, writing a diary was not just a unifying process involving the metaphorical incorporation, digestion, and transformation of their elders' writings. Foucault paradoxically argues that it was, instead, a literal process of embodiment: "writing transforms the thing seen or heard 'into tissue and blood.' It becomes a principle of rational action in the writer himself" (Foucault *Ethics*, 213). The essay both presupposes and develops a notion of the self as more than its physical constitutive parts, but also as a self whose excess is always substance: a substance that cannot be reduced to desires or thoughts. It is fairly clear that Foucault's paradoxical "bios," defined by his biographer as "life in its chaotic, prepersonal flux," is akin to the Freudian notion of the drive, always described as a force that is also a flow of energy or substance.[6]

Foucault has been an important influence on contemporary critical thought about Latin America. Theorists working on Latin American culture and literature such as Angel Rama, Roberto González Echevarría, Doris Sommer, and Sylvia Molloy owe many of their insights on modern subjectivity in Latin America to Foucault's diagnosis of the Western subject.[7] This critical tradition, however, also succeeds in reading Foucault in a very particular way. While Foucault's account of subjectivity as force leads him to represent the Western subject with metaphors that combine organic and inorganic parts, theorists such as Rama and González Echevarría, for example, represent the colonial and postcolonial subject as the inorganic result of a struggle against organic elements.

In his 1984 *La ciudad letrada,* Rama developed his now famous definition of the *letrado:* the educated member of an elite in Latin America in part responsible for, and in part the result of, a momentous change in the configuration of Western culture.[8] This change in the configuration of culture had wide implications for its colonial subjects. Drawing from Foucault's *The Order of Things,* Rama argued that the colonial cities in Latin America were built at the periphery of a Western epistemic break between words and things, between signifiers and their signifieds. The break signaled the emergence in Europe of a rationalism that freed itself from the constraints of the material world which simulated an autogenic and autotelic nature. This analogic thought, or Western consciousness, Rama went on to suggest, was both imposed on and willingly interiorized by the educated elites of the seventeenth century in Latin America. The subjugation was reproduced in some shape or form in the eighteenth and nineteenth centuries and is still with us even today. The planning grids or concentric shapes of cities in Latin America are, for Rama, both a symbol of the abstract, rationalistic, and idealistic nature of this subject and a measure of its desire to erase the material conditions of its own possibility of existence. In keeping with this reading of Foucault, Rama calls nineteenth-century cities bathyscaphes: precarious deep-diving chambers surrounded by ever increasing material pressures that threaten to overcome the internal pressures configuring it.[9]

Rama's metaphor and the analysis leading up to it were felicitous, and we find a slightly altered version of his bathyscaphe four years after the publication of *La ciudad letrada,* in an essay by literary critic González Echevarría. In a critical text that focuses on the close link between the novel and scientific discourse, González Echevarría compares the influential nineteenth-century European travel accounts of the New World to the submarine of captain Nemo and extends that metaphor to the Latin American narratives, informed by their struggles with Western science ("Redescubrimiento," 396–397). In that essay, González Echevarría sets that metaphorical capsule against the accidental and catachrestic language of an American literature. Significantly, González Echevarría marks the scientific model with rational attributes and the literary model with corporeal and material ones. He then goes on to describe the modern subject that arises from these struggles between America and Europe as a geometric asymptote: a line that is the limiting position of a tangent to a curve as its point of contact recedes indefinitely along an infinite branch of the curve. In other words, the modern subject in Latin America is a position that draws the limits of an unbridgeable breach between nature and culture, body and reason.

The rational or *letrado* consciousness of Rama's text and the submarine metaphors used to describe it are but one side of the process of subject formation described by Foucault. In his work "What Is an Author," Foucault describes the subject as a "function" of an *inorganic* struggle between forces, discourses, or power. Indeed, Foucault's work is filled with mechanical and inorganic metaphors for the subject, which he describes not only as a "function," but also as a "device" and a "technique." Foucault also, however, describes the process of subject formation organically. In "What Is an Author," Foucault also calls the subject an "interstice," an *organic* network of tensions, between forces, discourses, or power. In other words, Foucault uses the metaphor of the "interstice" not just in its spatial sense of aperture but also in its medical sense as fibrous tissue that is situated within but is not restricted to a particular organ. Drawing from Nietzsche, Foucault argues that one can shed light on the nature of the subject only if one resists the temptation to reduce the subject to either nature or culture. The subject, like the network of discourses configuring it, is both inorganic and organic, function and interstice, process and site, language and matter. Thus Foucauldian metaphors for the Western subject tend to be combinations of organic and inorganic elements. Principal metaphors from his work, such as the panopticon in *Discipline and Punish* and the clinical gaze in *The Birth of the Clinic,* are good examples of this combination. Such metaphors foreground the Western subject as an inorganic architectural object, as a medical technique, and as an all-surveying organic eye.

The metaphors for the modern subject used by Rama and González Echevarría are a discriminating collection drawn from this Foucauldian archive about the subject. Their metaphors lack Foucault's ambivalence between the inorganic and organic aspects of the subject. The metaphor of the technologically wondrous bell jar diving into deep, profound, and powerful waters, the metaphor of the geometric asymptote between nature and culture, resolves the implicit tension in Foucault's metaphors. Foucault's *inorganic* interstices and *organic* functions are turned by these critics into a series of oppositions that perhaps can be reduced to an *inorganic* inside and an *organic* outside. The inside of the inorganic capsule represents the ordered world of culture, solids, and science, while its organic outside represents the catachrestic world of nature, liquids, and literature. Thus the submarine metaphors are part of a long tradition of thought theorizing the struggle in Latin America between a self-identical culture and a dispersed and ungovernable nature. The tradition dates back at least 150 years. In fact, it goes back to the literary work that occupies both González Echevarría and Rama. I am referring to *Facundo: Civilization and Barbarism,* an essay by the Argentinean Juan D. Sarmiento that has received much critical attention since it was written in the mid-nineteenth century.

In a more recent (originally published in 1990 and reprinted in 1998) and fascinating theoretical piece, González Echevarría further develops and significantly complicates the notion of a Western (Latin American and European) subject along Foucauldian lines, but in the end subjectivity continues to be explained in binary oppositions between natural and social orders, between jungle and writing. These oppositions can be reduced again to a primary one between organic and inorganic forces.

In "A Clearing in the Jungle: from Santa Mónica to Macondo," González Echevarría describes the hermeneutics of self in Latin America as a Foucauldian process of subjection.[10] He argues that the subject in Latin America is the result of "strategies of textual engenderment similar to those governing literature, which in turn reflect those of language itself" (this volume, 51). These strategies are violent cuts and wounds suffered by the subject in its struggle with language and in its search for self-knowledge. This search for the origin of subjectivity leads to a secret knowledge, an arcana both perilous and liberating. It leads to an empty space that González Echevarría fills with organic metaphors: an "eschatological abode," "an empty space," "a repository of bones," "a crypt filled with relics." It leads to the Archive: a storehouse of "ideological coagulations" of "embryonic presences" at the center of which and in whose perimeter we find death. The secret of Archive (the origin of subjectivity) is that within its ground zero "death and birth are conjoined as correlative moments of incommunicable plenitude" (this volume, 68). As is suggested by his choice of imagery, the reproductive body is the unacknowledged metaphorical quarry where González Echevarría excavates to find the raw material for his archival theory of language and writing.

González Echevarría argues that despite the constitutive mortality and radical historicity of the temporal and embodied subject, its dying body is eventually united to and becomes identical with transcendental otherness. The subject breaks open the Pandora's box–like container of the Archive and a radical (and I would add liturgical) dispersion occurs: "ghostly figures" of negation are unleashed, the forbidden knowledge of the Other as oneself is gained. The mythic power that lurks behind the temporality of history and writing is released, and transcendence, the phantasm of the mortal self, is achieved. The self as voided presence replaces and becomes identical with the clearing in the jungle, with the Archive. The voided presence of the self, however, also transcends the Archive.

On the one hand, by exhuming the archival crypt, by opening its doors and letting its disassembled bones escape and its coagulated blood run, the subject is again bound to the skin of the Archive. On the other hand, phoenixlike, Christlike, the subject is also born again, "creates itself anew in the image of another text" (this volume, 97). It is this ability to rewrite itself into "another text," to recover from its wounds, the ability to resurrect, to re-create, to transubstantiate itself, that sets the subject apart from the passive and voided presence of the wounding natural Archive.

The opposition suggested by both Rama and González Echevarría—between an organic object/Other that contains and is at the origin of an inorganic subject/self that paradoxically gives birth to itself—is dependent on a critical blind spot. These critics do not seem aware that their oppositions are based on unexamined notions of sexual difference. Members of what can perhaps be described as a different school of critical thinking choose instead not to leave such notions unexamined. Critical thinkers such as Doris Sommer and Sylvia Molloy belong to this group. Also influenced by Foucault's thought, they pay particular attention to his analysis of the history of sexuality. Their work is also inflected by psychoanalysis in such a way that it is more attentive than the work of Rama and González Echevarría to the importance of the bodily drives in the process of subject formation.

A careful reader of Foucault, attuned to the gender-bending possibilities of his theory, Sommer nevertheless returns to the opposition between passive nature and active culture in her highly influential 1991 book *Foundational Fictions*. In that insightful work (excerpted as chapter 5 of this volume), Sommer makes a strong case for the need to understand the modern civic subject in Latin America as the result of Foucauldian strategies ordering the body: "It is possible that the pretty lies of national romance are . . . strategies to contain the racial, regional, economic, and gender conflicts that threatened the development of new Latin American nations" (Sommer *Foundational Fictions*, 29). Unlike Rama and González Echevarría, Sommer argues that the modern subject emerges in Latin America as the result of an interlocking relationship or a marriage of erotics and politics, sexuality and nationalism: "Everyone not only 'has' a nationality and gender in the same imagined way, but these imaginings constitute us as modern subjects" (this volume, 111). Drawing from Foucault's first volume of *The History of Sexuality,* Sommer understands the modern subject as a sexual assemblage, an erotic, sexual invention. Desire, she writes, is the motivating force behind the assembly of the subject. Desire, she concludes, is not raw or natural. Instead, desire is learned, it is "cooked up" by fiction or romance (this volume, 119).

The metaphor of desire (the subject's constitutive force) as an event that has been "cooked" and the implicit definition of the subject as a sexual and desiring being suggest that for Sommer the subject is both organic and yet never really raw. Similarly, Sommer's focus on Eros, desire, and the body as a founding site for what she will go on to call the national subject turns her away from the tradition in Latin America that represents the modern subject as a geometric, rational abstraction forever keeping a distance from its corporeal forms, specifically represented here by the examples of a submarine surrounded and threatened by external organic pressures (see discussion of Rama above) and of a transcendental subject cut away from its organic origins (see discussion of González Echevarría above).

And yet her use of the corporeal is not altogether different from Rama's or González Echevarría's. She also concludes that the subject is allegorical, that its formation is fundamentally rhetorical and violent. For Sommer, the subject is both a palimpsest of pretty lies and also a subject haunted by the guilt of its bad conscience. In other words, it is a subject that suspects an originary self-deceit, an originary exclusion, and a violence done to a body: "a self-serving vanishing act for the originary scene of rape" (Sommer *Foundational Fictions*, 28). These conclusions combine to reinscribe her in the tradition of subject formation from which she is departing. It leads her to accept González Echevarría's description of subjectivity in Latin America as a series of adjustments to a master code or a dominant narrative, of accommodations and impressions of a violent writing process, or as a body wounded unto death and reified into the myth of subjectivity.

In her groundbreaking 1991 book *At Face Value: Autobiographical Writing in Spanish America,* Sylvia Molloy goes further than Sommer in her meditations on the influence of the corporeal drives in the process of subject formation.[11] Inflected by a foundational rift between signified and signifier, Molloy's theory is a diagnosis of a linguistic crisis suffered by the subjects produced in Spanish American autobiographies. For Molloy, subjects exist only in language and only at the moment of reading, enunciating, voicing, or writing (at the moment when the person reads, writes, or says "I.") Molloy's definition of subjectivity, however, is not solely linguistic. Instead, the subject is both a linguistic event and something more than a linguistic event: the subject is a network of signifying practices and psychic material (including memory traces and sexual drives).

A possible comparison emerges between Molloy's notion of autobiography, Freud's notion of screen memory, and Foucault's notion of technique. Like a Freudian screen memory, the autobiographical gesture is a memory trace that hides and reveals subjectivity; it is marked and shaped by the anxiety that results from the impossibility of being as a self-contained and stable subject. Like a Foucauldian technique, the autobiographical gesture is a validating strategy of self-constitution and a repressive strategy of self-defense. Whether validating or repressive, revealing or masking, memory or technique, autobiography always displaces and dramatizes the imminent threat of nonbeing at the core of a temporally unrepeatable and a spatially unique subject.

Thus, bolstering this simultaneously grammatical and corporeal definition of the subject, the reader finds a temporal and spatial presupposition. The subject for Molloy is as inherently transitory in time as it is unique in space. It exists momentarily in a present that is always receding and is always-already past. It similarly occupies a space that cannot be simultaneously occupied by an Other. Indeed, I would argue that the time and space of the subject according to Molloy are the result of a primal scene of prohibition. Subjectivity is subjection to a divine prohibition or law. The subject is literally and metaphorically faced with the divine Law of the Father. The Father's fundamental Law rules against the transcendence in life of the mortal coil; He rules against eating the fruit from the Tree of Knowledge. Immortality, eternity, resurrection, and transubstantiation are the exclusive provinces of the divine. Unrepeatable time and unique space are the prison of the subject.

If Molloy's subject constitutes itself within its assigned province, in doing so, however, the subject also appropriates and transforms the uniqueness and specificity that imprisons it. For Molloy, the process of writing the self in autobiography becomes a sacrilegious epiphany or transubstantiation. Modeled after Christ's exclusive and miraculous transubstantiation of body and blood into the sacred host of ritual, the subject is the all-too-human and everyday translation of bodily drives into language. Subjectivity for Molloy is the repetition of a human and transgressive act first performed as a prohibition by the paternal divinity.

Molloy gives us a convincing example of this model for subjectivity when discussing the ineffectiveness of parental censorship on Victoria Ocampo, an Argentinean writer. Her father (Ocampo writes in her autobiography) used to show early Max Linder films at home. But she adds that during love scenes her mother would censor the images by planting herself before the projector. In her essay, Molloy emphasizes the significance of this gesture of prohibition:

> The mother's purpose is clearly to censor all intimations of sexuality, in their graphic, physical representation. But in so doing she also obscures the words (those silent movie subtitles the viewer reads as if he were hearing them being

said) and deletes the meaning of the story. The intercepting gesture inadvertently merges body and reading, the two main components of Ocampo's autobiographical writing. (this volume, 217)

The moment is emblematic of the way Molloy conceives of self-constitution. In a Foucauldian move, Molloy transforms the prohibition into a model for the self. Like her mother, Ocampo also merges body and reading in her autobiography. Molloy astutely reminds the reader that throughout her autobiography Ocampo repeatedly intermingles *Lo leído* (literary experience) and *Lo vivido* (lived experience). But the foundational role played by prohibition in self-constitution is not the only Foucauldian point of reference for Molloy. She also compares Ocampo's autobiography to the method of self-expression described by Foucault as the transformation of what is seen or heard into strength and blood (this volume, 227). She quotes from Foucault's essay on writing the self to emphasize his overall point: that the references to the body in what Foucault calls self-writing are neither merely metaphorical nor strictly corporeal.

Instead, Molloy reads Victoria Ocampo's references to the body in her autobiography "as signifying something more complex—something that surely includes the concretely physical but goes beyond it, something more like a presence (the way one speaks of a presence on stage) that society would have her repress and for which her body is the most visible sign" (this volume, 224). Presence, for Molloy, is an amplification of the visible. It is a corporeal excess that screens and hides. But presence is also the representation of the invisible. It is the return of the repressed. The body is then the most visible sign of this presence, but it is not its only sign. Reading and writing texts, speaking and listening to voice, are other signs or simulacra for presence. For Molloy, subjectivity amounts to the vicissitudes suffered in the attempt to signify and appropriate presence. Presence is like the Foucauldian *bios*: it is the prepersonal flux of life.

Like Sommer, then, Molloy also describes the origin of the process of subjectivity as an act of subjection, as an originary exclusion and a violence done to a body constituted of forces in flux. Like Sommer, Molloy understands subjectivity as a process that produces a certain desire. In order to be a speaking subject, one behaves like a cruel divinity and represses the unspeakable presence, one inserts the self into the space and time of the person, one imprisons oneself in one's mortal coil. In other words, the subject is substance (understood here as presence) transformed into owned property: substance become one's language or voice. The process of appropriating or incorporating substance, however, also leads inevitably to the loss of the excess that makes presence distinct. That loss, concludes Molloy, creates in the subjected self a want that is never satisfied (this volume, 229). The want or the lack we experience in our core, Molloy suggests, is the price we pay for making ourselves into subjects.

While this definition of subjectivity echoes Foucault's challenge to the Cartesian notion of the subject, it also departs from the Foucauldian suggestion that the subject can occupy a space outside the Hegelian struggle for mastery. Instead, Molloy identifies signification or representation with appropriation. Indeed, Molloy quotes Foucault to exemplify a fundamental process of appropriation and consumption on which depends the production of a subject. Thus, despite her emphasis on excess, at work in Molloy's text is a narcissistic economy of scarcity. As in the *hypomnemata*,[12] presence can be produced or translated only through the appropriation and transformation of what is read and heard into the self. Molloy emphasizes that the subject is altered by this appropriation, but clearly it is not altered to the extent that it stops struggling to appropriate, to make the other into the same, to subject the self through a violent process. The subject described by Molloy does not become altered to the extent that it gives itself over to alterity in the generous gesture described by Foucault in his commentary on correspondence (Foucault *Ethics*, 213).

A close analysis of the critical appropriations of Foucault by Rama, González Echevarría, Sommer, and Molloy has shown that despite their differences, they all resolve the paradoxes of Foucault's theory of subjectivity and shy away from his provocative definition of the process of subjectivity as an enhancement of force. If Rama and González Echevarría resolve the tension in Foucault between his organic and inorganic metaphors for the subject and return to the disembodied Cartesian subject, Sommer and Molloy resolve the tension between self-mastery and self-offering and return to the Hegelian master/slave dialectic. Both versions of subjectivity seem to remain within what Krzysztof Ziarek has called its modern and technological mode of emergence: a notion of subject formation permeated by forces or power characterized by a will to dominate, know, or master. This leads to the question of the particular appropriations of Foucault's theories on subjectivity.

Perhaps the answer to this question can be divided into two parts. As pertains to Rama and González Echevarría, what seems to be at stake in their appropriation of discursive analysis is self-mastery—in their repeated construction of the divide between feminine and masculine, nature and culture, self and other. Self-mastery is achieved through the separation of consciousness from its body and eternal life from material death. It predetermines the subject as an abstractly ordered and disembodied event (an event that sometimes takes the form of an inside, made of a solid, scientific, consciousness, while at other times it takes the form of a disseminating literary force liberated from a constricting inside). Self-mastery is what produces Rama's precarious *letrado* and González Echevarría's threatened geometric subject. The struggle for self-mastery and domination is also what overdetermines the search for self-knowledge and the Pandora's box–like opening of the Archive famously described by González Echevarría.

Self-mastery and self-domination depend on the abjection of a natural and organic body, of Pandora's body and metaphorical "box." The body—whether it is described as an interior natural space or an external organic force—opposes the possibility of a consciousness based on domination. A subject based on mastery must imagine itself to be qualitatively different from a material body. Because the body always represents a potential "fall" from an ideal and infallible consciousness, bodies threaten authority with their materiality. The master's opposition to the body, then, is not due to the threat of a quality of the body, but to the threat of difference that puts into question the very concepts of quality and subject. Indeed, a defense from the corrosive body is already embedded in the master's opposition to it. In other words, the master's opposition to the body is essentializing. The opposition to the body presupposes a disembodied subject. But by the same token, the master's opposition to the body paradoxically puts into question the very ability to represent or describe consciousness. For the master subject, the body stands for the very inability to presuppose or to represent subjectivity.

The works of González Echevarría and Rama are fateful twentieth-century reinscriptions of a master subject that is also present in the critical discourses of the nineteenth century, in its divides between nature and culture, organic and inorganic, object and subject, language and reality, masculine and feminine. As such, they fall into similar quandaries that affected the work of nineteenth-century writers from Latin America. Despite its intentions, the master subject has a bad conscience. It hides in its very center the suspicion of a fatefully organic event, an original wound, a carving-out, which the master turns into an inorganic form, a machine, a geometric, allegorical, or mythical figure.[13] The inorganic nature of the master subject is, then, the result of a double move. On the one hand, the master subject emerges in opposition to this displaced organic act. On the other hand, the same subject emerges as the result of the insistent suspicion that at its origins there is a deadly violence inflicted on its own body. This double move leads to a master subject that is always the encasement for its missing body.

Matters stand somewhat differently in the case of Sommer and Molloy. These critics do not abstract the subject from its corporeal encasement. Instead their meditations on subjectivity depart from an explicit consideration of forces (or drives) that find their source in the body even if they are not limited to the body: desire in Sommer and presence in Molloy. And yet the metaphors they use to describe the process of subject formation are just as violent as those used by Rama and González Echevarría: a wounded and violated self in the case of Sommer, an appropriating and devouring self in the case of Molloy. This violence, I argue, leads them back to the Hegelian master/slave dialectic that I suspect Sommer and Molloy are trying to escape.

Why do these critics choose not to appropriate Foucault's emphasis on inter-subjectivity that not only makes the subject into an object but makes the process of subjection into a radical offering of the self? What is at stake in their description of the process of subject formation?

The defense of the economy of scarcity that drives the Freudian model of primary narcissism is what is at stake. The belief in a notion of the subject as constituted of calculable units as radically scarce as unrepeatable time and unique space seems to trap these critics, too, within the mode of modern technological subjectivity that Foucault and Freud both diagnose and seek to escape.

Other notions of subject formation are, however, possible. Constitutive knowledge about the subject need not be linked to the essential forms of cruelty, as Foucault believed (*Mental Illness,* 73). The fact that such master subjects are privileged in the critical theory of Latin America should give us pause. The tendency of the Foucauldian model to reproduce an authorial model of subject formation should also give us pause. Consider, for example, the models and metaphors based on an economy of exclusion developed by Judith Butler and Nikolas Rose.[14] But subjectivity need not be reduced to this model. Foucault's own focus on intersubjectivity, and recent attempts (like those of Kelly Oliver and Krzysztof Ziarek) to introduce the notions of an ethical subjectivity, and of subjectivity as a power to be, represent philosophical alternatives to the master's model of subjectivity.

In Latin America, we can look to a tradition of works that engages with the pugilistic premises of the master's model of subjectivity. Novelists such as Elena Garro, Julia Álvarez, and Irene Vilar propose an alternative version of subject formation in their work, a version that also leaves behind the notion of a subject mastering a trauma that is found at its very origins, a version of subjectivity that makes the given separation from a maternal body into a problem. These women's writing locates that abjected body deep within the self. However, they are also attempts to work through or to name and to give voice to the unnamable loss of what Kristeva has called the Thing. To do so, I would argue, is also to participate in the hopeful work of mourning.

The melancholy novel is a subject which merits more considered attention than I can give within the limits of this essay and greater consideration than it has received to date. Suffice it to say for now that its turn away from relations of the self to itself despite its conception of subjectivity as constitutively melancholic inserts this novel into a nexus of relations and situations that reopen the promising space foreclosed by a dominating trend in critical theory. Unlike Rama, González Echevarría, Sommer, and Molloy, the novelists of the melancholy novel shift away from self-mastery to face instead the impossible but nevertheless necessary task of remembering the wounded bodies left in the wake of the unrelenting pursuit of self-mastery.

NOTES

This essay was first published in the *Revista de Estudios Hispánicos*. I would like to thank Kelly Oliver, Elzbieta Sklodowska, and Fred Evans for their invaluable help with this essay.

1. For a convincing narrative of the differences between Foucault's and Freud's account of subjectivity, see Patrick Hutton, "Foucault, Freud, and the Technologies of the Self."

2. I owe many of my insights into Foucault's notion of force as a modality of biopower to Krzysztof Ziarek's essay "Powers to Be." For a similar interpretation of the concept of excess or enhancement of force in Foucault, see Deleuze *Foucault.*

3. Foucault *Mental Illness,* 45, 56.

4. James Miller writes that during the early eighties: "friendship became one of [Foucault's] explicit concerns. On more than one occasion, in interviews and composed texts, he returned to the theoretical possibility that two people, in spite of differences in age, status, and calling, might nevertheless be able to bridge the gaps between them through a reinvented "art" of friendship. By speaking frankly with someone who was neither a sycophant nor a coward, neither a lover nor a student, one might expand the reach of one's feelings, and test the value of one's own opinions, in the process confiding a part of which one was to the care of another." James Miller, 328.

5. In his fascinating essay on the debt owed by Foucault to Heidegger in his later reflections on the care of the self and the use of pleasure, Krzysztof Ziarek theorizes this mysterious self-offering or objectification of the soul in terms that are not only reminiscent of Heidegger's theory of aesthetics but also of Freud's theory of the drives. Most important for the purposes of this essay is Ziarek's emphasis on the relations of forces that are internal to, but nevertheless are in excess of, what Foucault calls biopower, or the technological modality of the emergence of being. Like Freud, Foucault calls this excess life-force. Like Heidegger, Foucault also calls this excess an aesthetics of existence.

6. James Miller, 347.

7. Examples of these authors and of their insights on modern subjectivity in Latin America can be found in chapters 1, 3, 5, and 12 of this volume. These examples are discussed in this essay in the following order: Rama's "The Ordered City," González Echevarría's "A Clearing in the Jungle," Sommer's "Love and Country," and Molloy's "The Theatrics of Reading."

8. See chapter 1 of this volume.

9. As Fernand Braudel notes in his remarkable book, *Civilisation matérielle,* when the rules of the world economy are designed: "capitalism and the market economy coexist, they are interrelated but they never come together as one" in such a way that these unreal cities, detached from the needs of the environment, indeed true bathyscaphes, if not extraterrestrial at least intercontinental in character, will benefit from preexistent indigenous networks." The translation is mine. Rama *La ciudad letrada*, 16.

10. See chapter 3 of this volume.

11. See chapter 12 of this volume.

12. The *hypomnemata* were account books, public registers, or individual notebooks that served as memory aids and which Foucault contrasts with the correspondence between the Stoics. The *hypomnemata* emphasize writing as self-discipline rather than as the generous exchange of energy of correspondence.

13. For a comprehensive development of this idea, see my *Subjects of Crisis,* chap. 5.

14. For a persuasive critique of Butler's model, see Kelly Oliver's "What Is Transformative about the Performative?" As regards an European reader of Foucault such as Nikolas Rose, he will flesh out Foucault's insights into subjectivity and will call its process an invagination, engendering the process in a way that is not altogether different from that of the critics that occupy us here.

10

Subjectivity and Olavide's Sentimental Novels

FERNANDO UNZUETA

W hether he is considered an *afrancesado* (Defournaux), a Spanish *ilustrado* (Perdices Blas), or a colonial Latin American author (Sánchez, Núñez, Bendezú), the writings and reform efforts of the Peruvian-born Pablo de Olavide (1725–1803) can be framed profitably within Foucault's conceptualizations about modern subjectivity and subject formation.

Deploying largely a discursive perspective, Foucault's varied, suggestive, and often polemical texts touch on many topics but return to a handful of central issues, most notably truth, power/knowledge, and the self. His "late" writings gradually focused on the last topic. In a 1982 essay, two years before his untimely death, he stated: "the goal of my work during the last twenty years . . .

has been to create a history of the different modes by which, in our culture, human beings are made subjects" ("Subject and Power," 777). This is not to say that he ignored the other issues. On the contrary, the processes by which subjects are constituted for Foucault always take place within specific discursive formations, regimes of truth and power/knowledge relations. Nevertheless, for expository reasons perhaps, he noted that his work "has dealt with three modes of objectification which transform human beings into subjects." In the first modality, human beings are objectivized by being the subject of a body of knowledge that pretends to be scientific. In the second, individuals are objectivized by the "dividing practices" that separate the subject from him/herself or others. Finally, Foucault's last studies considered "the way a human being turns himself into a subject" ("Subject and Power," 777–778).

These three modes of objectification have discourse, the body, and the self, respectively, as their main foci for the articulation of subjectivities. Rabinow argues for a significant difference between the first two modalities for constituting subjects, and the last, calling it "subjectification." While the other modes imply forms of classification and techniques of domination constraining subjects largely to a passive position, under the third, "the person initiates an active self-formation" (Rabinow, 11). The dichotomies between passive and active, domination and agency, "subjection" and "subjectification," however, run counter to Foucault's own formulations: "There are two meanings of the word 'subject': subject to someone else by control and dependence; and tied to his own identity by a conscience or self-knowledge. Both meanings suggest a form of power which subjugates and makes subject to" ("Subject and Power," 781). Acknowledging a shift toward self-constitution in his thinking, it is also safe to say that both agency and power are present throughout Foucault's work. Human agency, particularly in terms of resistance, always challenges strategies of power and objectifying forces targeting individuals and their bodies.[1] Unlike Paul Smith, for instance, Foucault considers both agency and resistance (to power) as integral aspects of the notion of the subject. Thus, even in Foucault's late, care-of-the-self studies, processes of self-subjectification are necessarily linked to regimes of power/knowledge.[2]

Thus, keeping in mind Rabinow's warning "not to draw too sharp a line" between these different modalities because they "can be effectively combined, although they are analytically distinguishable" (11), I will suggest that some of Olavide's writings can be seen as participating in the three modes of subject formation outlined. His education and agricultural reform proposals, for instance, conceive new subjects of knowledge and production. His colonization project, on the other hand, and his reform-oriented work to rid Seville of vagrants by distinguishing between the "true and fake poor" (*pobres verdaderos y pobres falsos o fingidos*) (Perdices, 147, 516) deal mostly with the administration of bodies:

their relocation, classification, control, and discipline.[3] Finally, I will argue that Olavide's late writings, and his *novelas morales* in particular, are more closely related to what Foucault would call "technologies of the self."[4]

Three decades ago, Núñez "discovered" six sentimental novels by Olavide and republished them as *Obras narrativas desconocidas* in 1971. These works had been printed in New York (for reasons not well known) in 1828 but remained unstudied, even by such thorough Olavide scholars as Defournaux. As Alonso Seoane has shown, however, they were only some of the more than twenty *novel-las* Olavide began to publish in Spain in 1800 under the general title *Lecturas útiles y entretenidas,* using the pseudonym Atanasio de Céspedes y Monroy (Alonso Seoane "Adaptador"). This critic has also confirmed what many had long suspected (see Sánchez, 583): most of these works, if not all, are not "original" but rather translations of French texts, with different degrees of "adaptation" to a Hispanic cultural and literary context.

Further complicating matters, concurrent with Alonso Seoane's ongoing research, Núñez found and published a seventh work, *Teresa o el terremoto de Lima* (Olavide *Obras selectas,* 193–216). This "Peruvian novel" is based on "the author's personal experiences [of the 1746 earthquake] in his native country." According to Núñez, it proves Olavide's "authorship" *(autoría)* of the others, "even supposing they are adaptations or imitations of narratives by foreign authors" ("Una novela," 128). Such transliterations, it should be noted, were well within the Enlightenment literary cultural tradition. Furthermore, as a type of creative *imitatio,* it produced "palimpsests" that allowed the author to express "everything he wanted between the lines" (Bendezú, 18–19). The final result, Edmundo Bendezú Aibar suggests, is symptomatic of Peru's colonial condition (21–22), and makes Olavide the founder of the Peruvian novel and of a "subversive colonial literature" (29).

ETHICS AND SUBJECTIFICATION

Olavide's best-known work is his lengthy (four volumes and more than a thousand pages) epistolary novel *El evangelio en triunfo o historia de un filósofo desengañado* (1797–1798), a pious Christian apologia that was widely published, edited (mostly in abbreviated form), and translated well into the middle of the nineteenth century (see Goic, 394–395; Dufour, 13; and Valle "Estructura," 149). In the last letters of the philosopher-narrator, his life and conversion are presented as *exempla* for the moral education of others (Goic, 396). This confessional and didactic core of *El evangelio* is clearly present in the novels as well, which were written around the same time and published shortly after.[5] As their prologues note, they are *novelas ejemplares,* intended to "teach" an "example" or a "lesson" to the readers and urging them to "reflect" and to "learn" from them, particularly when it comes to following virtuous models and rejecting all vices.[6]

According to Goic, the themes of the novels are "ideologically related [to those in *Evangelio*], but strictly secular" (396). At first there seems to be a close parallel between, on the one hand, *El evangelio* and Saint Augustine's *Confessions,* in which a life is shown as "an *exemplum* of the glory of God and the workings of His spirit" (Gutman, 102), and, on the other, Olavide's novels and Rousseau's *Confessions,* where the purpose is "secular, not religious" (Gutman, 103). Whereas the religious work's ultimate goals are to praise the Lord and to save souls, Rousseau provides a road map for the creation of the modern self. As Gutman puts it, his *Confessions* elaborate a Foucauldian technology of the self, a mechanism to turn "man into a subject (an individuated self and a defined personage in the social order)" (103).

The analogy is nevertheless problematic. First, Olavide's *El evangelio en triunfo,* besides its Christian message, also includes an enlightened reform program (see Dufour), one clearly engaged in the modern processes of subjectification.[7] More specifically, the program articulates what Foucault calls the "political technologies of individuals" or the work of "police," understood as the techniques and practices of a new rationality in the late eighteenth century: "When people spoke about police at this moment, they spoke about the specific techniques by which a government in the framework of the state was able to govern people as individuals significantly useful to the world" ("Political," 154). As Foucault further adds, "life is the project of the police" (153); "the purpose of the police is . . . taking care of individuals living in society" (158). These are almost the same words Dufour uses to describe Olavide's "Enlightened, even revolutionary," reform program. Through a private Association for the Public Good (*Junta del Bien Público),* Olavide sought to regulate and improve "every aspect of the organization of social life" (Dufour, 17).[8] Thus the last five letters of *El evangelio* are not far removed from the discourses engaged in the constitution of modern subjects. Like the novels, they center both on the civic (public) education of individuals, and the policing of their (private) intimacy (see Olavide's *cartas*).

On the other hand, the novels may not as secular as Goic suggests. They certainly have personal and civic virtue at their core, even though this virtue remains connected to Christian morality. In Althusserian terms, religion still seems to be the most important Ideological Apparatus of State (ISA); as such, it plays a key role in the ideological interpellation of individuals as subjects (170–177).[9] In Olavide's novels, religion and religious authority remain at the core of their subjects, but so are the more secular notions of (social) sympathy, beneficence, and virtue. Consequently, the workings of other ISAs, such as family and an increasingly modern education system (as well as more informal means of education), are also highlighted.

As a way to explore the workings of virtue and some of the mechanisms of subjectification, I will consider the early education of one of the protagonists of *Paulina*, the homonymous orphan:

> Doña Clara was not able to provide her with more than a simple education; but she had accustomed her to virtue, and to the fear and love of God, to appreciate honesty, to consider honor as the supreme law, and one's conscience as the most respectable sovereign. . . . The good and innocent Paulina did not know that it was possible to be bad; in her heart's judgment, everyone was good, and she had figured that men were born only to serve God, to love and help each other. (*Paulina*, 86–87)

The potentially secular values of virtue, honesty, honor, and even conscience seem at first subservient to the service, love, and fear of God. The novel's central character, however, also shares a "secularized view of virtue," one with "reason and natural law" at its source. More than simply following theological virtues (faith, hope, and charity) with God as their object or the partially Christianized cardinal virtues (prudence, justice, fortitude, and temperance), Paulina thinks and acts appropriately simply for the goodness of the acts or thoughts and because doing so comes to her naturally. Finally, the end of the passage also hints at another secularizing tendency of the Enlightenment, a harmonious shift from individual to social morality and to civic virtue in particular.[10]

More importantly, the vocabulary used above by Olavide points to how subjects (both as individuals and social beings) are formed through the internalization of values and practices. Ideological constructs, discourses, and actions become a part of one's self, as a matter of a habit (*acostumbrado*) or a liking (*amar, estimar*), or because of fear (*temor*) or respect for the highest ordering or subjugating principles (*ley suprema, soberano*). According to Foucault, technologies of the self imply "certain modes of training and modification of individuals," providing them with certain "skills" and "attitudes." These technologies "permit individuals to effect by their own means or with the help of others a certain number of operations on their own bodies and souls, thoughts, conduct, and way of being, so as to transform themselves in order to attain a certain state of happiness, purity, wisdom, perfection or immortality" ("Technologies," 18). Olavide's novels, I suggest, provide a mode of subjectification close both to Foucault's concept of technologies of the self and to his interpretation of the Christian pastoral "process of confession and guidance" (*History of Sexuality* (b), 19).

It is also worth noting that Paulina, above, in spite of her "innocence" and lack of "worldly experiences" (*Paulina*, 87), has already been subjected, by her "simple education," or because there is no before or outside ideology (Althusser) or power (Foucault).[11] As Althusser summarily puts it: "individuals are always-already subjects" (176). In principle, this statement does not deny the possibility of change or, I would argue, the notion that subjects are always in a process of transformation. In Olavide's novels, however, there is an effort to sustain the myth of the unitary, autonomous, and unchanging subject. They articulate morality plays in which Rousseauistic—good-nature—characters are corrupted, or at least tempted, by society and, to a lesser extent, by their passions. Almost uniformly, these characters are rescued by the interpellation of the highest ethical standards (Christian and secular) and regain their integrity as virtuous subjects.

The protagonist of *Marcelo o los peligros de la corte* follows this pattern closely:

> Marcelo, even though he already was a father and a husband, still preserved the candor and purity of an innocent age. The heavens had endowed him with an invariable liking for everything that is solid, true and honest; and his upbringing and education had taught him to fulfill all of his obligations with precision, to contain his desires, and to temper his pleasures. His naturally fair spirit and his generous and kind heart made him consistently practice all types of virtues. (*Obras narrativas*, 129)

Like Paulina, Marcelo has maintained a primal "innocence." Nevertheless, he is subjected by his tastes, habits, and education. The internalization of these elements makes him act in certain ways, whether this leads to carrying out his "duties" or practicing his "virtues." The passage also alludes to the disciplinary nature of his training: he has to "contain his desires" and "temper his pleasures." Despite his moral rectitude, Marcelo is lured and corrupted by the pleasures of city life. He sins and demeans himself at the court, but he eventually repents and amends his family life, becoming an exemplary citizen: "This experience affirmed his virtue, and from then on he was once again a good husband, excellent father, good citizen, and a good-natured man (*hombre de bien*) in everyone's eyes" (169). Civic virtue once again seems to be one of the key goals of all personal transformations.

PASTORAL SUBJECTS AND CONFESSIONAL NARRATIVE

The pastoral subjects represented by Olavide share several traditional values: a natural goodness that is reinforced by religious and secular morality, and cultivated through education, broadly understood; living in a peaceful and simple country setting or, at least, away from the "corruption" of the city and the court; the utmost respect for authority, religious, political, and, more visibly, paternal; finally, an unquestioning understanding, if not a promotion, of a hierarchical society that uses caste and gender as its two basic ordering principles.

I use the term "pastoral subjects" both to refer to representations lodged in an ideal, bucolic setting, but more importantly, to relate them to Foucault's description of the "incitement to discourse" present in the Counter-Reformation's "confessions of the flesh" (*History of Sexuality* (b), 19):

> The Christian pastoral prescribed as a fundamental duty the task of passing everything having to do with sex through the endless mill of speech. The forbidding of certain words, the decency of expressions, all the censorings of vocabulary, might well have been only secondary devices compared to the great subjugation: ways of rendering it morally acceptable and technically useful. (*History of Sexuality* (b), 21)

I am not suggesting that Olavide's novels are (primarily) about sex. On the contrary, their moral charge and prudish and censored nature seem to point in the opposite direction. As Foucault notes, however, under a pastoral "process of confession and guidance," there was a tendency "to make the flesh into the root of all evil, shifting the most important moment of transgression from the act itself to the stirrings—so difficult to perceive and formulate—of desire. . . . Discourse, therefore, had to trace the meeting line of the body and the soul, following all its meanderings" (*History of Sexuality* (b), 19–20).

From this perspective, the novels are not only about virtue and morality but, precisely, about the denial of the flesh (and to that extent, about—repressed—sex). A character's virtue is defined, to a large extent, by how well most aspects associated with the body, bodily pleasures, and the senses are denied. In Olavide's words, a virtuous subject is one able "to contain his desires, and to temper his pleasures." Thus, in order to render sex "morally acceptable and technically useful," the novels turn to verbalize conflicts arising at the "meeting line of the body and the soul" and to explore the "stirrings of desire." The novels basically propose the self-control of the body, passions, and desires as a technique for edifying the soul (*Paulina* 112, 121). And the same vocabulary of "desire," "pleasure," and "seduction" is used when referring to love or other material (bodily) enticements that tend to corrupt reason and, ultimately, the soul (32).

The confessional dimension of the novels is evident when Marcelo repents, expresses his remorse and asks for forgiveness for his faults (166–67), but is more clearly articulated in *El Incógnito o el fruto de la ambición*, the longest and more complex of the novels in narrative terms (Goic, 397; see also Valle, "Duplicación"). In the opening level of a framed narrative, Mauricio, a young nobleman, has carriage problems on his way to Paris, where his father sends him to see the world and meet people as a way to better his education (*perfeccionar su educación*). He encounters a "venerable" old man sighing with grief in a cemetery, asks him about the cause of his sorrows, and volunteers to help him "feel his pain" if he would share his concerns (*El Incógnito,* 3). The unnamed man, *el Incógnito,* offers him hospitality for the night and agrees to tell his "sorry story" for two explicit reasons: he perceives his interlocutor has a "sensitive heart," and he wants to show him "good examples" (4). While it may help to communicate the reasons for his grief to a kindhearted person, he knows this action will reopen his wounds. In a sense, recounting the events seem to be part of the Incógnito's penance. In any case, the confessional motive is also present when he agrees to tell about his misfortunes and his crimes (6): "I now see all the horror of my actions. . . . I wanted to satisfy my ambition at the expense of all crimes" (74). The core of the novel consists of his detailed retrospective narration of how he came to betray his family and friends when he tried to marry his daughter to a wealthy nobleman (thus the charge of "ambition") instead of his close friend's virtuous son, of more modest means, to whom she had been promised at an earlier stage and whom his daughter loved deeply.[12]

In Rousseau's *Confessions,* "the self is the subject of the discourse. His aim is not to glorify God but to provide the truth about himself by revealing himself *in all his completeness* to the gaze of the reader. . . . Time and again, Rousseau refers to this triumvirate of compunction, external gaze and the need for complete disclosure" (Gutman, 104, 106). Olavide's novel shares, to a large extent, these basic elements of the writing of the self of the "modern secular confessional."[13] Before beginning his narrative, the *Incógnito* warns his interlocutor: "my sorry story will destroy your heart, and you may conceive the most hateful loathing for me; but no, be sorry for me instead: I am very unhappy: I was a father, and now I am no more than the most miserable of all men" (5). The emotional narrative striptease of the old man constitutes his (divided) self. But it can be argued that his self is not the main subject of his discourse. His sins, his repentance, and even his sharing the story with others are equally important. While the events he recounts are part of who he is, his self is the focus of the story only in the frame of the novel (and in some recurring apostrophes to his interlocutor). The novel, after all, is conceived as an *exemplum* (*novela ejemplar,* according to the prologue [3]); as such, its immediate target is the narratee, Mauricio, and the hope he learns from the *Incógnito's* misfortunes (24, 84). More broadly, the subject of the discourse is anyone like Mauricio, who possesses a *corazón sensible* (4, 5, 84) and is open to bettering his (moral and sentimental) education (3).

In a sense, Olavide's novels, unlike Rousseau's *Confessions,* are not primarily concerned with the "complete" representation of *one* self. Not even *El Incógnito,* the longest of them and the one with the clearest confessional structure, fully explores the individuated nature of a self. They are, however, totally committed to the business of constituting subjects and they pay particular attention to the role of these subjects in a community. In addition to appealing to the readers' moral sensibilities, the novels provide models of behavior internally. That is, some characters, witnesses to the same exemplary metanarratives as the audience, respond exactly in the same terms Olavide proposes for the readers of his texts. Mauricio, therefore, with his "generous soul," his predisposition toward "all sorts of virtues" (5), and his willingness to learn and help his fellow humans, is the ideal reader figured by Olavide. Several other characters also respond with a helping hand and a compassionate soul when faced with situations or narratives of suffering.[14] Not only do they offer to feel the pain of those in anguish, like Mauricio, but more importantly, they are moved to improve the circumstances and even the material conditions affecting the less fortunate. Yet again the social dimension of individual virtue is privileged.

CHALLENGING THE (AUTONOMOUS) SUBJECT

As I have suggested throughout this essay, Olavide's novels attempt to portray autonomous subjects that are unitary and unchanging. These subjects have a seemingly solid place and role to play in a basically fixed social order. Their "external" appearances are supposed to be in harmony with their "interiors" and their education (see *Paulina*, 91, 109). Likewise, they are expected to remain true to themselves, even when faced with adversity or with different circumstances. Rufina, for example, when her father breaks her original engagement, tells her lover: "I will always be your Rufina. I am the one you have always seen" (*El Incógnito*, 49). Similarly, when Paulina's reputation is questioned, she affirms: "I am the same person I was, and no one can criticize me for anything" (*Paulina*, 103). Indeed, Olavide's subjects are always confronted with moral and sometimes social conflicts, which they use to improve themselves through means of self-control and the practice of personal and civic values. Those characters who "fall" after facing troubling experiences normally reestablish their lost innocence and virtuous selves through moral repentance and, when possible, the social undoing of bad deeds.

   At the same time, I will continue to argue that these subjects' autonomy is relative, at best, and that their apparent unity is not only challenged but also inherently marked by internal contradictions. I already mentioned that subjects, besides being agents of their own destiny (within certain limitations), are always-already subject to (or are subjected by) someone or something else. In Olavide's novels, the various authorities, Christian values, personal and social ethics, the social order, and the processes of formal and informal education are among the most obvious subjecting elements. The repeated advice to submit to God's or to a father's will, for instance, or a student's obedience to his or her teacher, like discipline, produce "practised, 'docile' bodies."[15]

   Olavide's *sentimental* novels are among the first to introduce emotional depth to the representation of characters in Spanish and Latin American literary tradi-

tions. Feelings and emotive life, considered characteristic of modern individuality (see Gutman, 100–101), can also play a subjecting role for the protagonists,
particularly when the subject has to discipline his or her emotions, or when passion takes hold of a lover (*El Incógnito,* 41; *Paulina,* 95). But the life of the heart
can be liberating as well. Paulina's feelings are a case in point. Under the moral
imperative of the novels, or the pastoral requirement to render sex "morally
acceptable," her love at first has to be restrained by reason (*Paulina,* 97).
Eventually, however, she is able to declare her passion in a way that allows her
to be at peace with herself and the world (119).

As far as the social order is concerned, Paulina's love for the Marquis is
vetoed by a hierarchical society where individuals are supposed to remain in
their respective "spheres" (*Paulina,* 101). Even the impoverished Marquis is
"enslaved" by the generosity of a wealthy relative (121). Only when he becomes
rich himself can he dispose of his feelings as he wishes: "now that God has made
me a rich man, I can follow the inspirations of my heart" (126). In the last
analysis, both the happy ending of a cross-class marriage in *Paulina* and, more
broadly, the emphasis the novels place on education and self-improvement
undermine their efforts to maintain a society organized by caste.[16]

In these novels it is also evident that a subjects' position depends to a large
extent on his or her situation or place in society, whether in terms of "reputation," ability to act, or how a self is defined by or in relation to the gaze and positions of others. As I noted before, there is an effort to preserve social hierarchies
and to reinforce the respect for authority. In *El Incógnito,* for instance, when
"the law of the father" is first questioned, it is supported by a wise and respected
priest *(venerable eclesiástico),* even though the father is clearly acting in pursuit
of his ambition (34–36). Nevertheless, Albano, against his own father's call for
resignation, voices his strong opposition to an unjust decision based on "reason"
and the principles of natural law, the foundations of secular virtue (Coughlin,
86). Whereas the questioning of authority ends up being muted by the novel's
resolution, as Sinfield notes: "Readers do not have to respect closures. . . . We
can insist on our sense that the middle of such a text arouses expectations that
exceed the closure" (248). Thus Olavide opens the possibilities for the emancipation of subjects from unjust authority.

Finally, the novels also hint at the modern sense of a subject's separation from
the world and society, and even a division from his or her own self: "The first, and
essential, move in the constitution of the self is division" (Gutman, 107). In spite
of Olavide's efforts to highlight the importance of social sympathy and civic virtue
as ways to provide a sense of community, a subject's position within a social order
often produces alienating effects. Paulina, for instance, carefully nuances a previous affirmation of her unchanging character in a letter to the Marquis: "I have not
changed, I am the same person; but I have learned what I ignored, and I do not

fear you but fear myself. I am young, I owe you everything I am, and I love you" (*Paulina*, 119). While ignorance may be bliss, in this context knowledge implies an awareness and an acceptance of the role of the others in the constitution of the self (through reputation or otherwise) and of a social hierarchy that divides. The first part of the statement (*no me he mudado, yo soy la misma*) is totally undermined by the rest. Both situating (or relocating) the self in a (newly "learned") social order, and the also-new and clear awareness of her feelings (*te amo*) necessarily change the subject. This is so even to the point that it creates a division and a contradiction within the subject herself (*me temo a mí misma*).[17]

A divided self can nevertheless act as an agent and even as an agent of change. Paulina, once again, acknowledges social limitations and ultimately rejects them (*Paulina*, 107, 124), and so does the Marquis (126). Thus, while the subjecting effects of sentimental and particularly romantic love are widely recognized, the same feelings can also be empowering. Both Paulina and the Marquis, for instance, are able to choose for themselves and, at least in this instance, to break with tradition by contesting restrictive social codes with their actions.

Olavide's novels engage in the complex processes of subjectification and mediate between individuals and society, both within the text and, potentially, outside. More concretely, they provide models and technologies for the articulation of a subject's position within his or her circumstances. As part of a moralistic project, they privilege certain positions—those of the virtuous individual—as the most coherent response to those circumstances and ideological underpinnings. Nevertheless, by appealing to an emotive life and to the imagination, and by including some challenges to authority and the social order, they allow for the constitution of agents of emancipatory projects. Likewise, while promoting civic values and a sense of community, they allude to the increasingly individualistic, sentimental, and ultimately problematic character of modern subjectivities.

NOTES

1. Patton makes this argument clearly. For a concise discussion of "power" by Foucault, besides "The Subject of Power," see *The History of Sexuality* (b), 92–98.

2. Besides Rabinow, Goldstein (43–44) argues this point forcefully.

3. Both Defournaux and Perdices provide detailed analyses of Olavide's multiple reform projects. In the hospices Olavide proposed, and the one he directed in Madrid, the poor were not only confined but also forced to work (see Perdices, 143–155).

4. See, in particular, Foucault's *Ethics: Subjectivity and Truth.* Also, his "Technologies of the Self" (one of the key essays included in *Ethics*) and "The Political Technology of Individuals" (in Martin, *Technologies of the Self*). In Spanish, see his *Hermenéutica del sujeto.*

5. See Alonso Seoane ("Las últimas") for some of the details about the censure process of approval (in 1799–1801) and publication of these works.

6. While the prologues were in all likelihood not written by Olavide, they nevertheless express the conventions for the reception of these works, or the "horizon of expectations of the literary experience of contemporary and later readers, critics, and authors" (Jauss, 22). See the prologues of *El Incógnito o el fruto de la ambición, Paulina o el amor desinteresado, Marcelo o los peligros de la corte, Sabina o los grandes sin disfraz, Lucía o la aldea virtuosa, Laura o el sol de Sevilla* (in *Obras narrativas,* 1, 85, 128, 171, 218, and 244, respectively), and *Teresa o el terremoto de Lima* (in *Obras selectas,* 193). From now on, the page numbers for quotes of the novels will be included in the text and will refer to these editions. (I should nevertheless note that all seven novels are included in Olavide, *Obras selectas*). All translations will be mine.

7. The reform program of *El evangelio* is contained in its last five letters (XXXVI–XLI). They have been published by Dufour as Olavide, *Cartas de Mariano a Antonio. "El programa ilustrado de 'El evangelio en triunfo.'"*

8. Both Dufour (21) and Perdices (523) consider this reform program a "privatized" extension of Olavide's earlier efforts.

9. Religion, considered by Olavide as the institution better able to "improve the customs of the people" (see his *Cartas* 138–139), is at the center of his reform and subjectification program.

10. I have relied heavily on Coughlin's article for this discussion of virtue. His work, however, centers on the writings of Jovellanos and the Salamanca School, and does not mention Olavide.

11. Not even resistance can escape power: "Where there is power there is resistance, and yet, or rather consequently, this resistance is never in a position of exteriority in relation to power" (Foucault *History of Sexuality* (b), 95).

12. The confessional impulse of the novels is normally introduced in more subtle ways, through the characters' personal reflections upon their own actions or by way of interpellating questions (and guidance) from other characters.

13. "The modern secular confessional, as invented by Rousseau, involves nor merely the recital of sins but the enumeration of each and every experience that has made one what and who one is" (Gutman, 107).

14. I will only mention two of the many possible examples. In *Paulina,* Doña Clara adopts the abandoned Paulina (86); in *El incógnito,* the central couple, after helping an old, destitute woman, is praised for their "constant acts of beneficence" and their "good deeds" (11).

15. See Foucault, "Docile Bodies" (*Discipline & Punish* (b), 138). In *El incógnito,* after his father asks him to respect God's will, "the docile and excellent Albano follows him like a child" (44). In *Paulina,* both Paulina and then the Marquis are "docile" disciples when they are learning to paint (88, 93).

16. Perdices notes a similar contradiction: while Olavide defended a hierarchical state society, his social and economic reform programs implied the destruction of such a social order (515).

17. In *El incógnito,* Albano expresses his isolation from the world: "I am finally alone in the middle of the universe" (54), and the *Incógnito* manifests the contraditions (and guilt) within himself: "how could I forgive myself?" (80).

11

Author-(dys)function:
Rereading *I, Rigoberta Menchú*

ELZBIETA SKLODOWSKA

The author—or what I have called the 'author-
function'—is undoubtedly only one of the possible
specifications of the subject and, considering past
historical transformations, it appears that the form,
the complexity, and even the existence of this function are far from immutable. We can easily imagine a
culture where discourse would circulate without any
need for an author.

—Michel Foucault, "What Is an Author?"

*T*his essay explores the articulation of authorship and authority in *I,
Rigoberta Menchú: An Indian Woman in Guatemala* within the context
of a recent debate that has been unleashed around this now-classic
Latin American *testimonio* after the publication of David Stoll's *Rigoberta
Menchú and the Story of All Poor Guatemalans*. In his book Stoll accuses
Rigoberta Menchú of misconstructing some of the crucial facts and events
described in her powerful indictment of the victimization of the indigenous
population of Guatemala in the 1970s and early 1980s. After an endorsement
from a front-page story in the *New York Times* of December 15, 1998, Stoll's

arguments generated a myriad of responses, mostly from North American and Latin American intellectuals, and the debate is still gathering force.

Latin American *testimonio* stands in particular relation to issues such as the constitution of the subject, authorship, and authenticity. Since testimonial texts base their claims to truth primarily on the credibility of the witness, the very concept of the testimonial pact enters into crisis whenever the "character" of the witness is put into question. As a form of life writing that attempts to "interface" several disciplines (literature, ethnology, historiography) with a progressive political agenda, *testimonio* does not fit comfortably within the contours of any single disciplinary paradigm. And yet, since the publication in 1966 of Miguel Barnet's/Esteban Montejo's "foundational" *testimonio, Biography of a Runaway Slave,* there has been a consistent effort on the part of critics and writers to attribute a distinct Latin American identity to a vast array of nonfictional texts whose production "involves the recording and/or transcription and editing of an oral account by an interlocutor who is a journalist, writer, or social activist" (Beverley and Zimmerman, 173). Consequently, *testimonio* has been canonized as a unique narrative form, one that can be seen to represent both the creative vitality of Latin American culture and its power to express defiance of subordinate groups and recover historically muted voices.

This view of *testimonio* echoes postcolonial critics like Benita Parry, for whom the creation of "an oppositional discourse" depends on securing "a speaking position" for the subaltern. On the other side of the spectrum, critics following Gayatri Spivak's more skeptical approach perceive *testimonio* as a form of manipulation of the subaltern who has already been constructed "according to the colonizer's self-image and can therefore not simply be given his/her voice back" (Mordorossian, 1071). Due to the mediated character of *testimonio*—the witness is both the subject and the object of the narrative, with the editor positioned as mediator between story and discourse—the "intertwined issues of authorship, representation and self-reflection" should be of particular interest to readers and critics of such texts (Logan, 203). However, as Logan further indicates, these questions are seldom considered in any detail. Even the editors of Latin American testimonies published in recent years—acutely aware of political and ethical implications of mediated texts—"rarely discuss the significant part played by the recorder-editor in creating the structure of the final document. Nor is much said about the social relationship between the authors of the testimonies and those who record and edit them" (Logan, 203). Logan illustrates her point with two mediated women's testimonials: *Hear My Testimony: María Teresa Tula, Human Rights Activist of El Salvador* (edited and translated by Lynn Stephen, 1994) and *Celsa's World: Conversations with a Mexican Peasant Woman* (by Thomas C. Tirado, 1991).

Published in Spanish in 1983 and translated into several languages, including

English, *Me llamo Rigoberta Menchú, y así me nació la conciencia (I, Rigoberta Menchú: An Indian Woman in Guatemala)* exemplifies many of the "intertwined issues" of authorship.[1] Such multilayered nature of authorship emerges with exceptional clarity in Philippe Lejeune's widely known study on autobiography:

> the status of author has different aspects, which can be dissociated and possibly also shared: the juridical responsibility, the moral and intellectual right, literary ownership (with the financial rights related to it), and the signature, which, at the same time that it refers to the juridical problem, is part of a *textual* device (cover, title, preface, etc.) through which the reading contract is established. (192)

Lejeune's model of authorship has obvious implications for *I, Rigoberta Menchú*. In a prologue that frames most editions, Elisabeth Burgos-Debray, the editor, candidly admits to have altered Menchú's oral account in order to produce a readable narrative: "I followed my original chronological outline, even though our conversations had not done so, so as to make the text more accessible to the reader" (xx). Such lack of respect for boundaries between self and other is not without consequences for the dissociation of authorship, especially in the politically charged space of collaborative life writing, ostensibly devoted to empowering a subaltern.

That Stoll does not address these issues for most of his book poses both problems and temptations for literary scholars like myself who have found the powerful appeal of Rigoberta Menchú's story in "the truth of possibility" rather than in "the truth of material events" (Portelli, 38). *Testimonio* students are in considerable accord as to the problematic status of authorship of *I, Rigoberta Menchú*, and some go as far as to argue that Menchú is the product rather than the producer of her book. The recent controversy requires, however, a more concerted analysis of comments strewn across a variety of sources. In my attempt to address these questions in a more systematic manner I will take up Foucault's discussion of "author function" from his influential essay "What Is an Author?" Questions of power and subject positioning are central to Foucault's thought, hence their relevance for the study of discursive agency in *testimonio*. On the other hand, a deep sense of the specificity of the context of Spanish American *testimonio* gives me a strong sense of ambivalence involved in an attempt to "apply" Foucault's ideas to testimonial texts. Consequently I will close my essay with a brief self-reflection on the validity of such an approach.

In his now "classic" essay, Foucault separates the categories of "author" and "biographical subject" and analyzes authorship as a function of discourse. "If by accident or design a text was presented anonymously," continues Foucault, "every effort was made to locate its author. Literary anonymity was of interest only as a puzzle to be solved as, in our day, literary works are totally dominated by the sovereignty of the author" ("What Is an Author?" (b), 236–237). Foucault insists on defining the author as a textual function which, by referring readers to a named source, acts as one of the controls within and between texts: "An author's name is not simply an element of speech. . . . Its presence is functional in that it serves as a means of classification. A name can group together a number of texts and thus differentiate them from others" ("What Is an Author?" (b), 234).

Even though Rigoberta Menchú has achieved a symbolic status as a spokesperson for the indigenous people of Guatemala and her testimony has mobilized both outrage and solidarity, it is important to remember that what stands in the way of the "sovereignty of the author" in *I, Rigoberta Menchú* is that, for all practical purposes, it is a collaborative text. The autobiography composed in collaboration, as Lejeune is right to conclude, "introduces a flaw" into the autobiographical contract practiced in Western culture since the time of Rousseau: instead of "facilitating a confusion between the author, the narrator, and the 'model' and in neutralizing the perception of the writing . . . the autobiography composed in collaboration . . . calls to mind that the 'true' and that the 'author' is a result of the contract" (Lejeune 187–188).

At any given time, at least two "authorial" names are attached to Menchú's testimony, appearing in different configurations in various editions. Most Spanish publications of the book bear two names: that of Rigoberta Menchú (author, witness, narrator) and that of Elisabeth Burgos-Debray (interviewer, journalist, editor). However, several editions by Seix Barral that appeared in the aftermath of Menchú's Nobel prize (1992) signal an attempt to clarify the division of labor between the two women by specifying in a subtitle that what follows is "La autobiografìa de Rigoberta Menchú contada a Elisabeth Burgos" ("Autobiography of Rigoberta Menchú as told to Elisabeth Burgos. As far as the editions in English are concerned, Stoll indicates that even though Burgos-Debray's name "is not on the cover of the current edition in English, appearing on the title page as editor, . . . she figures prominently on earlier covers" (182).

If we go beyond the packaging of the book for different audiences, we are bound to see that behind the title, I, *Rigoberta Menchú,* which allocates testimonial authority to one voice, lurk numerous political and cross-cultural complications involved in the making of the book and of the author. It is common knowledge that Rigoberta Menchú—the already constructed self of the original interview—was further "reconstructed" by several advisors and editors, although the actual details of this complicated process are still in dispute.[2] According to Lejeune, "Collaboration blurs in a disturbing way the question of responsibility, and even damages the notion of identity. The model and the writer both tend to believe that they are the principal, if not the only, 'author' of the text" (192). While this gradual dissolution and disempowering of Menchú as author does not absolve her from the responsibility for a text that names her as a source, according to Stoll Menchú is accountable for every word and for every omission in the published product.

That Stoll saves the discussion of authorship of *I, Rigoberta Menchú* for the last third of his book should make us leery of the integrity of his argument. In the first twelve (out of twenty) chapters he treats Menchú as if she were *the* author of the text, solely responsible for whatever discrepancies he has uncovered between her story and his own findings. By the time when, in Chapter 13 ("The Construction of *I, Rigoberta Menchú*) he asks himself, rather disingenuously: "But is *I, Rigoberta Menchú* really her voice? Since her taped stories were edited by anthropologist Elisabeth Burgos-Debray, could they have been seriously distorted?" (178), we know that had he asked this question at the outset, he would not have written the book he wrote. While I do not expect from an anthropologist a "literary" interpretation that celebrates the proliferation of gaps, ambiguities, and differences of meaning, Stoll's self-imposed goal of "separating truth from falsehood" (274) certainly calls for a more rigorous approach than the one he has to offer.

Stoll does not dwell on the usual misgivings in relation to testimonial mediation or "collaboration" voiced by most literary scholars of *testimonio*. While he perceives the editor's presence as disquieting, his goal is not to analyze what happens when a committed intellectual uses his or her own political agenda to create a readable story based on the experience of the disenfranchised. Rather, he uses his findings as a springboard to launch a vitriolic critique of the academic left: "Although they are willing to entertain certain issues, on close examination their conception of peasants and political violence is so bound up with romantic notions of authenticity, collectivity, resistance, and revolution that they have no patience with contradictory evidence" (242). The author of *Rigoberta Menchú and the Story of All Poor Guatemalans* is ill at ease in front of a mediated testimony traversed by various voice registers and discursive codes. Consequently, he chooses to impose a reading that is both reductive and manipulative.

In his belated discussion of authorship, Stoll quotes Menchú's statement in which she contends that *I, Rigoberta Menchú* is not her own book:

> It does not belong to me morally, politically or economically. I have respected it greatly because it played an immense role for Guatemala. . . . But I never had the right to say if the text pleased me or not, if it was faithful to the facts of my life. Now my life is mine, therefore I believe that now it is opportune to say that it is not my book. . . . Anyone who doubts about the work should go to [Elisabeth] because, even legally, I do not have author's rights, royalties or any of that. (quoted in Stoll, 178)

By evoking these words, Stoll at least concedes that the ambiguities involved in this particular transaction are far from being resolved. Since Menchú has not been granted formal protection of copyright legislation, it is by no means clear that she has the status of an owner of intellectual property (author) as defined by Mark Rose in a Foucauldian vein:

> The name of the author becomes a kind of brand name, a recognizable sign that the cultural commodity will be of a certain kind and quality. No institutional embodiment of the author-work relation, however, is more fundamental than copyright, which not only makes possible the manufacture and distribution of books, films, and other commodities but also, by endowing it with legal reality, helps to produce and affirm the very identity of the author as author. (Rose, 1–2)

In his critique of Menchú, Stoll conflates Menchú with *I, Rigoberta Menchú,* a life with a text, a person with an "author-function." Curiously enough, his *modus operandi* seems both to illustrate and challenge some important points made in Foucault's essay. For a start, Stoll's understanding of Menchú's author-function is inconsistent with Foucault's thesis that "unlike a proper name, which moves from the interior of discourse to the real person outside who produced it, the name of the author remains at the contours of texts—separating one from the other, defining their form, and characterizing their mode of existence" ("What Is an Author" (b), 235). On the other hand, Stoll's manipulation of author-function through dissociation of authorial entitlements from duties is consistent with Foucault's understanding of the pliability of "author-function":

> "author-function" is . . . not formed spontaneously through the simple attribution of a discourse to an individual. It results from a complex operation whose purpose is to construct the rational entity we call an author. Undoubtedly, this construction is assigned a "realistic" dimension as we speak of an individual's "profundity" or "creative" power, his intentions or the original inspiration manifested in writing. Nevertheless, these aspects of an individual, which we designate as an author (or which comprise an individual as an author), are projections, in terms always more or less psychological, of our way of handling texts: in the comparisons we make, the traits we extract as pertinent, the continuities we assign, or the exclusions we practice. ("What Is an Author" (b), 237)

Finally, Stoll's questioning of Menchú's account echoes Foucault's thesis that the attribution of authorial identity becomes necessary so that authors can be punished for their transgressions: "Speeches and books were assigned real authors, other than mythical or important religious figures, only when the author became subject to punishment and to the extent that his discourse was considered transgressive" ("What Is an Author?" (b), 235).

What are, then, Menchú's transgressions? Stoll's approach to her testimony reflects an assumption that in her role as a *native informant* Menchú does not (or should not) make use of creative imagination, even though it is now commonly accepted that *authors* of factually based narratives—such as biographies, memoirs, diaries, or autobiographies—routinely transfigure facts.[3] The role of the native informant is to function as a source of information and to fit and follow an imposed script—of a discipline, of a political agenda, of a literary genre. What bothers Stoll most of all is that Menchú hardly conforms to any script.

One curious aspect of Menchú's authority or lack thereof has to do with the category of name. As I have already mentioned, Foucauldian "author-function" is defined by the *name* of the author. Indeed, subjecthood as such, as Kamala Visweswaran reminds us, "requires a category or name" (60). It is in this context that Rino G. Avellaneda asks an important question: "Why does it seem so natural, in our discourse about Rigoberta Menchú, to speak of her as Rigoberta?" While the designation of "Rigoberta" may be natural in terms of friendship and solidarity, as Avellaneda suggests, it is also a tactic of positionality and a stratagem "to address the subaltern" (Book Review, 426). Beverley echoes similar concerns in a more confessional mode:

> In deference to political correctness, not to say politeness or respect for a person I have met only formally, I make it a point to say Rigoberta Menchú or Menchú. But I have to keep reminding myself on this score. My inclination is also to say Rigoberta. What is at stake in the question of how to address Menchú is the status of the testimonial narrator as a subject in her own right, rather than as someone (or some thing) who exists essentially *for us.* (*Subalternity and Representation,* 68).

It is certainly not a coincidence that Latin American mediated *testimonios* are rife with naming, renaming, and refusing to name. Rachel, a protagonist of Barnet's testimonial novel *Rachel's Song* is "baptized" as she is reinvented by the author-interviewer. So is Jesusa Palancares in *Hasta no verte Jesús mío* whose real name, according to Elena Poniatowska, who wrote the book, was Josefina Borque. In Barnet's classic *testimonio, Biography of a Runaway Slave,* there is a discrepancy between the narrator's "real" name and the one he chooses to use: "One of my surnames is Montejo," he explains, "after my mother who was a slave of French origin. The other is Mera. But hardly anyone knows this. Well, why should I tell people, since it is false anyway? It should really be Mesa, but what happened is that they changed it in the archives" (17). And Rigoberta

Menchú, as we all remember, refuses to reveal the secret name of her protective spirit, her *nahual.*

Like many other mediated testimonial texts that have come from Latin America in the last three decades, *I, Rigoberta Menchú* is prefaced with a commentary by the editor. According to Foucault, a commentary is one of the internal controls which—along with the author and the discipline—regulate discourse ("The Order of Discourse"). The role of a commentary (introduction) in mediated testimonials clearly goes beyond providing a user's guide to a text: such introductions discipline reading, they tend to petrify the text and to impose the ideology of correct interpretation. Furthermore, these "paratexts" explicitly problematize the authority of the speaker and point to the need for an interpretive tool and to the desire to control the witness. Burgos-Debray's prologue further exacerbates the ambivalence of Menchú's "author-function" by demonstrating that the act of bearing witness had to fit the mold of a guided dialogue, while the fragmentation of the original account acquired the overall coherence of discourse primarily through the discursive mastery of the editor. Curiously enough, despite Burgos-Debray's insistence—echoed by Stoll—as to Menchú's almost magical storytelling abilities, her agency of speech is constantly diminished. In Stoll's quote of Burgos-Debray, the editor defines her own interventions with merciless precision:

> Her Spanish was very basic . . . yes, I corrected verb tenses and noun genders, as otherwise it would not have made sense, but always trying to retain her own powerful form of expression. Rigoberta's narrative was anything but chronological. It had to be put in order. And the passages about culture that I elicited had to be inserted into the narrative of her life. I had to reorder a lot to give the text a thread, to give it the sense of a life, to make it a story, so that it could reach the general public, which I did via a card file, then cutting and pasting. It was hard to give it a sense of continuity in Rigoberta's own words. (Stoll, 185)

Given this division of labor, Menchú's story cannot stand on its own. Unlike Barnet or Poniatowska—professional authors and editors of mediated *testimonios* already mentioned here—Menchú has not been actively involved in the process of canonization (production and reproduction) of the testimonial mode in Latin America, and her Nobel prize is for her activism, not for her writing. On the other hand, after the enormous success of *Biography of a Runaway Slave*, Barnet formulated a theory of *testimonio* in his influential essay, "La novela-testimonio: socio-literatura" ("The Testimonial Novel: Socioliterature"). Originally conceived as a lecture, the text was appended to his testimonial novel *Rachel's Song* (*Canción de Rachel,* 1969), inspiring a series of critical debates concerning the amorphous identity of the genre. It is only in light of Barnet's commentary attached to the Spanish edition of *Canción de Rachel* that the reader becomes aware of Barnet's technique of amalgamation of real witnesses into a fictional persona. So, whereas Barnet and Poniatowska are renowned also as authors of numerous accompanying discourses—prefaces, lectures, critical essays—that reinforce the authority of *testimonio* and their own agency of speech, Menchú's metacommentaries are, for the most part, contained in a highly regulated format of interviews.

Following Foucault's lead, we could venture yet another hypothesis about testimonial authority. As most literary scholars would agree, upon the publication of his first *testimonio* and subsequent essays, Barnet was credited with the creation of a model of Latin American mediated testimony that continued to be reworked in powerful ways by author-editors such as Noema Viezzer, Burgos-Debray and Ruth Behar, to name only a few. Because of his "inaugurative" role in the history of *testimonio,* Barnet, unlike Menchú, could qualify perhaps as an "initiator of discursive practices," a metaauthorial figure who, according to Foucault, also establishes "the possibility and the rule of formation" (240) for texts other than his or her own.

Despite its own internal contradictions—amply discussed by numerous critics (see Seán Burke)—Foucault's "What Is an Author?" undoubtedly provides some critically productive insights into the articulation of authorship within the context of Menchú-Stoll controversy. How far can we get, however, with a reading inspired by Foucault's ideas without grounding them in or testing against history, culture, gender, class, and ethnicity of Latin America? Can a case be made at all for "applying" Foucault's conceptualization to Latin American mediated testimonies? In sum, an awareness of the fact that "universal" or "global" theories cannot possibly give their due to the specificity of Latin American culture created an uneasy—yet necessary—context for my contribution to this volume.

On the basis of the Foucauldian concepts employed here, it should be evident that his "author function" would easily qualify, in Roberto Schwarz's terms, as a "misplaced idea." Even though Foucault admits that the form and the existence of the "author-function" are "far from immutable," his theory is inextricably linked to the modern Western literary history and, as such, has limited application to Latin American cultural practices and traditions. Furthermore, despite their indebtedness to Foucault's thought, leading postcolonialist critics (Spivak; Bhabha *Location of Culture*) make us acutely aware of his disregard for the problem of colonialism altogether.

After formulating his attractive theory of "misplaced ideas" Schwarz is quick to points out that such transplanted concepts can be adapted in ways that are both creative and transgressive. I am not convinced, however, that theories or methodologies can be used with the same antidisciplinary twist of "creative difference" that another Brazilian critic, Silviano Santiago, identifies as the most

salient characteristic of Latin American literature. From Avelar's succinct summary of Santiago's ideas we learn that he envisions Latin American literature as
"the space of the in-between" that would counterweigh "both the servile submission to the paradigms of sources and influences as well as a naive nativism that
eludes confrontation with cultural dependency through facile affirmations of
originality" (Avelar "Angel of History," 188). Could a literary scholar operate in
the same transgressive vein of a creative writer who, according to Santiago, must
start "between sacrifice and play, prison and transgression, submission to code
and aggression, obedience and rebellion, assimilation and expression—there, in
this seemingly empty site, its temple and locus of clandestineness, the anthro-
pophagous ritual of Latin American literature takes place" (Santiago, quoted in
Avelar "Angel of History," 188)?

The answer, I am afraid, is no, although the question is certainly being pon-
dered. To be sure, in the last two decades the interlacing between literary theory
and Latin American literature has become increasingly complex and markedly
politicized. According to Hernán Vidal, two rival camps of literary critics—the
"technocratic" and the "culture oriented"—have been locked in a struggle over
the interpretation of Latin American literary production. Whereas the first group,
explains Vidal, relies on imported theories that little have to do with Latin
American realities, the second one "sets as its goal direct contributions to the cultures from which its material for study comes, addressing itself to the academic
establishment only as a very secondary interlocutor" (Vidal, 115). In his article
Vidal builds his case against the first trend, which he accuses of being obsessed
with endless innovation for innovation's sake (116 passim). While Vidal's model
registers a very important split in the Latinamericanist critical thought as practiced in North America, it does not give its due to the position of those Latin
American intellectuals who have been voicing their concern about the overpowering presence of metropolitan theories, including those "culture oriented."

Walter Mignolo takes Vidal's argument a step further when he points out in
"Postoccidentalismo: el argumento desde América Latina" that many of the
debates during the 1997 Latin American Studies Association Congress in
Guadalajara were animated by a confrontation between cultural and postcolo-
nial studies, on one side, and the emerging "latinamericanist fundamentalism"
focused on defying theoretical colonization, on the other *(Teorías sin disciplina)*.
For many critics, the "supreme test" of validity of a theoretical approach is, as
Hallward indicates, its sensitivity to the particular or specific, its emphasis on
the "embeddedness of every utterance in its particular social context" (441).
Scholars working on Latin American cultural production *from* Latin America—
Hugo Achugar, Nelly Richard, Roberto Schwarz, Beatriz Sarlo, to mention only
a few—have warned us that it is all too easy to lose sight of separate identities
and disparate traditions while pursuing transnational paradigms and borrowed

concepts: "How can we make use of international theoretical concepts, knowing that they come from the metropolitan center—and, at the same time, not surrender to the grammar of their authority?" (Richard quoted by Moreiras in *Tercer espacio* 41; my translation).

In this context Idelber Avelar's bold statement that the academic practice of North American Latinamericanism reinforces "the perverse division of labor according to which certain national traditions produce thought and other produce objects for the thought" ("Cultural Studies," 52) should ring a cautionary note for all of us engaged in this practice.

NOTES

1. John Beverley does not hesitate to consider the title of the English edition as "dramatically mistranslated" (*Subalternity and Representation*, 68).

2. In a recent review of Stoll's book, Peter Canby summarizes the contradictory accounts of the editorial process as recounted by Arturo Taracena and Burgos-Debray, two people most directly involved in the making of *I, Rigoberta Menchú*.

3. What follows is a good summary of recent trends—both in life writing and criticism—that acknowledge the fact that the transfiguration of lived experience is part and parcel of autobiographical writing: "Beginning with Paul John Eakin's now standard *Fictions in Autobiography*, which argued that 'the self that is the center of all autobiographical narrative is necessarily a fictive structure' (3) and that 'fictions and the fiction-making process are a central constituent of the truth of any life as it is lived and of any art devoted to the presentation of that life' (5), most scholars have come to agree that the presence of fiction within autobiography is no more problematic than the presence of nonfiction within the novel. Focusing more on the autobiographical act, including its fictive impulse, than on the historicity of the text, theorists have in recent years given their books on the genre such titles and subtitles as *Fabricating Lives* (Leibowitz), *Inventing the Truth* (Zinsser), *Figures in Autobiography* (Fleishman), *Constructions of Self-Representation* (Folkenflik), *Rewriting the Self* (Freeman), *Metaphors of Self* (Olney), *Marginality and the Fictions of Self-Representation* (Smith), and *Imagining a Self* (Spacks)" (Adams, 459).

SEXUALITY

12

The Theatrics of Reading:
Body and Book in Victoria Ocampo
From *At Face Value: Autobiographical*
Writing in Spanish America

SYLVIA MOLLOY

I experienced everything through the transmuted substance of my body. . . . I had no other thing to offer
under the species of linked words, under the bread
and wine of the spirit we call literature. That, in sum,
could well be the epigraph of every one of my
texts. . . . The more I strayed from it, childishly heed-
ing who knows what convention of the *hateful "I,"* the
weaker my writing was—flabby, without substance.

—Victoria Ocampo, *Autobiografía*

*B*ooks, many books are mentioned throughout Victoria Ocampo's texts. If
autobiographics are wont to highlight the privileged encounter with the
written word as a symbolic beginning for their life stories, an acknowledgment of the very tools for self-definition, this highlighting usually occurs,
emblematically, close to the beginning of their narrative. In the case of Victoria
Ocampo, however, there is no such clear-cut inception of the readerly into the

life story; not one, not two, but many encounters with books are described in her text. The significant gesture is tirelessly repeated: one scene of reading brings on another, book follows upon book and discovery upon discovery, so that we are left with many beginnings; so many, in fact, that they blur into a dizzying contin-uum in which the bare gesture—reading—perpetuates itself as the self-sustaining motion of one consistent autobiographical act.[1]

Among Ocampo's earliest childhood recollections we find recorded an initial version of the scene of reading. Under the entry "Book" she writes: "I carry a book that has been read aloud to me and pretend I am reading it. I remember the story perfectly, I know it is behind those letters I cannot understand" (Autobiografía I, 81). I wish to dwell on the precise phrasing of this recollection, for it contains many elements specific to Ocampo's scene of reading. Much like Sarmiento, she favors the Hamlet-like posture—the young reader with a book in hand. Yet in Ocampo's recollection of the scene, the theatricals of the pose are stressed. She sees herself performing: *carrying* the book (as an actor would carry a prop onstage) and *pretending* to read. Distance is emphasized in the scene, but so is familiarity: the child carries a book full of letters to which she has no access, but it is a book with whose contents she is quite familiar since it has been read to her many times.[2]

It may be argued that this parading with a book in hand is no more meaning-ful than any other example of childhood make-believe: as one might "play doc-tor," one "plays book." For that matter, Ocampo is not unique amongst autobiographers in playing this game: Sartre, to give one memorable example, recalls a similar imposture in *Les Mots*.[3] As a point of reference, the latter text proves useful to evaluate Ocampo's experience. Sartre's childhood mimicry has a precise model at its source: the child's maternal grandfather is a writer, has a library full of books and, when taking a book from a shelf, follows a set pattern of trivial gestures on which the child spies avidly. The first time the boy pretends to read from a book, he performs a "ceremony of appropriation": he opens the book "to the right page" as he has seen his grandfather do, fully expecting a revelation which, to his dismay, does not occur.[4] Moreover, for Sartre, books are a perma-nent and gender-affiliated presence: on the one hand, there are the serious "cul-tural objects" revered by his grandfather; on the other, the frivolous *"colifichets"* that fuel the erotic imagination of his grandmother and his mother.

Ocampo's posturing with the book in hand, while clearly imitative, differs from that of Sartre in that she has no clear reader, in her immediate entourage, either "seriously" male or "frivolously" female, on whom to model her own read-ing. No one adult in her childhood is associated with books in any exemplary way, nor does reading appear to play a prominent part in family tradition beyond the conventional reading practiced by the well-to-do: "Despite the fact that, like Virginia Woolf's Orlando, I had 'bestowed my credulity' on writers from childhood, I had the misfortune of barely knowing professional writers or people who were interested in books" (Autobiografía II, 71). When the parents' library is described, books are made to appear as ornaments, objects appealing more than anything to the senses (Autobiografía I, 94). The adults who read to her, hardly identified, do not seem to have any special connection to books beyond story-telling. A blurry French governess, Mademoiselle Guérin, is credited with teach-ing her the alphabet; *showing* may be a better term, since the learning process itself (French is Ocampo's first reading language) is presented as an undirected, spontaneous event: "I learn the alphabet I don't know how . . . I learn French I don't known how" (Autobiografía I, 83). A favorite great-aunt, Vitola, is also mentioned as reading to the child in Spanish, but little more is said.

It is obvious that we are not faced here with a situation such as, again, that of the young Sarmiento, born to parents of rudimentary culture, who taught him-self to read and took pride in his status as an autodidact. The family into which Ocampo was born, in 1890, was both socially prominent and wealthy. Together with her five younger sisters, she received at home the privileged if restricted education of the upper-middle-class—training in languages and music, plus a smattering of general knowledge that conspicuously excluded Argentine litera-ture, history, and current events. Despite this limited formation, Ocampo is far from being culturally deprived. Yet it is clear, from the numerous passages throughout her autobiographical texts that echo that first recollection of the child posturing as reader, that books take on for Ocampo an importance well beyond the one her milieu is willing to assign to them. They are not marks of conventional culture nor are they means to achieve the formal education to which, as a woman, she has no right: "'If she had been a boy she would have taken up a career,' my father would say of me, probably with sadness" (Autobiografía II, 16).[5] It is not suprising, then, that, like Sarmiento, Ocampo referred to herself as an autodidact:[6] she had to teach herself new ways of read-ing and of relating to a canon to which, because of her gender, she had limited access. The inordinate intensity with which Ocampo successively fills out the first version of her scene of reading, giving life to the childhood posturing and turning that posture into an expression of self, betrays a relation with books that goes will beyond—and even goes against—the tame and ideologically limited cultural landscape in which she was raised.

Ocampo has written extensively about her voracious childhood reading, and I shall not go into it in detail here.[7] Although her appetite for books is constant, the reading itself follows different patterns. In early childhood there are the books one is read to from; later on, the "classics," read in the classroom and elic-iting a prescribed response; finally, there are the books that one reads for one-self, those that Ocampo appropriates more directly and turns into vehicles of self-expression: "Books, books were a new world in which blessed freedom reigned. I lived the life of books and had to account to no one for that life. It was my thing. *[Era cosa mía]*" (Autobiografía I, 177).

Like Proust's scene of reading to which Ocampo refers often, this private reading is a solitary ritual observing specific rules. However, reading does not escape contamination with the outside world and even seems to encourage it. If French and English books are devoured inside the house, the reading experience also incorporates the specifically Argentine surroundings, so that, in memory, the two live combined, in a constant interplay of the exotic and the familiar: the Brontës' Yorkshire moors will "forever smell of the Argentine summer and echo with the amorous duets of *hornero* birds and the resonant presence of cicadas,"[8] while "The Fall of the House of Usher" will always be associated with the mooing of cows and the bleating of sheep.[9] This very elementary contamination between what Ocampo will later set up as complementary and often interchangeable categories, *lo vivido* and *lo leído,* carries over into other domains. As *lo vivido* seeps into the book, so at other times does *lo leído* parry the onslaught of direct experience and even replaces that experience. When Ocampo reads *David Copperfield,* she has already lost her great-grandfather; yet it is Dickens's description of Steerforth's body on the beach at the end of the novel—"I saw him lying with his head upon his arm, as I had often seem him lie at school"—that gives her her first "real" contact with death and with personal loss:

> [I] wept also for myself. I wept for the childhood I knew was leaving me since I had already begun to look back on it; and I wept for the childhood that did not completely let go of me, that in vain resisted triumphant adolescence, as Steerforth's familiar posture, with its appearance of life, in vain resisted death. (Autobiografía I, 179–180)

From adolescence on, Ocampo will read most major events of her life through books. This is not to say that hers is a primarily bookish existence lived in seclusion, nor that because of books, to transpose the phrase Borges wrote of himself, "life and death are lacking from [her] life." Books do not do her living for her but they are, in a way, the space in which her life is enhanced and can be lived more fully than anywhere else. Referring to the modelling function of readings done early in life, Ocampo highlights empathy and identification. The theatrical terms she uses provide a helpful clue to the self-representational potential she attributes to books:

> All imaginative and highly sensitive children are fascinated by certain heroes and tell themselves stories in which they play an important role in relation to their hero—they are pursued, loved, betrayed, saved, humiliated or glorified by him. Later, once that stage is left behind, they usually act out in life those

scenes so often rehearsed in childhood. When the magnificent or terrible moment finally arrives, the reply comes naturally, on cue. Impossible to change it, impossible to get it wrong. . . . There have been too many rehearsals. It is no longer possible to choose another, it was never possible to choose another reply. Each being carries within himself the same scene, the same drama, from the moment he awakens to consciousness till the end of his days, and he plays out that scene, that drama, no matter what events or what characters come his way, until he finds his own plot and his own character. He may never find them. But that does not stop him from playing out his scene, bestowing on the events and characters least likely to fit his play the shape of the events and character that are his own. He was born to play but one scene and one drama, and cannot help repeating them as long as he lives.[10]

Reading is a vital performance but a performance that continuously seeks new settings. "From my adolescence onwards," writes Ocampo, "I was dissatisfied with the books I was given. I began to read all those I could lay my hands on."[11] One of the first examples of this new, unfettered manner of reading that remains in her memory for its modeling impact is Rostand's *L'Aiglon,* a text that she hears and sees before actually reading it, much as she had heard the book she carried around as a child. At age fifteen, she sees a performance of *L'Aiglon* with Marguerite Moreno (who would later give her acting lessons) in the title role, and recognizes herself wholeheartedly in the young hero. The fact that the role of the Duke of Reichstadt was usually played by a woman—Sarah Bernhardt, in one of her most famous performances, and now Marguerite Moreno—must have had, one suspects, some part in this spontaneous reaction. However, there was more that bonded Ocampo to the protagonist:

> I immediately recognized myself in the hero. Why? The whole thing seemed preposterous. The plight of Napoleon's son was not my own. However, that sick boy (his ravaging consumption seemed to me then an enviable illness) was as much a prisoner at Schoenbrunn as I was in the house on Florida and Viamonte. He was a *pas-prisonnier-mais.* He could not go out riding without "the sweet honor of an invisible escort." His mail was censored. He was allowed to read only those books that had been chosen for him. Someone lent him books clandestinely:

> Le soir, dans ma chambre, je lisais, j'étais ivre.
> Et puis, quand j'avais lu, pour cacher le délit
> Je lançais le volume au haut du ciel de lit.
> My bed had no canopy but it did have a mattress and under that mattress
> I hid my private library. (100)[12]

Ocampo reads herself not only into a character but into a character *who reads:* like Hamlet, Napoleon's son is a prince with a book in his hand. However, unlike Hamlet, who reads with impunity, the young duke's unsupervised reading, his only means of liberation, is an offense in the eyes of his guards. It is in this illegality, assumed defiantly as a liberating act, that Ocampo recognizes the mark of her own reading.

The theatrical nature of the experience is to be noted. Rostand's text is discovered not on the printed page but on a stage—through voice and representation, through active posturing. What Ocampo "reads" (and what she reads herself into) is, in sum, a performance: an actress playing the role of a character who rejects the role others would impose on him and turns reading into rebellion. If reading is performance, this particular reading of *L'Aiglon* is the performance of a performance. And it is also, of course, a translation; a passage not only from text to life, or from French theatrical convention to Argentine everyday experience, but from one gender to the representation of the other: the young Ocampo identifies herself with a boy but also with a woman playing the role of a boy.

The presence of the theatrical in Ocampo's scene of reading, from the posturing with the book as a child, through the dazzled recognition of self in *L'Aiglon,* to the unceasing search for her "own plot and [her] own character," reveals Ocampo's obsessive preoccupation with self-representation, a preoccupation that informs all of her work and reflects a gender-related cultural predicament. But this presence of the theatrical should also be seen quite literally, as the expression of a vocation—"I was born to *act.* I have theatre in my blood."[13]—that was thwarted early on, leaving its diffuse trace in her life and in her writing. Ocampo's life story casts her early on as a misfit, constantly at odds with the real-life roles society had to offer, roles that did not include, needless to say, that of actress or writer. Instead of public acting, for example, she is allowed recitation in private; a pale and insufficient substitute, it is allowed, even encouraged, as a decorous manifestation of talent. That Ocampo wished to go beyond those private spectacles and devote her life to acting, that she strived to achieve her goal by coaching with a reputed professional, that, when faced with strong parental opposition, she did not assert herself, appears in her autobiographical writing as one of her more poignant defeats; a defeat that occasional and very successful public performances in later years, as the *récitante* in Honegger's *Le Roi David* and in Stravinsky's *Perséphone,* doubtless rendered more unpalatable.[14]

Literature was not an easy career, even for men, at the turn of the century. The caricatures of the uncomprehending, self-assured bourgeois that pepper the texts of Spanish American *modernismo,* the discomfort shown by that bourgeois himself when he became a writer, as did the members of the Argentine generation of 1880, are proof of the unease with which society looked on the institutionalization of literature and on the professional status claimed by writers. For women wishing to write, the issue, foreseeably, was infinitely more thorny.[15] As an adolescent, Ocampo complains vehemently to her friend and confidante of those years, Delfina Bunge:

> Man of letters is a word that is taken pejoratively in our midst. "He is a man of letters" (or what is worse, "she is a woman of letters") means a good-for-nothing. . . . (Unless he's a professor and has a chair: they respect that kind of title.) If it's a woman, she is a hopeless bas-bleu [bluestocking], a poseuse, she borders on perversion or, in the best of cases, she is a badly put together Miss Know-It-All. Conversely, the word landowner [estanciero] has prestige. As in the fable, it means veau, vache, cochon, couvée. (Autobiografía II, 104)

For women, the dividing line between the permissible and the perverse, in areas pertaining to literature or theater, clearly reproduces the separation between public and private. Theatrical performances are limited to domestic interiors—safe places where, precisely, one does not make a spectacle of oneself. The same applies to literary performances—reading and writing—albeit in a more complex way. Reading from a censored list is permitted, even encouraged, but the censorship itself is arbitrary. Many books were on the family index but others, unaccountably, escaped it: Anna Karenina, for example, and also Shakespeare and Dante because, "although all sorts of things happened there, they eluded censorship because of the rhyme, as operas did on account of the music" (Autobiografía II, 62). An autobiographical footnote, tucked away in an essay by Ocampo on Virginia Woolf, is expressive of her parents' shortsightedness. The father used to show early Max Linder films at home:

> [I]f there were love scenes accompanied by kissing, my mother . . . planted herself before the projector, intercepting the image. We protested but she would not budge. As she couldn't guess how long the amorous outbursts lasted (these were silent movies and in covering the image she covered the subtitles), her shadow remained longer than necessary on the screen, just in case, and made us lose the gist of the story."[16]

For all its comicality, the passage is significant. The mother's purpose is clearly to censor all intimations of sexuality in their graphic, physical representation. But in so doing she also obscures the words (those silent movie subtitles the viewer reads as if he were hearing them being said) and deletes the meaning of the story. The intercepting gesture inadvertently merges body and reading, the two main components of Ocampo's autobiographical writing.

As with the plays staged in private, Ocampo's first publication was very much an entre nous affair. Two of her poems, in French, were published anonymously in 1908; the Buenos Aires newspaper in which they appeared merely identified her as a young woman from a distinguished family. In no manner, however, was writing or even interest in literature to be personalized and made public, to be *signed*. In 1910, during an extended stay with the Ocampo family in Paris, the parents allowed their eldest daughter to audit courses at the Sorbonne and, as was fashionable, attend lectures at the Collège de France. Ocampo heard Bergson and Faguet, and was particularly taken by Hauvette's course on Dante. Also during that stay, arrangements were made for Ocampo to sit for different artists then in fashion, amongst them Troubetzkoy and Helleu. One of the artists, Dagnan Bouveret, struck by her love of books and by the passion with which she quoted from the *Commedia*, decided to place a small head of Dante on the table on which she leaned while posing. Ocampo wryly recounts the consequences of his idea:

> [My parents] tactfully told him that his new ornament was not suitable for a nineteen-year-old girl and that it might seem pretentious or would be interpreted as a ridiculous show of *basbleuisme.* Dagnan answered that my love of Dante seemed to him to justify fully "the ornament" but that he was ready to erase it and replace it by some pansies or a laurel sprig in a vase. So he did. Thus we were separated, Dante and I, in effigy, and the vegetable kingdom occupied his place but could not (in my memory) "briser son absence." So much could it not shatter it that my first article, in *La Nación,* was a commentary on the *Commedia.* It was published ten years later—that is, after ten years of navigating against wind and tide. (Autobiografía, 151)

If Ocampo did not become an actress, she did become a writer, "against wind and tide," as she so enjoyed saying, against the Argentine literary establishment and against the better judgment of the social group to which she belonged. The displacement of one vocation by another doubtless affected her writing and her general demeanor within a field she would always perceive as not entirely her own. Despite the importance she would achieve in literary circles, both at home and abroad, despite the fact that she founded and for many years directed *Sur,* one of the most influential literary journals in Latin America, despite her self-assured stance when she advocated women's rights and founded the Argentine Women's Union in 1936 with two other women, María Rosa Oliver and Susana Larguía,[17] when Ocampo speaks of herself as a writer, there is always malaise, a reluctance to accept herself fully in that role. As is well known, such self-disparagement is not uncommon in women writers of the nineteenth (even the twentieth) century.[18] In Ocampo's case, the deprecating gesture may also echo, unconsciously, the very class prejudice she believed she was battling—contempt for the professional writer and devaluation of "paid" work. But the gesture is further compounded by the fact that Ocampo the actress is always behind Ocampo the writer or, rather, that the writer is an actress in disguise, living out a *rôle manqué.* The text she reads will always be a partition waiting to be performed, a quiescent word in search of expression, a *chose possible,* as she notes much later, quoting Valéry: "the poem is an abstraction, a text that awaits, a law that has no life but in the human voice. . . ."[19] So is the self perceived as a *chose possible,* another word—"I"—in search of its script. If the theatre cannot provide a suitable scene for the encounter of the two, then literature—writing as a performance of reading—will have to suffice.

Ocampo's living and writing her life through books and through authors has been routinely interpreted as a desire to identify with the male models offered by a patriarchal society.[20] While this interpretation is *in part* true, it suffers from oversimplification and needs to be qualified on several levels. In relation to the literary *characters* with whom Ocampo bonds through her reading, such an interpretation falls short. For example, it ignores the young Ocampo's reading of self in *Corinne* and her sympathy for Madame de Staël, often mentioned in the second volume of her autobiography.[21] Furthermore, that interpretation—living through books as a way of identifying with male models—sidetracks the most interesting and intricate bonding of them all, that of Ocampo with Dante's Francesca.

Describing her first encounter with the *Commedia,* at age sixteen, Ocampo recalls the drastic nature of her reaction to "some passages from the *Inferno*":

> The impression made on me by that reading is only comparable to what I experienced as a very young child when, in the sea for the first time, I was swept off my feet and rolled over in the sand by a magnificently impetuous wave. In all of my being I received the baptism of those *parole di colore oscuro,* as the poet himself so fittingly writes, and I emerged from that immersion staggering, my lips wet with bitter salt.[22]

Two years later, in a letter to Delfina Bunge in which she speaks of her attraction for the man she will eventually marry (with disastrous consequences), she begins by quoting from Canto V and adds: "These verses sing in my mind like a catchy tune" (Autobiografía II, 97). In spite of its adolescent pretentiousness (the eighteen-year-old Ocampo is courting literary approval from an older, budding *femme de lettres*),[23] the letter illustrates the process that Ocampo's subsequent writing will tirelessly repeat. *Lo vivido* and *Lo leído* form a system of interconnecting vessels, flowing, being translated, into one another. One calls effortlessly to the other: the connection is automatic, "like a catchy tune." If the flow seems to favor at times one direction over the other, it is only because time or social circumstances so demand;[24] what is important is that contact, intermingling, and mutual reinforcement between the two—life and literature—are unceasing.

Sustained by the *Commedia,* the third volume of Ocampo's *Autobiografía* stands out as the one that best expresses, celebrates even, this intermingling between literature and life in one passionate performance. Narratively speaking, this volume constitutes the high point of Ocampo's story; devoted to the great love of her life and also (not by chance, as will be seen) to her literary beginnings, it also marks the passage from the private individual of the first two volumes to the more public adult of volumes IV, V, and VI. Less digressive than the other volumes, volume III is, in all senses of the word, the most *dramatic:* it dynamically sets forth a plot and plays the self into that plot as protagonist. From the Stendhalian echoes of its title, *La rama de Salzburgo,* it proclaims its literary texture and functions like a many-layered script through which Ocampo reads herself. Whereas the script is composed of many voices, the figure that holds those literary echoes together, the model that will center the performance and serve as an emblem for the autobiographical "I," is, once more, Dante's Francesca.[25]

Why Francesca? The reference to Stendhal's *De l'amour* in the title announces the text for what it indeed is, a narrative of *amour passion,* devoted in its near entirety to the account of a long, secret relationship with her husband's cousin, Julián Martínez. That in itself might justify the translation into Ocampo's life of Francesca, of a particular version of Francesca—Francesca the eternal lover, as popularized by nineteenth-century readings of Dante. The fact that the affair Ocampo narrates, with a mixture of passion and directness rare in Spanish American autobiography by male or female, in a way parallels the episode in Dante (two cousins instead of two brothers) provides further grounds for the comparison. Yet neither the superficial resemblance nor the clandestine character of the relationship wholly accounts for the presence of Canto V in this text. Many other references to jealous husbands and doomed lovers (*Tristan, Pelléas et Mélisande, Anna Karenina,* the *Princesse de Clèves*) have their part in this concert of voices through which Ocampo writes herself.

More to the point, it is the illicit nature of this love that connects it to other transgressive gestures in Ocampo's life. On more than one occasion, when pressed by her lover to brave public opinion and leave her husband, Ocampo holds back for fear of parental rejection. This combination—vital attraction for the forbidden curbed by fear of authoritarian repression—immediately prompts the reader to rank this love with the other interdictions imposed by (or attributed to) parental and, by extension, social intolerance. Relegated to the limits of the permissible, like the child who hides her books under the mattress, the woman meets her lover in an apartment on the outskirts of the city. Ocampo inscribes the three forbidden passions—the theater, literature, and love—in the margins of convention.

As the coded language of flowers is ritualized in nineteenth-century novels, so books, from the very beginning and especially *at* the very beginning of Ocampo's relationship, convey meaning. When all other possibilities of exchange are barred, books become a privileged means of communication—better still, of conversation and confabulation. Before effectively becoming lovers, Ocampo and Martínez use reading as a clear substitute for physical contact:

> I soon got into the habit of calling him, sometimes from my singing teacher's house. We spoke briefly. We recommended books to each other. We read Colette, Maupassant, Vigny. We set up rendezvous to read them at the same time. "At ten, tonight. Can you do it?" Twenty blocks apart, I at home, he in his house, we read. Next day we discussed our reading. . . . On occasion we would make a date to meet in a bookstore, to see each other from a distance. We did not greet each other. We did not go beyond looks. (Autobiografía III, 29)

In this fecund junction of love and literature and, more specifically, in the use of the book as mediator in the unfolding of love, the presence of Francesca in Ocampo's text takes on full meaning—not only as a passionate lover, but as a reader whose sign is the book. Francesca recognizes an expression of self and the *prima radice* of her feelings as she reads. Furthermore, in an important gesture of reflection, she recognizes the mediating qualities of the book itself: "Galeotto fu il libro e chi lo scrisse."[26] As with *L'Aiglon,* Ocampo reads herself into a figure who reads and for whom reading is allied with interdiction. And, more importantly, she is reading herself into a figure who is aware of what the process of reading achieves.[27]

It is not impertinent to recall, at this point, the illustration on the cover of this third autobiographical volume. Although the role Ocampo had in the choice is hard to determine, all six volumes having been published posthumously, *La rama de Salzburgo* is strikingly different from its companion volumes. Whereas there are photographs on the covers of the others, there is an arresting full-length painting of Ocampo on the cover of this one—a sensuous, physically challenging Ocampo, the body very much in evidence, and *a book in her hand.* This is the very portrait by Dagnan Bouveret referred to earlier, the one from which a small bust of Dante was deleted by a parental ukase which had not succeeded, however, in deleting Dante from her mind. In a sense this cover, built around the absence of Dante, turns that absence into a presence, and *re-presents* Francesca: the painting binds love's body to the body of the book, defiantly expressing—as an actress on a stage—the union of the two.

"I lived Dante, I did not read him. I received baptism from certain verses; they had been written to name me. I took notes so I would learn to read him better" (Autobiografía III, 98). If one discounts the mediocre French sonnets turned out at some governess' bidding, writing, for Ocampo, had been until then only a possible sequel to reading, not its systematic complement. The scribblings in the margins of Dante now mark a transition. On the one hand, they are the logical continuation "in literature" of the haphazard private journal she has kept since adolescence; on the other, they prepare her for a more sustained, visible effort: the writing, in French, of her first book, *De Francesca a Beatrice,* which was published during this love affair. That writing should finally find its form and become a public gesture at this stage in Ocampo's life is not a coincidence. It is a way of completing the meaning of Dagnan Bouveret's painting, of exhibiting, through a now triple mediation—a book about a book in a language that is not her mother tongue—that which society denied her: to speak her body and to speak her mind.[28] "This book was a substitute for a confession, for a confidence" (Autobiografía III, 105). Significantly, *De Francesca a Beatrice* is dedicated to Ocampo's lover in a coded inscription, a subversive gesture that effectively succeeds in calling attention to itself.

If Dante's Francesca is the major mediating text that governs self-portrayal in *La rama de Salzburgo,* it is by no means the only one. Not surprisingly, this third volume of the autobiography, by far most personal and stirring of all six volumes, is also the one in which the most reading gets done, in which the most quotations appear, in which literary reference is at its most dense. The very excess of feeling—"passion is beautiful only in its excess and can only be conceived in that excess" (Autobiografía III, 32)—is matched by the excess of voices that mingle in the text. Dante, yes, but Dante contaminated: not only read through French nineteenth-century readings but read in conjunction with Stendhal (the crystallization of love), Proust (the violence of retrospective jealousy), Shakespeare ("Make thee another self, for love of me"), Eliot, when all passion is spent ("What is actual is actual only for one time"), Péguy, when her lover is dead ("C'est le sang de l'artère et le sang de la veine/Et le sang de ce coeur qui ne bat déjà plus").

In a sense, one might apply the Stendhalian notion of crystallization not only to the love that is narrated here but to the process of narration itself, an accumulation of fragmentary quotes that gradually take on meaning. Indeed, this prolific annotation of life through texts is a dilated process occurring at different stages. Resort to texts takes place at the time of the experiences themselves, for *lo vivido* goes hand in hand with *lo leído,* as has been noted: Ocampo thinks and feels "in literature." But it also takes place, even more conspicuously, at the time of the autobiographical act itself. Ocampo subjects her retrieval of the past to the very same contact with literature to which she had exposed life itself: memory of life also follows a path of texts. I give but one example. At the time of her relationship with Julián Martínez, Ocampo states, she had not yet read Proust. It is when she looks back on those years in order to narrate them that Proust's text, which she has since read, allows her to recognize and name within that relationship one of the sources of its undoing—her retrospective jealousy.

Resorting to literature in that retrieval of the past allows for something more: it permits a reinterpretation from afar in which literature is astutely used to give the self the best part, glossing over events that might reflect on it adversely, and channeling the reading of the autobiography away from potentially thorny issues. Again, I consider Ocampo's reference to Proust. Retrospective jealousy provides one of the more poignant scenes in this volume: Ocampo, being fitted for a dress, feels jealousy arise within her as the designer's assistant innocently describes for her in detail the body of the woman who had been Martínez's lover before her. The scene, subtly combining retrospective voyeurism and rekindled desire, is remarkably effective; so much so that, for a moment, it steers the reader's attention away from another, more immediate issue that affects the relationship in a manner no less adverse—the fact that Julián himself was jealous, not precisely of past lovers Ocampo might have had but of a very concrete man with whom she was flirting in the present.

In speaking of the publication of *De Francesca a Beatrice*, I purposefully compared it to an exhibition and meant it explicitly, in a near-physical sense. Indeed, this is the sense in which the verb surfaces in the negative reactions greeting Ocampo's first literary attempt. The criticism to which she was subjected proved, at the very least, that her reading was unexpected. Ocampo showed her manuscript before publication to two prominent figures of the Argentine establishment: Paul Groussac, the acerbic French critic turned self-appointed mentor of the Argentine intelligentsia, and Angel de Estrada, the highly respected aesthete and *modernista* writer who wrote for *La Nación*. Groussac, from his lofty magisterial stance, dismissed the piece as pedantic:

> [He] mocked my choice and assured me that if I really felt a literary itch (an itch he clearly considered masculine) it was better to choose *"personal"* topics. Personal? This good man did not understand that *Dante for me was a personal topic*. (Autobiografía III, 107)

For reasons precisely opposite,[29] Angel de Estrada also criticizes Ocampo's piece and recommends caution:

> You tell me that these pages are written this way because this is how you feel Dante. I know, it suffices to read them. However, this is not what makes the publication difficult, it is the excessively personal form, *utterly straightforward*. . . . When women bared their shoulders to go to the theatre and to balls, everyone screamed. Now there are fewer screams and he who screams does so against all of society. It has become a general *state of body*. But you are the only innovative woman who is on familiar terms with designers of spiritual fashion and, being alone, you will reveal a *state of mind*." (Autobiografía III, 106)

Despite the comparison with the world of fashion, highly revealing of a generalized opinion on women's writing, this judgment, in an odd way, is not inaccurate. Estrada perceives something untoward that smacks of exhibitionism, of unseemly revelation, of *excess,* and not being able to name it precisely, he translates it into physical terms: showing one's mind, if one is a woman, is as unacceptable as, in the past, showing one's body. But then, showing body and mind, through the reading of Dante, was precisely Ocampo's purpose.

When I speak here of body, as I have in the past pages, I am not vindicating for Ocampo a notion of woman's writing based on physical pleasure or physiological difference—a notion held by certain French feminists which I find perilously close to essentialist formulations of the feminine and do not happen to share.[30] Nor, of course, am I celebrating Ocampo's body against her, considering *it* in lieu of her writing, as not a few masculinist critics are prone to do when discussing women's texts and as some of Ocampo's male friends and would-be suitors did. Ocampo tells the story at her expense of the time when, as a young woman in Rome, she was invited by a courtly Italian *senatore,* who shared her passion for Dante, to see "his most precious treasure." "I imagined" she writes "that it was some rare edition of Dante. He brought me, instead, a plaster mold of Pauline Borghese's breast. . . . This man did not take my love for Dante seriously. To hell with the senator and to hell with the breast *[Al diablo et senador y el seno]*" (Autobiografía III, 15). Similar misunderstandings, less ludicrous albeit more painful, abound in Ocampo's life. Ortega y Gasset, sensitive to her physical attraction, extravagantly sang her "feminine" virtues while subtly putting her down intellectually in his epilogue to *De Francesca a Beatrice* (a book he himself had published); Hermann von Keyserling never accepted that Ocampo's passion for his books did not prepare a way into her bed.[31] That there is a strong physical, both sensual and sexual, drive in Ocampo, the woman—what Drieu La Rochelle, her friend and, in the early 1930s, her lover, called her *génie charnel* (Autobiografía II)—is certain: she manifests it often enough and in different ways throughout the six volumes of her autobiography, never reluctant to speak of erotic desire, of the physical urge to have a child by her lover, of menstrual blood. Yet I read her references to her body in the autobiography as signifying something more complex—something that surely includes the concretely physical but goes beyond it, something more like a *presence* (the way one speaks of a presence on stage) that society would have her repress and for which her body is the most visible sign.

Ocampo speaks complacently of the more evident, even frivolous aspects of that presence in visual terms, narcissistically referring to the way in which others look at her, desire her, flatter her. Her sheer size and good looks, those commanding proportions so imposing to acquaintances and admirers in real life ("the Gioconda of the Pampas," Ortega would call her) are translated in her autobiographical text into an overwhelming persona. Yet there is an odd imbalance between that physical self-assuredness and the anxiety of speaking found so often in these writings, an anxiety compounded by a basic situation that repeats itself in the text: Ocampo, tongue-tied (*callada, inarticulada, muda,* are her expressions) before a voluble, eloquent writer. These interlocutors are frequently male but not always: Gabriela Mistral, María de Maeztu, Virginia Woolf have the same effect of cowing her into silence. Ocampo's description of herself and Woolf, in the very first volume of her *Testimonios,* is an accurate reflection of these flawed dialogues:

> Tavistock Square, this past month of November. A small dark green door, very English, with the number squarely placed in the middle. Outside, all of London's fog. Inside, upstairs, in the light and warmth of a living-room, the panels of which have been painted by a woman, two women speak of women. They look each other over, they ask each other questions. One of them is curious; the other, delighted.
>
> One of them has found expression, because she has been able to find herself, magnificently. The other has tried, lazily, feebly, but something within her keeps her from doing so. Precisely because she has not found herself, she cannot move further.[32]

In life, Ocampo often compensated for that lack of eloquence with gestures. They were usually munificent (selling a tiara to pay for Tagore's stay in Buenos Aires, showering Virginia Woolf, who made fun of her in return, with extravagant gifts) and often overbearing. It was as if, when the writer faltered, the *grande dame* stepped in, asserting herself where the writer could not. This too-easy shifting of roles worked its way into her writing with infelicitous consequences: moments of rare literary effectiveness are succeeded by petty grievances or imperious statements, often bearing the imprint of class. In addition to her gender, and perhaps even more than her gender, it is this hesitation between two very different forms of self-validation—literary competence and social standing—that may well account for Ocampo's final lack of writerly *authority.* It certainly accounts for the way she is so often perceived by the least kind of her critics: as a rich woman, at once fascinating and exasperating, who writes.

At their best, Ocampo's *Testimonios,* essays on subjects ranging from current world events (women's rights, the Nuremberg trials) to everyday minutiae which she considered no less worthy (traffic in Buenos Aires, the smell and colors of trees), to her encounters with books and their authors (usually her most memorable pieces) turn her lack of eloquence into an advantage. In these scattered writings, the role of the witness is Ocampo's mask of choice: if she cannot easily speak, then she will testify to the words of others. Ten collections of essays, published under a title that emphasizes that testimonial stance, record her meetings, conversations, interviews with figures as diverse as Ravel, Mussolini, Malraux, García Lorca, Anna de Noailles, Nehru, Stieglitz. And, when the *Testimonios* do not deal directly with live interlocutors—those figures Ocampo calls "men-books-ideas"—they deal, for the greater part, with reading and books. In all these encounters Ocampo plays Galeotto for the reader: she is the go-between transmitting the voices of others. The *Testimonios* are, in a sense, mini-performances in which Ocampo, to use a metaphor taken from the French classical theatre she knows so well, plays the role of a *suivante* to the hero or heroine of her choice.[33] Yet as in paintings in which the artist, while ostensibly painting another, paints himself, too, in the corner of the picture, so Ocampo uses these *testimonios* as vehicles for oblique self-figuration: these texts are no less autobiographical, finally, than the autobiography itself. Her own tendency to silence is replaced by the voices of others, voices that will become, as she writes them down, her own voice. Besides testifying to the people and events in her life, Ocampo's *Testimonios,* as well as her autobiography, testify to her quest for expression, to finding a *voice* for her *presence* so that her performance will be complete.[34]

That Ocampo's choice of a writing language was so riddled with anxiety surely contributed in great measure to her difficulties. Torn between a native language which she was taught to consider inadequate (Spanish words were not "words with which one thinks")[35] and the second language, French, in whose comforting cadences and prestigious rhetoric she seemed to perform best, she would start out in literature by posturing as a "French" writer.[36] If Ocampo would gradually come to master her own language, to the point of attaining that seemingly effortless juncture of the spoken and the written that Borges identifies as a typically Argentine *entonación,*[37] a good part of her writing, and most importantly her autobiography, would rely to the end on duplication as a necessary vehicle for self-expression: Ocampo continued to write first in French, then to rewrite herself in Spanish.

(A close examination of her style throughout the six volumes of the autobiography sheds light on how the process worked. Ocampo lived long enough to translate—to repossess—only the first three volumes, which read admirably well. The other three were published posthumously *as if she herself had also translated them,* although it is clear, from the inferior translation, that someone other than Ocampo performed the task. While a disservice, prompted perhaps by a misguided sense of loyalty, the anonymous translation of the last three volumes proves, through its flaws and by comparison with the first three, to what point Ocampo rewrote her texts and rendered her linguistic duplicity unnoticeable.)

Until the end, then, the process is the same—the appropriation of texts and voices of others. Self-expression is, necessarily, a process of *alteration*: one speaks through the voice of an *Other* even if that Other—as in the case of Ocampo's self-translation—is a simulacrum of oneself. Could one not compare the autobiographical venture, asks Ocampo, resorting once more to the theatre, to what Jouvet says of actors? "One enters a role, slides into it, one wields the text, one wields it cunningly, *surreptitiously one replaces oneself*" (Autobiografía, VI, II). The process of reconstituting this *altered* voice, the culling of literary fragments and "great" voices for the purpose of self-expression, brings to mind the method of Seneca's *hypomnemata*, as described by Foucault:

> The role of writing is to constitute, with everything that has been constituted by reading, a "body" *(quicquid lectione collectum est, stilus redigat in corpus)*. That body must be understood not as a body of doctrine but rather—and following the so often quoted metaphor of digestion—as the very body of him who, on transcribing his reading, makes that reading and its truth his own. Writing transforms that which is seen or heard "into strength and blood" *(in vires, in sanguinem)*.[38]

In this light, Ocampo's best-known cultural venture, the founding in 1931 of *Sur* (a review that was to be, for the next forty years, one of the most influential literary journals of the Spanish-speaking world), becomes another form of (distanced) self-writing, an extension of a presence that increasingly needed to be made public.[39] The concert of voices that Ocampo transforms *in vires, in sanguinem* for her own self will become her other body, that of the review to which her name is permanently allied.

I am aware that a successful argument could be made in favor of the dependent nature of Ocampo's reading. Such an argument would highlight the fact that the reading to which she turned in search of self-expression was taken mainly from a male-authored canon; the fact that Francesca, the readerly emblem of her choice, was a character in a text within that male-authored canon; the fact that the writers she befriended as mentors were mostly men. To this perceived dependency of Ocampo as a woman one could add her excessive dependency, as a Latin American, on European models; a dependency evinced not only in the texts she quotes in her own writing but in the preference for the oddly anachronistic assortment of foreigners—Gramsci next to Denis de Rougemont, for example—that became the hallmark of her review. Beatriz Sarlo perceptively interprets this "*bovarysme* with regard to European writers" as a delayed response: "One might say that *Sur* is the review that Victoria Ocampo would have wanted to read as an adolescent and a young woman. It responds, more than twenty years later, to her unfinished struggle for initiation."[40] It is not, however, my intention to evaluate *Sur* in itself, as a cultural product of a period.[41] I wish to consider instead the first aspect of Ocampo's dependency, which affecting her reading, writing, and composition of self as a woman.

It is true that male presences inform Ocampo's system of self-defining voices. If Ocampo does refer frequently to women—Woolf, Anna de Noailles, the Brontës, Mistral, María de Maeztu, Adrienne Monnier—either for their live presence or for their equally live texts, she never *quotes* these women, except in those pieces she devotes specifically to them. In other words, although sympathetic to women's texts—witness the admirable intermingling of Ocampo's voice and that of Woolf in "Virginia Woolf in My Memory"[42]—Ocampo does not incorporate them into that larger and freer system of quotations on which she relies for voice. There appears to be a contradiction here, one that betrays a conflict between two modes of self-representation.[43] On the one hand, there is Ocampo's desire to "some day write, more or less well, but *like a woman*," because "a woman cannot unburden herself of her feelings and thoughts in the style of a man, anymore than she can speak with a man's voice";[44] on the other hand, there is the fact that Ocampo most often speaks, if not *with* a man's voice, *through* men's voices. Ocampo never resolved this ambivalence; nor did she ever refer, she who was aware that her writing was marked not only by her gender but by her Latin American origins, to other Latin American women writers (Gabriela Mistral being the exception) embarked on a similar quest for self-expression. This silence should be read less as a sign of snobbery, I suspect, than as what could be called an "anxiety of sorority," a case of literary sibling rivalry.[45] Like Sarmiento, Ocampo creates distance around her in order to be perceived alone.

The question is, though, do the voices appropriated by Ocampo continue to be solely men's voices? A possible solution to the predicament created by Ocampo's ambiguity takes us back to the scene of reading; to Ocampo not only as reader but as woman reader. Discussing Artemisia Gentileschi's painting within a male pictoric tradition, Mary Jacobus writes: "In order to see herself or be seen she has to insert herself into a preexisting narrative."[46] The same might be said of Ocampo who, as a reader and autobiographer who seeks self-definition through reading, can insert herself only in a masculine lineage of texts and a masculine system of representation—the only one available to her—all the while wishing for another.

What might be judged Ocampo's weakness could well be, given her time and her circumstance, proof of her resourcefulness. Lacking a voice of her own and a feminist system of representation, she repossesses voices of the male-authored canon and, by the sheer fact of enunciating them from a feminine "I," succeeds, much in the way Pierre Menard did when rewriting Cervantes, in differentiating her text. The constant misunderstandings between Ocampo and the "men-books-ideas" she seeks so passionately (and inadvisedly) to dialogue with, the unfamiliar slant given by her comments to canonically "correct" texts, the feeling, so often experienced by her reader, that her quotations, while impeccably accurate, are somehow off-key, are all symptomatic signs, I believe, of that difference. A different way of reading it is also a different way of reading oneself into being. "The alterity of feminist reading is posited, not simply in opposition to masculinist reading, not simply as a move that carries off familiar readings and puts them to strange uses, but rather as a move that installs strangeness (femininity) within reading itself," writes Jacobus.[47] The alterity of self-figuration through reading, I would argue, is a move introducing a similar uncanniness in the autobiographical venture. It is not surprising then that, behind these readings that Ocampo appropriates in her autobiography in order to compose her own voice, lies a question, a *want* that echoes throughout her text and is never satisfied: "I am the *other*. But what?" ("Soy lo *otro*. Pero qué?" (Autobiografía I, 61).

NOTES

1. The autobiographical nature of the entire works of Victoria Ocampo is patent. My study will focus on the posthumously published *Autobiografía* comprising six volumes:

   I.   *El archipiélago*
   II. *El imperio insular*
   III. *La rama de Salzburgo*
   IV. *Viraje*
   V.   *Figuras simbólicas. Medida de Francia*
   VI. *Sur y cia.*

   Subsequent references to these editions appear in the text. I shall also discuss a good number of Ocampo's first-person chronicles and essays collected in ten volumes under the general title of *Testimonios*.

2. Another version of this first scene of reading may be found in "De la cartilla al libro" in *Testimonios*, 6a serie: "Before learning [the alphabet], I so loved stories, and books because they had stories in them, that, according to my mother, I would settle down to read, with an open book in my hands, repeating a story that I knew by heart and turning the pages at the right moment" (137).

3. "[I] pretended to read. My eyes followed the black signs without skipping a single one, and I told myself a story out loud, being careful to utter all the syllables" (Sartre, 48).

4. Sartre, 44.

5. The second volume of the autobiography, *El imperio insular*, presents an incisive critique of the education of Argentine women in the late nineteenth century. To back it, Ocampo includes the letters she wrote to her friend Delfina Bunge in adolescence: "I wanted to stress how much I suffered, how much I was mentally tortured, early on in my adolescence, by the situation of women. That suffering was not without cause. I was wasting my time, I was hopelessly wasting my time. And those lost years are impossible to recover later on (I mean in discipline, in seriousness towards study)" (II, 143).

6. "Malandanzas de una autodidacta" in *Testimonios,* 5a serie.

7. In addition to her autobiography, specific references to childhood reading may be found in "Ordenar el caos," a review article on Graham Greene's autobiography (*Testimonios,* 9a serie, 58–67) and in "La influencia de la lectura sobre nuestra infancia" in the same volume of *Testimonios.*

8. *Testimonios,* 6a serie, 143.

9. "Palabras francesas," in *Testimonios* (Madrid:), 35.

10. "Emily Brontë, terra incognita" in *Testimonios,* 2a serie, 115–116.

11. "El aguilucho" in *Testimonios,* 8a serie, 100. Subsequent references to this piece appear in the text.

12. For an almost identical version of this discovery, see Autobiografía II, 62–63.

13. Letter to Delfina Bunge, 3 August 1908, quoted in Meyer, 31.

14. In these performances, Ocampo notes rapturously: "I expressed myself fully, entirely. I *communicated," Autobiografía,* IV, 103. Of her concession to the wishes of her parents, she writes to Ortega y Gasset: "I have sacrificed to my parents convictions I should have sacrificed to no one. Given my character, the sacrifice should have been not to sacrifice myself but to sacrifice them. That is, to sacrifice the false view they had of things (in MY opinion) even if it made them suffer. But I was a coward out of love. It's a fault I still have and I don't know that I'll ever be rid of it" (letter to Ortega, cited in Autobiografía II, 175).

15. "In those years, the attitude of Argentine 'society' towards a woman writer was not particularly indulgent. . . . [Writing] was considered scandalous, as much as driving a car in the streets of Buenos Aires. For the latter I was showered with insults. And what passers-by shouted at me when they saw me go by at the wheel of my car, others thought when they read my articles" (Autobiografía III, 105).

16. *Virginia Woolf,* 44–45.

17. A detailed, personal account of the political struggle for women's rights in that period may be found in the second volume of María Rosa Oliver's autobiography, *La vida cotidiana,* 350–355.

18. Sandra M. Gilbert and Susan Gubar, "Infection in the Sentence: The Woman Writer and the Anxiety of Authorship," 45–92.

19. *Testimonios,* 8a serie, 195. Ocampo quotes from Valéry's "De la diction des vers," 1255.

20. Thus, for example, Doris Meyer writes: " . . . Victoria had identified her adolescent heroes. Not surprisingly, they were all characters in her favorite books, and all of them were men. . . . [F]emale roles were singularly uninspiring at the turn of the century. Both in life and literature, the Victorian age fostered the notion that a woman should be chaste and long-suffering . . ." (Meyer, p. 27). The statement implies a view of identification that is strictly mimetic and coeval: it does not allow for the possibility of anachronism in the process of *literary* identification.

21. Meyer does not mention Madame de Staël in her biography of Ocampo. Yet Ocampo writes to Delfina Bunge in 1906: "Mme Necker de Saussure was right to observe in a footnote: *'In writing, she wished to express what she carried within her far more than to achieve a work of art.'* More than ever have I had the familiar feeling of living what I was reading. I was *Corinne.* Her fate was mine" (Autobiografía II, 166). Later in the same volume, Ocampo again resorts to Madame de Staël "because I find her so useful to determine my own position" (Autobiografía II, 179).

Drieu la Rochelle, a friend and sometime lover of Ocampo, compares her in his journals to Madame de Staël. The comparison, in fact, is far from flattering: "Victoria will have been my Madame de Staël. But she was less substantial; in a few months, I was practically free from her grip" (Drieu la Rochelle, 208). Ocampo defends herself gallantly (Autobiografía II, 167). For further reference to Madame de Staël and politics, see Autobiografía IV, 14.

22. *De Francesca a Beatrice*, 27.

23. Delfina Bunge, nine years Ocampo's senior, wrote poetry in French at the time these letters were exchanged. The friendship would soon die out due to Bunge's growing religious prejudice and the protofascist ideology she shared with her husband, the writer Manuel Gálvez. Besides poetry and essays on religion, Bunge published a childhood memoir in Spanish, *Viaje alrededor de mi infancia.*

24. Years later Ocampo tells an interviewer: "In my childhood, in my adolescence and in my first plunge into young adulthood, I lived in books what I could not live in life, because life was full of absurd taboos for a girl or a young woman when I was at either stage. After that, I lived in life what I had lived before in literature and literature paled. It was used to relate, more or less indirectly or directly, what was lived *[lo vivido]*" (interview with Fryda Schultz de Mantovani in *Testimonios*, 8a serie, 297).

25. Nora Domínguez and Adriana Rodríguez Persico, in a generally thoughtful article, suggest Racine as Ocampo's intertext in this third volume, with the character of Hermione as her emblem. Their notion that Ocampo "performs" her text is convincing. However, since Racine's text is never summoned in *La rama de Salzburgo* in any constructive way, the suggestion seems rather hasty ("Autobiografía de Victoria Ocampo. La pasión del modelo").

26. As a point of curiosity, I quote from a footnote in an Argentine translation of the *Commedia*, a translation sponsored by the Fondo Nacional de las Artes on whose board of directors Ocampo served: "A similar role [that of go-between] is played by an inanimate object, the book, in the relationship between wife and brother-in-law. The episode constitutes an early but unquestionable example of the harmful influence of certain readings." Dante Alighieri, *La divina comedia*, 313, n. 137. The narrowness of the translator and critic ironically echoes the parental and societal repression Ocampo fought all her life.

27. Marcelle Thiébaux argues that women's reading is intolerable to patriarchal discourse and that it is constantly interrupted, redirected, and incorporated into the (patriarchal) text. "Dante records Francesca's own story of how reading about adultery stirred her and her lover's passion. The fateful kiss interrupts the reading: 'That day we read no further.' Now she is a text in hell" (53). I take issue with some points of this particular interpretation while not disagreeing with its general argument. Francesca's and Paolo's reading is less an act of voyeuristic titillation than a moment of knowledge (indeed, Dante uses the verb *conoscere* twice); reading does more than arouse the two lovers, it allows them to recognize and to name. Thus "the fateful kiss" does not interrupt the reading but in a sense continues it. Greenberg concurs with Thiébaux's interpretation of the Francesca episode and, extending it to Ocampo, speaks of a voyeuristic dimension in Ocampo's reading of Dante (150), a view I do not share.

28. The additional fact that she enters the literary scene with a text in French prompts Beatriz Sarlo to comment shrewdly: "Foreign language was the language of feminine consumption not of production. Victoria Ocampo subverts it, making it productive—to read, to receive, is also to quote, to give back. . . . She gives back what her family had given her in childhood

but changes its sign: what her social milieu considered an ornament, Victoria Ocampo turns into an instrument" (*Una modernidad periférica: Buenos Aires 1920–1930*, 91).

29. The predicament of male critics when confronted with women's texts is not infrequent, nor are the contradictory statements they issue on the texts themselves. For a similar situation, see Gilbert and Gubar on the conflictive reception of Emily Dickinson, *The Madwoman in the Attic*, 541–543.

30. For a lucid critique of some versions of this position, see Jones, 361–377.

31. Of her misunderstanding with one of those men, Ocampo writes: "Maybe he ignored (as do most men) up to what point I was capable of feeling passion (dissociated from amorous passion) for a book, an idea, for a man who would incarnate that book, that idea, without having that passion invade other regions of my being. Those regions seemed to have their own laws, their requirements, their rights to veto in accordance with their nature. If the man-book-idea was not accepted by that other part of myself . . . distance became definitive and frontiers were set up. This is what happened to me with Ortega" (Autobiografía III, 110). On her particularly irksome misunderstanding with Keyserling she wrote *El viajero y una de sus sombras* and also devoted a good portion of the fourth volume of her autobiography to the subject.

32. "Carta a Virginia Woolf" in *Testimonios* (Madrid), 9.

33. On Ocampo's *Testimonios* as subjective and ahistorical constructs, see Marta Gallo.

34. Thus Cortázar comments on the immediacy of Ocampo's *Testimonios* as verbal performances: "All I know of her are her books, her voice and *Sur*." He adds: "This book *[Soledad sonora]* forces us to accept the role of direct interlocutors. . . . Each chapter bites into its subject matter with an impulse that is both confidential and defiant. . . ." (Julio Cortázar, "Soledad sonora").

35. "Palabras francesas" in *Testimonios* (Madrid), 34. In this same piece, an interesting example of linguistic soul-searching, she adds: "Add to this that our society was somewhat indifferent to matters of the mind, even quite ignorant. Many of us, unconsciously, had ended up believing monstrosities. For example, that the Spanish language was incapable of expressing what lay beyond the purely material, practical aspects of life; a language in which it was a bit ridiculous to strive for precision, that is, nuance. . . . Many of us used Spanish like those travelers who learn a few words in the language of the country they are visiting because those words are useful in getting them out of trouble in their hotels, at the station, in shops. But that is as far as they go" (36).

36. It is interesting that the other Ocampo sister to become a writer, Silvina, went through a similar struggle, torn between an inadequate command of written Spanish and the ease with which she wrote in the other language—English, in her particular case. See Noemí Ulla, 16.

37. A way of "speaking the written" that Ocampo admired in her favorite performers, Marguerite Moreno (whose acting she preferred to the declamatory style of a Sarah Bernhardt) and Laurence Olivier. (*Soledad sonora*, 194–195).

38. Michel Foucault, "L'écriture de soi," 8, 12.

39. On *Sur* as a form of "personal writing," see María Luisa Bastos, "Escrituras ajenas, expresión propia" and "Dos líneas testimoniales: *Sur*, los escritos de Victoria Ocampo."

40. Beatriz Sarlo, *Una modernidad periférica*, 89.

41. The most complete evaluation of *Sur*'s merits and shortcomings is that of John King, *Sur*.

See also María Luisa Bastos; Eduardo Paz Leston; Beatriz Sarlo *et al.*, "Dossier: La revista *Sur*"; Nicolás Rosa; Blas Matamoro.

42. "Virginia Woolf en mi recuerdo" in *Testimonios*, 2a serie, 415–428. English version in Doris Meyer, *Victoria Ocampo. Against the Wind and the Tide*, 235–240.

43. For competing self-representations in autobiographies written by women, see Sidonie Smith, especially chap. 3: "Woman's Story and the Engendering of Self-Representation."

44. *Testimonios*, (Madrid) 12.

45. This attitude, one should add, is not exclusive to Ocampo. See Sandra M. Gilbert and Susan Gubar, "'Forward into the Past': The Female Affiliation Complex." On Ocampo's attitude in particular, see Matamoro, 80.

46. Mary Jacobus, 132.

47. *Ibid.*, 286.

13

"One Nail Takes Out Another":
Power, Gender, and Revolution in
Julia Alvarez's Novels

KELLY OLIVER

Between every point of a social body, between a man
and a woman, between the members of a family,
between a master and a pupil, between everyone
who knows and everyone who does not, there exist
relations of power . . .

—Michel Foucault[1]

*O*ne of the central themes in Julia Alvarez's novels is the way that power
dynamics shift according to race, class, and gender positions. Alvarez's
reflections on power, resistance, and domination in *How the Garcia
Girls Lost Their Accents, In the Time of the Butterflies,* and *¡Yo!,* can be produc-
tively used to exemplify both the strengths and limitations of Michel Foucault's
analysis of power, resistance, and domination. On the one hand, Alvarez's reflections on power, in her novels bring to life Foucault's notion of local transformation and immanent resistance. On the other hand, her focus on the power
dynamics of race, class, and gender in the private domestic sphere unsettles a
Foucauldian analysis more concerned with disciplinary techniques in public

institutions such as schools, churches, prisons, and hospitals. Alvarez's use of the conventions of domestic femininity, womanhood, and motherhood, to resist patriarchal authority both at the level of private family life and in public institutions, including government, at once demonstrates Foucault's thesis that resistance to domination must take localized forms and at the same time makes all the more striking the Foucaultian blind spot in terms of sexual difference in relation to power.[2]

In addition, Alvarez's attempts to fragment the authority of a unified centered narrative voice through her use of changing perspectives and voices, and the tensions between domination and resistance raised by such an attempt that become explicit in her latest novel ¡Yo! are symptomatic of the Foucaultian notion of power which is necessarily both the power to dominate and the power to resist. ¡Yo! can be read as a literary exercise in the necessary tension between the attempt to open one's own discourse onto the voice of the others, on the one hand, and the solipsistic world that attempt can engender, on the other— between having a voice and being silenced, between resisting domination and dominating through resistance.

POWER AND RESISTANCE

Foucault suggests that resistance does not have to originate from outside the system of dominance. In fact, it can't. To say, as Foucault does, that one cannot get outside power is not to say that it is necessary to accept an inescapable form of domination (*Power/Knowledge*, 141). Foucault insists that "resistance to power does not have to come from elsewhere to be real, nor is it inexorably frustrated through being the compatriot of power. It exists all the more by being in the same place as power. . . ." (*Power/Knowledge*, 142). Moreover, "[i]t would not be possible for power relations to exist without points of insubordination" (*Dreyfus*, 225). Power demands resistance and resistance requires power.

To say that everyone is caught in the machine of power is not to say that there aren't those who benefit and those who suffer. For Foucault, "everyone does not occupy the same position; certain positions preponderate and permit an effect of supremacy to be produced" (*Power/Knowledge*, 156; *Dreyfus*, 223) "Every relationship of power puts into operation differentiations which are at the same time its conditions and results" (*Dreyfus*, 223). The oppressive effects of power relations are very real. And although resistance is part of this power relation, it too is very real:

> [T]here is a plurality of resistances, each of them a special case: resistances that are possible, necessary, improbable; others that are spontaneous, savage, solitary, concerted, rampant, or violent; still others that are quick to compromise,

interested, or sacrificial; by definition, they can only exist in the strategic field of power relations. But this does not mean that they are only a reaction or rebound, forming with respect to the basic domination an underside that is in the end always passive, doomed to perpetual defeat. (*The History of Sexuality* (a), 96)

In fact, Foucault's analysis points to the fragility of systems of domination. They do not have one central power and therefore they do not have only one central weak spot. Rather, they have weakness everywhere. There is potential for resistance on every level. Because power is not possessed and because it doesn't just emanate from the top down, even those disenfranchised by the dominant system are empowered. Power is not possessed; it is not something that belongs exclusively to the oppressors (*Discipline and Punish* (a), 26). Foucault says that "power is not a thing, it is a relationship between two individuals, a relationship which is such that one can direct the behavior of another or determine the behavior of another" ("What Our Present Is," 155).

Foucault suggests that "local, specific struggles" against local forms of power and resistance on all levels can affect change (*Power/Knowledge,* 130–131). If the state is the effect of a multiplicity of institutions, it can be changed by changing those institutions. Changes can ripple through the system. Just as disciplinary patterns are repeated on different levels and cascade upward through the system, so too changes and resistance can move from one location to another throughout the system. Foucault's local strategies provide the hope that individuals can make a difference. Because power dynamics are fluid and always shifting, resistance to domination is possible. In *The History of Sexuality* Foucault concludes that: "one is dealing with mobile and transitory points of resistance, producing cleaves in a society that shift about, fracturing unities and affecting regroupings, furrowing across individuals themselves, cutting them up and remolding them, marking off irreducible regions in them, in their bodies and minds" (*The History of Sexuality* (a), 96).

SHIFTING POWER RELATIONS

Julia Alvarez's first novel, *How the Garcia Girls Lost Their Accents,* is in one sense a study in mobile and transitory points of resistance and shifting power dynamics that fracture unity and affect regroupings. Throughout this novel, Alvarez shows shifting power relations between race, class, and gender. The same individual in different contexts occupies positions of power and disempowered positions. For example in the first chapter, "Antojos," Yolanda Garcia returns to the Dominican Republic after five years without a visit and ventures into the countryside to pick fresh guavas. The first chapter opens with the narrator describing the color-coding of class hierarchy: old aunts in greys and blacks of widowhood, cousins in bright colors, nursemaids in white uniforms, and kitchen help in black uniforms (3). This chapter and the book as a whole repeatedly recount the deferential gestures that signal power relations between race, class, and gender. When scolded for not having matches on hand to light the candles on the cake, one of the maids, Iluminada, makes a pleading gesture with her hands clasped against her breast (4). When another maid, Altagracia, is asked to explain the word "antojo" to Yolanda, she "puts her brown hands away in her uniform pockets" and "says in a small voice. You're the one to know" (8). These deferential gestures signal class hierarchy and the differential power relation in terms of class privilege.

Later in this chapter, when Yolanda is picking guavas and she gets a flat tire, gender hierarchy displaces class hierarchy and the power dynamics shift. Alone with her car, Yolanda is terrified when two men appear out of the grove with machetes hanging from their belts. She considers running, but she is paralyzed with fear and rendered speechless (19). The narrator describes her repeating the same pleading gesture of Illuminada, hands clasped on her chest (20). Yolanda's class privilege in relation to the maid, and in relation to the young boy, José, who has taken her to pick the guavas, shifts in relation to these two men whose gender privilege is threatening to Yolanda. Now she is the one using deferential gestures.

The power dynamics again suddenly shift in this scene when she begins speaking in English and the two men conclude that she is American. At this point, they are "rendered docile by her gibberish" and when she mentions the name of her aunt's rich friends, the Mirandas, "their eyes light up with respect" (20–21). In this scene of shifting power relations, class privilege has given way to gender privilege, and then the relation between gender hierarchy and class heirarchy is reversed again. In the end, when Yolanda tries to confirm her class privilege and express her gratitude by paying the men, they refuse and look at the ground, as the narrator tells us, with the same deferential gestures of Illuminada and the little boy José (22). The chapter ends with José returning from the Mirandas' slapped, shamed, and accused of lying when he tells the guard that a woman is out picking guavas alone. Even Yolanda's dollar bills can't cheer him. The collusion of rigid gender and class structures results in José's punishment, which is just intensified when Yolanda offers him money. Even in her attempts to make José happy, Yolanda reaffirms her class dominance over him.

Although the novel is full of this type of power reversal and shifting power dynamics, I will mention just one more example of shifting power relations between race, class, and gender from the tenth chapter, "Floor Show." As the novel moves back in time, this chapter takes place in New York when the Garcia girls are young, shortly after their family has fled the Trujillo dictatorship. Here, the Garcias have been invited to join Dr. Fanning and his wife for dinner at a restaurant. Dr. Fanning had arranged the fellowship that allowed "Papi" Garcia to take his family to New York and was trying to help Papi get a job. For days "Mami" gave the girls instructions on how to behave, and on the evening of the dinner she dressed them in binding braids and tights in the hopes of disciplining not only their behavior but also their bodies. The dinner scene is very tense because the Garcias, used to having class privileges in the Dominican Republic, are financially beholden to the Fannings. In their presence both Mami and Papi Garcia display deferential gestures and repeatedly look down at the floor.

This chapter displays several reversals between race, class, and gender hierarchies. First, because Mami Garcia studied in the United States as a girl, her English is better than Papi's and this gives her more power than him in social situations: "Mami was the leader now that they lived in the States. She had gone to school in the States. *She* spoke English without a heavy accent" (176). The power dynamics between mother and father are reversed by the power of linguistic access. Class dynamics shift when the Garcias, struggling to make ends meet in the United States, no longer have class privilege. Papi no longer has the honor of paying for dinner. The Fannings, who appeared in the Dominican Republic as silly-looking tourists speaking bad Spanish, now make the Garcias look small (184). Gender dynamics shift when Mrs. Fanning kisses Papi Garcia on the way to the bathroom. In this context his class and race deference to Mrs. Fanning make him powerless to object to her flirtations. Power dynamics shift again when Sandi, who witnessed the kiss, uses what she saw to blackmail her father into allowing her to get a doll that they cannot afford and for which the Fannings end up paying. In this chapter Sandi recognizes the value of passing as a white American when she studies her fair-skinned and blue eyed beauty in the mirror after she has seen the power Mrs. Fanning exercised over her father with the kiss.

Shifting power dynamics are also central to Alvarez's second novel, *In the Time of the Butterflies.* Here, there is a scene similar to "Floor Show" where a daughter becomes more powerful than her father when he wants her to keep a secret from her mother. When Minerva Mirabal discovers that her father has a secret second family, she gains power over her father; gender and generation power relations shift. In the end, it is this second illegitimate family, much poorer and less powerful than the first, that smuggles letters and care packages back and forth between the girls in prison and their family at home; the power dynamics of class shift when the lower-class family has access to the guards in a way unavailable to the upper-class family.

The narrative structure of Alvarez's third novel, *¡Yo!,* is motivated by shifting power dynamics. Like her earlier two novels, *¡Yo!,* is written from different perspectives and in different voices, but with the third novel, perspective and voice become the focus of the novel itself; even the plot revolves around the question of narrative voice. In the first novel, the story of the Garcia girls is told as the stories of the four daughters and their parents. The chapters are written about each of them and, with the exception of Yolanda's chapters written in the first person and the unidentified "we" of the chapter "A Regular Revolution," the narrator refers to them all in the third person. We still have one omniscient narrator who sees and describes the inner lives of the different protagonists. In the second novel, the chapters are written from different first-person perspectives. Although there is still a thin narrator, each chapter is written from the perspective of one of the four Mirabal sisters. While the first novel gives us different perspectives by telling different stories, it does not give us different voices. The second novel gives us different perspectives by giving us different voices. This shift in perspective as well as voice unsettles the power of the narrator or any one character to direct the point of view of the novel. In the third novel, perspective and voice even become plot themes. Characters in the novel challenge the narrator's authority. In addition, for the first time in Alvarez's novels, chapters are written from the perspectives and in the voices of minor characters, who challenge the point of view of major characters and the narrator.

Alvarez's fictional account of shifting power relations embodies Foucault's theory of mobile and transitory sites of resistance that reconfigure always shifting power relations. These novels exemplify some of the ways in which, as Foucault says, individuals are furrowed by intersecting axes of power, cut up and remolded and marked by their various positions in shifting power relations that constantly regroup them in terms of race, class, and gender, among other alliances. While Foucault's genealogies are peopled with boys and men locked into mental and penal institutions, Alvarez's novels are peopled with girls and women locked into patriarchal conventions. The contrast between the everyday lives of ordinary women incarcerated in their own homes and disciplined through mundane practices and Foucault's descriptions of public disciplinary practices used to crush "insane," "criminal," and "perverted" boys both expands a Foucauldian notion of power to include domestic space and highlights the lack of attention to this feminine space in Foucault's own work. While the logic of power determines that it shifts between resistance and dominance, Alvarez's novels make clear that the differential norms for masculinity and femininity within patriarchal cultures circumscribe power relations differently for men and women.

In her depiction of shifts in power relations, Alvarez is not only sensitive to the ways in which individuals move between positions of relative power but she also shows how individuals are marked and excluded by group identities that divide them against themselves. Alvarez's focus on shifting power relations of race, class, and gender show how these group identities work as what Foucault calls "dividing practices" that split individuals and individuality itself (*Dreyfus,* 208). Foucault describes how the individual needs to be recognized in his individuality but not to the point that his identity or individuality is used to exclude him. Individuality itself is a dividing practice that divides us against ourselves. Foucault says that the power of dividing practices: ". . . applies itself to immediate everyday life which categorizes the individual, marks him by his own individuality, attaches him to his own identity, imposes a law of truth on him which he must recognize and which others have to recognize in him. It is a form of power which makes individuals subjects" (*Dreyfus,* 212). Alvarez's fiction is a study in how individuals become subjected to race, class, and gender in ways that mark them, cut them up, remold them, and reconfigure them relative to their position in relation to the shifting power dynamics of racist, classist, and patriarchal cultures.

REVOLUTION

Revolution is a recurring trope in all of Alvarez's novels. Like Foucault, Alvarez is concerned with local resistance to domination and exclusion. The revolutions of Alvarez's novels, however, are not monumental actions that overthrow governments but the everyday struggles with authority that enable and empower resistance. Alvarez's revolutions are localized sites of resistance that often use the very structure and traditions of domination itself against domination. They are Foucauldian revolutions. As Foucault says: "points of resistance are present everywhere in the power network. Hence there is no single locus of great Refusal, no soul of revolt, source of all rebellions, or pure law of the revolutionary. Instead, there is a plurality of resistances, each of them a special case. . . ." (*The History of Sexuality* (a), 95–96). More specifically, Alvarez is concerned with the ways in which the very trappings of femininity, womanhood, and motherhood can be used against patriarchy in order to open up a space for women's resistance to patriarchal domination.

How the Garcia Girls Lost Their Accents documents various localized struggles of women against patriarchal domination. In a chapter entitled "A Regular Revolution," Alvarez suggests that revolution is a matter of "constant skirmishes" on an everyday mundane level (111). She compares the four daughters' revolt against their parent's authority and against patriarchal authority to their father's participation in the revolt against the Trujillo dictatorship. This comparison itself suggests that revolution happens continually through everyday resistance rather than "global" overthrow. The girls plot their revolution using the accepted patriarchal codes for chaperones and young ladies' proper behavior against those very codes. Alvarez shows how the patriarchal traditions are turned against themselves in order to undermine patriarchal authority. Everyday practices of domination also open up everyday modes of resistance. Alvarez's novels deliver the Foucauldian message that power is not only the power to dominate but also the power to resist.

In "A Regular Revolution" three sisters, Carla, Yolanda, and Sandi, are trying to rescue the fourth, Fifi, from getting pregnant and stuck marrying their very traditional sexist island cousin Mundín. Here, Mundín is called a "tyrant" and the girls are staging a "revolution," "a coup on the same Avenida where a decade ago the dictator was cornered and wounded on his way to a tryst with his mistress" (127). The girls use the traditional restrictions on girls and women to their advantage when they insist that their cousin and chaperone Manuel take them home early without the lovers Mundín and Fifi. They use Manuel's responsibility for them to combat the "male loyalty" that "keeps the macho system going" (127). Manuel is forced to take them home without the lovers, which blows their cover. The "first bomb" explodes on women's side of the patio when the girls answer that Fifi is with Mundín and then "there is an embarrassed silence in which the words *her reputation* are as palpable as if someone had hung a wedding dress in the air" (129). The girls use the patriarchal convention that girls are not to be left alone without their chaperone to expose the breach of another convention that girls are not to be left alone with their *novios*. Their motives, however, are not to protect their sister's reputation or virginity but to protect her from the oppressive patriarchal culture that would demand and circumscribe marriage, family, and subservience to her husband.

The plot of Alvarez's *In the Time of the Butterflies* revolves around revolution, specifically the Mirabal sisters' involvement in the underground revolution against Trujillo. Again revolution and resistance are not painted in the broad strokes of bloody battles and guerilla uprisings but in the mundane makeup of femininity. Alvarez's story of the Mirabal sister's revolution against Trujillo is as much about their own local revolutions against the restrictions of patriarchy as it is about a rebellion against the restrictions of dictatorship. In fact, the dictator's authority is depicted as founded on the macho image of a patriarch who has his ways with women.

Like *How the Garcia Lost Their Accents, In the Time of the Butterflies* describes how patriarchal conventions are used to undermine patriarchy and how the trappings of femininity are used to fuel revolution, this time political as well as personal revolution. The church, crucifixes, and praying become forms of rebellion (237). The sisters use the script they learned from the nuns for writing out Bible passages to list the ammunition in their hiding places (168). The sisters' mental and physical discipline while in prison is compared to keeping the baby on a feeding schedule (235). Maté uses her long hair and hair ribbons to smuggle news stories to other prisoners and secret notes detailing the human right's abuses of the Trujillo regime to the Organization of American States's representatives when they visit the prison (246, 252). A young woman's diary becomes incriminating evidence against the dictatorship's human right's abuses. The election of "Miss University" becomes the promise of democratic elections;

Minerva tells Maté that "this country hasn't voted for anything in twenty-six years and it's only these silly little elections that keep the faint memory of democracy going" (136).

For the Mirabal sisters, love, family, and revolution are inseparable. Passion between lovers feeds passion for revolution, and the common struggle against the dictator fuels personal passion. The struggle for freedom keeps Minerva and Manolo together through difficult personal times. Maté falls in love with Leandro when she meets him delivering ammunition for the revolutionaries. She sees the revolution as her chance for personal independence from a family that treats her like the baby. More than that, she realizes that her looks and easy manner with men can serve the revolution. She writes in her diary: "now I can use my talents for the revolution" (143). Patricia becomes involved after her church group witnesses young guerillas attacked by Trujillo's soldiers. She sees the face of her own son Nelson in the face of a dying young guerilla and from that moment on is committed to saving her family by fighting Trujillo. While these women are fighting against the national patriarch, Trujillo, they are also fighting against their own local patriarchs at home. They all have various skirmishes with their father and their husbands in order to assert themselves against patriarchal conventions.

If, as Minerva Mirabal says of the dance that cures her headache, "one nail takes out another," then she is the hammer (97). She knows how to strike one nail of patriarchy against another in order to get what she wants. When her father won't let her leave the farm to go to law school, and when El Jefe (Trujillo) wants to make her his mistress, she eventually convinces Trujillo to allow her go to law school to be near him in the city (98). She pits the authority of Trujillo against her father's authority. When Trujillo suggests private meetings, she uses the patriarchal conventions of propriety and honor to argue that it would not be honorable of her to meet him alone (111). One nail of patriarchy takes out another.

GENEALOGY AND SUBJUGATED KNOWLEDGE

In his own work, Foucault attempts strategically to recall points of resistance in the form of subjugated knowledges. "Subjugated knowledges," he says, are those "blocs of historical knowledge which were present but disguised within the body of functionalist and systematizing theory." Subjugated knowledge is by definition differential knowledge. It is oppositional knowledge. It is knowledge which is concerned with historical struggles (*Power/Knowledge*, 82–83). Foucault suggests that the genealogist uses subjugated discourses in order to effect a resistance to domination. Genealogy, says Foucault, is the "union of erudite knowledge and local memories which allow us to establish a historical knowledge of struggles and then make use of this knowledge tactically today" (*Power/Knowledge*, 84).

Julia Alvarez's *In the Time of the Butterflies* is a type of Foucauldian genealogy. In her fictional account of the Mirabal sisters' participation in the resistance to the Trujillo dictatorship, Alvarez documents/imagines a resistance not only to the patriarchal power of the dictator but also localized and more mundane patriarchal power that subordinates women in their everyday lives. In her postscript to the novel, Alvarez says that she presents neither the real Mirabal sisters of fact nor the Mirabal sisters of legend, but tries to demythologize their courage by describing ordinary people. Perhaps paradoxically, even as she creates them in her fiction, she wants to avoid making these women into deities under the sway of "the same god-making impulse that had created our tyrant" (324).

Alvarez's novel describes the ways in which femininity and women's restricted and stereotypical roles as guardians of the family and of religion are put into the service of revolution—revolution against the dictatorship and revolution against patriarchy. Confessional diaries become means not only for personal therapy and Foucauldian self-surveillance but also for testimonies of injustice and suffering. The trappings of femininity, for instance, beautiful long hair, become means to deliver secret messages to the outside world. In a Foucauldian vein, Alvarez's *In the Time of the Butterflies* not only documents the subjugated knowledge of women subject to patriarchal oppression, but also shows some of the ways in which the very trappings of domination can be used to resist that domination. Insofar as women's knowledge is subjugated knowledge within patriarchal cultures, all of Alvarez's novels in various ways give voice to the subjugated knowledge of girls and women.

Alvarez's third novel, *¡Yo!,* attempts to give voice to knowledge and perspectives subjugated within her first novel, *How the Garcia Girls Lost Their Accents.* The book begins with one of the Garcia sisters, Fifi, complaining about her sister Yolanda becoming a famous novelist and at once exposing and distorting the family history. Many of the subsequent chapters in the novel are written from the perspectives of both major and minor characters from the first novel—a cousin Lucinda, the maid's daughter Sarita, the mother, the father, the sister Fifi. Often these characters correct and revise the story as told by Yolanda, the famous novelist. Both Alvarez's use of the first person only from Yolanda's perspective in her first novel and the depiction of Yolanda as a famous author who wrote a book about "the hair and nails cousins" and other characters from *How the Garcia Girls Lost Their Accents,* suggest that as readers we are to identify Alvarez with the character Yolanda.

Yet, *¡Yo!* makes us suspicious of Yolanda and of our author. The novel is written not only from different perspectives but also from those perspectives that challenge the perspective of the novelist character, Yolanda. Even when they don't challenge Yolanda's story, Yolanda is the center of attention, so much so that if we are supposed to identify Alvarez with Yolanda, this third book

seems self-indulgent. For example, the last chapter begins with the father saying "of all my girls, I always felt the closest to Yo" (292). Characters throughout
the novel question the stories told by others. The reader is continually told that
an author lies, exaggerates, and manipulates the truth. This move within the
novel itself to challenge the authority of the novel puts the reader in the liar's
paradox: Do we believe what the characters tell us, that the novel is not telling
the truth? Or, do we disbelieve what the characters tell us, and believe that the
novel is telling the truth? We are caught within a paradox of saying that the
truth is that there is no truth.

The reader is put into an even more problematic position in relation to the
alternative perspectives presented by the minor characters insofar as they are
also the creations of Julia Alvarez, identified with Yolanda Garcia. If Alvarez (as
Yolanda) is trying to give a voice to the silent minor characters of her first novel
in her third novel, she does so by co-opting their voices, speaking for them, and
thereby manipulating her readers. This tension between opening up space for
voices other than the author's unified individual voice and speaking for others is
symptomatic of the Foucauldian project of giving voice to subjugated knowledges. How is it possible to write or speak or describe subjugated knowledge
without also reinscribing it within another dominant discourse and subjugating
it even while attempting to liberate it? In other words, how can Foucault or anyone else write about subjugated knowledge or discourse silenced by other dominant discourses without reinscribing the subjugated discourse within his own
discourse, and, more than that, reinscribing it *as subjugated?* So, too, how can
the author of *¡Yo!* speak for all of the characters who didn't have a chance to tell
their stories in the first novel (*How the Garcia Girls Lost Their Accents?*) without, as Fifi accuses Yolanda, putting words in their mouths. This tension is
inherent in all attempts to speak for others, even if those attempts are motivated
by a concern to give voice to subjugated knowledge.

With *¡Yo!* we have the mind-bending situation of a character telling us that
her husband didn't speak the way that he does until he read her sister's novel,
which put the words into his mouth. This novel, which begins with one sister
making fun of the other for mouthing clichés on the radio about art mirroring
life, ends up confusing the relation between life and art. At the end of *How the
Garcia Girls Lost Their Accents,* in a chapter entitled "Yoyo" the first-person narration concludes: "I grew up, a curious woman, a woman of story ghosts and
story devils, a woman prone to bad dreams and bad insomnia. There are still
times I wake up at three o'clock in the morning and peer into the darkness. At
that hour and in that loneliness, I hear her, a black furred thing lurking in the
corners of my life, her magenta mouth opening, wailing over some violation that
lies at the center of my art" (290). Who is the author? Whose words and voices
are these? In *¡Yo!* Alvarez ties the text in knots around the question of the

author's authority. By so doing, she at once challenges and fragments the authority of the author and at the same time exposes the fiction of speaking for and as others. This double movement again suggests the Foucauldian lesson that the power to resist is also the power to dominate, and visa versa.

At this point, the postscript to *In the Time of the Butterflies* reads as a warning. Alvarez, presumably now in her own voice, tells us that "a novel is not, after all, a historical document, but a way to travel through the human heart" (324), and that an epoch of life, at least that of the Trujillo regime in the Dominican Republic, "can only be understood by fiction, only finally be redeemed by the imagination" (324). Fiction, then, tells us something about life that history can't. It speaks to the heart in a way that "immerses" readers in an epoch and helps them to "understand" it. Like a Foucauldian genealogy, Alvarez's fiction uses and creates local memories "which allow us to establish a historical knowledge of struggles and then make use of this knowledge tactically today" in order to understand the dynamics of patriarchal oppression.[3]

NOTES

Thanks to Benigno Trigo for helpful suggestions and continuing a dialogue from which this essay is formed.

1. Foucault *Power/Knowledge*, 187.

2. Although Foucault analyzes the normalization of heterosexuality, he pays little attention to the effects of patriarchal power on women. For feminist criticisms of Foucault on the question of sexual difference see: Alcoff; Butler, *Gender Trouble*; Diamond and Quinby; Fraser; Heckman; Biddy Martin; McNay; McWhorter; Sawicki.

3. Benigno Trigo has suggested that there is a tension between what Alvarez says she does in her novels—provides what is missing in history, the story of the human heart—and what she actually does in her novels. The tension between what Alvarez says she is doing and what she does points to tensions between any author's intentions and her products, especially when those intentions are to speak what has not been spoken or heard within dominant culture. Foucault has problematized any straightforward discussion of the transparency of the author's intentions or authority in ways that speak to this tension in Alvarez's writing. While Alvarez describes the feminine domestic space that Foucault ignores, she is not as self-reflective about the ways that her writing is inscribed in a process of the production of truth and authority as is Foucault.

14

"Race Woman":

Reproducing the Nation in

Gabriela Mistral

LICIA FIOL-MATTA

*T*he Chilean poet, educator, and Nobel laureate Gabriela Mistral (1889–1957) is an example of a lesbian intellectual who was instrumental in instituting sexual and racial normativity through nationalist discourse in Latin America. Mistral is best known as the icon of Latin American motherhood. She also enjoyed a brilliant career as a diplomat. This article expands the scope of the inquiry into Mistral's sexual identity by examining her status as "race woman"—a public position that she fiercely claimed, as opposed to any public nonnormative sexual stance.[1]

Within the Latin American public, Mistral upheld the heterosexual matrix. But was her queerness completely out of public view? Certainly Mistral alluded to reproductive sexuality every time she spoke of race. She consistently portrayed herself as the spokesperson of Latin America—which she referred to as *"nuestra raza,"* our race—posing as the mixed-race mother of the nation. Mistral devoted many prose pieces to the subject of a Latin American unified culture achieved through individual and social reproduction. Well known for her defense of the indigenous peoples of Latin America, she frequently and vigorously alluded to the process of *mestizaje.*

Through the stance of race woman, Mistral aided the state in managing Latin America's racially heterogeneous populations, regarded as a problem since the Wars of Independence. Both publicly and privately, she addressed topics ranging from the classification and hierarchical ordering of racial "mixings" to the status of black Latin Americans in nationalist discourse, from desirable *mestizaje* in the Latin American territory to dangerous *mestizaje* beyond the watchful purview of the state.

It is tempting to separate Mistral's sexual and racial identities—envisioning one as private and the other as public, one secret and the other on strident display. Typically, the quandary of a subject such as Mistral is to be analyzed one identity at a time. The story of her romantic life is separated from the story of her public career, even as her public figure unfolds in accordance with the narrative of republican motherhood. Salacious attention to the invented details of her private existence meshes happily with a hagiographic view of her role in world affairs. But to understand Mistral's complexity more fully, it is useful to view her private and public identities less as discrete segments of self and more as spliced and interdependent.

Examining the intersection of race and sexuality in Mistral is vital in more senses than one. Dispelling myths about her is important, but understanding a mythology put at the service of the state is critical. Both racial mixing (collective sexuality) and Mistral's ambiguous sexuality (seen as a private affair) involve the *social* demarcation of acceptable and unacceptable sex; in both instances, sex is coded as reproduction. In the state project that Mistral helped articulate, reproduction meant not only maximizing women's bodies to produce fit laborers and manage productive, patriarchal, heterosexual families, but also establishing and enforcing the parameters of who belonged, racially speaking, in the nation. This was true of the restricted sense of the emerging nation-state—*What* is a Chilean? *Who* can be considered a Mexican?—and of the expansive, indeed massive, sense of Americanism *(latinoamericanismo).* Enforcing the stricture of belonging entailed a submerged but no less potent role for Mistral's "silent" sexuality. As I have discussed elsewhere, the language of reproduction and child care functions as a kind of closet that paradoxically has made public what was to remain private (Fiol-Matta 1995). In the more far-reaching context of public or collective sexuality, Mistral deploys the same language to draw a firm, frequently onerous line of national belonging.

An intersectional analysis reveals that Mistral's symbolic heterosexuality was meant to guarantee or benefit not heterosexuality *per se* (that is, not all heterosexuals equally) but a particular heterosexuality tailored to the state's project. Mistral offered her own body as the representation of an entire race—a race created from an invented tradition. But how could a woman who bore no biological children for the race, who was always coupled with women, become the lasting symbol of the national mother? Her lived sexuality did not coincide with the national prescription, but was her queerness the linchpin of her national pose?

In "The Politics of Posing," Sylvia Molloy classifies queer Latin American posing as perverse posing—that is, posing as effeminate or as a sodomite, for example, in the face of prescriptive masculinities. Expanding the concept of posing to include poses such as Mistral's, this article articulates a notion of display more closely linked to deployment. Molloy discusses the pose of the *"raro"* (queer) as a type of gender and sexual resistance to a prescriptive nationalist ideology: "I want to think about *posing* in Latin America differently, not as the vapid posturing of some ghostly *fête galante,* a set of bodily or textual affectations at odds with national and continental discourses and concerns from which Latin America ultimately recovers, but as an oppositional practice and a decisive cultural statement whose political import and destabilizing energy I will try to recuperate and assess" (142). Mistral made use of a straightforward posing, as mother, as mestiza, but her posing abetted—instead of destabilizing—the national discourse. Indeed, posing is part of nationalism's effectiveness, for it engages the complicated question of identification. Conservative Latin Americans may have felt that their identity as national subjects suffered no threat from the elevation of a queer like Mistral, but there is more. As Foucault established, power is at its weakest when it does no more than negate. Mistral's figure enabled citizens to take part in the productive nature of power, specifically in the pleasures of identification—pleasures that underwrite both liberationist and repressive actions, to be sure. It was not simply a posing *pro patria* of the kind Molloy observes in José Enrique Rodó's *Ariel*—a posing meant to hide homoerotic desire, visible only at the moment when Prospero caresses the bronze statue of Ariel and "finds Rodó out" (150–151). Mistral's example provides a model for the incorporation of queerness into the state's project, and makes the case that Latin American queerness was not as invisible as one may have thought.

It is paradoxical and extraordinary, at the very least, that Mistral attained the status of symbolic guardian of the national family. Had she chosen to emphasize her variance publicly—her masculinity, her choice of intimate arrangements, her failure to marry and have children—without engaging the play of identification on a national and transnational scale, the state, with its ample resources, would have crushed her ambitions. The state, however, was attracted to her queerness—to what she and only she could accomplish within a biopolitical realm of power. So the union was consummated: Mistral would perform in the public sphere as the state's star attraction, posing as so married to the national cause that she had sacrificed her most personal fulfillment for the good of her and the state's "national children," the citizens.

Mistral most definitely planned and executed her participation in the state agenda. Consider her avowal of her own potential, as well as her intense self-focus, in a 1923 letter to Pedro Aguirre Cerda: "Of all the South American nations, Chile does the least for its propaganda in the exterior. It doesn't care about its image, or it believes that only the ministers and consuls can generate this propaganda; but they only live the good life and don't divulge things Chilean. I believe I can do what they have not yet done, and that I can do it with the only tools of effective propaganda: the *schools* and the *press*" (Emphasis added. *Antología mayor,* 100).[2] Undoubtedly, Mistral's almost mercenary assumption of culture entailed a measure of self-protection. However, could it have exceeded the demands of self-protection? Additionally, did it signify beyond naked self-advancement? Did Mistral identify with the national project?

In 1918 Mistral was sent to the southernmost province of Chile, Magallanes, with a specific mission: *"chilenizar,"* to Chileanize: "I had to Chileanize your homeland, on orders of my Minister and friend" (*La desterrada,* 18). Such statements, in conjunction with a knowledge of the period's significant acts of protest against the state,[3] reveal much about the state's racial project: assimilate or anni-hilate indigenous peoples in the province, promote immigrations from northern Europe to Chile to "whiten" the race (Mistral mentions Yugoslavs and Germans in the same text), and symbolically implant the idea of citizen allegiance to a Chilean nation, targeting most specifically the working classes. Mistral spoke rancorously about her stay in Magallanes, yet the same national prerogatives that she occasionally decried governed her public and private discourse until her death. Though Mistral evinced perplexity at her role in this endeavor, she inter-nalized and enacted it thoroughly—to the point that her own feelings meshed with the state's racial project.[4]

Mistral was, arguably, fueled by a desire to erect herself as a pillar in dis-courses of mass appeal and as a player in the transformations that ensued partly through the deployment of these discourses. Her difficult experiences of gender and sexuality, while very real, did not counteract the maturing of an early racial identification with the nation-state. Indeed, her "open secret" interacted with her identification with the Chilean racial project and her overwhelming ambi-tion to anchor the racial state. It is essential to note that Mistral's racial identifi-cation was not a reflection of her unique personality; her treatment of racial others and of *mestizaje* may seem idiosyncratic at times, yet she was shaped by the racial project as much as she shaped it when she became its active enuncia-tor. *Collective racial identifications in flux*—experienced by the majority of Latin

American citizens during a period of uneven modernization—*were refracted uniquely through Mistral,* hardening into a common national identification tailored to the state's desire.

MESTIZAJE AND BLACKNESS

Mistral is commonly heralded as the champion of the indigenous peoples of Latin America, particularly of the mestizo. *"Mestizaje,"* as it appears in her essays, is both a spontaneous racial mixing dictated by movements and contacts between peoples and a phenomenon that the state should administer. Mistral employs a strong biologistic interpretation but does not exclude *mestizaje*'s social characteristics. Racial mixing was an entire arena of social policy and discursive practice, requiring classification, expertise, and policing.[5] Michel Foucault's 1976 lectures at the Collège de France on the genealogy of racism, specifically his notion of violence in biopower, are singularly suited to this discussion. According to Foucault, violence in biopower has less to do with overt acts of killing than with a series of institutionalized exclusions and hierarchies designed to guarantee that only some have "the capacity to live" in a society of normalization.[6] A Foucauldian genealogy of *mestizaje* in Mistral's work—an attempt to define the conditions for and to locate its precise emergence—indicates that she took this concept directly from José Vasconcelos and the great project of nation-building after the Mexican Revolution. Moreover, it strongly suggests that for Mistral, *mestizaje* essentially meant marshaling a cultural notion of "unity" in the service of an integrationist agenda.

Mistral's notion of Latin American *mestizaje* implies a binary that marginalizes Latin Americans of African descent. At best, they are folklorized as an "exotic" minority; at worst, they are literally eliminated. But before exploring the treatment of the black (Latin American) subject, it is instructive to revisit a critical issue in Mistral's racial discourse: the status of her "defense" of the indigenous people.

Shocking as it may be to us today, the young Mistral was attracted to white-supremacist beliefs. Ana Pizarro reports that very early in her career, Mistral spoke of *"la salvación del blanco"* ("saving the white man") and *"la pureza de la raza"* ("the purity of the race") on, of all holidays, "el Día de la Raza," Columbus Day.[7] Interestingly, she abandoned this virulent discourse and began speaking on behalf of the indigenous peoples only after her first visit to Mexico in 1922, when Vasconcelos invited her as part of his educational reform. But was this change heartfelt and humanitarian or was it a strategic adoption of a discourse of normalization? Pizarro believes that it was the former.[8] At the very least, Mistral's change of heart was impeccably timed.

The essay "El tipo del indio americano" ("The Type of the Indian of the Americas") (1932) is often cited as an example of her "defense":

> One of the reasons for the native repugnance to confess the Indian in our blood, one of the origins of our fear of telling the world that we are loyal mestizos, is the so-called "ugliness of the Indian." We hold this as an irrefutable truth; we have accepted it without question. It goes hand in hand with such phrases such as "The Indian is lazy" and "The Indian is evil." . . . We should have taught our children about the differentiated and opposed beauty of the races. A long and slender eye is beautiful in the Mongolian, while in the Caucasian it debases the face. A yellowish color, ranging in shade from straw to sheepskin, accentuates the delicate nature of the Chinese face. In the European it suggests sanguine misery. Curly hair is a glorious crown on the head of the Caucasian; in the mestizo it hints at *mulataje,* and we prefer the flat locks of the Indian. (179)

Apart from interpreting beauty racially in this essay, Mistral analyzes racial mixings for their advantages and disadvantages through binaries. The binary of beauty/ugliness and the Vasconcelian idea of "aesthetic selection" informs all of her writings after 1922, and could well be interpreted as the subtext of her own subsequent, increasing, and deeply problematic self-description as *"india"* or "mestiza." So profound was her discursively produced racial transformation that it became commonplace in the public record to refer to Mistral as mestiza. Her biographers and critics took this identification to be a biographical fact, and it persists to this day.

Mistral's negation of "the so-called ugliness of the Indian" ("la llamada fealdad del indio") is generally regarded as a defense of the "indigenous element" in the racial configuration of the universal Latin American subject. In an insightful essay, Amy Kaminsky recognizes Mistral's problematic use of racial stereotypes as she fashioned a symbolically beautiful Indian (118–119); her well-known essay "Silhouette of the Indian Woman," for example, "does little more than bring the Indian woman into the field of vision and make of her an object of beauty" (121). Kaminsky believes, however, that essentially Mistral cared for the indigenous peoples and that championing their cause made her a social "outsider." But might this not be a superficial reading? It is vital to contextualize Mistral's "defense" and to discern where the idea of ugliness emerged. To uncover what the defense enabled—or at least glossed over—it is fruitful first to ponder Vasconcelos's considerable influence.[9]

In his treatise *La raza cósmica* ("The Cosmic Race") (1925), Vasconcelos presented a true exceptionalist narrative, placing Latin America squarely at the center of world affairs through a racial construction, or in Omi's and Winant's terminology, a "racial project." *Mestizaje,* Vasconcelos argued, constitutes Latin America's racial specificity and claim to centrality. This region alone contains the four races of the world, which means that the next (and, according to him, last) leading race—the fifth or cosmic race—will originate in Latin America.

Notably, the process of mixing is not haphazard; it is a meticulously selective. In a highly questionable but fascinating passage, Vasconcelos predicts that "uglier races" will voluntarily "phase themselves out" through the principle of "aesthetic eugenics," or the criterion of "taste":

> The lower types of the species will be absorbed by the superior type. In this way, for example, the Negro will be able to redeem himself, and, little by little, through voluntary extinction, the uglier races will pave way for the most beautiful. The inferior races, through education, will reproduce less, and the best specimens will ascend on the scale of ethnic improvement. On this scale, the uppermost type is not the white man but a new race, to which the white man will also have to aspire for the synthesis to be achieved. The Indian, by being grafted onto a race of affinity, will take the leap over the million-year gap that separates Atlantis from our time. In a few decades of *aesthetic eugenics* the Negro will disappear, along with the types that the free instinct of beauty signals as fundamentally recessive and, for that very reason, unworthy of survival. In this way a process of *selection by taste* will take place. It will be much more efficient than the brutal Darwinist criterion of selection, which may be relevant, at best, to inferior species, but not to man. (emphasis added, 42–43)[10]

The phrase *aesthetic eugenics* attempted to make an unsavory social action philosophically palatable. The management of social life entailed the elimination of certain social subjects and the eradication of their cultures. This loss of life—the life of people, the life of cultures—must be masked as the continuation of another life—that is, the life of a nation so vital that it is glorious.

Mistral clearly retained the concept of nationality and adhered to the idea of Latin America as a "race." But her simultaneous championing of "biological patriotism" in other contexts betrayed the eugenicist understanding of populations as shaped by elements from superior and inferior races.[11] Essays in which she copied the Mexican model of *mestizaje* may not obviously demonstrate this fact, but when her essays on the Argentinean paradigm of white immigration are taken into account, it is impossible to maintain with confidence that Mistral held the indigenous peoples in the same esteem as white people.[12] Even white immigrants were a sore point for her on occasion; in "El folklore argentino" ("Argentine Folklore") she speaks of folklore as "the defense of the race against dangerous immigration," apparently taking a page from United States policy: "'Argentina for the Argentineans,' plagiarizing Monroe; conquering the immigrant and the native . . . through folklore" (58–59).

In her important study of the eugenics projects of early twentieth-century Latin America, Nancy Leys Stepan summarizes the relationship between race and national belonging as follows:

> The desire to "imagine" the nation in biological terms, to "purify" the reproduc-
> tion of populations to fit hereditary norms, to regulate the flow of peoples
> across national boundaries, to define in novel terms who could belong to the
> nation and who could not—all these aspects of eugenics turned on issues of
> gender and race, and produced intrusive proposals or prescriptions for new
> state policies toward individuals. Through eugenics, in short, gender and race
> were tied to the politics of national identity. (105)

Mistral was attracted to the problem of the national population and who should
be part of it and to the sexual reasoning that authorized this discourse. Her views
constituted a subtle, insidious form of eugenics; far from confined to a small circle of specialists with influence only in medicine and health, Mistral's views were
naturalized across nations as "the thing to do." Accessible in mass venues such as
the schools and the press, her "race-speak" became synonymous with a national
understanding of self and essential to the affective register of national belonging.

Critics have held that when Mistral mentions "the race," she means a civilization, not biological characteristics or the separate populations within *mestizaje*.[13]
Her references to a mestizo Latin American race, they argue, represent a recognition of four hundred years of *mestizaje* that, presumably, had arrived at a final
point more or less coinciding with the advent of the modern Latin American
state, sealed in a liberal social contract that needed no revision. Nevertheless, it is
clear that Mistral's racial worries were not primarily, but only tangentially, about
the survival of one civilization under pressure from others, especially its feared
northern neighbor. Her worries gravitated around three key issues: whether
blacks and immigrants were part of Latin American *mestizaje*, what to do if they
were, and how to privilege the indigenous over the black in a binary construction
that exalted Latin American heterogeneity while tightly controlling its impact.

Mistral understood the connection, and contrast, between indigenous and
black racial constructions within the context of the state project. The condition
assigned to the indigenous woman revolves around it. In an early, pedagogical
essay, "A la mujer mexicana" ("To the Mexican Woman") (1922): "You have been
told that your purity is a religious virtue. It is also a civic virtue: your womb sustains
the race; the citizen masses are born out of your breast quietly, with the eternal
flowing of the springs of your fatherland." (*Lecturas,* 173) In other words, the
indigenous woman is the sealed receptacle in which the race is kept pure. She is
sheer reproduction, but she is also the acceptable vessel of reproduction.
Projections about making the Indian woman feel pure resonate instantly with the
eugenicist project to improve the quality of the population. The link between the
indigenous woman's body and the black woman's body is crucial. While the indigenous woman is a receptacle of the race, a national mother, the black woman is a
vehicle through which the national seed and thus national life are lost.

Latin American ideologies of racial democracy rested on a conceptualization of Latin American slavery that held it as more benign because it was supposedly more affective and erotic.[14] Queers are not exempted from this legacy. Queer desire is not immune to racialized constructions of eroticism or to the lure of achieving national belonging through a collective exercise of racial fetishization. Globally, queer desire has often been associated with private acceptance and public shame. Within a liberal order, racial condescension or hatred often appears uncensored in private venues while it is tempered or silenced in public discourse. Thus one unspoken citizen prerogative under liberalism is to accede to a private sphere where prohibited queer desires interact with racialized, hierarchical eroticism. Mistral exoticizes and sexualizes the black subject in this private sphere. Her letters to the Cuban anthropologist and ethnographer Lydia Cabrera offer an example. Before traveling to Brazil, Mistral shared her intentions with Cabrera: "Look, seriously, whenever you want to go there, please, don't hesitate to come to our house. I am Consul in Nitcheroy, a beach in Rio, across from the city as you traverse the beautiful bay. It's only half an hour away. It's a sinecure, because I will hardly have any work to do. My State is the most beautiful and has the most inhabitants. People there seem courteous and with good manners. And of course there's the magnificent Negro" (*Cartas a Lydia Cabrera,* 77).

Molloy (1995) has demonstrated that the exchange of letters between Mistral, Cabrera, and the Venezuelan novelist Teresa de la Parra is coded as lesbian. Molloy refers to Mistral's participation in some of their "lovers' quarrels" and to her urging them to "patch things up." Mistral's startling racial references and lack of self-censorship invite further reflection, and, because they are directed at a lesbian addressee, they may signify as a common viewpoint about "black people." Mistral assumes that the black man and black woman, whom she thinks of as "blackness," are objects of desire for Cabrera and Parra.[15] The fellow lesbian, who shares the bond of secrecy and the fear of social retribution, participates in a discourse forbidden in other quarters. Perhaps Mistral's own fear of retribution in and consequent silence on sexual matters enabled her uninhibited declarations in racial matters. It is peculiar that Cabrera—a well-known author of seminal books on Afro-Cuban religions and "folklore"—is the recipient of Mistral's racial and racist fantasies, since Cabrera explicitly seeks to portray the black people of Cuba in "respectable" terms as profoundly religious people.

Cabrera's and Parra's model of the national writer—individuals freed from the shackles of iconicity—resonated deeply with Mistral's own troubled subjectivity. Mistral, electing to represent a kind of Latin American work ethic, had chosen to emphasize the utilitarian relationship between citizen and state. Furthermore, she had gendered and racialized this relationship of acquiescence to the common good, implanting it in the national psyche by posing as a mixed-race person. Cabrera and Parra, by contrast, remained resolutely white.

Mistral's letters to Cabrera inscribe eroticism as a racialized fantasy directly engaging black people. The first letter opens with a reference to a presumably shared racial discourse: "Dear Lydia: I have not forgotten about you. Connie always thinks of you as well. Believe me, both of us experience a sweet desire: that of knowing that you are a little happy, but not only with the Negroes. . . ." (*Cartas a Lydia Cabrera*, 73). [16] Racial discourse functions as erotic teasing between couples who are "in the know" about each other. The connection between "happiness" and an unspecified group of "Negroes" (*"los negros"*) is laced with this obvious erotic tone.

In this passage, Mistral explains the substance of her own desire for a readily available, docile "blackness":

> I love you very much, even though I am mostly silent about it. I've had to move a few times; I've had an enormous amount of correspondence to deal with, as well as sicknesses of my own. And now the conflict of our people stuck in France without any money. I think I will soon leave this place; I know not when, or where I will go. I've had—it's been a few months now—a violent desire, to go to the countryside; I think I will do everything possible to go to a place where there are very few people, where a foreign language is spoken, and where I can live with cows, pasture, and guinea-hens. I feel ashamed at asking; sometimes I feel like trying out a great adventure and going off without any paid employment to live in a semi-tropical, American land, and be a farmer. Do you know that Bernanos, desperate as he was, has gone to Brazil, and lives there, in a beautiful and barbaric land, which cost only 200 Francs per hectare? I feel sorry for you. This time around you were very much the citizen, the lady of Lyon or Blois; but I increasingly feel that a field with black witch doctors, banana trees and pineapple groves is my solution as well as yours. I hope I can offer you as much in a short period of time: a place without the European cold, without the decadent white man, and full of the many beasts of your [illegible].
>
> I will tell you as soon as I have it. Connie has begun to arrange my consular papers; to let me sleep and offer my happiness to black men, black women, and the grass. Don't think I have gone crazy because of the war; I've thought about it quite a lot. (74)

Black people occupy a space parallel to that of women and indigenous people, since all three are deployed in Latin Americanist discourse as representations of archaic times before "modernity." Moreover, for Mistral as well as for the Americanist discourse that she helped consolidate and eventually represented, black people occupied space in a remarkably different way from the indigenous peoples. Certainly, both blacks and Indians are part of spectacle. Indians belong in the theater of labor; they are circumspect and detached from social life even as they materially contribute to it and anchor the national subject in an originary time. Blacks, though, exist in an unspecified but clearly ludic—and not precisely childlike—relationship to Mistral. Their interaction occurs in dream time, and it is to be played out in a pastoral setting, in "the grass." Nowhere in Mistral's known and published correspondence and prose works is there similar derision of or condescension toward indigenous peoples. They are rendered childlike in another way: in the racist imaginary, they require parental intercession to be modernized. The state must supervise their labor. Black people, by contrast, are sexualized, as in Baker and the "witch doctors," or criminalized, a characterization that became personal with the death of her adopted son.

MULATAJE AND IMMIGRATION

Mistral's writings about her stay in Brazil, where the Chilean government posted her at her own request at the outbreak of World War II, are markedly negative. Mistral did not experience her racial fantasy while consul in Petropolis, and her adopted son, Juan Miguel Godoy, committed suicide in 1943. These two events—the dissolution of her fantasy and the trauma of real-life loss—led Mistral to level strident accusations of xenophobia at a generalized delinquent Brazilian "*mulataje*," negating Brazil's inclusion in the rhetoric of *mestizaje:* (To Tómic, 1951) "I have no intention of leaving Italy. I hate myself for . . . having gone off to live out the xenophobia of the Brazilian *mulataje*. . . . I sacrificed Juan Miguel to that country. . . . There I became acquainted with the most hateful and tribal xenophobia" (*Vuestra Gabriela*, 150); (To Reyes, 1948) "In that horrible country that you like so much—Brazil—three doctors ruined me when they treated me for diabetes, for tropical amoebas. *They are bastards, like most of the population*" (emphasis in original. Mistral *Tan de usted*, 160).

The word *mulataje* first appeared in Mistral's article "The Type of the Indian of the Americas" in 1932, just prior to the Cabrera correspondence. To understand the full implications of Mistral's often-remarked championing of *mestizaje*, it is essential first to understand *mulataje*'s conceptual implications. The word *mulataje* is not merely a descriptor of a particular racial mixing—white with black—but also denotes the presence of a racial threat: the destruction of white children and the white family. Indigenous women may function as receptacles to carry the seed of the white man. Their racial mark is rationalized as minor compared with the degrading and deforming mark attributed to black people. The sexualization of blacks changes to their pathologization as murderers.

Central to Mistral's racial narrative of Brazil is her recollection of the death of her son, affectionately referred to as "Yin Yin," who died when he was sixteen. Yin Yin had ingested a lethal dose of arsenic, and his death was ruled a suicide.

Mistral, who never reconciled herself to this fact, created a narrative around his death by which she exonerated herself for his actions. In the following excerpt of a 1954 letter to Reyes, for instance, Mistral recasts the events as a racially motivated murder by a "gang" of black youngsters:

> Come Christmas, the gang that had tormented him in school came to my house. All four of them. I summoned the courage to ask them why they had killed such a sweet soul, who had been such a good friend to each one of them. This was their reply:
>
> —We know that Madam is still upset over this matter but *it had to be.* I bolted out of my chair and replied: Why did it "have to be"?
>
> —He had more than his fair share of things.
>
> —What did he have "more than his fair share of"? I had to trick him so that he would go out with me. I had to tell him we would be buying clothes and shoes for me.
>
> —He had his name, your writer's name, which gave him prestige. He was also too white for his own good.
>
> —Villains, I said. His being white and your being black were not his fault. (emphasis in original. Mistral *Tan de usted,* 218)

Mistral believes that her child's death resulted from three factors: jealousy over his material possessions, the privilege of his whiteness, and the prestige of his writer-mother. Mistral positions herself at the center of the tale as the reason for the alleged murder and the ultimate source of whiteness.

This excerpt represents the other side of Mistral's racial fantasy of excess. In this scenario, the mother-child dyad is broken. *Mulataje,* a derogatory word indicating the racial mixing of white and black, is responsible for the disappearance of the (white) family. In other words, it interrupts the harmonious mix of *mestizaje* and destroys the national family. The black subject becomes excessive once again, but this time it is overtly rendered as violent, criminal, and cynical.

The guilty party becomes an entire country marked as black, Latin American, non-Spanish-speaking, and criminal. Brazil is portrayed as a dangerous and criminal country. Mistral codes its black identity in official language as xenophobic—and hatred of the foreigner becomes hatred of whiteness. The formerly mestiza Mistral is now white—"too white for [her] own good." And Mistral, the national writer of Latin America, is in danger. She epitomizes Latin America, and Latin America—at least the one that must survive—is white.

Notable Latin American queers such as Mistral were just as notably invested in maintaining their status as "white people." Some of the most important queer writers and intellectuals turned their attention to immigration as a solution to the nation's racial problematic. The discursive manipulation of *mestizaje, mulataje,* and immigration happened at one and the same time, conforming the subjectivities and shaping the writing of much of Latin America's "queer" canon.

In discussing Mistral's stay in Veracruz, the Mexican scholar Luis Mario Schneider refers to a 1948 interview of her conducted by Salvador Novo for the Mexican press. Schneider excerpts only a few brief lines from the interview. The complete text contains a telling exchange:

Novo: And then I heard a defense from her lips, which I transcribe here, and subscribe to with the greatest fervor:

Mistral: "There is one thing that I should like to call to the attention of President Alemán. It is a grave and dangerous situation, and a very painful one, for those Mexicans who cross the border to work in California. It is urgent and necessary that this situation be taken care of immediately."

Novo: Gabriela Mistral lives in Santa Barbara, California, a State of the Union whose laws prohibit the marriage of Mexicans—"colored"—with white women. When they happen, they are annulled and [the participants] fined, but they don't happen too often. The trucks with cattle are loaded with Mexican work-ers. Single men, destined to live in special neighborhoods, where they are dis-criminated against. The only contact they are allowed is with black women, ugly, of the worst species. As the years go by, the entire region boils with mes-tizo creatures of black and Mexican blood, [a mixture] that degrades and effaces the fine Mexican race.

Mistral: "Why in God's name do they not let the Mexicans take their women with them?" . . .

Novo: Connie listened to our conversation, and she offered new and painful examples of this tragic situation. ("Ventana," 4)

Here Mistral believes that the matter of national reproduction is at risk; she finds that sex between Mexican men and black women, as well as their offspring, is unacceptable and not Latin American. There are other, more subtle and fasci-nating issues at stake as well. First, Mistral addresses Novo, another prototype of the national writer and, like Mistral, gay and employed by the state (in the Ministry of Education, no less). Second, the anecdote concludes with a reference to "Connie," Mistral's companion. A triangle of queer intellectuals discusses the possible disappearance of the Mexican race, caused by unregulated blackness—specifically, by black women. All lay claim to women nationals as "theirs," serving one function, reproduction, which has one end: to produce the best nationals, mestizos. But none of these three queer subjects produced any biological children, much less mestizos. Even Mistral's son was emphatically represented as white. Their conversation raises a question: Why should the offspring of Mexican men and (presumably American) black women not be considered mestizos too?

The idea of ugly races expressed by Vasconcelos survived in Mistral's work to the end. Despite the accolades heard in her official discourses, Mistral never abandoned the private belief that Afro-Latin Americans were not Latin Americans and did not meet the aesthetic requirements of "the race." While Vasconcelos believed in the voluntary phasing out of "inferior" races (of which his example is black people), Mistral claimed that Mexican-black couples brought unacceptable children of mixed mestizo and black heritage into the world, children who by definition could not be Latin American because they failed to meet the aesthetic criterion. Notably, this was not only Mistral's belief. It was shared by other important pillars of the ideal of Latin American *mestizaje*. Queer Latin American writing, then, is at least on some important occasions imbricated with heteronormative desire.

CONCLUSION

Three critical operations are at work throughout Mistral's writings on the subject of the Latin American "race." The first is the disavowal of blackness. Simply stated, black populations have existed since colonial times in all the viceroyalties. The fact that the communities did not survive in the Southern Cone after the nineteenth century indicates that the founding of these nation-states depended on a process of forgetting and reinvention, not unlike that of repression in psychoanalysis. How should the fact that Mistral praised blacks publicly and despised them privately be addressed? Should scholars simply dismiss this as a minor point, in consideration of Mistral's championing of the Indian ("el indio") and of women and children? It is extraordinary that Mistral acted as if she had never known of the black populations of Latin America prior to her travels to the Caribbean in the 1930s, and that she responded to the black subject with predictable white responses: anxiety, sexualization, and pathologization. The celebrated Freudian formula of disavowal perfectly describes this operation. Mistral knew that there were Latin Americans who were black, but for her, Latin Americans were indigenous, period. The discursive operations of Latin Americanism obliterated the black subject from aesthetic and also political representation.

The second operation in Mistral's writings is the complicity of the language of diversity in the practices of white supremacist thinking.[17] Some critics have dismissed Mistral's story of Yin Yin's death as mere "madness," or as a "personal" deviation. The genealogy of *mestizaje* in her thinking demonstrates, however, a bifurcation between what Mistral publicly declared and what she privately believed. The confidences shared in less formal venues such as correspondence and interviews were not, of course, entirely private; their circulation among a select group of intellectuals and newspaper readers suggests, at the very least, public racial ambivalence. Mistral's cry of racial murder in the death of Yin Yin, while certainly inflected with grief and possibly guilt, cannot be attributed solely to these feelings. That is, one can be either aggrieved or mentally unstable and still be a racist. While critics have discounted the seriousness of Mistral's accusations due to the extreme circumstances that gave rise to them, they have effaced another extreme: Mistral's characterization of black national subjects.

The third operation is the role played by Mistral's queerness in her racialized nationalism. Mistral "queered" the nation, to be sure, yet this "queering" advanced not only heteronormativity but also the unspoken Latin Americanist racial project. Her maternal grief and any allusions to her personal feelings should supplement, not obscure, the analysis of her nationalist maternal discourse and how much it had to do with securing "the reproduction of the nation." While Mistral's official discourse celebrates the abstract qualities of the mother and the child, some of her other speech genres leave no doubt that certain women could never be mothers in this sense and that their children would never be counted as Latin American children. There are no necessary, certain, or predictable alliances between sexually oppressed people and racially oppressed people. Mistral as a queer, but also Mistral's nationally projected queerness helped articulate the state discourse about the reproduction of the nation, an example of Foucault's "right to life" within biopower. Between a prohibited sexual identity and a racist national identity lie the contradictions of Mistral as a race woman: proclaiming *latinoamericanismo*'s tenets, doing the work of its gendered and heteronormative formulations, and reproducing the racist and homophobic state.

NOTES

Special thanks to Benigno Trigo and Gayatri Patnaik. This article is an abridged version of a longer chapter from my book, *Schooling Sexuality: The State and Gabriela Mistral* (University of Minnesota Press, forthcoming).

1. *Race woman,* a term borrowed from African-American studies, refers to a militant woman who upholds or defends the race.

2. All translations of Mistral are my own.

3. Acts of organized protest included the worker revolts in Puerto Natales and Punta Arenas in 1919 and 1921, respectively. The state violently suppressed both, massacring workers and indigenous peoples alike. Mistral was stationed in Punta Arenas during the former

revolt and had already left the region by the time of the latter. See Teitelboim, *Gabriela Mistral pública y secreta*, 87–91.

4. See Mistral's prologue to Scarpa, *La desterrada en su patria*. This prologue was written almost three decades after Mistral left Magallanes.

5. For varied accounts of this pervasive preoccupation with "right and wrong" racial mixing, see Nancy Leys Stepan, *The "Hour of Eugenics": Race, Gender, and Nation in Latin America*; Richard Graham, ed., *The Idea of Race in Latin America 1870–1940*; and Thomas E. Skidmore's *Black into White: Race and Nationality in Brazilian Thought*.

6. See also Ann Laura Stoler's brilliant analysis of Foucault's lectures in *Race and the Education of Desire: Foucault's History of Sexuality and the Colonial Order of Things*.

7. Quoted in Ana Pizarro, "Mistral, ¿qué modernidad?" ("Mistral: What Modernity?"), 49.

8. Pizarro also notes that Mistral changed her white-supremacist stance after her visit to Mexico in 1922, but at this point our views diverge. Pizarro writes: "Mistral's gaze changes, of course, in Mexico, and this new gaze reaffirms itself in Brazil, in a period when Gilberto Freyre and Sergio Buarque de Holanda had undertaken the fundamental reconsideration of black culture" (49). Freyre and Buarque de Holanda were part of the trend towards normalization and contributed to what Foucault labeled "governmentality." With respect to black people, Mistral's racist views remained unchanged. If anything, they became more murderous. Her references to Brazil precisely crystallized this dangerous racism.

9. Though I single out Vasconcelos, he was not the only practitioner of this ideology of *mestizaje*, and much less its formulator. See Alan Knight for an introduction to the genealogy of this model in Mexico: "Racism, Revolution, and *Indigenismo*: Mexico, 1910–1940."

10. My translation. I thank Julio Ramos for calling this passage to my attention.

11. Mistral's remarks on "biological patriotism" are quoted in Lavrin, *Women, Feminism, and Social Change*, 163–164.

12. On Mistral's admiration for Argentina's racial project, see "La pampa argentina" ("The Argentinean Pampa"), "Recado de una maestra argentina" ("Message about an Argentinean Schoolteacher"), and "Madrinas de lectura" ("Godmothers of Reading") in *Magisterio y niño* (*Teaching and Children*).

13. See, e.g., Patricio Marchant, "Desolación," 60–61, in Olea, ed., *Una palabra cómplice*.

14. The most famous proponent of the "racial harmony" theory is the influential Gilberto Freyre. See Michael Hanchard, "Racial Democracy: Hegemony, Brazilian Style," *Orpheus and Power*.

15. Mistral may not have simply invented this commonality. Cabrera and Parra may indeed have shared this imaginary of fetishized and subservient black people, which may have had something to do with the gestation of Cabrera's works, especially the *Black Tales of Cuba*.

16. The letters to Cabrera quoted here are found in Hiriart's edition; none are dated but they were all written in the 1930s.

17. I thank Janet Jakobsen for the phrasing of this point in my work.

15

Sadomasochism in *Paradiso*:
Bound Narratives and Pleasure

B. SIFUENTES JÁUREGUI

Thus, it is not through sexuality that we communicate with the orderly and pleasingly profane world of
animals; rather, sexuality is a fissure—not one which
surrounds us as the basis of our isolation or individuality, but one which marks the limit within us and
designates us as a limit.

—Michel Foucault[1]

*J*osé Lezama Lima's *Paradiso* undoubtedly signals a watershed moment in
the (literary) history of (Latin American) sexuality. Certainly the political
discussions in *Mundo Nuevo* and elsewhere among Latin American writers and intellectuals about the status of the novel as a queer masterpiece framed
the reading of this text greatly; this debate tiptoed around the now (in)famous
"capítulo VIII." In this essay, I propose a close reading of a seminal scene in the
novel (Farraluque's weekend sexual escapades) as well as of those debates surrounding the Farraluque episode to capture a moment in a history of sexuality.
Such a reading will highlight *Paradiso*'s function as a receptacle of exclusion and

inclusion of what will be deemed a "normative" sexuality, both within the confines of a national imaginary and an aesthetic space.

CHAPTER VIII, OR THE UNSPOKEN SCENE

I would like to begin by shaping a critical narrative of (sado)masochism to underscore some important points. First, sexuality is a means of knowledge; it provides a peculiar epistemology. Thus subjectivity is animated through narratives of sexuality. Second, masochism is a difficult case of how subjectivities are formed—socially, politically, culturally—that permits the emergence of narratives that effect different identities. Nonetheless, I hope to argue that this very difficulty enables us to refunction the very scene of S/M as a space wherein identifications may occur on both personal and political levels.

I would like to sketch here some of the signposts and critical contours that make *Paradiso* so interesting to read and useful to theorize about sadomasochism, and masochism in particular. From within, the work shows us several places where corporeal violence, aggressive sexuality, and sexy power trips are at play. It also displays how identities (master/slave, teacher/disciple) are set up. I intend to read the spectacular masochism of *Paradiso* as a symptom of neo-Baroque tendencies, and alongside Foucault's paradox of *assujettissement*. Additionally, I would like to look at the metatextual reinscriptions of the novel by Vargas Llosa and Rodríguez Monegal in *Mundo Nuevo* and Cortázar in *La Vuelta al día en ochenta mundos,* reinscriptions which impinge a certain cultural capital on *Paradiso* and which show how sadomasochist aesthetics function at multiple levels.

These many layers of signification address both the inner and outer workings of masochism as a strategy for self-figuration—(auto)biographical, literary, national, postcolonial, and cultural, to name a few—in Lezama Lima's oeuvre. It is my contention that masochism as a regulating strategy of self-figuration exerts centrifugally a powerful rethinking of the Latin American subject and his disciplining at this moment of the Latin American literary "Boom."

The whole mess as to what degree *Paradiso* really is or is not a "homosexual" text began with a review by Mario Vargas Llosa, where he omits reference to the "homosexual episodes" in the text. Emir Rodríguez Monegal writes a letter where he expresses bewilderment as to the "inexplicable omission of all reference to the clearly homosexual aspect of the novel," especially "as we know, Lezama Lima dedicates a good fourth of his book describing in the most deliriously metaphoric manner the characters' hetero and homosexual relations" ("Sobre el *Paradiso*," 90). Then Vargas Llosa proceeds to give a whole series of reasons for the "omission": "The truth of the matter is that I do not find this silence a low blow in any way; it was a deliberate product of a sense of irritation." Irritation, which Vargas Llosa goes on to explain, was caused by "tens of opinions" which "almost all alluded—in praise or criticism—exclusively to the already legendary eighth chapter of *Paradiso*. . . ." ("Sobre el *Paradiso*," 89) Furthermore, he argues that:

> Hearing all these presumptive readers of Lezama, I had the impression that this was a novel centered essentially on a homosexual theme, one which does not seem to me more or less legitimate than any other. My surprise was great in reading the book and realizing that this theme in truth occupied a relatively modest space in the novel. . . . This complex work, arduous to read, and for the same reason hard to "interpret," can be considered many different things, as all mayor works may be, but, under *no* case is this a treatise, a manual or a defense of homosexualism. ("Sobre el *Paradiso*," 89; translation mine)

Rodríguez Monegal takes this and returns to his point that any reviewer cannot dismiss the homosexual element in the work; thus he follows up with a "page by page" catalog enumerating the main episodes and homosexual allusions in *Paradiso* ("Sobre el *Paradiso*," 91–92). Before engaging with Rodríguez Monegal's critique, let's read carefully Vargas Llosa's "irritation," which has to do with the emphasis on Chapter VIII. Vargas Llosa seems to assume that reading the work as possessing a homosexual theme somehow makes the work appear commonplace. That reading, he states, is "one which does not seem to me more or less legitimate than any other." What he forgets is that homosexuality as a theme functions just like any other, for it marks the very notion of difference—and more so in the history of Latin American writing, where that difference has remained largely silent or has been absented. Thus the loudness with which homosexuality emerges in the text irritates Vargas Llosa (as it will others) because it is a double figure: an inscription of difference as well as the *resistance* to the very erasure of that difference. Furthermore, Vargas Llosa's cavalier dismissal of the homosexual theme reminds us over and again of the ways in which certain themes are imagined as central while others are represented as marginal.[2]

In *Paradiso*'s Chapter VIII, we learn the story of a certain Farraluque, son of a Basque and a Havana woman, "a leptosomatic adolescent, with a sad and baggy-eyed face, but endowed with an enormous cock." He is quite proud of his tool. While performing his duties as bathroom monitor of the younger students at the school, he shows it off:

> [Farraluque] raised his arms as if beating on aerial castanets, always keeping his cock outside his zipper. He used to roll it in his fingers, on his forearm, pre-

tending as if he were hitting it, reprimanding it, or caressed it as if it were a
hungry child. (P: 199–200; P(E): 197)[3]

One of these "ceremonies" is witnessed by a lazy maid, "from the Persian screens
of the second floor" who reports him so that he will be appropriately disciplined.
During his absence from "service" we learn about Leregas, a classmate of the
novel's protagonist, José Cemí. Leregas's member was equally impressive in
length, like "the forearm of a manual worker" (P: 200; P(E): 198). Unlike the
rows of students who would stare at his massive phallus, I will forgo discussion
of Leregas's powerful dick, which could hold up three books, and focus on
Farraluque's. What is important for my argument is that Leregas represents
Farraluque's double; his presence introduces this idea of doubleness that I hope
to elaborate throughout this essay.

As part of his punishment, Farraluque is not allowed to leave the school
grounds for three consecutive Sundays. On the first Sunday, he meets with
the maid who had accused him. Unaware that she is responsible for his fate,
Farraluque agrees to help her "whitewash" the walls of the director's house.
While supposedly helping her, he notices in a room next door the director's
cook, a "nineteen-year-old mestiza mamey," apparently sleeping. Her luscious
back and buttocks become an invitation: "The salt deposited in each of her
body's crevices seemed to burn glowingly. It awakened the reflections of temptations . . ." (P: 203; P(E): 201). The young man strips and jumps into a
tableau vivant of delights *(saltó sobre el cuadrado de las delicias),* at which time
the young cook turns over—still sleeping—and offers her pubis, "the normality of her body," to the newly arrived man (P: 204; P(E): 201). Once finished,
he goes and peeks in the second bedroom where he finds the maid, *"la
españolita,"* who had brought him there. She is exposing her breasts and her
"aracnid mound," which requires "the carnal cylinder of a powerful adolescent . . . to split the aracnid through its center" (P: 204; P(E): 202). When
Farraluque goes to jump into "the feathery *tableau* of the second room *(el
cuadrado plumoso del segundo cuarto),* the rotation of the españolita was the
inverse of the mestiza's turn" (P: 204; P(E): 202). By giving herself anally, she
is caring for her virginity "theologically." Anal penetration protects her honor
and against pregnancy. This is a felicitous encounter because "the phallic configuration was extremely propitious to this retrospective penetration, since his
spear had its exaggerated predominance on the length near its bearded root"
(P: 204; P(E): 202). She proudly takes control of the situation and handles the
massiveness of the young man in a heroic divide-and-conquer fashion, first
taking the glans, then the shaft, finally, she enters "permanent undulation"
which continues after he withdraws and leaves; in effect, she experiences an
endless anal orgasm.

I would like to look momentarily at the first set of encounters. The "mestiza mamey" begins by seducing him with her back and then turns to offer him the "normality of her body." Really the first tableau into which Farraluque enters is one of heteronormativity.[4] The second tableau with *la españolita* represents its literal turn, perverse heterosexual desire, as well as entrance into the realm of fantasy, here manifested as a "permanent undulation" or quiver. *La españolita* sexually *rides* the Basque youth; she *writhes* in the *jouissance* provoked by a fantasy of anal eroticism.[5] Indeed, this fantasy signifies on the young man sexually; she *writes* him as Other. The scene of riding/writhing/writing is a magnificent moment in the Lezamian text where pleasure and pain and marked identity meld into the throes of a permanent undulation.

The next day, the cook tells a servant across the street what happened, and she tells her bored mistress about the youth's massive gift. The lady of the house presses her servant for details. The following Sunday, a monkeylike boy comes to look for Farraluque to inform him that the lady across the street from the school also needed her house painted. "Painting the house" or whitewashing has become, thus far, the euphemism for fucking. When he gets there "as if in a stage set," he discovers that "the mature Madonna faked without skill a sensual drowsiness." She stretches her arms to form a square with her index and middle fingers, a square which is broken by the proximity of the "phallic Niké." Again, we notice, as before, the arrival and entrance into each staged setting: "Farraluque jumped into the foamy *tableau (el cuadrado espumoso)* . . . " (P: 206; P(E): 204). This time however, the sexual act involves a more aggressively active participation by the sleeping beauty: she specializes in "two of the eight parts of which oral sex consists." First she engages with talent in the "biting of the borders," then, in "whirling the carpet of her tongue on the cupola of the head" (P: 207; P(E): 204–205). When she thinks his orgasm was immanent, she draws him toward her vagina only to have the young man yank her away from the hair so that she could see his orgasm, "the excited gorgon squishing the sweat produced in its depths" (P: 207; P(E): 205). This encounter has left him a bit unsatisfied, he feels that "his energy had not manifested itself freely" (P: 207; P(E): 205). As he haughtily leaves the room, he anticipates what would come next, and sure enough in the next room is Adolfito, the monkey-boy, waiting for him: "He feigned sleep, but with visible malice, since with one uncovered and naughty eye he wandered around Farraluque's body, stopping afterwards on the culminating point of the spear" (P: 208; P(E): 205). Indeed, the phallus is the final point of every encounter with Farraluque. And again;

> Before Farraluque penetrated the joyous *tableau (el cuadro gozoso),* he notices that, while turning, Adolfito . . . showed the phallus hidden between his legs, leaving behind a hairy concavity, tense by the pressure produced by the phallus

in its hideaway. Upon beginning the encounter, Adolfito turned with incredible sagacity. . . . But pleasure for the monkey-boy seemed to consist in hiding himself, in reproducing an invincible difficulty in the sexual aggressor. . . . The search of a bay made Farraluque crazy. . . . (P: 208; P(E): 206)

Finally, in the process of finding the hole, the Basque squirts over the boy's chest, who then spins over to show his "diabolically spread-eagle legs" and to smear the useless cream over the sheets.

I would like to review certain elements from this dance. We notice again that Farraluque "penetrates" a *tableau jouissant,* but not the boy. This is an important moment because it signifies an initiation to the scene of S/M, for as we know pleasure in sadomasochistic act is located in the very setting and choreography of the event, not in the *telos* of an orgasm. The boy presents himself but hides his penis and turns over and over to prevent Farraluque from penetrating him. So, strangely, the boy's turns come to signify his sexuality differently. He turns obsessively to figure as "castrated," thereby seducing a presumptive heterosexual gaze, and then he re-turns to anal eroticism, thus confusing and infuriating the other youth. Adolfito's body allows for an erotic and sexual refunctioning, which destabilizes the identificatory practices involved in possessing the other. Furthermore, we learn that for Adolfito pleasure consists in hiding himself, "in reproducing *(en hacer nacer)* an invincible difficulty in the sexual aggressor." Pleasure is enacted via a provocation; it is elicited by making the other perform as you want him to perform. This very notion of provoking the other would then call into question the status of the "sexual aggressor." It would seem that the boy, seen from outside as the masochist, is in control—but, then again, the masochist is always in control.

Now if we can plot out Farraluque's sexcapades, we can see a pattern develop. First, he has sex with the cook, your basic heterosexual framing of "man-on-top." Second comes the *españolita* who offers her bottom, as a way to protect a particular imaginary of virginity. Third, Farraluque gets blown (away) by the "mature Madonna." What is important in this scene is that his orgasm is accompanied by his violently yanking her hair and making her watch the flow from his man-meat, thus demonstrating that the scene is all about the man's pleasure. This leads us to the scene with the boy, who hides his penis to provoke the other. With each scene we see a modulation of erotic perversion, and we see Farraluque's sexual identity change depending on the *tableau* he enters. We could imagine that he begins identifying as heteronormative, having sex with the nineteen year-old, followed by a perverse heterosexual connection with the *españolita*. Then Farraluque's sexuality is no longer about penetration, as we witness in his encounter with the Madonna; finally, Farraluque ends up in a homosexual scene with Adolfito. With each encounter his sexual identity shifts—he covers a wide spectrum from heteronormative to homoerotic. What unites these scenes is the trope of waste, because each time he reaches orgasm outside the erotogenic zone.[6] Also, each first encounter (the cook, the Madonna) has a double (*la españolita* and Adolfito—each a diminutive) that deconstructs the first. For instance, in the first set of encounters, the security of heteronormativity (the normality of sexual penetration with the cook) is problematized by the promise of anal eroticism (which is always bisexual).[7] In the second set, heterosexual identity (as visibly manifested with sex with a woman) becomes further destabilized by the change of the object of desire (sex with the boy). Even between the two sets there is a change. Penetration as the paragon of genital sexuality (the aim of the first two encounters) is complicated by fellatio (in the third encounter). If we trace Farraluque's experience in a linear fashion, we discover that what began as an initiation to heteronormative sexuality ends in a complex whereby he is made Other, unable to be neatly classified into any one sexual identity.

NARRATIVES OF MASOCHISM

The third Sunday also takes Farraluque to another realm, fully into a scene of sadomasochism. Before we enter it, let us survey what sadomasochism means socially, culturally, and theoretically.

Readers of Freud know that one of his most important impasses is the question of masochism as a strategy of self-figuration. In his early writings, Freud discusses masochism as derivative of sadism; he would not conceive of a primary masochism until much later.[8] In 1924, in "The Economic Problem of Masochism," Freud gives his most complete analysis of this phenomenon. He identifies three forms of masochism, *erotogenic* ("pleasure-in-pain"), *feminine,* and *moral.*[9] Freud seeks to read masochism as a perplexing "economic problem" within the principle of constancy:[10] "For if mental processes are governed by the pleasure principle in such a way that their first aim is the avoidance of unpleasure and the obtaining of pleasure, masochism is incomprehensible" ("Economic," 159). In other words, he asks: How does subjectivity emerge in the scene of masochism? How does the "I" claim agency through its very debasement?

In a completely different manner, Foucault meditates on this paradox in his discussions of *assujettissement,* the process of becoming a subject and the process of subjection.[11] Though I am aware that I am linking the Foucauldian notion of "discipline" with a distinct practice of sadomasochism, I do this deliberately by placing momentarily the differences aside, with the intention of showing a continuum between both practices and theories. I want to create a critical slippage between "the strategic use of power differentials to produce effects of pleasure instead of domination," which is how Halperin sees a major difference between sadomasochistic eroticism and discipline in Foucault's work (85). According to Halperin: "Foucault emphasizes that what goes by the name of 'domination' in S/M is a strategy for creating pleasure, not a form of personal or political subjugation" (86). So in effect, Foucault presents separate fields—pleasure and domination—which are enacted differently through a variety of practices of relational power. I am interested in the perversion of the question of pleasure as form of domination, not just domination as pleasure (the classic definition of sadism). I want to keep in mind this idea that by acknowledging pleasure, the subject controls, resists, stops the flow of domination. One way to begin looking at this question would be to ask whether or not the fields of pleasure and domination also operate and implicate one another *metaphorically*. If so, how is the metaphor written and read, meaning: What are the consequences of the act of metaphorization, especially in relation to subjectivity?

THE MASOCHIST'S PLEASURE

If the scene with Adolfito suggests the initiation of Farraluque into the space of S/M, "[t]he third Sunday of punishment" certainly shows S/M in its plenitude (P: 208–211; P(E): 206-209).[12] On that morning, Farraluque is met by Adolfito and given a key to a place where he is to meet a nameless "*someone,* seduced by his art of whitewashing" (P: 208; P(E): 206). Farraluque is already well able to read into what "whitewashing" meant. However, we could add further that the white of his semen writes the *tableaux* in which he is invited to participate. He is given a key and an address, where, late that afternoon, Farraluque goes to visit. We are told that:

> . . . he had arrived to a forest of fog. In what depths had he fallen? After his sight became more accustomed to its surroundings, he realized that he was in a coalhouse. The first partitions that surrounded the entire square were full of coal already separated. . . . (P: 209; P(E): 207)

The *mise-en-scène* is quite different from the earlier two scenes. We are no longer in the comfort of domesticity but, rather, in the darkness of a coal house. The scene, which is thought of as a hell, is described as dark and difficult to see through. If he was, in effect, going to whitewash the place, the space presented quite a challenge. As he walks through the coal bins, he comes to a small room barely lit. There he finds a man of around fifty who is naked, wearing only his shoes and socks—and a mask. The man quickly and ceremoniously begins stripping the young man, and immediately takes him:

> The mastery of the serpent's incorporation was complete; as [the masked man] allowed himself to be won over by the penetrating body, he became red, as if, instead of receiving, he were giving birth to a monstrous animal.

The apoplectic tone of this so powerful incorporator of the outside world grew
in a crescendo to the point of acquiring truly oracular roars. With his hands up
high, he gripped the ropes that fastened the carbon sacks until his fingers began
to bleed. (P: 210; P(E): 207)

There is no effort to flirt with Farraluque here. I would suggest that this flirtation
had already happened *narratively* through the stories that were circulating
around the priapic one. Rumors and phantasies about Farraluque's dominion
had been circulating around the school playground; and, when they reached the
masked man, these narratives had acquired the form of a speech act that would
attract him to Farraluque. In other words, the seduction of the masked man was
accomplished *performatively* by the circulation of rumors about the big boy.

What is most important here is seeing who is given and who claims agency in
the sexual act, not the endowed man, but the one who gets fucked, "the powerful incorporator." The older man merely puts this scene or fantasy of masochism
into motion. What we witness here is a classic S/M erotic narrative—the mask,
the darkness, the raw sexuality, the blood. It is a scene of sexual domination that
has been enacted *for pleasure*. Again, pleasure lies not in the graffiti of the
orgasm or the blood, but in the prior narrative that frames the scene—as well as
in the spin-off narratives that the scene will evoke. In other words, pleasure has
already been accounted for in the old man's construction of the S/M fantasy narrative, a narrative that has been told prior to the encounter and that gets retold
over and over after the event. The enactment and totality of this event are articulated "in *crescendo* to the point of acquiring truly oracular roars." The true narrative of the event at the very moment of its realization is (dis)articulated, it
cannot be told, and this marks the entrance into the Lacanian Real. It is that
moment of "dreams-come-true," where the subject cannot fully comprehend the
overwhelming nature of the event, nor does he possess the language to begin
speaking of it and to start symbolizing the event.[13]

Read *from outside,* this scene produces the kind of devaluation through horror
and panic that exemplifies Vargas Llosa's commentary as well as the uneasy
superficial catalogs that Rodríguez Monegal presents,[14] when in actuality, it is
imperative to underscore that this scene of masochism obeys the law of
Lezamian poetics or his *eras imaginarias*—a series of image worlds that flow
across time and space. Furthermore, this reading from the inside is what makes
Julio Cortázar's 1967 reading of *Paradiso* so brilliantly relevant: he proposes "that
Paradiso's characters always speak *from inside the image,* since Lezama projects
them from a poetic system that has its key in the potentiality of the image as a
supreme secretion of the human spirit in search of the reality of an invisible
world" (61, emphasis in the original). The idea of speaking *from within* the literary image is very compelling when thinking of Farraluque, who constantly enters

the *tableaux,* sees himself, and projects an identity from inside the visual. This entrance into the *tableau* has connections with Foucault's discussion of the panopticon. He notes that "a real subjection *(assujettissement)* arises mechanically from a fictitious relation" (*Naissance,* 204). Within panoptic institutions— and I would define these in the broadest sense possible as not just the prison, but the school, the house across the street, exhibitionist relations, and so on— Foucault finds:

> He who is submitted to a field of visibility, *and who knows it,* takes again into his account (realizes) the constraints of power; he allows them to play spontaneously upon him; *he inscribes in himself the power relation in which he simultaneously plays both roles* [subject and subjected]; he becomes the principle of his own subject-formation/subjection *(assujettissement).* (*Naissance* 204, italics mine)

Foucault's brilliant insight helps us to see that Farraluque positions himself inside a scene and from there projects outwardly: he becomes a subject by submitting to the place of the other. The difference that we can see between both authors is that Foucault focuses on the simultaneity of the *assujettissement,* thereby producing a relational vision of power, whereas Lezama places and *displaces* (really, oscillates) *the degree of priority given to the subject versus the image-world.* In other words, the Lezamian subject and his image-worlds clash and transform each other violently, producing a distinctive voice and/in narrative.

I want to return and listen a bit longer to the *rugidos oraculares*—oracular moans or roars—as the struggle by *someone* to articulate something. We should remember that earlier, when the maid was telling her boss (the mature Madonna) over and over again of "the fever in the ecstasy in receiving such a huge spear," she finally says "with extreme humility":

> Madam, that can only be described well when one has it before oneself, but, believe me, then right away one forgets about it all and afterwards, one cannot describe anything in detail. (P: 206; P(E): 203)

The story of the phallus is also the story of a trauma ("such a huge spear") which cannot be described. What follows this trauma is a repetition compulsion, the circulation of the story as well as everyone's desire to receive or incorporate that traumatic event. This compulsion to repeat (the many dualities in the chapter) produces a restricted economy of the traumatic event. Repetition is, then, a formula containing the violence of the traumatic spear. The narrative of repetition (compulsion) produces the very broken, fragmented, incomplete structure it is trying to repair. Sadomasochism is a structure which tries to contain a phallic trauma, which of course exceeds the confines of this S/M narrative. The power of the Real thus deconstructs reality as fiction.

WHO'S YOUR DADDY?; OR, THE ABSENT QUESTION

THAT STRUCTURES THE SUBJECT

In the last section I looked at the S/M scene between Farraluque and the masked man; however, I shifted the focus of my reading from the visual inflection of the tableaux to a more linguistic inflection. Also, the critical narrative I constructed suggests that the duality of the earlier encounters (cook/*la españolita* and Madonna/boy) no longer continued on the third Sunday. In this section, I want to return to the visual dimension of my reading and "round off" my narrative by reading the scene of Farraluque's final orgasm, the impossibility of repetition—and the repetition of an impossibility.

Just before reaching orgasm, Farraluque notices with humor and laughter the penis of the "receptive subject"; the masked man's penis is "concealed by indifference, disdained flaccidity" (P: 210; P(E): 207–208). At that point:

> . . . his phallus, accustomed to ejaculate without the heat of a carnal envelopment, became agitated by the levity of a soft breeze. . . . He pushed his vacillating cock in a crack in the coal, his exasperated movements in the final moments of passion caused coal dusk to scatter. He yanked the ropes, punched the concave sacks, kicked the coal. . . . His frenzied hardness caused the final fall of the coalhouse. (P: 210; P(E): 208)

As the men run to safety from the falling coal, they are marked by "irregular black stripes on [their] bodies" (210). This scene brings up again important issues regarding Farraluque's virility. I would like to suggest that penetrating the carbon is a desire to return to the origin. Rather than display the money shot, as he has done before with the Madonna, it appears as though Farraluque is trying to give his semen to the organic matter, thus reenacting another beginning of life, where semen and carbon become the *materia prima* of creation. I am tempted to return to Cortázar's (masculinist) rendering of the Lezamian image-world—"the image as a supreme secretion of the human spirit in search of the reality of an invisible world." Cortázar's description of the Lezamian image-world is just like the figure of Farraluque trying to penetrate the mystery of the origin of life. However the disturbance of this act, literally *contra natura,* ends up in a disaster which leaves the two men's bodies beaten and marked (or written upon).

The masked man leaves the scene of the crime, and Farraluque follows a bit later. Outside, he meets Adolfito, who reveals the identity of the someone, that *someone:* "'Well, behind the mask you would have found the husband of the lady across the street from the school. The one you had to pull by the hair. . . .' Thus Adolfito finished, smiling" (211). Revealing the identity of the masked man also reveals the circular knowledge that has emerged around Farraluque's member. We discover that Adolfito had witnessed Farraluque and the lady, and that he may have been involved in constructing the fantasy for the masked man. Thus we learn that the encounter with the endowed man was already predetermined by a particular narrative about the phallus and this narrative is repeated in an incomplete manner in the afterthoughts of those who seek to come close to it. There appears to be a symmetrical narrative before and after the phallus. This symmetry between the stories before and after the scenes of encounter frames and, in this sense, also closes up the narrative and the circulation of desire for the phallus. But the containment or possession of phallic power is, nevertheless, made impossible because the multiple narratives produced by the phallus become increasingly ungraspable.[15] Even sadomasochistic eroticism, and especially its aggression, cannot contain the fantastic narrative.

Earlier I suggested that this final erotic scene has a double. The chapter ends, and in the critical edition we find a felicitous footnote: "In the text's manuscript, a larger space between the last sentence of this paragraph and the beginning of the next indicates the end of a section and the beginning of another; this was not taken into consideration in either the *Unión* (1966) [the first] or the *Era* (1968) [the previously authoritative] editions" (P: 211; not in English edition). This blank space that follows Farraluque's erotic scenes is the visual performative double of the S/M encounter with the masked man. It brings together a textual reconciliation and Lezama's representation of the Real. It is at once the failure of language to capture the Real, as well as the success of silence, as an affirmation of muteness, to represent (visually) the Real. The blank space is Farraluque's final painting, the whiteness of his semen, the whiteness of his excuse. The whiteness of textual representation is pure image, pure meaning: ungraspable, yet knowable; unknowable, yet narratively and visually graspable as a restricted economy.

NOTES

1. Foucault *Language, Counter-Memory,* 30.

2. For an important discussion on the relation of gay and lesbian studies to the literary and historical canon, see Sedgwick, 48–59; also Sifuentes Jáuregui, 298–300.

3. All translations are mine. Citations are taken from Cintio Vitier's critical edition of *Paradiso* (Colección Archivos, 1988). For a good, not to mention valiant, translation please refer to Gregory Rabassa's work. To facilitate referencing to both the original and Rabassa's translation, I will use the following convention to quote pages from the critical edition, followed by pages from the Rabassa's English translation, e.g., (P: xx; P(E): yy).

4. By heteronormative, I want to underscore the guarantee of normativity secured by compulsory heterosexuality. See Warner "Introduction."

5. I want to retain a critical awareness that, given biological difference between men's and women's bodies, anal eroticism may signify differently. On a phantasmatic level, I suspect that that the difference between the sexes may amount to a different register on a *plaisir/ jouissance* spectrum. For instance, for a (gay) male, anal eroticism may represent a pleasure that is biologically inflected; whereas for a woman, it may be a question of fantasy and *jouissance.* Following this, I am proposing that for *la españolita,* this anal eroticism hinges more on a fantasy, than on a biological fact.

6. On this question, Pellón summarizes that "Lezama and Sarduy conceive of the erotic in sex and in language as *dépense,* as the cultivation of the superfluous, the goal-less, for which the waste of the seed—whether as semen or seme—is essential" (28–29).

7. What I mean here is that for a man, anal eroticism as the *aim* of sexual practice and pleasure signifies on him the orientation of "bisexual," whereas the genital sexuality would do so as either homo/heterosexual.

8. Early in his *Three Essays* (a), Freud states that "the most remarkable feature of this perversion [sadism/masochism] is that its active and passive forms are habitually found to occur together in the same individual" (159). Freud discusses masochism as a reversal of sadism in "Instincts and Their Vicissitudes." He never commits to a masochism emerging independent from sadism. It is only after *Beyond the Pleasure Principle* (in 1920) where he begins to note the possibility of a "primary masochism" (55).

9. In this discussion, I make primary reference to the first and third forms; feminine masochism presents certain issues and questions of social, historical, and cultural attachment with which I do not engage in my reading of *Paradiso.*

10. The best presentation and reading of the psychosexual dynamics in Freud's essays on masochism is Noyes's (140–163).

11. See Foucault *Naissance,* esp. Part Three; *Discipline,* section 2, "The Means of Correct Training," and Section 3, "Panopticism." For a helpful discussion of the paradox of *assujettissement,* see Butler *Psychic Life,* chap. 3, on Freud and Foucault.

12. In the description of the scene that follows, I will focus primarily on masochism. Following Deleuze's *Masochism,* I want to break apart the conjunction between sadism *and* masochism as proposed by Freud. Each practice is not the opposite of the other; both have the same end to produce a subjectivity. I would deem more challenging the language of the structuration of the subject that emerges in and from masochism.

13. One of the most lucid readings of Lezama is Chiampi's "Proliferación barroca." She performs a reading of Baroque proliferation in *Paradiso;* among the different forms she discusses, there are syntactic, semantic, and verbal proliferations. I agree that Baroque proliferation is a central practice in neo-Baroque writings and, indeed, that Lezama (also Sarduy) puts into play a whole series of proliferations in his narrative context. I have gone in a different direction with Chiampi's particular example of verbal proliferation of the "sexual organ." She correctly lists the many metaphoric substitutions of Leregas's phallus (her example from Chapter VIII, though it can be said about Farraluque as well), and adds that: "on the one hand, this metaphoric constellation [constructed by the phallic proliferation] connotes laughter and derision; on the other, it installs the unfulfillment (*desrealización*) of the object, by hyperbolizing its dimensions" (86). As I have been arguing, the very proliferation of the object is the result of other subject's inability to grasp the object,

hence, my Lacanian reading of encountering the Real. She concludes that: "[i]n order to describe the referent, the narrator is forced to produce an aphasia, a stutter, to designate that which cannot be spoken (*lo indecible*)" (86). This aphasia provoked in the speaking subject, *lo indecible,* is another name for disarticulation by the Real. I would add that, in my reading, I am more concerned not so much with naming *what* is the object of desire (this being always already an impossibility), but rather with understanding *how* this unnamed and unknowable object *signifies on the other.*

14. After the catalog, Rodríguez Monegal argues that: "[w]hat determines the central homosexual nature of a considerable part of the book (when I spoke of a fourth of the book, I may have underestimated the matter) is not just the abundance of direct references; it is the entire system of allusions and metaphors that constitute the linguistic plot of the text" ("Sobre el *Paradiso,*" 92). Although he makes this adjustment to his argument, the critic continues cataloguing those "allusions and metaphors," thereby preserving a closed circularity or a hermetics of queerness, without fully engaging the more provocative homographetic implications of his insight. For a provocative discussion on the inscription of homosexuality in the literary, see Edelman (1989). On a related conceptualization of textual inscriptions, see Roberto González Echevarría ("Lo cubano"), where he traces the ways in which the national (inflected as *lo cubano* in the novel) is laced throughout Lezama's textuality.

15. We remember that José Cemí was named after his father, José Eugenio Cemí. Santí notes that: "[t]odo el capítulo VI de la novel está repleto de escenas que subrayan esta relación incierta entre padre e hijo. Las diferencias los separan, muy a pesar de los deseos a lo contrario del Coronel" ("Parridiso" 95). And, later on, Santí emphasizes that the father-son differences are inscribed in their names, José and José Eugenio: "El hijo parece marcado por la ausencia del segundo nombre: Eugenio, *eugenes,* el bien nacido. El hijo no es, no puede ser, el 'bien nacido,' que sería el padre" ("Parridiso" 95). Cruz Malavé intelligently points out that: "[e]l destino del hijo será 'intentar lo más difícil': aclarar el 'oscuro' creado por la muerte de su padre, José Eugenio Cemí, 'transfigurándose' en el 'testimonio'" (51). My position is closer to Cruz Malavé's. Following my reading of Farraluque's identity, I would not see the absence of the middle name as a *sujet-manqué* (as suggested by Santí), always wanting to be (like) the father, but rather I tend to privilege that blank/white space in the name José [ ] Cemí, for it represents a certain totality (as privilege) and its impossibility. In fact, the whiteness is a visual sign of the semen, so, in effect, we read his name José [whiteness=semen=Cemí] Cemí. The son carries the father's name as the sign of the double; he is the figure of dissemination/de-Cemí–nation, the figuration of the *petit histoire* (the son) as the *grand récit* of the Nation (the father), "the Cemí Nation," Cuba.

BIBLIOGRAPHY

Abelove, Henry, "Towards a History of 'Sexual Intercourse' during the 'Long Eighteenth Century' in England," *Genders* 6 (November 1989): 125–130.

Achugar, Hugo. *Uruguay: cuentas pendientes: dictadura, memorias y desmemorias.* Montevideo: Trilce, 1995.

———. "Prólogo." *La ciudad letrada,* by Angel Rama. Hanover: Ediciones del Norte, 1984. 9–16.

Adams, Timothy Dow. "Introduction: Life Writing and Light Writing; Autobiography and Photography." *Modern Fiction Studies* 40.3 (1994): 459–492.

Adorno, Rolena. "*La ciudad letrada* y los discursos coloniales." *Hispamérica* 16.48 (1987): 3–24.

Ahmad, Aijaz. *In Theory: Classes, Nations, Literatures.* London: Verso, 1992.

———. "Jameson's Rhetoric of Otherness and the 'National Allegory,'" *Social Text* 17: 3–25.

Alcoff, Linda. "Cultural Feminism Versus Post-Structuralism: The Identity Crisis in Feminist Theory," *Signs* 13.3 (1988): 405–436.

Alberdi, Juan Bautista. *Bases y puntos de partida para la organización política de la República Argentina,* ed. Jorge Mayer. Buenos Aires: Editorial Sudamericana, 1969.

———. *Peregrinación de luz del día, o, viajes y aventuras de la verdad en el nuevo mundo.* Buenos Aries: Secretaría de Cultura de la Nación en coproducción con ediciones Theoria, 1994.

Alighieri, Dante. *La divina comedia,* trans, prologue and notes by Angel Battistessa. Buenos Aires: Ediciones Carlos Lohlé, 1972.

Alonso, Carlos J. "Rama y sus retoños: Figuring the Nineteenth-Century Spanish America" *Revista de Estudios Hispánicos* 28(1994): 283–291.

———. *The Spanish American Regional Novel: Modernity and Autochthony.* Cambridge: University Press, 1989.

Alonso Seoane, María José. "Las últimas obras de Olavide a través de los expedientes de censura." *Elsiglo que llaman ilustrado,* comp. Joaquín Alvarez Barrientos and José Checa Beltrán. Madrid: Consejo de Investigaciones Superiores Científicas, 1996. 47–54.

———. "Olavide, adaptador de novelas: una versión desconocida de Germeuil, de Baculard d'Arnaud." *Actas del X Congreso de la Asociación Internacional de Hispanistas,* ed. Antonio Vilanova. Barcelona: Promociones y Publicaciones Universitarias, 2 (1992): 1157–66.

Altamirano, Ignacio M., "La literatura nacional" *La literatura nacional,* ed. José Luis Martínez. México: Edit. Porrua, Col. de Escritores Mexicanos, 1949. 9–40.

Althusser, Louis. "Ideology and Ideological State Apparatuses (Notes towards an Investigation)." *Lenin and Philosophy,* trans. Ben Brewster. New York: Monthly Review Press, 1971. 127–186.

Alvarez, Julia. *How the Garcia Girls Lost Their Accents.* New York: Plume Books, 1991.

———. *In the Time of the Butterflies.* New York: Plume Books, 1994.

————. ¡Yo! New York: Plume Books, 1997.

Anderson, Benedict. *Imagined Communities: Reflections on the Origin and Spread of Nationalism*. London: Verso, 1983.

————. "Census, Map, Museum: Notes on the Origins of Official Nationalism in Southeast Asia," draft of January 1989.

Anderson, Warwick. "Where Every Prospect Pleases and Only Man is Vile": Laboratory Medicine as Colonial Discourse." *Critical Inquiry* 18. 3 (1992): 506–529.

————. "Excremental Colonialism: Public Health and Poetics of Pollution." *Critical Inquiry* 21 (1995): 641–669.

Anonymous. ed. "Condición de los obreros." *El Progreso* October 19, 1850, in Grez Toso, Sergio, *La Cuestion social en Chile. Ideas y debates precursores (1804–1902)*. Santiago: Direccion de Bibliotecas Archivos y Museos and Centro de Investigaciones Diego Barros Arana, 1995. 121–123.

————. *La Vida de Lazarillo de Tormes y de sus fortunas y adversidades*, ed. Antonio Rey Hazas. Madrid: Castalia, 1986 [1554].

————. "Necesidades de la clase pobre a que debe atender el intendente de Santiago." *El Amigo del Pueblo* May 15, 1850. Ed. Grez Toso, Sergio. ed. *La cuestion social en Chile. Ideas y debates precursores (1804–1902)*. Santiago: Direccion de Bibliotecas Archivos y Museos and Centro de Investigaciones Diego Barros Arana, 1995. 113–115.

————. "Nuestra visita al Insituto de Medicina en Utuado." *Puerto Rico Ilustrado* 8 November 1913: 11–12

————. "Una visita al Instituto de Medicina Tropical." *Puerto Rico Ilustrado.* 18 October 1913: 12–17.

Anzaldúa, Gloria. *Borderlands: The New Mestiza = La Frontera*. San Francisco: Spinsters/Aunt Lute, 1987.

Apter, David E. ed. "Ideology as a Cutlural System." *Ideology and Discontent*. New York: Free Press, 1964.

————. The Interpretation of Cultures, New York, Basic Books, 1973.

Arac, Jonathan. "Afterword: Lyric Poetry and the Bonds of New Criticism." *Lyric Poetry: Beyond New Criticism*, ed. Chaviva Hosek and Patricia Parker. Ithaca, N.Y.: Cornell University Press, 1985. 345–355.

Argan, Giulio. *The Renaissance City*. New York: George Braziller, 1969.

Armstrong, Nancy. *Desire and Domestic Fiction: A Political History of the Novel*. New York: Oxford University Press, 1987.

Arnau, Carmen. *El mundo mítico de Gabriel García Márquez*. Barcelona: Ediciones Península, 1971.

Arnauld, Antoine, and Pierre Nicole. *La logique ou l'art de penser*, eds. Pierre Clair and Francois Girbal. Paris: P.U.F., 1965.

Arnold, David. *Colonizing the Body. State Medicine and Epidemic Disease in Nineteenth-Century India*. Berkeley: University of California Press, 1992.

Arteaga, Alfred. *Chicano Poetics: Heterotexts And Hybridites*. Cambridge, England; New York: Cambridge University Press, 1997.

Ashford, Bailey K. *Uncinariasis in Porto Rico. A Medical and Economical Problem.* Washington D.C.: Government Printing Office, 1911.

————. *Informe parcial de la Comisión de la Anemia sometido al gobernador William Hunt.* 4 November 1904: 1–7.

————. *Informe parcial de la Comisión de la Anemia sometido al gobernador Winthrop.* 31 May 1905: 1–5.

————. *Informe parcial de la Comisión de la anemia sometido al gobernador Winthrop.* 5 January 1906: 1–7.

————. *A Soldier in Science*. Río Piedras: Editorial de la Universidad de Puerto Rico, 1998.

Asturias, Meguel Angel. *Leyendes de Guatemala*. Prologue Paco Tovar. Buenos Aires: Losada, 2000 [1930].

Avalle-Arce, Juan Bautista. "Introducción." Vol. 2 of *Novelas ejemplares,* by Miguel de Cervantes Saavedra, ed. Avalle-Arce. 3 vols. Madrid: Castalia, 1987. 7–40.

Avelar, Idelber. "The Angel of History's Forged Signature: The Ruins of Memory and the Task of Mourning in a Brazilian Postdictatorial Novel." *Modern Fiction Studies* 44.1 (1998): 184–214.

———. "The Clandestine Ménage a Trois of Cultural Studies, Spanish and Critical Theory." *Profession* (1999): 49–58.

Avellaneda, Rino G. Book review of D. Grugelberger *The Real Thing: Testimonial Dicurse and Lation America. Modern Fiction Studies* 44.2 (1998): 424–428.

———. "The Clandestine Ménage a Trois of Cultural Studies, Spanish, and Critical Theory." *Profession* (1999): 49–58.

Bakhtin, Mikhail. *The Dialogic Imagination,* ed. Michael Holquist. Austin: University of Texas Press, 1981.

———. *Rabelais and His World,* tr. Helene Iswolsky. Bloomington: Indiana University Press, 1984.

———. "Speech Genres." *Speech Genres and Other Late Essays.* Austin: University of Texas Press, 1986. 60–102.

Balderston, Daniel, and Donna J. Guy. *Sex and Sexuality in Latin America.* New York: New York University Press, 1997.

Barnet, Miguel. *Biografía de un cimarrón.* La Habana: Instituto de Etnología y Folklore, 1966.

———. "The Documentary Novel." *Cuban Studies/Estudios Cubanos* 11.1 (1981): 19–32.

———. *Biography of a Runaway Slave,* trans. W. Nick Hill. Willimantic, Conn.: Curbstone Press, 1994.

———. *Canción de Rachel.* La Habana: Instituto Cubano del Libro, 1969.

———. *Rachel's Song.* Willimantic, Conn.: Curbstone Press, 1991.

Barrán, José Pedro. *Historia de la sensibilidad en el Uruguay.* Montevideo: Ediciones de la Banda Oriental, 1989, volume I.

Barthes, Roland. "The Photographic Message." *A Barthes Reader,* intro by Susan Sontag. New York: Hill and Wang, 1982. 194–211.

Bastos, María Luisa. "Escrituras ajenas, expresión propia: Sur y los Testimonios de Victoria Ocampo." *Revista Iberoamericana* 110–111 (1980): 123–137.

———. "Dos líneas testimoniales: *Sur,* los escritos de Victoria Ocampo." *Sur* 348 (1981): 9–23.

———, and Eduardo Paz Leston. *El proyecto de la revista Sur, Capítulo.* 106. Buenos Aires: Centro Editor de América Latina, 1981.

Behar, Ruth. *Translated Woman: Crossing the Border with Esperanza's Story.* Boston: Beacon Press, 1993.

Bendezú Aibar, Edmundo. "Pablo de Olavide." *La novela peruana. De Olavide a Bryce.* Lima: Lumen, 1992. 11–29.

Benítez Rojo, Antonio. "¿Cómo narrar la nación? El círculo de Domingo Delmonte y el surgimiento de la novela cubana." *Cuadernos Americanos* 3 (1994): 103–125.

Benjamin, Walter, "Central Park," trans. Lloyd Spencer. *New German Critique* 34 (1985): 32–58.

———. *The Origin of German Tragic Drama,* trans. John Osborne. London: NLB, 1977.

———. "Theses on the Philosophy of History." *Illuminations,* ed. Hannah Arendt, New York: Shocken, 1969. 253–264.

Bergmann, Emilie L., and Paul Julian Smith. *¿Entiendes? Queer Readings, Hispanic Writings.* Durham: Duke University Press, 1995.

Bersani, Leo. "Representation and Its Discontents." *Allegory and Representation,* ed. Stephen J. Greenblatt. Baltimore: Johns Hopkins University Press, 1981. 145–162.

Beto, Frei. *Fidel y la religión. Conversaciones con Frei Beto.* La Habana: Editorial Sí–Mar, 1994.

Beverley, John. *Subalternity and Representation: Arguments in Cultural Theory.* Durham-London: Duke University Press, 1999.

————, and Marc Zimmerman. *Literature and Politics in the Central American Revolutions.* Austin: Texas University Press, 1990.

Bhabha, Homi K. *Nation and Narration.* London: Routledge, 1990.

————. *The Location of Culture.* London: Routledge, 1994.

Blest Gana, Alberto. *Martín Rivas (Novela de costumbres politico-sociales),* ed. Jaime Concha. Caracas: Biblioteca Ayacucho, 1977 [1862].

Bloom, Harold. *The Western Canon: The Books and School of the Ages.* New York: Harcourt Brace, 1994.

Borges, Jorge Luis. *Other Inquisitions 1937–1952.* Austin: University of Texas Press, 1995 [1952].

————.*Ficciones.* Buenos Aires: Emecé, 1987.

————. *El Aleph.* Buenos Aires: 1999.

Boyne, Peter. *Foucault and Derrida: The Other Side of Reason.* London: Unwin Hyman, 1990.

Brau, Salvador. "Las clases jornaleras de Puerto Rico." *Ensayos.* San Juan: Edil, 1983 [1882]. 9–75.

Braudel, Fernand. *Civilisation matérielle, économie et capitalisme, XVe-XVIIIe siècle, t. 3, Le temps du monde.* Paris: Armand Colin, 1979.

Breuilly, John. *Nationalism and the State.* Chicago: University of Chicago Press, 1985.

Bunge, Delfina. *Viaje alrededor de mi infancia.* Buenos Aires: Imprenta Guadalupe, 1941.

Burchell, Graham, Colin Gordon, and Peter Miller, eds. *The Foucault Effect. Studies in Governmentality* Chicago: The University of Chicago Press, 1991.

Burke, Kenneth. *The Rhetoric of Religion: Studies in Logology.* Boston: Beacon Press, 1961.

Burke, Seán, ed. *Authorship from Plato to the Postmodern: A Reader.* Edinburgh: Edinburgh UP, 1995.

Butler, Judith. *Gender Trouble.* New York: Routledge, 1990.

————. *Subjects of Desire. Hegelian Reflections in Twentieth-Century France.* New York: Columbia University Press, 1999.

————. *The Psychic Life of Power: Theories in Subjection.* Stanford: Stanford University Press, 1997.

Cabrera, Lydia. *El monte.* LaHabana: Editorial Si-MAR, 1996 [1954].

Calasans Rodriques, Selma. "*Cien años de soledad* y las crónicas de la conquista." *Revista de la Universidad de México* 38, 23 (1983): 13–16.

Camhis, Marios. *Planning Theory and Philosophy.* London: Tavistock Publications, 1979.

Campos Harriet, Fernando. *Desarrollo educacional 1810–1860.* Santiago: Editorial Andres Bello, 1960.

Canby, Peter. "The Truth about Rigoberta Menchú." *The New York Review of Books* (April 8, 1999): 28–33.

Carey-Webb, Allen, Stephen Benz. *Teaching and Testimony: Rigoberta Menchú and the North American Classroom.* Albany: SUNY Press, 1996.

Cariola, Carmen, and Osvaldo Sunkel. *Un siglo de historia económica de Chile. 1830–1930.* Santiago: Editorial Universitaria, 1991.

Carpentier, Alejo. *El arpa y la sombra.* Mexico: Siglo XXI Editores, 1979.

————. *La consagración de la primavera.* Mexico: Siglo xxi, 1978.

————. *The Lost Steps,* tr. Harriet de Onis. New York: Alfred A. Knopf, 1956.

————. *Los pasos perdidos,* ed. Roberto González Echevarría. Madrid: Ediciones Catedra, 1985 [1953].

————. *El reino de este mundo.* Barcelona: Seix Barral, 1997 [1949].

————. *El siglo de las luces.* Barcelona: Seix Barral, 1983 [1962].

————. *Tientos y diferencias.* Montevideo: Arca, 1967.

Cascardi, Anthony J. "Cervantes and Skepticism: The Vanishing of the Body," eds. Sylvia Molloy and Luis Fernandez Cifuentes. *Essays on Hispanic Literature in Honor of Edmund L. King.* London: Tamesis, 1983.

Cervantes Saavedra, Miguel. *The Adventures of Don Quixote,* tr. J.M. Cohen. Baltimore: Penguin Books, 1968.

————. *Novelas ejemplares*, ed. Juan Bautista Avalle-Arce. 3 vols. Madrid: Castalia, 1987 [1613].

Chandravarkar, Rajnarayan. "Plague Panic and Epidemic Politics in India, 1896–1914." *Epidemics and Ideas. Essays on the Historical Perception of Pestilence,* eds. Terence Ranger and Paul Slack. Cambridge: Cambridge University Press, 1992. 203–240.

Chaunu, Pierre. *L'Amerique et les Ameriques.* Paris: Armand Colin, 1964.

Chiampi, Irlemar. 1979. "La proliferación barroca en *Paradiso.*" *José Lezama Lima: Textos críticos,* ed. Justo C. Ulloa. Miami: Ediciones Universales. 82–90.

————. 1991. "Sobre la lectura interrupta de *Paradiso.*" *Revista Iberoamericana.* LVII, 154: 63–76.

Clifford, James. *The Predicament of Culture: Twentieth Century Ethnography, Literature, and Art.* Cambridge: Harvard University Press, 1988.

Colección de documentos inéditos relativos al descubrimiento, conquista y colonización. Madrid, 1864–1884.

Collier, Simon. *Ideas y politica de la independencia chilena.* Santiago: Editorial Andres Bello, 1977.

Corominas, Joan. *Breve diccionario etimológico de la lengua castellana.* Madrid: Gredos, 1961.

Corral, Wilfrido H. "Carta de Estados Unidos: el negocio de Rigoberta." *Cuadernos Hispanoamericanos* 587 (1999): 129–134.

Cortázar, Julio. "Para llegar a Lezama Lima." *La vuelta al día en ochenta mundos.* Vol. II. 6th Ed. Mexico: Siglo XXI Editores, S.A., 1972 [1967]. 41–81.

————. "Soledad sonora." *Sur* 192, 3–4 (1950): 294.

Coughlin, Edward. "On the Concept of Virtue in Eighteenth-Century Spain." *Dieciocho* 15, 1–2 (1992): 83–94.

Craft, Linda J. *Novels of Testimony and Resistance from Central America.* Gainesville: UP of Florida, 1997.

Crimp, Douglas, "Pictures," *October* 8 (Spring, 1979): 75–88.

————. "On the Museum's Ruins," *October* 13 (1980): 41–57.

Cruz Malavé, Arnaldo. "El destino del padre: *Künstlerroman* y falocentrismo en *Paradiso.*" *Revista Iberoamericana* LVII, 154 (1991): 51–64.

da Cunha, Euclides. *Os sertões.* Saò Paulo: Circulo do Livro, 1975 [1902].

Davitt Bell, Michael. *The Development of American Romance: The Sacrifice of Relation.* Chicago: University of Chicago Press, 1980.

de Certeau, Michel. *The Practice of Every Day Life.* Berkeley: University of California Press, 1984.

de Hostos, Eugenio María. *La peregrinación de Bayoan.* Rio Piedras: Ediciones Edil, 1970.

de la Campa, Román. *Latin Americanism.* Minneapolis: University of Minnesota Press, 1999.

de la Vega, Garcilaso. *Comentarios reales de los Incas,* ed. M. Serna. Madrid: Editorial Castalia, 2000 [1609].

de Man, Paul. *Allegories of Reading: Figural Language in Rousseau, Rilke, Nietzsche and Proust.* New Haven: Yale University Press, 1979.

————. *Blindness and Insight: Essays in the Rhetoric of Contemporary Criticism.* New York: Oxford University Press, 1971.

————. "Pascal's Allegory of Persuasion." *Allegory and Representation,* ed. Stephen J. Greenblatt. Baltimore: Johns Hopkins University Press, 1981. 1–25.

Debray, Régis. *Revolución en la revolución. Mi defensa ante el consejo de guerra en Camini, Bolivia; experiencias con el "Che."* Cali: Editorial Pacífico, 1968.

Defournaux, Marcelin. *Pablo de Olavide (1725–1803) ou l'afrancesado.* Paris: PUF, 1959.

del Valle Atiles, Francisco. *Inocencia.* San Juan: Imprenta El Asimilista, 1884.

Deleuze, Gilles. "Coldness and Cruelty." *Masochism.* New York: Zone Books, 1989.

————. *Foucault,* trans. and ed. Seán Hand. Minneapolis: University of Minnesota Press, 1986.

Derrida, Jacques. *Of Grammatology*, trans. Gayatri Chakravorty Spivak. Baltimore: Johns Hopkins University Press, 1976.

————. *Spectres of Marx: The State of the Debt, the Work of Mourning, and the New International.* New York: Routledge, 1994.

Diamond, Irene, and Lee Quimby, eds. *Feminism and Foucault.* Boston: Northeastern University Press, 1988.

Dimock, Wai-chee. *Empire For Liberty: Melville and the Poetics of Individualism.* Princeton: Princeton University Press, 1989.

Dominguez, Nora, and Adriana Rodriguez Persico. "Autobiografía de Victoria Ocampo: la pasión del modelo" *Lecturas Críticas* 2 (1984): 22–33.

Donoso, Armando. *Bilbao y su tiempo.* Santiago: 1913.

Doyle, Sir Arthur Conan. *The Lost World.* Oxford: Heinemann ELT, 1998 [1912].

Dreyfus, Hubert and Paul Rabinow. *Beyond Structuralism and Hermeneutics.* Chicago: University of Chicago Press, 1983.

Drieu la Rochelle, Pierre. *Sur les écrivains,* ed. F. Grover. Paris: Gallimard, 1964.

Dufour, Gérard. "Introducción." *Cartas de Mariano a Antonio,* by Pablo de Olavide. Provence: Publications de l'Université de Provence, 1997. 5–29.

Eagleton, Terry. *The Ideology of the Aesthetic.* London: Basil and Blackwell, 1991.

Edelman, Lee. "Homographesis." *Yale Journal of Criticism* 3.1 (1989): 189–207.

Edwards, Paul, ed. *The Encyclopedia of Philosophy.* Vol. 1. New York: MacMillan Pub. Co. Inc., 1967.

El-Saffar, Ruth. *From Novel To Romance.* Baltimore: Johns Hopkins University Press, 1971.

Felstiner, Mary Lowenthal. "Kinship Politics in the Chilean Independence Movement." *Hispanic American Historical Review* 56:1 (1976).

————. "Family Metaphors: the Language of an Independence Revolution." *Comparative Study of Society and History* 25 (1983).

Fernández de Lizardi, José Joaquín. *El periquillo sarniento,* ed. Carmen Ruiz Barrionuevo. Madrid: Cátedra, 1997 [1816].

Fineman, Joel. "The Structure of Allegorical Desire." *October* 12 (1980): 47–66.

Fiol-Matta, Licia. "The 'schoolteacher of America': Gender, Sexuality and Nation in Gabriela Mistral." *¿Entiendes? Queer Readings, Hispanic Writings,* eds. Emilie L. Bergmann and Paul Julian Smith. Durham: Duke University Press, 1995. 201–229.

Fish, Stanley. "Interpretation and the Pluralist Vision." *Texas Law Review* 60.3 (1982): 494–505.

Forcione, Alban K. *Cervantes and the Humanist Vision: A Study of Four Exemplary Novels.* Princeton: Princeton UP, 1982.

Foster, George M. *Culture and Conquest: America's Spanish Heritage.* New York: Wenner-Gren Foundation for Anthropological Research, 1960.

Foucault, Michel. *The Archaeology of Knowledge and The Discourse on Language,* trans. A. M. Sheridan Smith. New York: Pantheon Books, 1972 [1969].

————. *The Birth of the Clinic. An Archaeology of Medical Perception.* New York: Vintage Books, 1994.

————. *Discipline & Punish: The Birth of the Prison* [1975].
(a) Trans. Alan Sheridan. New York: Random House, 1979.
(b) New York: Vintage Books, 1995.

————. *Ethics: Subjectivity and Truth,* ed. Paul Rabinow. trans. Robert Hurley, et al. New York: The New Press, 1997.

————. *The Foucault Reader,* ed. Paul Rabinow. New York: Pantheon Books, 1984.

————. *Genealogía del racismo: de la guerra de las razas al racismo de Estado.* Madrid: Las Ediciones de la Piqueta, no date.

————. *Hermenéutica del sujeto,* ed. and trans. Fernando Alvarez-Uría. Madrid: La Piqueta, 1987.

————. *The History of Sexuality* [1976].
(a) *An Introduction.* Vol.I, trans. Robert Hurley. New York: Random House, 1980.
(b) *An Introduction.* Vol. I, trans. Robert Hurley. New York: Vintage Books, 1978.

(c) *The Care of the Self. Vol. III*, trans. Robert Hurley. London: 1990.

(d) *Vol. I.* New York: Vintage, 1980.

———. *Language, Countermemory, Practice*, ed. Donald Bouchard, trans. Bouchard and Sherry Simon. Ithaca: Cornell University Press, 1977.

———. *Las palabras y las cosas.* Mexico City: Siglo XXI, 1968.

———. "L'ecriture de soi" *Corps écrit.* 5. Paris: Presses Universitaires de France, 1983.

———. *Les mots et les choses, une archeologie des sciences humaines.* Paris: Gallimard, 1966.

———. *Madness and Civilization: A History of Insanity in the Age of Reason.* New York: Vintage Books, 1973.

———. *Mental Illness and Psychology*, trans. Alan Sheridan. New York: Harper Colophon Books, 1976.

———. "Omnes et singulatim: Towards a Critique of Political Reason." *Tanner Lectures on Human Values II*, ed. Sterling McMurrin. Salt Lake City: University of Utah Press, 1981.

———. "The Order of Discourse." *Untying the Text*, ed. Robert Young. Boston: Routledge, 1981. 48–78.

———. *The Order of Things.* New York: Vintage, 1970 [1966].

———. "The Political Technology of Individuals." In *Technologies of the Self*, ed. Martin et al. Amherst: University Massachusetts Press, 1988. 145–62.

———. *Power/Knowledge: Selected Interviews and Other Writings*, ed. Collin Gordon. New York: Pantheon Books, 1980.

———. "The Subject and Power." *Critical Inquiry* 8.4 (1982): 777–795.

———. *Surveiller et punir. Naissance de la prison.* Paris: Éditions Gallimard, 1975.

———. "Technologies of the Self." In *Technologies of the Self*, ed. Martin et al. Amherst: University Massachusetts Press, 1988. 16–49.

———. "What Is an Author?"

(a) *Textual Strategies: Perspectives in Post-Structuralist Criticism*, ed. and intro. by Josué Harari. Ithaca: Cornell U. Press, 1979. 141–160.

(b) *Authorship from Plato to the Postmodern: A Reader*, ed. Seán Burke. Edinburgh: Edinburgh University Press, 1995. 233–244.

———. "What is Enlightenment." *Foucault Reader*, ed. Paul Rabinow. New York: Pantheon Books, 1984. 32–50.

———. "What Our Present Is," interview with André Berten, trans. Lysa Hochroth. In *The Politics of Truth*, ed. Sylvère Lotringer. New York: Semiotext(e), 1997. 147–168.

Fox, Claire F. *The Fence and the River: Culture and Politics at the U.S.-Mexico Border.* Minneapolis: University Of Minnesota Press, 1999.

Fran, Manfred. *What Is Neostructuralism?* Minneapolis: University of Minnesota Press, 1989.

Franco, Franklin J. *Trujillismo: Génesis y rehabilitación.* Santo Domingo: Editora Cultural Dominicana, 1971.

Franco, Jean. "Un viaje poco romántico: viajeros británicos hacia Sudamerica, 1818–28." *Escritura* 4.7 (1979): 129–141.

Franqui, Carlos. *Cuba: el libro de los doce.* Mexico City: Ediciones Era, 1966.

Fraser, Nancy. *Unruly Practices.* Minneapolis: University of Minnesota Press, 1989.

Freccero, John. "Reader's Report," Cornell University. *John M. Olin Library Bookmark* Series, no. 36. April 1968.

Freedman, Ralph. "The Possibility of a Theory of the Novel." *The Disciplines of Criticism: Essays in Literary Interpretation and History*, eds. Peter Demetz, Thomas Greene and Lowry Nelson Jr., New Haven: Yale University Press, 1968. 57–77.

Freud, Sigmund. "'A Child Is Being Beaten': A Contribution to the Study of the Origin of Sexual Perversions" (1919). *The Standard Edition of the Complete Psychological Works of Sigmund Freud*, ed. James Strachey. London: The Hogarth Press and The Institute of Psycho-Analysis XVII, 1995, 1966, 175–204.

———. *Beyond the Pleasure Principle* (1920). *The Standard Edition of the Complete Psychological Works of Sigmund Freud*, ed. James Strachey. London: The Hogarth Press and The Institute of Psycho-Analysis XVIII, 1995, 1996.

————. "Character and Anal Erotism" (1908). *The Standard Edition of the Complete Psychological Works of Sigmund Freud,* ed. James Strachey. London: The Hogarth Press and The Institute of Psycho-Analysis IX, 1995, 1996, 167–176.

————. "The Economic Problem of Masochism" (1924). *The Standard Edition of the Complete Psychological Works of Sigmund Freud,* ed. James Strachey. London: The Hogarth Press and The Institute of Psycho-Analysis XIX, 1995, 1996, 157–170.

————. *From the History of an Infantile Neurosis* (1918 [1914]). *The Standard Edition of the Complete Psychological Works of Sigmund Freud,* ed. James Strachey. London: The Hogarth Press and The Institute of Psycho-Analysis XVII, 1995, 1996, 1–124.

————. *General Psychological Theory,* intro. by Philip Rieff. New York: Touchstone, 1995, 1996, 1997.

————. "Instincts and Their Vicissitudes" (1915). *The Standard Edition of the Complete Psychological Works of Sigmund Freud,* ed. James Strachey. London: The Hogarth Press and The Institute of Psycho-Analysis XIV, 1995, 1996, 127–129.

————. "On Transformations of Instinct as Exemplified in Anal Erotism" (1917). *The Standard Edition of the Complete Psychological Works of Sigmund Freud.* Ed. by James Strachey. London: The Hogarth Press and The Institute of Psycho-Analysis XVII, 1995, 1996, 125–134.

————. *Three Essays on the Theory of Sexuality.*
(a) (1905). *The Standard Edition of the Complete Psychological Works of Sigmund Freud,* ed. James Strachey. London: The Hogarth Press and The Institute of Psycho-Analysis. VII. 123–246.
(b) Trans. James Stachey, intro. by Steven Marcus. n.p.: Basic Books, 1975.

Frye, Northrop. *Anatomy of Criticism.* New York: Atheneum, 1968.

————. *The Secular Scripture: A Study of the Structure of Romance.* Cambridge: Harvard University Press, 1976.

Fuentes, Carlos. *Aura.* México City: Ediciones Era, 1999 [1962].

————. *New York Times Book Review* (April 6, 1986): 34.

————. *Terra Nostra.* Mexico: Joaquín Mortíz, 1998 [1976].

Fusco, Coco, and Paula Heredia. *The Couple in the Cage: A Guatinaui Odyssey.* Authentic Documentary Productions, 1993.

Gage, Thomas. *Nueva relación que contiene los viajes de Thomas Gage en la Nueva España.* Guatemala: Biblioteca Guatemala, 1946 [1948].

Gallagher, Catherine. *Industrial Transformations in the English Novel.* Chicago: University of Chicago Press, 1985.

Gallo, Marta. "Las crónicas de Victoria Ocampo." *Revista Iberoamericana* 132–133 (1985): 679–686.

García Canclini, Néstor. *Consumidores y ciudadanos.* Mexico City: Grijaldo, 1995.

García Marquez, Gabriel. "Address Accepting the Nobel Prize." *Gabriel García Márquez: New Readings.* Cambridge, Endland: Cambridge University Press, 1987: 207–11.

————. *Cien años de soledad.* Buenos Aries: Editorial Sudamericana, 1967.

————. *Crónica de una muerte anunciada.* Bogotá: Grupo Editorial Norma, 1993.

————. "Discurso de acceptación del premio Nobel." *El Mundo* San Juan de Puerto Rico, Sunday, December 12, 1982: 21–C.

————. *El olor de la guayaba. Conversación con Plinio Apuleyo Mendoza.* Bogotá: Editorial La Oveja Negra, 1982.

————. *Los funerales de la Mamá Grande.* Buenos Aires: Editorial Sudamericana, 1967.

————. *One Hundred Years of Solitude,* trans. Gregory Rabassa. New York: Harper and Row, 1967.

Garro, Elena. *Recollections of Things to Come,* trans. Ruth L. C. Simms. Austin: University of Texas Press, 1981 [1963].

Gay, Peter. *The Enlightenment: An Interpretation. The Rise of Modern Paganism.* New York: The Norton Library, 1977.

Geertz, Clifford. "Ideology as a Cultural System." *Ideology and Discontent,* ed. David E.
    Apter. New York: Free Press, 1964.
————. *The Interpretation of Cultures.* New York: Basic Books, 1973.
————. *Works and Lives: The Anthropologist as Author.* Stanford University Press, 1988.
Gellner, Ernest. *Nations and Nationalism.* Ithaca: Cornell University Press, 1983.
Gilbert, Sandra M., and Susan Gubar. "'Forward into the Past': The Female Affiliation
    Complex." *No Man's Land. The Place of the Woman Writer in the Twentieth Century, Vol.
    I: The War on Words.* New Haven and London: Yale University Press, 1987. 165–224.
————. "Infection in the Sentence: The Woman Writer and the Anxiety of Authorship." *The
    Madwoman in the Attic.* New Haven and London: Yale University Press, 1979.
Glissart, Edouard. *Caribbean Discourse,* ed. A. J. Arnold, trans. J. Michael Dash.
    Charlottesville: University Press of Virginia, 1989.
Goic, Cedomil. "La novela hispanoamericana colonial." *Historia de la literatura hispanoameri-
    cana. Epoca colonial.* Tomo I. Comp. Luis Iñigo Madrigal. Madrid: Cátedra, 1982. 369–
    406.
Goldstein, Jan. "Foucault's Technologies of the Self and the Cultural History of Identity."
    Cultural History after Foucault, ed. John Newbauer. New York: Aldine de Gruyter, 1999.
    37–54.
Gómez-Peña, Guillermo. *The New World Border: Prophecies, Poems, and Loqueras for the End
    of the Century.* San Francisco: City Lights, 1996.
————. "The Multicultural Paradigm: An Open Letter to the National Arts Community."
    Negotiating Performance: Gender, Sexuality and Theatricality in Latin/o America, Diana
    Taylor and Juan Villegas, eds. Durham: Duke University Press, 1994. 17–29.
————. *Warrior For Gringostroika: Essays, Performance Texts, And Poetry.* St. Paul, Minn.:
    Graywolf Press, 1993.
————, and Isaac Artenstein, dir. *Border Brujo.* Cinewest Productions, 1990.
————, Roberto Sifuentes, and Philip Brookman. *Temple of Confessions: Mexican Beasts and
    Living Santos.* New York: Powerhouse Books, 1996.
Góngora, Mario. *Ensayo histórico sobre la noción de estado en Chile en los siglos XIX y XX.*
    Santiago: Editorial Universitaria, 1992.
González, Eduardo. *Alejo Carpentier: el tiempo del hombre.* Caracas: Monte Avila, 1978.
Gonzalez, Marcial. "La moral del ahorro." *La cuestión social en Chile. Ideas y debates precur-
    sores (1804–1902),* ed. Sergio Grez Toso. Santiago: Dirección de Bibliotecas Archivos y
    Museos and Centro de Investigaciones Diego Barros Arana, 1995. 297–307
González Echevarría, Roberto. *Alejo Carpentier. The Pilgrim at Home.* Ithaca: Cornell
    University Press, 1977.
————. "Lo cubano en *Paradiso.*" *Coloquio Internacional sobre la obra de José Lezama Lima.
    Vol. II: Prosa,* ed. Cristina Vizcaino and Eugenio Suárez Galbán. Poitiers: Centro de
    Investigaciones Latinoamericanas, Universidad de Poiters, 1984. 31–51.
————. *Myth and Archive: A Theory of Latin American Narrative.* Durham: Duke University
    Press, 1998 [1990].
————. "Redescubrimiento del mundo perdido: el *Facundo* de Sarmiento." *Revista
    Iberoamericana* 43 (1988): 385–406.
————. "With Borges in Macondo." *Diacritics* 2.I (1972): 57–60.
González Stephan, Beatriz. *La historiografía literaria del liberalismo hispanoamericano del siglo
    XIX.* Habana: Casa de las Americas, 1987.
Goodman, Edward J. *The Explorers of South America.* New York: The Macmillan Co., 1972.
Gordon, Colin. "Governmental Rationality: An Introduction." *The Foucault Effect. Studies in
    Governmentality,* eds. Graham Burchell et al. Chicago: The University of Chicago Press,
    1991.
Graham, Richard, ed. *The Idea of Race in Latin America, 1870–1940.* Austin: University of
    Texas Press, 1990.

Greenberg, Janet Beth. "The Divided Self: Forms of Autobiography in the Writings of Victoria Ocampo." Unpublished Dissertation. University of California Berkeley, 1986.

Greenblatt, Stephen J. *Allegory and Representation*. Baltimore: John Hopkins University Press, 1981.

Grez Toso, Sergio. *De la "Regeneracion del pueblo" a la huelga general. Génesis y evolución histórica del movimiento popular en Chile (1810–1890)*. Santiago: Dirección de Bibliotecas Archivos y Museos and Centro de Investigaciones Diego Barros Arana, 1997.

———, ed. *La cuestión social en Chile. Ideas y debates precursores (1804–1902)*. Santiago: dirección de Bibliotecas Archivos y Museos en coproducción con Centro de Investigaciones Diego Barros Arana, 1995.

Griffin, Robert J. "Anonymity and Authorship." *Configurations* 7.2 (1999): 279–290.

Gullón, Ricardo. *García Márquez o el olvidado arte de contar*. Madrid: Taurus, 1970.

Gutman, Huck. "Rousseau's Confessions: A Technology of the Self." *Technologies of the Self*, ed. Martin et al. Amherst: University of Massachusetts Press, 1988. 99–120.

Haller, John. "The Physician versus the Negro: Medical and Antrhoplogical Concepts of Race in the Late Nineteenth Century." *Bulletin of the History of Medicine* 44.2 (1970): 145–167.

Hallward, Peter. "Edouard Glissant: Between the Singular and the Specific." *The Yale Journal of Criticism* 11.2 (1998): 441–464.

Halperin, David M. *Saint Foucault: Towards a Gay Hagiography*. New York: Oxford University Press, 1995.

Hanchard, Michael George. *Orpheus and Power: the Movimento Negro of Rio de Janeiro and São Paulo, Brazil, 1945–1988*. Princeton, N.J.: Princeton University Press, 1998, 1994.

Hardoy, Jorge E. *El modelo clásico de la ciudad colonial hispanoamericana*. Buenos Aires: Instituto Di Tella, 1968.

———, ed. *Urbanization in Latin America: Approaches and Issues*. Garden City: Anchor Books, 1975.

———, and Richard Schaedel, eds. *Asentamientos urbanos y organización socioproductiva en la historia de América Latina*. Buenos Aires: SIAP, 1977.

———, and Richard Schaedel, eds. *Las ciudades de América Latina y sus áreas de influencia a través de la historia*. Buenos Aires: SIAP, 1975.

Hartman, Geoffrey, "Looking Back on Paul de Man," *Reading de Man Reading*, eds. Lindsay Waters and Wlad Godzich. Minneapolis: University of Minnesota Press, 1989. 3–24.

Heckman, Susan, ed. *Feminist Interpretations of Michel Foucault*. University Park: Pennsylvania State University Press, 1996.

Hegel, G.W.F. *Phenomenology of Spirit*, trans. A.V. Miller. Oxford and New York: Oxford University Press, 1977.

———. *Philosophy of Right*, Oxford: Oxford University Press, 1967.

Heiple, Daniel. "El licenciado Vidriera y el humor tradicional del loco." *Hispania* 66 (1983):17–20.

Hennessy, Alistair. *The Frontier in Latin American History*. Albuquerque: University of Mexico Press, 1978.

Hiriart, Rosario. *Cartas a Lydia Cabrera. Correspondencia inédita de Gabriela Mistral y Teresa de la Parra*. Madrid: Torremozas, 1988.

Hutton, Patrick H. "Foucault, Freud, and the Technologies of the Self." *Technologies of the Self; A Seminar With Michel Foucault*, ed. Gutman et al. Amherst: University of Massachusetts Press, 1988. 121–144.

Issacs, Jorge. *Maria*, ed. Donald McGrady. Madrid: Cátedra, 1996.

Jacobus, Mary. *Reading Woman. Essays in Feminist Criticism.* Bloomington: Indiana University Press, 1986.

Jameson, Fredric. "Third-World Literature in the Era of Multinational Capitalism." *Social Text* 15 (1986): 65–88.

Jan Mohamed, Abdul. "The Economy of Manichean Allegory: The Function of Racial Difference in Colonialist Literature." *Critical Inquiry* 12 (1985): 59–87.

Jauss, Hans Robert. *Toward an Aesthetic of Reception,* trans. Timothy Bahti. Minneapolis: University of Minnesota Press, 1982.

Jennings, Michael W. *Dialectical Images: Walter Benjamin's Theory of Literary Criticism.* Ithaca: Cornell University Press, 1987.

Jones, Ann Rosalind. "Writing the Body: Toward an Understanding of L'Ecriture féminine." *Feminist Criticism. Essays on Women, Literature and Theory,* Ed. Elaine Showalter. New York: Pantheon Books, 1985.

Kaiser, Walter. *Praisers of Folly.* Cambridge: Harvard University Press, 1963.

Kaminsky, Amy. "Essay, Gender, and *Mestizaje:* Victoria Ocampo and Gabriela Mistral." *The Politics of the Essay: Feminist Perspectives,* eds. Ruth-Ellen Boetcher Joeres and Elizabeth Mittman. Bloomington: Indiana University Press, 1993.

Kant, Immanuel. "What is Enlightenment?" *On History,* ed., trans. Lewis White Beck. New York: Bobbs-Merrill Co., 1963. 3–10.

Kantorowicz, Ernst H. "Pro Patria Mori in Medieval Political Thought." *Selected Studies.* Locust Valley, N.Y.: J.J. Augustin Publisher, 1965. 308–324.

Kerr, Lucille. *Reclaiming the Author: Figures and Fictions from Spanish America.* Durham: Duke University Press, 1992.

Kester, Grant H. "Rhetorical Questions: The Alternative Arts Sector and the Imaginary Public." *Afterimage* 20.6 (1993): 10–16.

King, John. *Sur. A Study of the Argentine Literary Journal and Its Role in the Development of a Culture. 1931–1970.* Cambridge, England, and New York: Cambridge University Press, 1986.

Knight, Alan. "Racism, Revolution, and *Indigenismo*: Mexico, 1910–1940." *The Idea of Race in Latin America, 1870–1940,* ed. Richard Graham. Austin: University of Texas Press, 1990.

Konetzke, Richard. *América Latina, II, La época colonial.* Madrid: Siglo XXI, 1972.

Krebs, Ricardo. "El pensamiento de la iglesia frente a la laicización del estado de Chile." Ricardo Krebs et. al. *Catolicismo y laicismo, seis estudios.* Santiago: Ediciones Nueva Universidad, 1981.

Kristeva, Julia. *Black Sun.* New York: Columbia University Press, 1989.

Kubayanda, Josaphat. "Order and Conflict: *Yo el Supremo* in Light of Rama's *ciudad letrada* Theory." *The Historical Novel in Latin America,* ed. Daniel Balderston. Gaithersburg, Md.: Hispamérica 15.45 (1986): 129–137.

Kuhnheim, Jill S. "The Economy of Performance: Gómez-Peña's *New World Border*" *Modern Fiction Studies* 44.1 (1998): 24–35.

Labarca, Amanda. *Historia de la ensenanza en Chile.* Santiago: Imprenta Universitaria, 1939.

Laclau, Ernesto. *New Reflections on the Revolution of Our Time.* New York: Verso, 1990.

Lastarria, José Victorino. *La América. Obras Completas,* vol. VIII. Santiago. Imprenta Barcelona, 1906–1934.

Latour, Bruno. "Give Me a Laboratory and I Will Raise the World." *Science Observed: Perspectives on the Social Study of Science,* eds. Kamin D. Knoor-Cetina and Michael Mulkay. Beverly Hills: Sage, 1983. 141–169.

Lavrin, Asunción. *Women, Feminism and Social Change in Argentina, Uruguay, and Chile, 1890–1940.* Lincoln: University of Nebraska Press, 1995.

Lejeune, Philippe. *On Autobiography,* ed. Paul John Eakin, trans. Katherine Leary. Minneapolis: University of Minnesota Press, 1989.

Levi-Strauss, Claude. *Tristes Tropiques*. Paris: Plom, 1977 [1955].

Levy, Anita, "Blood, Kinship, and Gender." *Genders* 5 (Summer 1989): 70–85.

Lezama Lima, José. *Paradiso*, ed. Cintio Vitier. Argentina: Colección Archivos, 1988 [1966].

———. *Paradiso*, trans. Gregory Rabassa. New York: Farrar, Straus and Giroux, 1974.

Lichy, René. *Yakú. Expedición Franco-Venezolana del Alto Orinoco*. Caracas: Monte Avila, 1978.

Liu, Eric. *The Accidental Asian: Notes of a Native Speaker*. New York: Random House, 1998.

Logan, Kathleen. "Personal Testimony: Latin American Women Telling Their Lives." *Latin American Research Review* 32.1 (1997): 199–211.

López-Baralt, Mercedes. "*Cien años de soledad*: cultura e historia latinoamericanas replanteadas en el idioma del parentesco." *Revista de Estudios Hispánicos*. San Juan de Puerto Rico, Year 6 (1979): 153–175.

Lowenthal Festiner, Mary. "Family Metaphors: the Language of an Independence Revolution," *Comparative Study of Society and History*, 25:1 (January, 1983).

———. "Kinship Politics in the Chilean Independence Movement," *HAHR*, 56:1 (February, 1976).

Lukács, György. *The Theory of the Novel: A Historico-Philosophical Essay on the Forms of Great Epic Literature*, trans. Anna Bostock. Cambridge: MIT Press, 1971.

Mañach, Jorge. *Historia y estilo*, Foreword by Rosario Rexach. Miami: Editorial Cubana, 1994.

Marchant, Patricio. "Desolación." *Una palabra cómplice*, eds. Raquel Olea and Soledad Fariña. Santiago: Editorial Cuarto Propio, 1996. 55–73.

Martin, Biddy. *Femininity Played Straight*. New York: Routledge, 1996.

Martin, Luther H., et al., eds. *Technologies of the Self. A Seminar with Michel Foucault*. Amherst: University Massachusetts Press, 1988.

Matamoro, Blas. "*Sur*: la torre inclinada." *Genio y figura de Victoria Ocampo*. Buenos Aires: Eudeba, 1986. 201–308.

McGuirk, Bernard, et al. *Gabriel García Márquez: New Readings*. Cambridge: Cambridge University Press, 1987. 207–211.

McNay, Lois. *Foucault and Feminism*. Boston: Northeastern University Press, 1992.

McWorther, Ladelle. *Bodies and Pleasures*. Bloomington: Indiana University Press, 1999.

Melville, Stephen. "Notes on the Reemergence of Allegory, the Forgetting of Modernism, the Necessity of Rhetoric, and the Conditions of Publicity in Art and Criticism." *October* 19 (1981): 55–92.

Mena, Lucila I. "La huelga de la compañia bananera como expresion de 'lo real maravilloso' americano en *Cien años de soledad*." *Bulletin Hispanique* 74 (1972): 379–405.

Menchú, Rigoberta. *Me llamo Rigoberta Menchú, y así me nació la conciencia*. Mexico: Siglo XXI, 1983.

———. *I, Rigoberta Menchú: An Indian Woman in Guatemala*, ed. Elisabeth Burgos-Debray, trans. Ann Wright: London Verso, 1984.

Menéndez Pidal, Ramón. "Idea Imperial de Carlos V." *Mis páginas preferidas. Estudios lingüísticos e históricos*. Madrid: Gredos, 1957. 232–253.

———. *La epopeya castellana a través de la literatura española*. Madrid: Espasa-Calpe, 1959.

Meyer, Doris. *Victoria Ocampo. Against the Wind and the Tide*. New York: George Braziller, 1979.

Mignolo, Walter. *The Darker Side of the Renaissance*. Ann Arbor: University of Michigan Press, 1995.

———. "Postoccidentalismo: el argumento desde América Latina." *Teorías sin disciplina (latinamericanismo, postcolonialdad y globilization en debate)*, eds. Santiago Castro-Gomez and Eduardo Mendieta. México City: Miguet Angel Porrúa, 1998.

Miller, D.A. *The Novel and the Police*. Berkeley: University of California Press, 1988.

Miller, James. *The Passion of Michel Foucault*. New York: Dobuleday, 1993.

Mistral, Gabriela. "A la mujer mexicana." *Lecturas para mujeres: destinadas a la enseñanza del lenguaje.* Madrid: Godoy, 1924. 172–175.

———. *Antología mayor: Cartas.* Santiago: Cochrane, 1992.

———. "El tipo del indio americano." *Gabriela anda por el mundo,* ed. Roque Esteban Scarpa. Santiago: Editorial Andrés Bello, 1978. 179–183.

———. "El folklore argentino." *Magisterio y niño,* ed. Roque Esteban Scarpa. Santiago: Andrés Bello, 1979.

———. "Imagen y palabra en la educación:" *Magisterio y niño,* ed. Roque Esteban Scarpa. Santiago: Editorial Andrés Bello, 1979. 195–205.

———. "Primer recuerdo de Isadora Duncan." *Gabriela anda por el mundo,* ed. Roque Esteban Scarpa. Santiago: Editorial Andrés Bello, 1978. 118–121.

———. "Prólogo." *La desterrada en su patria: Gabriela Mistral en Magallanes, 1918–1920.* 2 vols. Roque Esteban Scarpa. Santiago, Chile: Editorial Nascimento, 1977.

———. "Silueta de la india mexicana." *Gabriela anda por el mundo,* ed. Roque Esteban Scarpa. Santiago: Editorial Andrés Bello, 1979. 99–102.

———. "Sobre la mujer chilena." *Escritos políticos,* ed. Jaime Quezada. Santiago: Fondo de Cultura Económica, 1994. 61–65.

———. *Tan de usted. Epistolario de Gabriela Mistral con Alfonso Reyes,* comp. Luis Vargas Saavedra. Santiago: Hachette; Editorial de La Universidad Católica de Chile, 1991.

———. *Vuestra Gabriela: Cartas inéditas de Gabriela Mistral a los Errazuriz Echenique y Tómic Errazuriz,* ed. Luis Vargas Saavedra. Santiago: Zig Zag, 1995.

Molloy, Sylvia. *At Face Value: Autobiographical Writing in Spanish America.* Oxford: Cambridge University Press, 1991.

———. "Disappearing Acts: Reading Lesbian in Teresa de la Parra." *¿Entiendes? Queer Readings, Hispanic Writings,* eds. Emilie Bergmann and Paul Julian Smith. Durham: Duke University Press, 1995. 230–256.

———, and Robert I. Irwin, eds. *Hispanisms and Homosexualities.* Durham: Duke University Press, 1998.

———. "The Politics of Posing." *Hispanisms and Homosexualities,* eds. Sylvia Molloy and Robert Mckee Irwin. Durham: Duke University Press, 1998.

Montejo, Esteban. *The Autobiography of a Runaway Slave,* ed. Miguel Barnet, trans. Jocasta Innes. New York: Pantheon Books, 1968.

Moraga, Cherríe. "Art in América con acento." *Negotiating Performance: Gender, Sexuality, and Theatricality in Latino America.* Durham: Duke University Press, 1994. 30–36.

Morales Otero, P. "The Work of the Biological Laboratory of the Department of Health." *The Porto Rico Health Review* 2.9 (1927): 10–16.

Moraña, Mabel. "De *la ciudad letrada* al imaginario nacionalista: contribuciones de Angel Rama a la invención de América." *Esplendores y misterios del siglo XIX: cultura y sociedad en América Latina,* eds. Beatriz González Stephan, Javier Lasarte, Graciela Montaldo, and Maria Julia Droqui. Caracas: Monte Avila/Ediciones de la Universidad Simón Bolívar, 1995. 41–51.

Mordorossian, Carine M. "Shutting Up the Subaltern: Silences, Stereotypes, and Double-Entendre in Jean Rhys's *Wide Sargasso Sea.*" *Callaloo* 22.4 (1999): 1071–1090.

Moreiras, Alberto. *Tercer espacio: literatura y duelo en América Latina.* Universidad Arcis, 1999.

Morse, Richard. "A Framework for Latin American Urban History." *Urbanization in Latin America,* ed. Hardoy. Garden City: Anchor Books, 1975.

Mosse, George L. *Nationalism and Sexuality. Respectability and Abnormal Sexuality in Modern Europe.* New York: Howard Fertig, 1985.

Mumford, Lewis. *The City in History.* New York: Harcourt, Brace and World, 1961.

Newmark, Kevin. "Paul de Man's History." *Reading de Man Reading,* eds. Lindsay Waters and Wlad Godzich. Minneapolis: University of Minnesota Press, 1989: 121–135.

Nietzsche, Friedrich. *On the Genealogy of Morals,* ed. Walter Kaufmann. New York: Vintage Books, 1969.

Norris, Christopher. *Paul de Man: Deconstruction and the Critique of Aesthetic Ideology.* New York: Routledge, 1988.

———. *The Truth about Postmodernism.* Cambridge: Blackwell Publishers, 1993.

———. *Truth and the Ethics of Criticism.* Manchester: Manchester University Press, 1994.

Novo, Salvador. "Ventana: Con Gabriela Mistral I." *Novedades.* Mexico City, 1948.

Noyes, John K. *The Mastery of Submission: Inventions of Masochism.* Ithaca: Cornell University Press, 1997.

Núñez, Estuardo. "Una novela desconocida de Pablo de Olavide." *Cuadernos Hispanoamericanos* 459 (1988): 125–129.

———. "Estudio preliminar." *Obras selectas,* by Pablo de Olavide, ed. Estuardo Núñez. Lima: Biblioteca Clásicos del Perú/3, 1987. ix-cix.

Ocampo, Victoria. *El archipiélago.* Autobiografía, I. Buenos Aires: Ediciones Revista Sur, 1979.

———. *El imperio insular.* Autobiografía, II. Buenos Aires: Ediciones Revista Sur, 1980.

———. *La rama de Salzburgo.* Autobiografía, III. Buenos Aires: Ediciones Revista Sur, 1981.

———. *Viraje.* Autobiografía, IV. Buenos Aires: Ediciones Revista Sur, 1982.

———. *Figuras simbólicas. Medida de Francia.* Autobiografía, V. Buenos Aires: Ediciones Revista Sur, 1983.

———. *Sur y cia.* Autobiografía, VI. Buenos Aires: Ediciones Revista Sur, 1984.

———. *De Francesca a Beatrice.* Epilogue by José Ortega y Gasset. 2nd ed. Madrid: Revista de Occidente, 1928.

———. *El viajero y una de sus sombras.* Buenos Aires: Sudamericana, 1951.

———. *Soledad sonora.* Buenos Aires: Sudamericana, 1950.

———. *Testimonios,* Madrid: Revista de Occidente, 1935.

———. *Testimonios,* 2a. serie. Buenos Aires: Sur, 1941.

———. *Testimonios,* 3a. serie. Buenos Aires: Sudamericana, 1946.

———. *Soledad Sonora* (*Testimonios* 4a serie). Buenos Aires: Sudamericana, 1950.

———. *Testimonios,* 5a. serie. Buenos Aires: Sur, 1957.

———. *Testimonios,* 6a. serie. Buenos Aires: Sur, 1963.

———. *Testimonios,* 7a. serie. Buenos Aires: Sur, 1967.

———. *Testimonios,* 8a. serie. Buenos Aires, Sur, 1975.

———. *Testimonios,* 9a. serie. Buenos Aires: Sur, 1977.

———. *Testimonios,* 10a. serie. Buenos Aires: Sur, 1977.

———. *Virginia Woolf en su diario.* Buenos Aires: Sur, 1947.

Olavide, Pablo de. *Cartas de Mariano a Antonio. "El programa ilustrado de 'El evangelio en triunfo,'"* ed. Gérard Dufour. Provence: Publications de l'Université de Provence, 1997.

———. "El incógnito o el fruto de la ambición." *Obras narrativas desconocidas,* ed. Estuardo Nuñez. Lima: Biblioteca Nacional del Perú, 1971. 3–84.

———. *Obras narrativas desconocidas,* ed. Estuardo Núñez. Lima: Biblioteca Nacional del Perú, 1971.

———. *Obras selectas,* ed. Estuardo Núñez. Lima: Biblioteca Clásicos del Perú/3, 1987.

———. "Paulina o el amor desinteresado." *Obras narrativas desconocidas,* ed. Estuardo Nuñez. Lima: Biblioteca Nacional del Perú, 1971. 85–127.

Oliver, Kelly. *Subjectivity without Subjects: From Abject Fathers to Desiring Mothers.* New York: Rowman and Littlefield, 1998.

———. "What Is Transformative about the Performative? From Repetition to Working-Through." *Studies in Practical Philosophy.* 1.2 (1999): 144–166

Oliver, María Rosa. *La vida cotidiana.* Buenos Aires: Sudamericana, 1969.

Omi, Michael, and Howard Winant. *Racial Formation in the United States.* 2nd ed. New York and London: Routledge, 1994.

Ortiz, Fernando. *Contrapunteo cubano del tabaco y del azúcar.* Caracas: Ayacucho, 1978.

Owens, Craig, "*Einstein on the Beach:* The Primacy of Metaphor," *October* 4 (1977): 21–32.

———. "The Allegorical Impulse: Toward a Theory of Postmodernism," *October* 12 (1980): 67–86, and 2.13 (1980): 61–80.

Oyuela, Calixto. *Programa de literatura española y de los estados hispano-americanos.* Buenos Aires: Imprenta Biedma, 1884.

Padura Fuentes, Leonardo. *Paisaje de otoño.* Barcelona: Tusquets Editores, 1998.

Palencia Roth, Michael. "Los pergaminos de Aureliano Babilonia." *Revista Iberoamericana* 123.4 (1983): 403–417.

Parry, Benita. "Problems in current Theories of Colonial Discourse." *The Post-Colonial Studies Reader,* eds. Bill Ashcroft et al. London: Routledge, 1995. 36–44.

Parry, J. H. *The Cities of the Conquistadores.* London: Hispanic and Luso-Brazilian Councils, 1961.

Patton, Paul. "Foucault's Subject of Power." *The Later Foucault. Politics and Philosophy,* ed. Jeremy Moss. London: Sage Publications, 1998. 64–77.

Pellón, Gustavo. *José Lezama Lima's Joyful Vision.* Austin: University of Texas Press, 1989.

Peña y Cámara, José María de la. *Archivo General de Indias de Sevilla. Guia del visitante.* Valencia: Dirección General de Archivos y Bibliotecas-Tipografía Moderna, 1958.

Perdices Blas, Luis. *Pablo de Olavide (1725–1803). El ilustrado.* Madrid: Editorial Complutense, 1993.

Pérez-Firmat, Gustavo. *Life on the Hyphen: The Cuban-American Way.* Austin: University of Texas Press, 1994.

Picó, Fernando. *La Guerra después de la guerra.* Río Piedras: Editorial Huracán, 1988.

Pizarro, Ana. "Mistral, ¿qué modernidad?" *Re-leer hoy a Gabriela Mistral: Mujer, literatura y sociedad,* eds. Gastón Lillo and Guillermo Renart. Ottawa and Santiago: University of Ottawa: Editorial de la Universidad de Santiago, 1997. 43–52.

Poblete, Juan. "El Castellano: la nueva disciplina y el texto nacional en el fin de siglo chileno." *Revista de Crítica Cultural,* 15 (November, 1997).

———. "Lectura de la sociabilidad y sociabilidad de la lectura: la novela y las costumbres nacionales en el siglo XIX," *Revista de Crítica Literaria Latinoamericana,* 52 (2000). 11–34

Poniatowska, Elena. *Hasta no verte Jesús mío.* México: Era, 1969.

Poole, Ross. *Nation and Identity.* London and New York: Routledge, 1999.

Portelli, Alessandro. "Oral History as Genre." *Narrative and Genre,* eds. Mary Chamberlain, and Paul Thompson. London-New York: Routledge, 1998. 23–43.

Posner, Richard. *Law and Literature: A Misunderstood Relation.* Cambridge: Harvard University Press, 1988.

Posse, Abel. *Daimón.* Barcelona: Plaza and Janès, 1983 [1978].

Pratt, Mary Louise. "Linguistic Utopias." *The Linguistics of Writing: Arguments between Language and Literature,* eds. Nigel Fabb, Derek Attridge, Alan Durant, and Colin MacCabe. New York: Methuen, 1987. 48–66.

———. "Scratches on the Face of the Country; or What Mr. Barrow Saw in the Land of the Bushmen." *Critical Inquiry* 12 (1985): 119–143.

Programas detallados para las escuelas secundarias. Mexico: Secretaría de Educación Pública, 1933.

Quintero, Rodolfo. *Antropología de las ciudades latinoamericanas.* Caracas: Dirección cultura de la Universidad Central de Venezuela, 1964.

Rabasa, José. *Inventing America.* Norman: University of Oklahoma Press, 1993.

Rabinow, Paul. "Introduction." *The Foucault Reader,* ed. Paul Rabinow. New York: Pantheon Books, 1984. 3–29.

Rajnarayan, Chandravarkar. "Plague Panic and Epidemic Politics in India, 1896–1914." *Epidemics and Ideas. Essays on the Historical Perception of Pestilence,* eds. Terence Ranger and Paul Slack. Cambridge: Cambridge University Press, 1992. 203–240.

Rama, Angel. *La ciudad letrada.* Hanover: Ediciones del norte, 1984.

———. *Las máscaras democráticas del modernismo.* Montevideo, Uruguay: Fundación Angel Rama, 1985.

————. *The Lettered City*, ed. and trans. Charles Chasteen. Durham: Duke University Press, 1996.

————. *Transculturación narrativa en América Latina*. Mexico City: Siglo XXI, 1982.

Ramón, Armando de. *Santiago de Chile (1541–1992). Historia de una sociedad urbana.* Madrid: Editorial Mapfre, 1992.

Ramos, Julio. *Desencuentros de la modernidad en América Latina: Literatura y política en el siglo XIX.* México: Fondo de Cultura Económica, 1989.

Reyes, Alfonso, "Pasado inmediato." V.12. *Obras completas.* Mexico: Fondo de Cultura Economica, 1960.

Ricard, Robert. *La "conquête espirituelle" du Mexique.* Paris: Institut d'ethnologie, 1933.

Richard, Nelly. *La estratificación de los márgenes.* Santiago de Chile: Francisco Zegers, 1989.

————. *La insubordinación de los signos: cambio político, transformaciones culturales y poéticas de la crisis.* Santiago: Editorial Cuarto Propio, 1994.

Rincón, Carlos. *La no simultaneidad de lo simultáneo.* Bogotá, Colombia: Universidad Nacional de Colombia, 1995.

Rodó, José Enrique. *Ariel, liberalismo y jacobinismo, ensayos,* ed. Raimundo Lazo. México: Editorial Porrua, 1989 [1900].

Rodríguez-Luis, Julio. *Novedad y ejemplo de las novelas de Cervantes.* Madrid: José Porrúa, 1980.

Rodríguez Monegal, Emir. "*One Hundred Years of Solitude*: The Last Three Pages." *Books Abroad,* 47 (1973): 485–489.

————. "Sobre el *Paradiso* de Lezama." *Mundo Nuevo* 16 (1967): 90–95.

————. "*Paradiso* en su contexto." *Mundo Nuevo* 24 (1968): 40–44.

Rodríguez, Simón. *Pensamientos de Simón Rodríguez.* Caracas: Alfadil, 1955.

Rojas, Rafael. *Isla sin fin. Contribución a la crítica del nacionalismo cubano.* Miami: Ediciones Universal, 1998.

Rojas, Ricardo. *La restauración nacionalista.* Buenos Aires: Libreria de la Facultad, 1922.

Román Lagunas, Jorge. "Bibliografía anotada de y sobre Alberto Blest Gana." *Revista Iberoamericana* 112–113 (1980): 605–647.

Romero, Jose Luis. *Latinoamérica: las ciudades y las ideas.* Mexico: Siglo XXI, 1976.

————. *Asentamientos urbanos y organización socioproductiva en la historia de América Latina.* Buenos Aires: SIAP, 1977.

Romero, Luis Alberto. "Los sectores populares en las ciudades latinoamericanas del siglo XIX: la cuestión de la identidad." *Desarrollo Económico* 27 (1987): 201–222.

Romero de Castilla y Perosso, Francisco. *Apuntes históricos sobre el Archivo General de Simancas.* Madrid: Imprenta y estereotipia de Aribau y Co., 1873.

Rorty, Richard. "Comments on Castoriadi's 'The End of Philosophy.'" *Salmagundi* 82–83 (1989): 24–30.

————. *Objectivity, Relativism, and Truth.* Cambridge: Cambridge University Press, 1991.

————. "Tales of Two Disciplines." *Callaloo* 17.2 (1994).

Rosa, João Guimarães. *Grande sertão: veredas.* Rio de Janeiro: Nova Fronteira, 1994 [1956].

Rosa, Nicolás. "Sur, o el espíritu y la letra." *Los Libros* 15–16 (1971): 4–6.

Rosales, Luis. *Cervantes y la libertad.* Madrid: Graf. Valera, 1960.

Rose, Mark. *Authors and Owners: The Invention of Copyright.* Cambridge, Mass., Harvard University Press, 1993.

Rose, Nikolas. *Inventing Our Selves: Psychology, Power and Personhood.* Oxford: Cambridge University Press, 1996.

Rousseau, Jean Jacques. *Essay on the Origin of Languages,* ed. and trans. John T. Scott. Hanover: University Press of New England, 1998.

Ruiz, Carlos. "Escuela, politica y democracia. El caso de Chile en el siglo XIX." *Realidad Universitaria* Santiago, 7, 1989.

Ruiz, Roberto. "Las 'tres locuras' del licenciado Vidriera." *Nueva Revista de Filología Hispánica* 34 (1985–6): 839–847.

Ruthrof, Horst. *Semantics and the Body: Meaning from Frege to the Postmodern.* Toronto: University of Toronto Press, 1997.

Said, Edward. *Orientalism.* New York: Pantheon Books, 1978.

———. *Culture and Imperialism.* London: Chatto and Windus, 1993.

Saldívar, José David. *Border Matters: Remapping American Cultural Studies.* Berkeley: University Of California Press, 1997.

Sánchez, Luis Alberto. "Pablo de Olavide y Jáuregui." *Revista Iberoamericana* 38.81 (1972): 569–584.

Santa María, Fernando. "Ojeada sobre la condición del obrero y medios para mejorarla." Sergio Grez Toso. *La cuestión social en Chile. Ideas y debates precursores (1804–1902),* ed. Santiago: Dirección de Bibliotecas Archivos y Museos and Centro de Investigaciones Diego Barros Arana, 1995. 247–251.

Santí, Enrico Mario. 1979. "Parridiso." *José Lezama Lima: Textos críticos,* ed. Justo C. Ulloa. Miami: Ediciones Universales. 91–114.

———. *Pensar a José Martí. Notas para un centenario.* Boulder: Society of Spanish and Spanish American Studies, 1996.

Santiago, Kelvin. *"Subject Peoples" and Colonial Discourses. Economic Transformation and Social Disorder in Puerto Rico, 1898–1947.* Philadelphia: Temple University Press, 1994.

Santiago, Silviano. "O entre-lugar do discurso Latino-Americano." *Uma literatura nos trópicos.* São Paulo: Perspectiva, 1978. 11–28.

Sarduy, Severo. *Barroco.* Paris: Gillimard, 1991.

———. *De donde son los cantantes,* ed. Roberto González Echevarría. Madrid: Cátreda, 1997 [1967].

———. *Escrito sobre un cuerpo.* Buenos Aires: Editorial Sudamericana, 1969.

Sarlo, Beatriz. "Decir y no decir. Erotismo y represión." *Una modernidad periférica: Buenos Aires 1920–1930.* Buenos Aires: Nueva Vision, 1999.

———. *Escenas de la vida posmoderna.* Buenos Aires: Espasa Calpe, 1994.

———, et al. "Dossier: La revista *Sur.*" *Punto de vista.* 17 (1983): 7–14.

———. *Una modernidad periférica: Buenos Aires 1920 y 1930.* Buenos Aires: Ediciones Nueva Visión, 1999.

Sarmiento, Domingo F. *Facundo: civilización y barbarie.* Madrid: Cátedra, 1999 [1845].

Sartre, Jean-Paul. *The Words,* trans. Bernard Frechtman. New York: George Braziller, 1964.

Sater, William F. *The Heroic Image in Chile: Arturo Prat, Secular Saint.* Berkeley and Los Angeles: University of California Press, 1973.

Sawicki, Jana. *Disciplining Foucault: Feminism, Power, and the Body.* New York: Routledge, 1991.

Schmitt, Richard. "Edmund Husserl." *The Encyclopedia of Philosophy,* ed. Paul Edwards, vol. 4. New York: MacMillan, 1967. 98.

Schneider, Luis Mario. *Gabriela Mistral: Itinerario veracruzano.* Xalapa: Biblioteca de la Universidad Veracruzana, 1991.

Schwarz, Roberto. "Brazilian Culture: Nationalism by Elimination." *New Left Review* 167 (1988): 102–116.

———. "Misplaced Ideas: Literature and Society in Late Nineteenth-Century Brazil," *Comparative Civilizations Review* 5 (1979): 33–51.

———. *Misplaced Ideas: Essays on Brazilian Culture,* ed. John Gledson. New York: Verso, 1992. 19–32.

Scobie, James R. *Argentine: A City and a Nation.* New York: Oxford Press, 1964.

Sedgwick, Eve Kosofsky. *The Epistemology of the Closet.* Los Angeles: The University of California Press, 1991.

Serrano, Sol. *Universidad y nación. Chile en el siglo XIX.* Santiago: Editorial Universitaria, 1994.

Shakespeare, William. *Hamlet.* New York: Dover Publications, 1992.

Sifuentes-Jáuregui, B. "National Fantasies: Peeking into the Latin American Closet." *Queer*

    Representations: Reading Lives, Reading Cultures, ed. Martin B. Duberman. New York: New York University Press, 1997.

Silvestrini, Blanca. "El impacto de la política de salud pública de los Estados Unidos en Puerto Rico 1898–1913." *Politics, Society and Culture in the Caribbean. Selected Papers of the XIV Conference of Caribbean Historians.* Río Piedras: Editorial de la Universidad de Puerto Rico, 1983. 69–83.

Sinfield, Alan. "Reading Dissidence." *Twentieth-Century Literary Theory. A Reader,* ed. K.M. Newton. 2nd ed. New York: St. Martin's, 1997. 247–252.

Singer, Armand. "Cervantes' *Licenciado Vidriera*: Its Form and Substance." *West Virginia U. Philological Papers* 8 (1951): 13–21.

Singleton, Charles S., ed. *Interpretation: Theory and Practice.* Baltimore: Johns Hopkins University Press, 1969

Skidmore, Thomas E. *Black into White: Race and Nationality in Brazilian Thought.* Durham: Duke University Press, 1993.

Skrine, Peter N. *The Baroque.* London: Methuen, 1978.

Smith, Paul. *Discerning the Subject.* Minneapolis: University of Minnesota Press, 1988.

Smith, Sidonie. *A Poetics of Women's Autobiography: Marginality and the Fictions of Self-Representation.* Bloomington and Indianapolis: Indiana University Press, 1987.

Sommer, Doris. *Foundational Fictions: The National Romances of Latin America.* Berkeley: University of California Press, 1991.

———. "Allegory and Dialectics: A Match Made in Romance." Boundary 2,18, 1 (1991). 60–82.

Speak, Gill. "The *Licenciado Vidriera* and the Glass Men of Early Modern Europe." *The Modern Language Review* 4 85(4): 850–865.

Spivak, Gayatri Chakravorty. "Can the Subaltern Speak?" eds. Patrick Williams, Laura Chrisman. *Colonial Discourse and Postcolonial Theory.* New York: Columbia University Press, 1994. 66–111.

Stavans, Ilan. *The Hispanic Condition: Reflections on Culture and Identity in America.* New York: Harpercollins, 1995.

Stein, Stanley, and Barbara Stein. *The Colonial Heritage of Latin America.* New York: Oxford University Press, 1970.

Stepan, Nancy Leys. *The "Hour of Eugenics": Race, Gender and Nation in Latin America.* Ithaca: Cornell University Press, 1991.

Stephen, Lynn, ed., trans. *Hear My Testimony: María Teresa Tula, Human Rights Activist of El Salvador.* Boston: South End Press, 1994.

Stoler, Ann Laura. *Race and the Education of Desire: Foucault's History of Sexuality and the Colonial Order of Things.* Durham: Duke University Press, 1995.

Stoll, David. *Rigoberta Menchú and the Story of All Poor Guatemalans.* Boulder: Westview Press, 1999.

Suarez y Romero, Anselmo. *Francisco, el ingenio, o las delicias del campo, novela cubana.* Miami: Mnemosyne Publishing Inc., 1969 [1880].

Taylor, Diana. "A Savage Performance: Guillermo Gómez-Peña and Coco Fusco's 'Couple in the Cage.'" Cambridge: *The Drama Review* 42.2 (1998): 160–175.

Teitelboim, Volodia. *Gabriela Mistral pública y secreta. Truenos y silencios en la vida del primer Nobel latinoamericano.* Santiago: Ediciones BAT S.A., 1991.

Thiébaux, Marcelle. "Foucault's Fantasia for Feminists: The Woman Reading." *Theory and Practice of Feminist Literary Criticism,* eds. Gabriela Mora and Karen S. Van Hooft. Ypsilanti, Michigan: Bilingual Press/Editorial Bilingüe, 1982.

Tirado, Thomas. *Celsa's World: Conversations with a Mexican Peasant Woman.* Tempe: Center for Latin American Studies, 1991.

Tobin, Patricia. *Time and the Novel: The Genealogical Imperative.* Princeton University Press, 1978.

Todorov, Tzevetan. Michail Bakhtine. *Le principe dialogique.* Paris: Editions du Seuil, 1981.

Trigo, Benigno. *Subjects of Crisis: Race and Gender as Disease in Latin America.* New Hampshire: Wesleyan University Press, 2000.

———. "Anemia and Vampires: Figures to Govern the Colony, Puerto Rico, 1880–1904." *Comparative Studies in Society and History* 41 (1) 1999: 104–123.

Turner, Victor. *The Ritual Process.* Ithaca: Cornell UP, 1977.

Ulla, Noemí. *Encuentros con Silvina Ocampo.* Buenos Aires: Editorial de Belgrano, 1982.

Valéry, Paul. "De la diction des vers." *Pièces sur l'art, Oeuvres,* II. Paris: Gallimard, La Pléiade, 1966.

Valle, Enid. "La duplicación en *El incógnito o el fruto de la ambición* de Pablo de Olavide y Jáuregui." *Dieciocho* 21.2 (1998): 195–208.

———. "La estructura narrativa de *El evangelio en triunfo* de Pablo de Olavide y Jáuregui." *Pen and Peruke: Spanish Literature of the Eighteenth Century,* ed. Monroe Z. Hafter. *Michigan Romance Studies* 12 (1992): 135–151.

Vargas Llosa, Mario. "Angel Rama: La pasión y la crítica." *La ciudad letrada.* By Angel Rama. Hanover: Ediciones del Norte, 1984. 1–8.

———. *Histroria de Mayta.* Madrid: Alfaguara/Santillana, 2000 [1984].

———. *La guerra del fin del mundo.* Madrid: Alfaguara/Santillana, 2000 [1980].

———. "Sobre el *Paradiso* de Lezama." *Mundo Nuevo* 16 (1967): 89–90.

Varner, John G. *El Inca: The Life and Times of Garcilaso de la Vega.* Austin: University of Texas Press, 1968.

Vasconcelos, José. *La raza cósmica.* México: Espasa-Calpe, 1996 [1925].

———. *La raza cósmica.* Barcelona: Angencia Mundial de Librería, n. d. [1926].

Vattimo, Gianni. *The End of Modernity. Nihilism and Hermeneutics in Postmodern Culture.* Baltimore: The John Hopkins University Press, 1991.

Vidal, Hernán. "The Concept of Colonial and Postcolonial Discourse: A Perspective from Literary Criticism." *Latin American Research Review* 28.3 (1993): 113–119.

Viezzer, Moema, ed. *Si me permiten hablar: testimonio de Domitila, una mujer de las minas de Bolivia.* México: Siglo XXI, 1994.

Vigarello, George. *Concepts of Cleanliness. Changing Attitudes in France since the Middle Ages,* trans. Jean Birrell. Cambridge: Cambridge University Press, 1988.

Vilar, Irene. *The Ladies' Gallery,* trans. Gregory Rabassa. New York: Vintage, 1998.

Villaverde, Cirilo. *Cecilia Valdés, o, la loma del ángel.* Madrid: Cétedra, 1992 [1880].

Visweswaran, Kamala. *Fictions of Feminist Ethnography.* Minneapolis: University of Minnesota Press, 1994.

Wallerstein, Immanuel V. *The Modern World-System.* 2 vols. New York: Academic Press, 1974–80.

Warner, Michael. "Introduction: Fear of a Queer Planet." *Social Text* 29.9.4 (1991): 3–17.

———, ed. *Fear of a Queer Planet: Queer Politics and Social Theory.* Minneapolis: University of Minnesota Press, 1993.

Waters, Lindsay. "Paul de Man: Life and Works." In *Paul de Man Critical Writings 1953–1978.* Minneapolis: University of Minnesota Press, 1989.

Welch, Thomas and Myriam Figueras, eds. *Travel Accounts and Descriptions of Latin America and the Caribbean 1800–1920: A Selected Bibliography.* Washington, D.C.: OAS, 1982.

Zavala, Iris M. "*Cien años de soledad,* crónica de Indias." *Insula* 286 (1970): 3–11.

Zavala, Silvio. *La filosofía política en la conquista de América.* México: Fondo de Cultura Economica, 1947.

Zeno Gandía, Manuel. *La charca.* San Juan: Instituto de Cultura, 1968 [1894].

Ziarek, Krzysztof. "Powers to Be: Art and Technology in Heidegger and Foucault." *Research in Phenomenology* 28 (1998): 162–194.

Contributors

Aída Beaupied is Associate Professor of Spanish American Literature at Pennsylvania State University. She is the author of *Narciso hermético: Sor Juana Inés de la Cruz y José Lezama Lima* (Liverpool, 1997). She has published numerous articles on Golden Age and Contemporary literatures in journals such as *Hispania, Romance Notes, Latin American Literary Review, Hispanófila, Hispanic Journal, Chasqui, Anales Cervantinos, Revista de Estudios Hispánicos, Plaza: Revista de Literatura*. Her recent published articles, as well as her current research interest, address the topic of Cuban poetry and culture.

Román de la Campa is Professor of Hispanic Languages and Literature at SUNY, Stony Brook. He is the author of numerous books and articles on theatre, testimony, cultural theory and cultural diasporas. He is the author of *José Triana; Ritualización de la sociedad cubana* (Institute for the Study of Ideologies and Literature, 1979), *Latin Americanism* (University of Minnesota, 1999), *Cuba on My Mind* (Verso, 2001). His most recent edited title is *Late Imperial Cultures* (Verso, 1995).

Fernando Feliú is Associate Professor of Spanish at the University of Michigan, Dearborn. He is a specialist in Caribbean literature and science. He has published articles in journals such as *Confluencias, Cupey: Revista de la Universidad Metropolitana, Revista Bilingüe, Revista Interamericana de Bibliografía,* and *Revista de Estudios Hispánicos de la Universidad de Puerto Rico.* He is currently working on a book manuscript on Bailey K. Ashford and the Anemia Campaigns in Puerto Rico.

Licia Fiol-Matta is Assistant Professor of Spanish at Barnard College. She has a book under contract with University of Minnesota Press titled *Schooling Sexuality: The State and Gabriela Mistral*. She has published work on women's writing, gender issues, and queer studies in such prestigeous publications as *Revista Iberoamericana, Diálogo. Revista de la Univeridad de Puerto Rico, Social Text, Nomadías. Journal of the Program in Gender and Culture, University of Chile.* She has also contributed essays to collections including *Obras completas de Margot Arce de Vázquez,* Hugo Rodríguez Vecchini, ed.; and *¿Entiendes? Queer Readings, Hispanic Writings.* Emilie L. Bergmann and Paul Julian Smith, eds.

Roberto González Echevarría is Sterling Professor of Hispanic and Comparative Literature at Yale University. He has published extensively on colonial and contemporary Latin American literature. His works include *The Pride of Havana: A History of Cuban Baseball* (Oxford University Press, 1999), *Myth and Archive; A Theory of Latin American Literature* (Duke University Press, 1998), *Celestina's Brood: Continuities of the Baroque in Spanish and Latin American Literatures* (Duke University Press, 1993), *De donde son los cantantes* (Ediciones Del Norte, 1989), *Isla a su vuelo fugitiva* (Ediciones Del Norte, 1983).

Sylvia Molloy is the Albert Schweitzer Professor of Humanities at New York University. She is a distinguished critic and writer of fiction. Author of numerous books and articles, her titles include *La Diffusion de la littérature hispanoaméricaine en France au XXe siecle* (Paris: Presses Universitaires de France, 1972), *Las letras de Borges* (Buenos Aires: Editorial Sudamericana, 1970), *En Breve carcel* (Barcelona: Seix Barral, 1981), *Certificate of Absence* (University of Texas Press, 1989), *At Face Value: Autobiogrphical Writing in Spanish America* (Oxford University Press, 1991) and *Sign of Borges* (Duke University Press, 1994). She has also edited a number of volumes, such as *Hispanisms and Homosexualities* (Duke University Press, 1998), and *Essays on Hispanic Literature in Honor of Edmund L. King* (London: Tamesis, 1983).

John Ochoa is Assistant Professor of Hispanic Studies at the University of California, Riverside. His area of specialty is nineteenth-century Latin American literature and science. He has published in *Modern Language Notes.* He is currently at work on a project exploring the theme of failure in Mexican literature in connection with the development of national identity from the colonial period to the twentieth century.

Kelly Oliver is Professor of Philosophy and Women's Studies at SUNY Stony Brook. She is the author of *Witnessing: Beyond Recognition* (University of Minnesota, 2001), *Subjectivity without Subjects: From Abject Fathers to Desiring Mothers* (Rowman & Littlefield, 1998), *Family Values: Subjects between Nature and Culture* (Routledge, 1997), *Womanizing Nietzsche: Philosophy's Relation to "the Feminine"* (Routledge, 1995), and *Reading*

Kristeva: Unraveling the Double-Bind (University of Indiana, 1993). She has edited several books, including *Ethics, Politics and Difference in Kristeva's Writings* (Routledge, 1993), *Feminist Interpretations of Nietzsche* (Penn State Press, 1998), and *The Portable Kristeva* (Columbia, 1998).

Juan Poblete is Assistant Professor of Spanish at University of California, Santa Cruz. He has published articles on literary theory in journals such as the *Instituto Internacional de Literatura Iberoamericana, Revista de crítica literaria latinoamericana*

Angel Rama (1926–1983) was the author of hundreds of articles on Latin American literature. His prolific carreer included books such as *The Lettered City: Post-Contemporary Interventions* (Duke University Press, 1993), *Literatura y clase social* (México, 1984), *La novela latinoamericana* (Bogotá, 1982), *Transculturación narrativa en América Latina* (México, 1982), *Los gauchopolíticos Rioplatenses* (Buenos Aires, 1976), *Rubén Darío y el modernismo* (Caracas, 1970), *Los poetas modernistas* (Montevideo, 1969).

B. Sifuentes Jáuregui is Assistant Professor of Spanish American literature at Rutgers. His areas of research range from gender and queer studies to psycho-analysis. He has published articles in edited collections such as *Queer Representations: Reading Lives, Reading Cultures* (A Center for Lesbian and Gay Studies Book, 1997) and *Hispanisms and Homosexualities* (Duke University Press, 1998). Presently, he is completing a project entitled *Facing Masculinity: Transvestism and Spanish American Literature.*

Elzbieta Sklodowska is Professor of Spanish at Washington University in Saint Louis. Her more recent research focuses on the inscriptions of power in the Spanish-American novel: *Todo ojos, todo oídos; control e insubordinación en la novela hispanoamericana (1895–1935)* (Rodopi, 1997). She has done extensive work on testimonial literature, including *Testimonio hispanoamericano: historia, teoría, poética* (Peter Lang, 1992). She is also the author of *La parodia en la nueva novela hispanoamericana* (Purdue University Monographs, 1991). She is currently finishing a new book entitled *Uncharted Territories: Space and Memory in Cuban Literature* and, together with Ben Heller, she is editing a collection of essays *Homenaje a Roberto Fernández Retamar.*

Doris Sommer is Professor of Romance Languages and Literatures at Harvard University. She has published extensively on Latin American literature, race, and gender studies. Some of her published work includes *Proceed with Caution, When Engaged by Minority Writing in the Americas* (Harvard University Press,

1999), *Foundational Fictions: The National Romances of Latin America* (University of California Press, 1991), *One Master for Another: Populism as Patriarchal Rhetoric in Dominican Novels* (Lanham, 1983). Her edited books include *The Places of History; Regionalism Revisited in Latin America* (Duke University Press, 1999).

Benigno Trigo is Associate Professor of Hispanic Languages and Literature at SUNY, Stony Brook. He is the author of *Subjects of Crisis: Race and Gender as Disease in Latin America* (Wesleyan University Press, 1999). He has published articles on Latin American literature and culture in such journals as *Comparative Journal of Society and History, Journal of Latin American Cultural Studies, Revista Canadiense de Estudios Hispánicos.* He is presently completing a project entitled *The Melancholy Novel: Remembering the Abject Mother.*

Fernando Unzueta is Associate Professor of Latin American literatures and cultures at Ohio State University specializing in the nineteenth century. He is the author of *La imaginación histórica y el romance nacional en Hispanoamérica* (Latinoamericana Editores, 1996) and numerous articles in journals such as *Dispositio/n, Revista Iberoamericana, Estudios, Papers in Comparative Studies* and *Latin American Research Review.* He is presently working on a book-length project provisionally entitled "Subjects to Change: The Formation of National Subjects in Nineteenth-Century Spanish America."

Index